CW01024760

THE ARTHUR OF THE NO

ARTHURIAN LITERATURE IN THE MIDDLE AGES

V

THE ARTHUR OF THE NORTH

THE ARTHURIAN LEGEND IN THE NORSE AND RUS' REALMS

edited by

Marianne E. Kalinke

UNIVERSITY OF WALES PRESS

© The Vinaver Trust, 2011

Reprinted, 2012
Reprinted in paperback, 2015

All rights reserved. No part of this book may be reproduced in any material form (including photocopying or storing it in any medium by electronic means and whether or not transiently or incidentally to some other use of this publication) without the written permission of the copyright owner except in accordance with the provisions of the Copyright, Designs and Patents Act 1988. Applications for the copyright owner's written permission to reproduce any part of this publication should be addressed to The University of Wales Press, 10 Columbus Walk, Brigantine Place, Cardiff, CF10 4UP.

www.uwp.co.uk

British Library Cataloguing-in-Publication Data.
A catalogue record for this book is available from the British Library.

ISBN 978-1-78316-7876
e-ISBN 978-0-7083-2354-0

The right of the Contributors to be identified separately as authors of this work has been asserted by them in accordance with sections 77, 78 and 79 of the Copyright, Designs and Patents Act 1988.

Typeset by Mark Heslington Ltd, Scarborough, North Yorkshire
Printed by CPI Antony Rowe, Chippenham, Wiltshire

PUBLISHED IN COOPERATION WITH

THE VINAVER TRUST

The Vinaver Trust was established by the British Branch of the International Arthurian Society to commemorate a greatly respected colleague and a distinguished scholar

Eugène Vinaver

the editor of Malory's Morte Darthur. *The Trust aims to advance study of Arthurian literature in all languages by planning and encouraging research projects in the field, and by aiding publication of the resultant studies.*

ARTHURIAN LITERATURE IN THE MIDDLE AGES

Series Editor

Ad Putter

CONTENTS

PREFACE

This book forms part of the ongoing series Arthurian Literature in the Middle Ages. The purpose of the series is to provide a comprehensive and reliable survey of Arthurian writings in all their cultural and generic variety. For some time, the single-volume *Arthurian Literature in the Middle Ages: A Collaborative History* (ed. R.S. Loomis, Oxford, 1959) served the needs of students and scholars of Arthurian literature admirably, but it has now been overtaken by advances in scholarship and by changes in critical perspectives and methodologies. The Vinaver Trust recognized the need for a fresh and up-to-date survey, and decided that several volumes were required to do justice to the distinctive contributions made to Arthurian literature by the various cultures of medieval Europe. *The Arthur of the North: The Arthurian Legend in the Norse and Rus' Realms* is primarily devoted to medieval Arthurian texts composed in the Scandinavian peninsula and in Iceland, but it also takes account of later Arthurian material, such as the Arthurian ballads from Iceland, Denmark, Norway and the Faroe Islands, and of the Belarusian 'Tristan' story and its context.

The series is mainly aimed at undergraduate and postgraduate students and at scholars working in the fields covered by each of the volumes. The series has, however, also been designed to be accessible to students and scholars from different fields, who want to learn what forms Arthurian narratives took in languages and literatures that they may not know, and how those narratives influenced the cultures that they do know. Within these parameters the editors have had control over the shape and content of their individual volumes.

Ad Putter, University of Bristol
(General Editor)

INTRODUCTION

Marianne E. Kalinke

A monograph on Arthurian romance in the West Nordic region was published in 1981 bearing the title *King Arthur, North-by-Northwest.*[1] This was intended to indicate the transmission of French Arthurian narratives to the North, that is, Norway, and from there to Iceland, that is, the Northwest. The subtitle of the present volume expresses a broader initiative. The *Arthur of the North* is a study of the *matière de Bretagne* in a more extended linguistic and geographic region than that undertaken in the 1981 volume and first covered in the chapter on Scandinavia by P. M. Mitchell in Roger Sherman Loomis's *Arthurian Literature in the Middle Ages* (1959). The subtitle, *The Arthurian Legend in the Norse and Rus' Realms*, seeks to designate the broad geographical area in which the literature discussed in this volume was composed and transmitted and where variants of the Norse tongue flourished in the Middle Ages. Included are the vast Eastern regions of Rus', primarily the Kievan state, where Scandinavians and Slavs coexisted and the Norse, the Varangians or so-called Rus', settled, governed and conducted commerce from the middle of the ninth century to the middle of the twelfth century.

The term Norse refers both to the people and their language, a language that had currency when writing was first introduced into the area we know today as Denmark, Iceland, Norway and Sweden. Medieval sources indicate that the name Rus', which may be of Norse origin, was first applied to Scandinavians and subsequently to the eastern Slavic peoples and areas.[2]

The Arthur of the North covers a broad geographical area and chronologically more than half a millennium. The introduction of Arthurian literature in the North, primarily French romances and *lais*, is indebted largely to the efforts of King Hákon Hákonarson (r.1217–63) in thirteenth-century Norway and Queen Eufemia (d.1312), the German wife of Hákon Magnússon (r.1299–1319), Hákon Hákonarson's grandson (chapter 1). The earliest Arthurian text to have been translated, however, was the *Prophetiae Merlini* in Geoffrey of Monmouth's *Historia regum Britanniae*, known in translation as *Merlínússpá*, and this took place in Iceland around the year 1200. Presumably at the same time, or a little later, Geoffrey's *Historia* was also translated in Iceland and entitled *Breta sögur* (chapter 3). The last Arthurian narrative to be translated in medieval Scandinavia, albeit for a second time, was Chrétien de Troyes's *Yvain* at the behest of Queen Eufemia. Unlike the thirteenth-century Norse translators, who rendered French verse in prose, the anonymous translator of this unique Swedish Arthurian romance, *Hærra Ivan*, chose to employ German *Knittelvers* (chapter 7).

The earliest Arthurian romance to have reached the North is Thomas's *Tristan*. According to its incipit, *Tristrams saga ok Ísöndar* was translated in 1226 by a certain Brother Robert at the behest of King Hákon Hákonarson (chapter 4). The same king also had a collection of *lais* translated, including some ascribed to Marie de France. This Norse collection of twenty-one *lais*, entitled *Strengleikar*, contains four narratives the French sources of which are no longer extant. Presumably translated separately, but also commissioned by Hákon, is *Möttuls saga*, the Norse version of the *Lai du cort mantel* (chapter 5).

Three of Chrétien de Troyes's Arthurian romances were transmitted to the North, his *Erec et Enide*, *Yvain* and *Perceval* (chapter 6). In the manuscripts of *Ívens saga*, the Norse translation of *Yvain*, Hákon 'the Old' is identified as the patron, presumably so designated to distinguish him from his son who bore the same name and died six years before his father, in 1257, without succeeding to the throne. Scholars generally assume that *Parcevals saga*, the translation of *Perceval*, was also produced at the court of Hákon Hákonarson, given the similarity of style between it and the other works known to have been translated at the Norwegian court. Some scholars think that *Erex saga*, deriving from *Erec et Enide* and extant only in seventeenth-century Icelandic manuscripts, was also translated at Hákon's court, but the saga deviates so radically in content and structure from its French source and so markedly in style from the other works known to have been translated in thirteenth-century Norway, that it is doubtful that the preserved text represents a medieval Norse translation. More likely it is an extensively revised Icelandic redaction or perhaps even an Icelandic translation.

Most of the Arthurian narratives were imported to thirteenth-century Norway and translated in a courtly environment. Except for the two Arthurian *lais* in the *Strengleikar* compilation, however, which are preserved in a Norwegian manuscript, we know these texts today solely because Icelandic scribes and redactors transmitted them through the centuries. In most instances several centuries lie between the time of translation and the extant manuscripts of a work. Thus, a question that has repeatedly occupied scholars is whether the preserved texts represent the work of the thirteenth-century translators or the interventions of Icelandic copyists. If the former, then we are dealing with the culture of a royal court, similar to or attempting to emulate the royal courts of England and France; if the latter, then the issue becomes one of acculturation in a rural society and to indigenous literary practices that produced one of the great literatures of Europe, the *Íslendingasögur*, that is, Sagas of Icelanders, a literature quite distinct in both form and content from the courtly Arthurian literature. Chapter 2 deals with the texts translated, their sources, the Icelandic redactions and the transmission of manuscripts.

Unlike what happened on the continent, for example in the German-language area, the introduction of the *matière de Bretagne* in the North did not lead to the production of a corpus of indigenous Arthurian romances. In Iceland, however, the translated narratives inspired anonymous authors to incorporate Arthurian themes, episodes and motifs into their own compositions and in a number of instances to transform these borrowings in light of indigenous literary norms (chapter 8). Icelandic literature bears witness to the transformation that occurs when a literature is transmitted from one culture to another, in this case from a courtly culture to a rural society. Whereas with one possible exception, the *Saga af Tristram ok Ísodd*, Iceland did not produce original Arthurian narratives, the Arthurian romances and lais copied by Icelandic scribes nonetheless had an impact on the indigenous literature. Episodes from the Tristan legend, adapted to the native literary culture, found their way into a couple of Sagas of Icelanders. Tristanian motifs were also incorporated into a number of late medieval Icelandic romances composed under the impact of the translated literature.

Whereas the medieval translations of Arthurian romances did not generate a body of indigenous Arthurian compositions in either Norway or Iceland, they inspired the creation of late medieval and early modern ballads, especially Tristan ballads, in Iceland, Denmark and the Faeroe Islands, and ballads reflecting the *Yvain* tradition in the Faeroes and Norway. The Tristan legend also led to the composition of Icelandic folk tales and an eighteenth-century Danish chapbook, which in turn was translated into Icelandic and inspired the production of Icelandic narrative poems, called *rímur*, in the eighteenth and nineteenth centuries. In one instance a German chapbook, *Wigalois*, a late fifteenth-century prose version of a thirteenth-century Arthurian romance, was translated into Danish in the seventeenth century and this was subsequently translated more than once into Icelandic (chapter 9).

The earliest written Arthurian narratives in the Norse realm date to around 1200, but there is evidence that Icelanders also knew oral versions of the Arthurian legend. The Icelanders were fabled travellers and together with other Scandinavians they journeyed far and wide in the Middle Ages. A mid-twelfth-century Icelandic travel guide, *Leiðarvísir*, attributed to Abbot Nikulás Bergsson of Munkaþverá, details his journey from Iceland to Denmark and Norway, then overland via Germany and Switzerland to Rome, and finally across the Mediterranean to the Holy Land. The far-reaching travels of the Norse on the European continent – Icelandic pilgrims are recorded as having taken lodging at the abbey of Reichenau on Lake Constance in the second half of the twelfth century – must have provided an opportunity to become acquainted with tales circulating among other travellers and in other lands. Although not undisputed, it is thought that the Norse, or Varangians, founded Kievan Rus' in the 880s, and Varangian mercenaries earned fame for their military prowess in the tenth and eleventh centuries and served as the Greek emperor's bodyguard. The account of the Arab emissary Ibn Fadlan in the year 921 CE to the king of the Bulgurs of the Middle Volga relates his encounter with a people called the Rus', presumably of Swedish origin, who conducted commerce on the banks of the Volga.

The inclusion of a chapter on Arthurian literature in East Slavic in a volume otherwise dedicated to Scandinavian Arthuriana led to the subtitle of this volume.[3] Chapter 10 introduces the reader to the Belarusian *Tryščan*, produced long after the Rus' principalities had ceased to be, but most likely indebted to the heroic poetry of the Rus'. The Belarusian 'Tristan' shares its distinct characteristics, chiefly its lack of a romantic element, with the translations and adaptations of other romances, and this is indeed one of the defining features of the heroic court poetry, the *byliny*, in Slavonic. The discussion of this medieval genre of the Rus' in chapter 10 provides a context for the Belarusian *Tryščan* and its acculturation to indigenous literary norms. In this respect the Belarusian 'Tristan' romance bears some comparison with the Icelandic version of the 'Tristan' legend, that is, the *Saga af Tristram ok Ísodd* (chapter 8), the author of which introduced substantial changes, especially in the formulation of the love problematic, and thereby adapted the traditional courtly legend to a non-courtly culture.

Finally, a note on terminology. Throughout, we use Old Norse to refer to the language of the translations undertaken in Norway, and Old Icelandic to those known to have occurred in Iceland. The hyphenated form Old Norse-Icelandic refers to the Norwegian translations that are extant solely in Icelandic redactions.

Given the fact that most Icelanders do not have surnames but rather patronymics, we follow Icelandic practice and the Library of Congress system and alphabetize by given name in the bibliography, e.g., 'Finnur Jónsson', not 'Jónsson, F.', who is unidentifiable in the latter form. Similarly, references are always to both given name and patronymic, since a reference to 'Jónsson', that is, 'the son of Jón', is meaningless.

Notes

[1] M. E. Kalinke, *King Arthur, North-by-Northwest: The* matière de Bretagne *in Old Norse-Icelandic Romances*, Bibliotheca Arnamagnæana, 37 (Copenhagen, 1981).

[2] See A. Nazarenko, 'Rus'', *Lexikon des Mittelalters*, VII (Munich, 1995), cols 1,112–13; J. Shepherd, 'Rus'', in N. Berend (ed.), *Christianization and the Rise of Christian Monarchy: Scandinavia, Central Europe and Rus' c. 900–1200* (Cambridge, 2007), pp. 369–416.

[3] Ch. 10, 'Arthurian Literature in East Slavic', is complemented by A. Thomas, 'King Arthur and his Round Table in the Culture of Medieval Bohemia and in Medieval Czech Literature', in W. H. Jackson and S. A. Ranawake (eds), *The Arthur of the Germans: The Arthurian Legend in Medieval German and Dutch Literature* (Cardiff, 2000), pp. 249–56. Thomas discusses *Tandariáš a Floribella*, the Czech version of the Middle High German romance *Tandareis und Flordibel* by Der Pleier, and *Tristram a Izalda*, deriving from the German Tristan romances by Eilhart von Oberge, Gottfried von Strassburg and Heinrich von Freiberg.

1

THE INTRODUCTION OF THE ARTHURIAN LEGEND IN SCANDINAVIA

Marianne E. Kalinke

Ok eptir unnit Írland stefnir hann til Nóregs ok léttir eigi fyrr en hann hefir unnit allan Nóreg. Ok í þessi ferð lagði hann undir sik öll Norðrlönd – Nóreg, Danmörk, Hjaltland, Orkneyjar, Færeyjar, Suðreyjar, Skotland – ok skattgildi alla er þar réðu þeim.

(And after he had conquered Ireland, he proceeded to Norway and did not rest until he had conquered all of Norway. And in this campaign he vanquished all the Northern lands – Norway, Denmark, Shetland, the Orkneys, the Faroes, the Hebrides, Scotland – and laid tribute on all who ruled there.)[1]

According to the above excerpt from *Breta sögur*, the Icelandic translation of Geoffrey of Monmouth's *Historia regum Britanniae*, King Arthur conquered the entire North, Iceland excepted. Lacking in the translation is Geoffrey's statement that after his conquest of Ireland, King Arthur 'classem suam direxit in Islandiam eamque debellato populo subiugauit' (Reeve edn 2007, 205) (took his fleet to Iceland, where he defeated the natives and conquered their land) (Wright trans. 2007, 204). The omission is ironic, considering that King Arthur did indeed successfully conquer Iceland in the sense that with one exception the Arthurian narratives thought to have been translated in thirteenth-century Norway are preserved solely in Icelandic manuscripts. Without Iceland, King Arthur would be all but unknown in Scandinavian literature today.

As happened in England, the North first became acquainted with the world of King Arthur by way of historiography, or pseudo-historiography if you will. The earliest attested translation of the *matière de Bretagne* in the North is *Merlínússpá*, 'Merlin's Prophecy', a rendering of the 'Prophetiae Merlini' in the *Historia regum Britanniae* (Reeve edn 2007, 143–59). *Merlínússpá*, consisting of two parts, each headed in the manuscript by the title of the poem, was written around 1200 by Gunnlaugr Leifsson (d. 1218 or 1219), a monk in the Benedictine monastery of Þingeyrar in Iceland. The monastery was founded in 1133 and by the end of the twelfth century and the beginning of the thirteenth 'it was the chief centre of intellectual activity in northern Iceland, if not in the whole country' (Turville-Petre 1953, 190). Gunnlaugr wrote both in Latin and in the vernacular, including a life of the Norwegian king Olaf Tryggvason in Latin as also of the Icelandic saint Jón Ögmundarson. Neither Latin biography has been preserved, only their Icelandic versions. *Merlínússpá* is found in one of the two redactions of *Breta sögur*, in the so-called *Hauksbók* (AM 544 4to), a compendious codex produced between 1301 and 1314 and named after its compiler Haukr Erlendsson who ascribed the poem to Gunnlaugr Leifsson (*Breta sögur* 1892–96,

271). A longer redaction of *Breta sögur*, in the manuscript AM 573 4to, dated 1330–70, does not contain *Merlínússpá,* but at the place in the narrative where the Prophecies are located in the *Historia* the anonymous redactor notes that 'kunna margir menn þat kuæði' (many persons knew that poem) (*Breta sögur* 1849, 13, fn. 11).[2] Given the fact that on the whole the text in AM 573 4to transmits much more of Geoffrey's *Historia* than Haukr Erlendsson does, who systematically condensed the text, the comment suggests widespread acquaintance in the fourteenth century, and presumably already much earlier, with at least this part of the Arthurian legend.

Merlínússpá is unique not only by virtue of its presumably being the oldest translation of the *matière de Bretagne* in the North, but also because it is in the native Icelandic metre *fornyrðislag*, 'old story metre', one of the metres of the *Poetic Edda*, the great collection of Norse mythological and heroic poetry. Geoffrey's 'Prophetiae Merlini' was in prose, however, and its translation into verse is unusual, as we shall see. It is thought that Gunnlaugr was inspired to translate the 'Prophetiae Merlini' into verse by the first of the Eddic poems, *Völuspá*, the 'Prophecy of the Seeress', composed predominantly in *fornyrðislag*, from which he also borrowed some material for his translation (Eysteinsson 1953–55, 98–103). Gunnlaugr obviously considered the subject matter of *Völuspá* analogous to that of the 'Prophetiae Merlini'.

Scholarly consensus concerning the origin of the *Breta sögur* ('Sagas of the Britons') has been wanting. While some have placed the translation of Geoffrey's *Historia* at the court of King Hákon Hákonarson (r.1217–63) of Norway, who commissioned the translation of a number of French Arthurian romances (Halvorsen 1959, 23), it is more likely that the *Breta sögur* originated in Iceland at the beginning of the thirteenth century, possibly in tandem with or as a follow-up to Gunnlaugr's *Merlínússpá* (Würth 1998, 81–2; Kalinke 2009, 185). Certain information in *Merlínússpá* not found in the 'Prophetiae' is included, however, in the *Historia*, and this suggests that Gunnlaugr composed *Merlínússpá* with Geoffrey's *Historia* at his side (Eysteinsson 1953–5, 98–103; Turville-Petre 1953, 202). Whether Gunnlaugr himself also translated the *Historia*, or one of his fellow monks at Þingeyrar, it is indisputable that the *Historia* was available in Iceland at the end of the twelfth century, and a monastery like Þingeyrar, which was noted for producing historiography (Turville-Petre 1953, 190–202), would have had the expertise to translate it into Icelandic.

By the time Gunnlaugr Leifsson translated Geoffrey's 'Prophetiae Merlini', Iceland had a flourishing tradition of both translation from Latin and literary composition in the vernacular. Christianity was officially adopted in Iceland in the year AD 1000, and with the Church came literacy and the shift from an oral to a written culture. The earliest texts to be produced in the new manuscript culture, starting in the second half of the twelfth century, were of a religious nature and were translations of saints' lives (Quinn 2000, 30; Cormack 2005, 29). Among them were the *vitae* of such saints as Nicholas and Stephen, which were translated before 1200 (Ásdis Egilsdóttir 2006, 122). These were followed towards the end of the twelfth century and the beginning of the thirteenth by translations of learned works, for example, the *Physiologus* and the *Elucidarius*, and of Latin historiography, to wit the *Historia regum Britanniae* (Würth 1998, 187–8).

A remarkable feature of Old Icelandic literature is that from the very beginnings it was in the vernacular. In addition to translations, by the end of the twelfth century Icelanders were writing legal and historiographic texts. Especially the latter had a remarkable impact on the subsequent production of literature. The earliest known writer was the priest Ari Þorgilsson, called 'inn fróði', 'the learned' (1067/8–1148), considered the father of Icelandic prose (Turville-Petre 1953, 167). His only surviving work, the *Libellus Islandorum*, also called *Íslendingabók*, a brief summary of Icelandic history, is the oldest example of narrative prose in a Scandinavian language (Turville-Petre 1953, 90–1). Snorri Sturluson (1178–1241), the great Icelandic historiographer and author of *Heimskringla*, the monumental history of the kings of Norway, claimed Ari's work as one of his sources (Bjarni Aðalbjarnarson edn 1941, 5–7). Emulating Ari's history of early Iceland an anonymous author produced *Hungrvaka*, a synoptic history of the bishops of Skálholt in the period 1055–93.

The translations of Arthurian literature fall into the thirteenth century, which is regarded as the classical age of Icelandic literature. During this century the great biographies of the Norwegian kings, the *konungasögur*, Kings' Sagas, were produced as well as the better known *Íslendingasögur*, that is, Sagas of Icelanders (also called Family Sagas). Among the former we find *Sverris saga*, the life of King Sverrir Sigurðarson (1177–1202) of Norway, most of the biography believed to have been written by Karl Jónsson, twice abbot of Þingeyrar (1169–81; 1190–1207), who seems to have collaborated with King Sverrir in the writing of his biography (Þorleifur Hauksson edn 2007, 4; Turville-Petre 1953, 214). In any case, Karl Jónsson was a pioneer in the writing of Kings' Sagas and may in fact be considered a 'founding father' of saga writing (Ármann Jakobsson 2005, 393). Around 1220 an anonymous author produced the great synoptic history of the kings of Norway known as *Morkinskinna*, 'Rotten vellum'. This collection of biographies of kings, from the death of St Ólafr until perhaps 1177, is unique inasmuch as a number of short stories, *þættir*, are interpolated into the lives of the kings, many of them exemplary in character. *Morkinskinna* was followed by Snorri Sturluson's compilation *Heimskringla*, dated between 1220 and 1235, containing biographies of the kings of Norway from Hálfdan the Black (*c*.820–*c*.860) to Magnús Erlingsson (1156–84), and preceded by the stories of the Ynglingar, the legendary ancestors of the kings of Sweden. What makes these examples of historiography unique is that unlike most of the contemporary histories and biographies of continental Europe, they were not in Latin but rather in the vernacular.

The biography of King Haraldr Sigurðarson (1015–66) *harðráði*, 'the Ruthless' in *Morkinskinna* contains a number of tales that tell of the king's encounters with Icelanders. One of these gives a glimpse of how historiography or royal biography came to be. A young Icelander arrived at the court of King Haraldr one summer and asked for hospitality. The king agreed to grant it, provided the Icelander entertain the court by telling stories. This he did until Christmas drew nigh and the storytelling Icelander became downcast. Upon being pressed by the king, he confesses that he has run out of stories, except for one that tells of the king's foreign adventures. Haraldr tells him to start this account on Christmas Day and to continue through the holidays. On the thirteenth day the king gave his judgement and said that the Icelander's account accorded with actual events. When asked where he had heard about the king's adventures abroad, the Icelander said that he had learned this from Halldórr Snorrason who related the king's adventures at the assembly meetings every summer (Andersson and Gade trans. 2000, 222–3). This Halldórr Snorrason, together with other Icelanders, had accompanied King Haraldr on his travels and upon their return to Iceland they told what had occurred. In other words, they provided the oral material that was passed down for several generations and which was to go into writing the king's biography.

During the same time that the voluminous compilations of Kings' Sagas were produced, Icelanders also started to write down their own history in the *Íslendingasögur*. Just as the Icelanders created a history for Norway in the Kings' Sagas, they captured their own past in the lives of individuals and their families, from the settlement of Iceland to the establishment of a social order and through the conversion to Christianity and its consequences (Vésteinn Ólason 2005, 112). The earliest of the *Íslendingasögur* were composed at the same time that translations of Latin literature were already flourishing and the Kings' Sagas were compiled. Although there is scholarly disagreement concerning the dates when some of the sagas were first composed, some of the oldest were presumably written down in the early decades of the thirteenth century, among them *Egils saga*, the life of the great tenth-century Icelandic poet Egill Skalla-Grímsson (Andersson 2006, 14–15), which is commonly ascribed to Snorri Sturluson, as well as *Fóstbræðra saga*, *Hallfreðar saga* and *Kormáks saga*, sagas of skalds that bear traces of influence from the Tristan legend, as we shall see (Vésteinn Ólason 2005, 115).

The Icelanders' instinct for and interest in history is also evident in the production of another group of sagas, the so-called *fornaldarsögur*, that is, Legendary or Mythical-Heroic Sagas. Whereas the Kings' Sagas relate the biographies of kings from the beginnings of the Norwegian royal dynasty into the late eleventh century, and the thirteenth-century Sagas of Icelanders recount the lives of individuals and families from the settlement of the country into the early days of the eleventh century, the *fornaldarsögur* focus on legendary prehistory in the Germanic world. Undoubtedly the best-known of the *fornaldarsögur* is *Völsunga saga*, based on the heroic lays concerning Sigurd the Dragon Slayer in the *Poetic Edda*. Although the extant manuscripts of the *fornaldarsögur* are late – the earliest manuscripts are from around 1300 (Tulinius 2005, 449) – there is evidence that at least in their oral form some of these tales were already known and told in the twelfth century. Indeed, the aforementioned

King Sverrir of Norway, who died in 1202, is said to have appreciated listening to a *fornaldarsaga*.[3] One of the late *fornaldarsögur*, to judge by the manuscript evidence, is *Hrólfs saga kraka*, the protagonist of which is the legendary Danish king Hrólfr kraki, whose fate is also recorded in Saxo Grammaticus's (*c*.1150–1220) *Gesta Danorum* (*c*.1208) and in the Icelandic *Skjöldunga saga*, dated to around 1200. As in the Kings' Sagas and the *Íslendingasögur*, a primary concern in *Hrólfs saga kraka* and in some of the early *fornaldarsögur* is history, albeit legendary history.

It should therefore not come as a surprise that a work like Geoffrey of Monmouth's *Historia regum Britanniae* would have been of interest to Icelanders, given their penchant for historiography. Indeed, the author of *Skjöldunga saga* is believed to have known Geoffrey's *Historia* (Wolf 1993, 597). Through the translation of the *Historia*, the Icelanders' store of historiography, that is, the histories of the kings of Norway and of the legendary kings of Denmark, was enriched by British royal history. Geoffrey's life of King Arthur, replete as it was with battles against heathens, encounters with giants and the conquests of foreign territories, was in many respects comparable to the lives of the Nordic kings, both prehistoric and historic. And the prophecies of Merlin were a perfect counterpoint to those of the Seeress in *Völuspá*, the first poem of the *Poetic Edda*.

At the same time that Icelanders were compiling the lives of the Norwegian kings, namely *Morkinskinna* and *Heimskringla*, and began to record the histories of their own ancestors in the Sagas of Icelanders, King Hákon Hákonarson (r.1217–63) of Norway, grandson of King Sverrir Sigurðarson, commissioned the translation of mostly French fiction, including romances belonging to the *matière de Bretagne*. Hákon's accession to the throne in 1217 was contested and not until 1223, with the cooperation and affir-mation of the Church, was Hákon's legitimacy as the successor of his father King Hákon Sverrisson on the Norwegian throne accepted. Some had accused Hákon of not being the legitimate son of Hákon Sverrisson and were unwilling to accept him as king until his mother Inga underwent an ordeal and swore an oath as to her son's legiti-macy. This occurred in 1218, even though Hákon was already king in 1217. She had to carry a glowing iron and when the bandages were removed from her hand, everyone said that it was more beautiful than before. Both friends and enemies attested to this. The narrator reports that God worked great miracles in his mercy so that she was proven innocent. The source for this, indeed for the entire life of Hákon is *Hákonar saga Hákonarsonar* (Mundt edn 1977, 30), which was written by the Icelander Sturla Þórðarson (1214–84), the nephew of Snorri Sturluson, the author of *Heimskringla*. The biography was commissioned by Hákon's son Magnús Hákonarson (r.1263–80), called *lagabœtir* 'Law-mender' in recognition of his promulgation of a unified code of law for all of Norway.

Hákon Hákonarson's reign was characterized by extensive contact with foreign princes and their courts, especially that of Henry III (r.1216–72) of England. Hákon promoted trade, including most importantly the importation of foreign literature. It is generally thought that the texts he had translated at his court came by way of England.[4] In any case, Matthew Paris of St Albans refers to him approvingly as 'bene litter-atus',[5] which might suggest that Hákon's furtherance of literature was well known in England. Hákon made every effort to raise the standards of his court to a level enjoyed by other European monarchs. That he had to battle some misconceptions as to the culture of the North is made clear at his coronation by Cardinal William of Sabina, the pope's representative, in 1247, thirty years after Hákon began his rule. William had sailed to Norway via England, was well received by Henry III, but was then told by some Englishmen – they are not identified – not to expect a proper reception in Bergen, not even enough food, and they advised him not to go to Norway (*Hákonar saga Hákonarsonar* 1977, 139). The cardinal is not deterred. At the feast following Hákon's coronation, he holds a speech and says that he had been told that there would be few people present on this occasion and that those he encountered would be more like animals than men. But, he continues, this is not the case. He sees here innumer-able people not only from this country but also from abroad, and he has never seen a greater fleet of ships in a harbour. He had been told that he would get but little to eat and poor food at that and nothing to drink but water and some watered-down whey. But this has also proven not to be the case, for he has received nothing but the best (*Hákonar saga Hákonarsonar* 1977, 142–3). The account of Hákon's coronation is important for giving us a sense of the king's cultural ambitions and what he had achieved during his reign.

One of Hákon's most far-reaching initiatives was the importation of foreign litera-ture and its translation into Old Norse. The year 1226, thus scholarly consensus, is the year in which Hákon Hákonarson introduced the Arthurian legend at his court. According to the testimony of a seventeenth-century Icelandic manuscript, AM 543, 4to, the king commissioned the translation of the legend of Tristan and Iseult into Norse. *Tristrams saga ok Ísöndar*, the title by which the translation is known, opens as follows:

> Hér skrifaz sagan af Tristram ok Ísönd dróttningu, í hverri talat verðr um óbæriliga ást, er þau höfðu sín á milli. Var þá liðit frá hingatburði Christi 1226 ár, er þessi saga var á norrænu skrifuð eptir befalningu ok skipan virðuliga herra Hákonar kóngs. En Bróðir Robert efnaði ok upp skri-faði eptir sinni kunnáttu með þessum orðtökum, sem eptir fylgir í sögunni ok nú skal frá segja. (Jorgensen edn 1999, 28)

> (Written down here is the story of Tristram and Queen Ísönd and of the heartrending love that they shared. This saga was translated into the Norse tongue at the behest and decree of King Hákon when 1226 years had passed since the birth of Christ. Brother Robert ably prepared the text and wrote it down in the words appearing in this saga. And now it shall be told.) (Jorgensen trans. 1999, 29)

The text that follows is a translation of the courtly version by Thomas de Bretagne which today is extant, however, solely in fragmentary form. Since *Tristrams saga* was translated from a manuscript containing the complete work, it is an extraordinarily important witness to the French romance. It should be noted that the German version of Thomas's *Tristan* by Gottfried von Strassburg is incomplete. If the date is to be trusted, Hákon was twenty-two years old at the time of the translation; a year earlier he had married.

In the wake of *Tristrams saga*, or contemporaneously with its translation, a number of other Arthurian narratives were transmitted to the North. These include three romances by Chrétien de Troyes, his *Erec et Enide* (*Erex saga*), *Yvain* or *Le Chevalier au lion* (*Ívens saga*) and *Perceval* or *Le Conte du graal* (*Parcevals saga* together with *Valvens þáttr*, the latter transmitting the text from v. 6514 to the fragmentary conclusion of *Perceval*). Like *Tristrams saga*, *Ívens saga* was translated, according to the testimony of the manuscripts, at the behest of King Hákon (Kalinke edn 1999, 98),[6] and this is also the case for the anonymous *Lai du cort mantel* or *Le mantel mautaillié*, an Arthurian fabliau (Kalinke edn 1999, 6).[7] Finally, a collection of Breton lais, some ascribed to Marie de France, was also translated into Norse and has become known as *Strengleikar*, that is, 'Stringed Instruments'. Two poems in the collection are Arthurian, namely *Chèvrefueille*, so called after the tale's prominent motif, the honeysuckle, which is translated as *Geitarlauf*, and *Lanval*, entitled *Januals ljóð* in translation. The prologue to the Norse translation of the lais names King Hákon as the instigator and also explains the name of the collection:

> <En> bok þessor er hinn virðulege hacon konungr let norrœna or volsko male ma hæita lioða bok. þui at af þæim sogum er þæssir bok birtir gærðo skolld i syðra brætlande er liggr i frannz lioð-songa. þa er gærazc i horpum gigiom. Simphanom. Organom. Timpanom. Sallterium. ok corom. ok allzkonar oðrum strænglæikum er menn gera ser ok oðrum til skemtanar þæssa lifs. (Cook and Tveitane edn 1979, 4)

> (This book, which the esteemed King Hákon had translated into Norse from the French language, may be called 'Book of Lais', because from the stories which this book makes known, poets in Brittany – which is in France – composed lais, which are performed on harps, fiddles, hurdy-gurdies, lyres, dulcimers, psalteries, rotes, and other stringed instruments of all kinds which men make to amuse themselves and others in this world.) (Cook and Tveitane trans. 1979, 5)

Only *Erex saga* and *Parcevals saga* are silent as to how and why these two romances found their way to the North. Scholars assume that the translations of *Erec et Enide* and *Perceval* also occurred at Hákon's court, given what appears to have been a concerted programme of translation and the evidence of the other Arthurian texts, but the transmission of *Erex saga* is most problematic (see chapter 2). The Norwegian king's interest in the courtly literature of other countries is undeniable, however, as is his patronage of at least one translator. A single name has come down to us, that of Brother Robert, who presumably is the same person as the Abbot Robert named as the translator of *Elis saga ok Rósamundu*, the Norse rendering of the French *chanson de geste Elie de St Gille*.[8]

Hákon's interest in having French literature translated for his court was presumably as much social and political as literary. His translators, aside from Robert whose identity as a religious is attested, most likely were clerics. Although we do not know the name of the translator of the *Strengleikar*, his clerical status is suggested by a singular long commentary (extending to some fifty lines in the printed edition) that he interpolated before the concluding sentence of *Equitan*, one of the lais in the collection (Cook 1998, 108), and addressed to his listeners:

> EN sa er þessa bok norrœnaðe ræðr ollum er þessa sogu hœyra ok hœyrt hava at þæir girnicz alldregi þat er aðrar æigu rett fengit. huarke fe ne hiuscaps felaga. ne ovunde alldre annars gott næ gævo. (Cook and Tveitane edn 1979, 78)

> (He who put this book into Norwegian advises all who hear and have heard this story that they never covet that which others own by right, whether property or partner in marriage, and that they never envy another man's lot or luck.) (Cook and Tveitane trans. 1979, 79)

And the translator expressly reveals that he had indeed intended to teach a lesson, for he concludes his interpolation with 'ok lykr her nu sinu ærendi. sa er bok þessare sneri' (and here he who translated this book concludes his message) (Cook and Tveitane edn and trans. 1979, 82–3). In other words, he construed the tale he was translating as an exemplum. In his admonitory interpolation the translator warns not only against envy and covetousness, but also against deceiving, betraying and dishonouring others, and he exhorts his readers and listeners to atone for their misdeeds in this life so as not to be punished in the next.

The Arthurian romances and lais translated at King Hákon's court had as their focus a great king, Arthur, and they related the exploits of some of his knights who, finally, also became rulers. That the imported Arthurian literature, although most entertaining, might also have had a didactic function is already voiced in the Middle Ages by one anonymous Icelandic author of a romance. In the preface to the late fourteenth-century *Flóres saga konungs ok sona hans* ('The Saga of King Flóres and his Sons') the author essays a classification of the sagas known to him, among them sagas of powerful kings, and he notes that 'má þar nema í hæverska hirðsiðu eða hversu þjóna skal ríkum höfðingjum' (one can learn there courtly manners and how one should serve powerful chieftains) (Bjarni Vilhjálmsson edn 1954, 65). This opinion is shared by many a modern literary critic who understands Hákon's programme of translation as an effort to educate his court in the finer manners of the long-established courts, especially those of France and England (Lönnroth 1978, 57–9; Damsgaard Olsen 1965, 107–8). Presumably B. Bandlien's assessment is correct that Hákon's programme of translation was generated by 'his outward-looking politics, his goal being to become one of Europe's leading royal houses' (2005, 218).

Scholars believe that the same Robert whom King Hákon commissioned to translate Thomas's *Tristan* was asked by the king to translate the anonymous *Elie de St Gille*. In the Old Norse *Elis saga* the translator is named Robert and identified as 'Abbot' (Bjarni Vilhjálmsson edn 1954, 107) rather than 'Brother', as he is called in *Tristrams saga*. In any case, an interpolation suggests that the translated *chanson de geste* was read aloud during meals, for he exhorts his audience to listen carefully, since fine lore (*fögur fræði*) is better than filling the belly. During reading aloud one may eat but not drink too much: 'It is an honor to tell a story if the listeners pay attention, but wasted work if they refuse to listen' (Bjarni Vilhjálmsson edn 1954, 31).

The prologue to the *Strengleikar* informs us that King Hákon had the Book of Lais translated from French into Norse and that the stories contained therein were composed for amusement (*til skemtanar*). The conclusion of *Januals ljóð* reveals that these stories were told or read aloud, for the translator turns to his audience in thanks: 'haui þackir þeir er heyrðu' (thanks to those who listened) (Cook edn and trans. 1979, 226–7). Similarly, in the prologue to *Möttuls saga* the translator addresses the listeners (*yðr áheyrendum*) and remarks that his own work had been undertaken to provide *gaman* and *skemtan*, that is, entertainment and diversion, to the listeners, and states that Hákon's objective in having the *Lai du cort mantel* translated into Norse was to provide *nokkut gaman* (some entertainment) (Kalinke edn 1999, 6). Similarly, *Elis saga ok Rósamundu*, although not an Arthurian romance, was translated to provide entertainment, as the colophon informs us: 'Hákon konungur, son Hákons konungs, lét snúa þessi norrænubók yður til skemmt-anar' (King Hákon, the son of King Hákon, ordered this Norse book to be translated for your entertainment) (Bjarni Vilhjálmsson edn 1954, 107).

Not only the *matière de Bretagne* reached the North but also the *matière de France* and *matière de Rome*. In addition to the Arthurian romances and lais, Scandinavia was introduced via translation to *chansons de geste* and pseudo-historiographic works about Greek, Roman and British antiquity. Among the translations of *chansons de geste* we find such works as *Bevers saga* (*Boeve de Haumtone*); *Karlamagnús saga*, a compilation of a number of Carolingian *gestes*, chief among them the *Chanson de Roland*; *Mágus saga jarls*, the major portion of which derives ultimately from *Les quatre fils Aymon* (also known as *Renaud de Montauban*), another Carolingian *chanson de geste*; and the aforementioned *Elis saga*. Included among the pseudo-historiographic works are *Alexanders saga* (Gautier de Châtillon's *Alexandreis*) and *Trójumanna saga* (deriving chiefly from Dares Phrygius's *De excidio belli Troiani*). Also from the realm of pseudo-historiography comes *Breta sögur* (Geoffrey of Monmouth's *Historia regum Britanniae*) with its important Arthurian section (Kalinke 1985, 322; Kalinke 2009).

The translations of this rather varied literature are known as *riddarasögur*, sagas of knights or chivalric sagas, an appellation that already had currency in the Middle Ages. The term appears at the conclusion of the younger redaction of *Mágus saga jarls*, 'Saga of Earl Mágus', which has been transmitted in a shorter and a longer recension from around 1300 and 1350 respectively. The author states that people want to hear stories that they consider enjoyable and entertaining, such as *Þiðreks saga* and *Flóvents saga* as well as other *riddarasögur* (Bjarni Vilhjálmsson edn 1953, 429).[9] *Þiðreks saga* and *Flóvents saga* derive from German and French heroic epic cycles respectively. *Þiðreks saga* is a large compilation of German narratives revolving around Dietrich von Bern

(Theoderic), while *Flóvents saga* is an analogue to the French heroic epic *Floovant*. Thus, the term *riddarasaga* applies to both indigenous and foreign narratives relating deeds of chivalry by protagonists in pseudo-historiographic narratives (*chansons de geste* and German heroic epics) as well as romances.

Scholars have long argued that the translation of the so-called *riddarasögur* should be understood in the context of the civilizing and feudalizing efforts undertaken by Hákon Hákonarson at his court. Henry Goddard Leach believed that the translated literature was 'intended by Hákon as much for profit as for pleasure, to instruct those who surrounded him, in the ideals and customs, accoutrement and ceremonials of chivalry' (Leach 1921, 153). The position of contemporary scholarship is that 'transmission of the new chivalric ideology, as deliberately targeted by Hákon, could be achieved especially effectively through the medium of literature' (Glauser 2005, 375). Hákon, and subsequently also his son Magnús Hákonarson, who ruled together with his father from 1257 until Hákon's death in 1263, and alone until 1280, sought to raise the Norwegian court to the level of the more established European courts. During Hákon's reign a Norwegian *speculum regale* modeled on other Kings' and Princes' Mirrors, was composed, possibly also at the behest of the king. *Konungs skuggsjá*, 'King's Mirror', is believed to have been written by a cleric associated with the royal Norwegian court and to have been intended as a didactic work for Hákon Hákonarson's two sons, Hákon the Young (1232–57) and Magnús, who succeeded his father as king (Barnes 2007, 377–8; Holm-Olsen edn 1983, xi). The work contains a long section on the king and his court, and it includes among others segments on the courtiers' duties, good manners and ethical and moral rules for those serving the king (Larson trans. 1917, 162–92).

Certain aspects of Sturla Þórðarson's biography of King Hákon Hákonarson, *Hákonar saga Hákonarsonar*, suggest that the courtly ambience of the translated romances and lais may have had an impact on the manner in which Sturla Þórðarson presents Hákon and his court. For example, the depiction of Hákon's coronation feast in Bergen in 1247 is comparable to that of Arthur's coronation in Geoffrey of Monmouth's *Historia regum Britanniae*, as it is transmitted in the Icelandic transla-tion in *Breta sögur* in the manuscript AM 573 4to (Kalinke 2009, 190–1). Indeed, the description in *Hákonar saga Hákonarsonar* of Hákon's 'eight-day coronation feast in Bergen in the summer of 1247 rivals that of Arthur's feast in *Möttuls saga* for its splendor, political significance, and theatricality' (Larrington 2009, 523; *Möttuls saga* 1999, 8–9). Similarly, Sturla's depiction of the journey to and arrival of Hákon's daughter Kristín in Spain, where she is to be married to Felipe, a brother of King Alfonso X el sabio, is in the best tradition of Arthurian romance as is her reception at the royal court of King Jaime of Aragon and subsequently by King Alfonso in Castile (Sprenger 2000, 53–4, 119–20; Larrington 2009, 524–6).

That medieval Icelanders were aware of the esteem foreign literature enjoyed at Hákon's court is suggested in an indigenous Icelandic romance, *Blómstrvalla saga*, thought to have been composed before 1500. The saga opens with an account of how emissaries of Emperor Frederick II came from Spain courting Hákon Hákonarson's daughter Kristín for whom the emperor intended to find a suitable match. The Norwegian king agrees and the saga reports how Kristín is received in Spain where the emperor asks her to choose among his three brothers. Her choice falls on Hermann and they are married (Pálmi Pálsson edn 1892, 3–4). This does not comport with the facts, but the account suggests that the author was familiar, albeit not quite accurately, with *Hákonar saga Hákonarsonar* (Hugus 1993, 50). The prologue concludes with the statement that a certain Master Bjarni from Nidaros, who led the wedding party from Norway, heard the following *Blómstrvalla saga* read in German and that he subsequently brought the narrative to Norway. One group of German narratives did indeed originate in translation at Hákon's court, namely *Þiðreks saga* (Kramarz-Bein, 2002), and the author of *Blómstrvalla saga* borrowed freely from this work. It is improbable, however, that *Blómstrvalla saga* was indeed translated at Hákon's court. It is more likely that the prologue is a pseudo-historical fictional frame for the Icelandic saga (Kramarz-Bein 2002, 312–13).

There is one notable oddity about the Arthurian texts that were supposedly translated in Norway and presumably during Hákon Hákonarson's reign: except for the two lais in the *Strengleikar* collection, not a single Arthurian narrative has been preserved in a Norwegian manuscript.[10] Our entire manuscript evidence is Icelandic and what we know about these translations is based on texts copied in the late Middle Ages or early modern times and in a culture quite distinct from that obtaining at the thirteenth-century Norwegian court.[11] The oldest complete texts of *Ívens saga* and *Parcevals saga* are dated around 1400, while complete texts of *Erex saga*, *Möttuls saga* and *Tristrams saga* are transmitted in late seventeenth-century manuscripts (Kalinke 1985, 332–3). This has a distinct bearing on the scholarly discussion surrounding the nature of translation and the abilities of the translators; the motivation for the introduction of the *matière de Bretagne* in the North; the participation of Icelandic copyists in shaping the Arthurian narratives; in short, the problem of cultural transfer and acculturation.

That Iceland should have become acquainted with and appropriated texts that may originally have been intended for a courtly Norwegian audience is not surprising. From the earliest days of the settlement of Iceland in the late ninth century, mostly by Norwegians, Icelanders were frequent visitors to Norwegian courts and poets were especially welcome and honoured guests. Icelanders gave Norway its history, one might even say its identity, by memorializing it in their poetry and historiography. What we know about King Hákon Hákonarson, who gave the impetus to the import of Arthurian literature, we owe to an Icelander, Sturla Þórðarson, who wrote his biography. It should not be forgotten that Iceland, which for several centuries had been an independent commonwealth, became a part of the Norwegian kingdom in 1262, one year before Hákon's death. Indeed, it was Cardinal William of Sabina who, on the occasion of Hákon's coronation, had commented about Iceland that it was unjust that this country did not serve a king as did all other countries in the world (Mundt edn

1977, 144). With the support of the Church in Hákon's drive to subject Iceland to the Crown, Icelandic independence was doomed. Even before Iceland submitted to the Norwegian Crown, some Icelanders received titles of nobility from the king. Snorri Sturluson was in Norway in the years 1218–20 and before he returned to Iceland he was given the title of *lendr maðr*, 'royal vassal'. Snorri's son, Jón murtr, was in Norway in 1229 and at this time he received the titles of both *hirðmaðr*, 'retainer' and *skutilsveinn*, 'royal attendant'. That same year another Icelander, Gizur Þorvaldsson also became the king's *skutilsveinn*. In 1238 Norwegians were consecrated bishops in Iceland (Jón Jóhannesson 1958, 210–12). There was also a considerable import of Icelandic manuscripts in medieval Norway and a number of Norwegian manuscripts were actually written by Icelanders residing in Norway (Stefán Karlsson 2000, 202). Moreover, one or the other Icelander returning home or one or the other Norwegian taking up service in Iceland could have brought with him manuscripts containing translations of Arthurian literature. The ultimate irony of the cultural transfer is that the Arthurian literature translated in Norway became as a matter of fact Icelandic by virtue of its transformation at the hands of Icelandic copyists.

The translations of Arthurian literature in the North, whether they were undertaken in Norway or Iceland, bear, with one exception, one striking distinguishing characteristic: they are in prose. With the exception of Geoffrey of Monmouth's 'Prophetiae Merlini', which was a Latin prose text but which Gunnlaugr Leifsson rendered in verse, the Arthurian texts transmitted to the North were in verse but in translation they were transformed into prose, a prose that is rhetorically ornate, *Erex saga* excepted, and characterized by synonymous collocations that at times were enhanced by alliteration. The prose of the translations favours amplification through repetition, variation, parallelism and synonymy as a means of emphasis and ornamentation. It also employs grammatical variation and acoustical word play to accentuate a passage, be that for dialogue or in descriptive passages (see chapter 2). In this respect the Arthurian translations are quite different stylistically from the Sagas of Icelanders, but they proved to have a significant influence on the language of the indigenous Icelandic romances, the production of which was inspired by the foreign literary import.

A new genre developed in the first half of the fourteenth century in Iceland, the so-called *rímur*, literally 'rhymes', narrative poems divided into fits, each of which, known as a *ríma*, was composed in a differing pattern of rhyme and alliteration. The subject of these metrical romances came from the older saga literature, primarily the *riddarasögur*, both those translated from foreign sources and the indigenous imitations. Of the Arthurian narratives only *Möttuls saga* inspired a *rímur* version, most likely composed in the fourteenth century and known as *Skikkju rímur* 'Mantle Rhymes'. While the metrical version preserves the content of the saga, the serial nature of the plot presumably inspired the author to interpolate additional guests at Arthur's feast and women to be tested, notably from *Erex saga*, the Icelandic version of Chrétien de Troyes's *Erec et Enide* (see chapter 5).

Hákon Hákonarson is credited with having brought Arthurian narrative to the North. Some fifty years after his death, however, a second wave of translation occurred at the Norwegian court, this time at the behest of Queen Eufemia, the German wife of Hákon Magnússon (r.1299–1319), Hákon Hákonarson's grandson. In the period 1303–12 she commissioned the translation of three romances known collectively as *Eufemiavisor*, 'Eufemia poems', namely Chrétien de Troyes's *Yvain*; an anonymous narrative about Duke Frederick of Normandy, which was supposedly translated from French into German; and the romance about Floire and Blancheflor, which presumably is based on a Norwegian prose translation of the French romance. These three romances are distinguished in that unlike the translations undertaken during the reign of Hákon Hákonarson, they were rendered into Swedish and into verse, into so-called *Knittelvers*. Unlike *Ívens saga*, Chrétien de Troyes's *Yvain* was now translated not into prose but rather verse. This second translation, known as *Hærra Ivan*, may have been commissioned on the occasion of the betrothal of Eufemia's daughter Ingibjörg in 1302 to the Swedish duke Erik, brother of the king of Sweden. They were married in 1312. According to the manuscripts, Queen Eufemia had *Hærra Ivan* 'translated from French into our language', that is, Swedish (*Hærra Ivan* 1999, vv. 6435–7). With this translation a new genre, romance, was introduced into Sweden from France, at the same time that the verse form of the translation, the *Knittelvers*, was imported from Germany (see chapter 7).

While the main conduit of Arthurian literature to the North in the Middle Ages was Norway, the preservation of the Arthurian narratives was in the hands of Icelandic scribes, who were copying and transforming the translated texts well into the seventeenth century. With the exception of *Hærra Ivan* and the two Arthurian lais in the *Strengleikar* compilation, the Arthurian narratives transmitted to the North in the Middle Ages are known to us only in Icelandic redactions, and the degree to which these correspond to the original translations is debatable. Hence, scholarly discussion of the nature of translation into Old Norse is problematic and lacks consensus (see chapter 2).

Unlike the reception of Arthurian literature in the German-language area, where the translations led to the creation of new Arthurian romances, the impact of the Arthurian narratives in medieval Iceland was limited chiefly to modifying the translations through reduction of text, change of style, the occasional addition of material and in one instance recasting a prose narrative in metrical form. With one exception, the *Saga af Tristram ok Ísodd* (see chapter 8), the translations of the Arthurian narratives did not lead to the development of indigenous Arthurian romances in the North, but they did inspire the composition of late medieval and early modern ballads, *rímur* (Icelandic narrative poems) and folk tales (see chapter 9).

Notes

[1] *Breta sögur* in the manuscript AM 573, 4to, 51v; see also *Breta sögur*, Jón Sigurdsson edn, 1849, p. 94. The *Hauksbók* version reads: 'Artvr konvngr for en aðra herferð til Irlandz ok lagði þat vndir sig ok i þeiri ferð vann hann Orkneyiar ok Hialltland ok Svðreyiar Danmork ok Noreg Færeyiar ok Gotland ok lagþi skatt a oll þersi lond' (King Arthur undertook another expedition to Ireland and vanquished it. On that expedition he conquered the Orkneys, Shetland and the Hebrides, Denmark and Norway, the Faroes and Gotland, and taxed all these lands) (Finnur Jónsson edn, 1892–6, p. 289).

[2] No edition of the manuscript AM 573 4to has to date been published, but variants from the manuscript are found in the Jón Sigurdsson edn, 1849.

[3] On the occasion of a wedding feast, the anonymous author of *Þorgils saga ok Hafliða*, one of the sagas in the compilation *Sturlunga saga*, a chronicle of Icelandic history in the twelfth and thirteenth centuries, notes that King Sverrir considered some of the stories (*lygisögur*, 'lying' or 'fictional' sagas) told there amusing, *skemmtilegar* (*Sturlunga saga*, 1988, ed. Örnólfur Thorsson, Reykjavík, p. 22).

[4] On King Hákon's relationship to the English court and the importation of foreign literature to Norway, see H. G. Leach, *Angevin Britain and Scandinavia*, 1921; rpt Kraus, 1975, which is still an indispensable source on the subject.

[5] *Matthæus Parisiensis Monachi sancti Albani*, IV (1877), Rerum Britannicarum Medii Ævi Scriptores 57, p. 652.

[6] *Ívens saga* concludes with the statement: 'Ok lýkr hér sögu herra Íven er Hákon kóngr gamli lét snúa ór franzeisu í norrœnu' (And the saga of Sir Íven ends here, which King Hákon the Old had ordered translated from French into Norse) (Kalinke edn and trans. 1999, pp. 98–9).

[7] The prologue to *Möttuls saga* ends as follows: 'En þvílík sannindi sem valskan sýndi mér þá norrœnaða ek yðr áheyrendum til gamans ok skemtanar svá sem virðuligr Hákon kóngr, son Hákonar kóngs, bauð fákunnugleik mínum at gera nokkut gaman af þessu eptirfylgjanda efni' (And this true account, which came to me in French, I have translated into Norwegian as entertainment and diversion for you, the listeners, since the worthy King Hákon, son of King Hákon, asked me, ignorant though I be, to provide some entertainment through the following story) (Kalinke edn and trans., 1999, pp. 6–7).

[8] The translation ends as follows: 'En huersu sem Elis hratt þeim vandræðum og huersu hann kom heim til Franz með Rosamundam, þá er eigi á bok þessi skrifað. En Roðbert ábóti sneri, og Hákon konungr, son Hákons konungs, lét snúa þessi norænubók yður til skemmtanar' (Bjarni Vilhjálmsson edn 1954, p. 107) (But how Elis escaped from these difficulties and how he came back to France with Rosamunda is not written in this book. Abbot Robert translated it and King Hákon, son of King Hákon, had this Norse book translated for your entertainment). The statement above occurs at the end of the translation. The saga continues, however, with an addition composed by an Icelandic author.

[9] 'þat gera spakir menn, að þeir vilja heyra þær frásagnir, sem þeim þykir kátlegar til gamans, svo sem er Þiðriks saga, Flóvents saga eða aðrar riddarasögur.' The author of *Viktors saga ok Blávus*, an indigenous Icelandic romance states that Hákon Magnússon (r.1299–1319), the grandson of Hákon Hákonarson, had many *riddarasögur* translated from Greek and French into Norwegian: 'Hann lét venda mörgum riddara sögum í norrœnu ór girzsku ok franzeisku máli' (Jónas Kristjánsson edn 1964, 3).

[10] Scholars have assumed that the translations commissioned by King Hákon were undertaken in the environs of the Norwegian court. In her doctoral dissertation, however, '*Strengleikar* og *Lais*. Høviske noveller i omsetjing frå gammalfransk til gammalnorsk' (2009), I. B. Budal argues persuasively that the lais – including the two Arthurian narratives – were translated in Anglo-Norman England rather than in Norway (I, 415–26).

[11] It should be noted, however, that there was a considerable import of Icelandic manuscripts in medieval Norway and that a number of Norwegian manuscripts were actually written by Icelanders residing in Norway. See Stefán Karlsson (2000, 202).

Reference List

Texts and Translations

Blómstrvallasaga, ed. Pálmi Pálsson (Reykjavík, 1892).

Breta sögur, ed. Jón Sigurdsson, in *Annaler for Nordisk Oldkyndighed og Historie* (Copenhagen, 1849), pp. 3–145.

Breta sögur, ed. Finnur Jónsson, in *Hauksbók* (Copenhagen, 1892–96), pp. 231–302.

Elis saga ok Rosamundu, ed. E. Kölbing (1881; repr. Niederwalluf, 1971).

Elis saga ok Rósamundu, ed. Bjarni Vilhjálmsson, in *Riddarasögur*, IV ([Reykjavík], 1954), pp. 1–135.

Flóres saga konungs ok sona hans, ed. Bjarni Vilhjálmsson, in *Riddarasögur*, V ([Reykjavík], 1954), pp. 63–121.

Geoffrey of Monmouth. The History of the Kings of Britain: An Edition and Translation of De gestis Britonum [Historia regum Britanniae], ed. M. D. Reeve, trans. N. Wright (Woodbridge, 2007).

Hákonar saga Hákonarsonar etter Sth. 8 fol., AM 325 VIII, 4º og AM 304, 4º, ed. M. Mundt, Norrøne Tekster, 2 (Oslo, 1977).

Hærra Ivan, ed. and trans. H. Williams and K. Palmgren, in *Norse Romance*, III, ed. M. E. Kalinke (Cambridge, 1999).

Ívens saga (1999), ed. and trans. M. E. Kalinke, in *Norse Romance*, II: *The Knights of the Round Table*, ed. M. E. Kalinke (Cambridge, 1999), pp. 33–102.

The King's Mirror (Speculum regale – Konungs skuggsjá), trans. L. M. Larson (New York, 1917).

Konungs skuggsiá, ed. L. Holm-Olsen, 2nd rev. edn, Norrøne Tekster, 1 (Oslo, 1983).

Mágus saga jarls hin meiri, ed. Bjarni Vilhjálmsson, in *Riddarasögur*, II ([Reykjavík], 1953), pp. 135–429.

'Merlínússpá', ed. Finnur Jónsson, in *Hauksbók* (Copenhagen, 1892–6), pp. 272–83.

Morkinskinna: The Earliest Icelandic Chronicle of the Norwegian Kings (1030–1157), trans. T. M. Andersson and K. E. Gade, Islandica, 51 (Ithaca and London, 2000).

Möttuls saga, ed. and trans. M. E. Kalinke, in *Norse Romance*, II: *The Knights of the Round Table*, ed. M. E. Kalinke (Cambridge, 1999), pp. 1–31.

Snorri Sturluson, Heimskringla, ed. Bjarni Aðalbjarnarson, Íslenzk fornrit, 26 (Reykjavík, 1941).

Strengleikar: An Old Norse Translation of Twenty-one Old French Lais edited from the manuscript Uppsala De la Gardie 4–7 – AM 666 b, 4o, ed. and trans. R. Cook and M. Tveitane, Norrøne Tekster, 3 (Oslo, 1979).

Sverris saga, ed. Þorleifur Hauksson, Íslenzk fornrit, 30 (Reykjavík, 2007).

Tristrams saga ok Ísöndar (1999), ed. and trans. P. Jorgensen, in *Norse Romance*, I: *The Tristan Legend*, ed. M. E. Kalinke (Cambridge, 1999), pp. 23–226.

Viktors saga ok Blávus, ed. Jónas Kristjánsson, in *Riddarasögur*, II (Reykjavík, 1964).

Studies

Andersson, T. M. (2006). *The Growth of the Medieval Icelandic Sagas (1180–1280)*, Ithaca, NY.

Ármann Jakobsson (2005). 'Royal biography', in R. McTurk (ed.), *A Companion to Old Norse-Icelandic Literature and Culture*, Oxford, pp. 388–402.

Ásdís Egilsdóttir (2006). 'The beginnings of Icelandic hagiography', in L. B. Mortensen (ed.), *The Makings of Christian Myths in the Periphery of Latin Christendom (c. 1000–1300)*, Copenhagen, pp. 121–33.

Bandlien, B. (2005). *Strategies of Passion: Love and Marriage in Old Norse Society*, trans. B. van der Hoek, Turnhout.

Barnes, G. (2007). 'The "Discourse of Counsel" and the "Translated" *Riddarasögur*', in J. Quinn, K. Heslop and T. Willis (eds), *Learning and Understanding in the Old Norse World: Essays in Honour of Margaret Clunies Ross*, Turnhout, pp. 375–97.

Budal, I. B. (2009). '*Strengleikar* og *Lais*. Høviske noveller i omsetjing frå gammalfransk til gammalnorsk. I. Tekstanalyse. II. Synoptisk utgåve' (unpublished Ph.D. thesis, University of Bergen).

Cormack, M. (2005). 'Christian biography', in R. McTurk (ed.), *A Companion to Old Norse-Icelandic Literature and Culture*, Oxford, pp. 27–42.

Damsgaard Olsen, T. (1965). 'Den høviske litteratur', in H. Bekker-Nielsen, T. Damsgaard Olsen and O. Widding (eds), *Norrøn fortællekunst. Kapitler af den norsk-islandske middelalderlitteraturs historie*, Copenhagen, pp. 92–117.

Eysteinsson, J. S. (1953–5). 'The relationship of *Merlínússpá* and Geoffrey of Monmouth's *Historia*', *Saga-Book of the Viking Society for Northern Research*, XIV, 1–2, 95–112.

Gelsinger, B. E. (1981). 'A thirteeenth-century Norwegian–Castilian alliance', *Medievalia et Humanistica*, n.s. 10, 55–80.

Glauser, J. (2005). 'Romance (translated *riddarasögur*)', in R. McTurk (ed.), *A Companion to Old Norse-Icelandic Literature and Culture*, Oxford, pp. 372–87.

Halvorsen, E. F. (1959). *The Norse Version of the Chanson de Roland*, Bibliotheca Arnamagnæana, 19, Copenhagen.

Hugus, F. (1993). 'Blómstrvallasaga', in P. Pulsiano and K. Wolf (eds), *Medieval Scandinavia: An Encyclopedia*, New York and London, pp. 50–51.

Jón Jóhannesson (1958). *Íslendinga saga*, II: *Fyrirlestrar og ritgerðir um tímabilið 1262–1550*, Reykjavík.

Kalinke, M. E. (1985). 'Norse romance (*Riddarasögur*)', in C. J. Clover and J. Lindow (eds), *Old Norse-Icelandic Literature: A Critical Guide*, Islandica, 45, Ithaca; rpt. 2005, pp. 316–63.

Kalinke, M. E. (2006). 'Scandinavian Arthurian literature', in N. J. Lacy (ed.), *A History of Arthurian Scholarship*, Cambridge, pp. 169–78.

Kalinke, M. (2009). 'The Arthurian legend in *Breta sögur*: historiography on the cusp of romance', in Margrét Eggertsdóttir et al. (eds), *Greppaminni: Essays in Honour of Vésteinn Ólason*, Reykjavík, pp. 217–30.

Kramarz-Bein, S. (2002). *Die Þiðreks saga im Kontext der altnorwegischen Literatur*, Beiträge zur Nordischen Philologie, 33, Tübingen and Basel.

Larrington, C. (2009). 'Queens and bodies: the Norwegian translated *lais* and Hákon IV's kinswomen', *JEGP*, 108, 506–27.

Leach, H. G. (1921). *Angevin Britain and Scandinavia*, Harvard Studies in Comparative Literature, 6, Cambridge, MA; rpt. Kraus, 1975.

Lönnroth, L. (1978). *Den dubbla scenen. Muntlig diktning från Eddan till ABBA*, Stockholm.

Quinn, J. (2000). 'From orality to literacy in medieval Iceland', in M. Clunies Ross (ed.), *Old Icelandic Literature and Society*, Cambridge, pp. 30–60.

Sprenger, U. (2000). *Sturla Þórðarsons* Hákonar saga Hákonarsonar, Texte und Untersuchungen zur Germanistik und Skandinavistik, 46, Frankfurt am Main.

Stefán Karlsson (2000). 'Islandsk bogeksport til Norge i Middelalderen', in *Stafkrókar*. Ritgerðir eftir Stefán Karlsson gefnar út í tilefni af sjötugsafmæli 2. desember 1998, Reykjavík, pp. 188–205; rpt of *Maal og minne*, 1979, 1–17.

Tulinius, T. H. (2005). 'Sagas of Icelandic prehistory', in R. McTurk (ed.), *A Companion to Old Norse-Icelandic Literature and Culture*, Oxford, pp. 447–61.

Turville-Petre, G. (1953). *Origins of Icelandic Literature*, Oxford.

Vésteinn Ólason. (2005). 'Family sagas', in R. McTurk (ed.), *A Companion to Old Norse-Icelandic Literature and Culture*, Oxford, pp. 101–18.

Wolf, K. (1993). 'Skjǫldunga saga', in P. Pulsiano and K. Wolf (eds), *Medieval Scandinavia: An Encyclopedia*, New York and London, pp. 597–8.

Würth, S. (1998). *Der 'Antikenroman' in der isländischen Literatur des Mittelalters. Eine Untersuchung zur Übersetzung und Rezeption lateinischer Literatur im Norden*, Basel and Frankfurt am Main.

Würth, S. (2005). 'Historiography and pseudo-history', in R. McTurk (ed.), *A Companion to Old Norse-Icelandic Literature and Culture*, Oxford, pp. 155–72.

2

SOURCES, TRANSLATIONS, REDACTIONS, MANUSCRIPT TRANSMISSION

Marianne E. Kalinke

Study of the Arthurian matter translated in Norway and Iceland is complicated by the fact that in no case do we have the manuscript from which a text was translated, be that French or Latin, and in no instance has a manuscript been preserved that represents the actual translation, be that into Norwegian or Icelandic. Even the only Norwegian manuscript that postdates by only a few decades the translation of a group of short narratives has been shown to be an unreliable witness of the actual translation.

In the transmission of the *matière de Bretagne* to the North a twofold cultural transfer took place: on the one hand, the introduction of courtly romance, which heretofore had been unknown in both Iceland and Norway; on the other hand, the introduction of metrical narrative which, with the exception of the mythological and heroic Eddic poetry, was also foreign to the North. The normal form of narrative in Iceland and Norway was prose and the Arthurian rhymed romances underwent a formal acculturation by being rendered in prose. Complicating further the introduction of the Arthurian matter in thirteenth-century Norway is the fact that the translations are preserved, with but one exception, solely in Icelandic manuscripts, the complete texts of most dating from the seventeenth century.

Not only the fact that in most instances centuries intervened between a translation and its transmission in manuscript but also a peculiar propensity of some Icelandic copyists to understand their task more as that of a revising editor than a mindless scribe means that in quite a few instances the manuscripts transmitting the *matière de Bretagne* in the North cannot be considered to represent the thirteenth-century translations. Occasionally, recourse to all manuscripts of an Arthurian translation permits a reconstruction that brings us close to what the original text must have contained, but this is usually the case only for select passages, not an entire work. Consequently, scholarly debate on the Old Norse translations frequently focuses on the question whether they provide insight into the work of the translators in thirteenth-century Norway or the creative endeavours of later Icelandic scribes. Are the deviations of these texts from their sources, be that in content or structure, to be understood as evidence of acculturation at the court of King Hákon Hákonarson or in the rural environs of Iceland?

No other Arthurian literature has generated as much discussion concerning the relationship of translations and their sources as that transmitted in Old Norse-Icelandic texts. Repeatedly scholars have addressed the reliability of the extant texts not only for assessing the abilities of the translators but also for the insight they give into the cultural context and motivation that permitted the importation to Norway and Iceland of a literature quite foreign. Given the manuscript transmission of the translations undertaken in thirteenth-century Norway and Iceland, the crucial question is whether the Arthurian texts in the Icelandic manuscripts that preserve the medieval translations actually correspond to those translations or whether they are to be considered late medieval and early modern Icelandic reworkings of those translations. If the extant Icelandic manuscripts do not transmit more or less reliably the texts produced by thirteenth-century translators, mostly in Norway, then how is this corpus of Arthuriana to be understood: as a Norwegian product of a royal court or an Icelandic product of a rural society? The degree to which the Icelandic redactions approximate the Norwegian translations has been a contentious issue and the position taken by scholars has influenced their understanding of the purpose of the translated literature – for entertainment or edification or both – at King Hákon Hákonarson's thirteenth-century Norwegian court.

The translation and transmission of the *matière de Bretagne* in Norway and Iceland has confronted scholars with issues and problems absent in other Arthurian literatures, in part because of the drastic alterity of Arthurian narrative *vis-à-vis* the indigenous Norse literature, in part because of the vagaries of Icelandic manuscript transmission. This is unlike the transmission of French romance in the German-language area, for example, where the oldest Arthurian romance is Hartmann von Aue's (*c*.1160–*c*.1210) late twelfth-century version of Chrétien de Troyes's *Erec et Enide*. Hartmann's *Erec* is preserved in one (almost) complete manuscript, in the so-called *Ambraser Heldenbuch*, compiled by Hans Ried around 1510 and commissioned by Emperor Maximilian I (Gibbs and Johnson 1997, 135). Despite a gap of three centuries between the time of composition and this copy, scholars accept the manuscript as representing more or less Hartmann's *Erec*. The case is otherwise in the North, where not only the interval between translation and copy but also the significant discrepancies among the preserved manuscripts prove to be major obstacles to assessing the character of the thirteenth-century translations.

Translations and their sources

Not a single manuscript from which an Arthurian text was translated in either Norway or Iceland has been either preserved or identified. The translations deviate in many respects from the sources available to us in editions. The question at all times is whether the deviations, be they modifications of content or additions, are to be ascribed to the unknown source manuscript, the translator or a later copyist. The one certainty about the *matière de Bretagne* in the North is that the text as it exists in any one manuscript is a text that was known and enjoyed in Iceland at a particular time.

A case in point is *Breta sögur*, the Icelandic version of Geoffrey of Monmouth's *Historia regum Britanniae*, which is extant in two fourteenth-century redactions, AM 573 4to and AM 544 4to, the latter generally referred to as *Hauksbók* after its redactor Haukr Erlendsson (d. 1334), who transmits a greatly reduced version of *Breta sögur*. Geoffrey's *Historia* was known in Iceland by the end of the twelfth century, and it is safe to assume that the translation of the *Historia* occurred around the year 1200, presumably in the Benedictine monastery of Þingeyrar, a centre of historiography in late twelfth- and early thirteenth-century Iceland, and the home of the monk Gunnlaugr Leifsson (d.1218 or 1219), the author of *Merlínússpá*, the translation of Geoffrey of Monmouth's 'Prophetiae Merlini'. We do not know whether the text of the 'Prophecies' was a separate work or whether it was available to Gunnlaugr as part of the *Historia*.

The AM 573 redaction of *Breta sögur* transmits a version of Geoffrey's Arthurian matter that approximates in many respects the narrativization and fictionalization that we are wont to associate with courtly romance rather than historiography. This redaction of *Breta sögur* pays heed to emotions, to courtly ceremonial, to the dramatic interaction of characters and to visual detail. A comparison with Geoffrey's *Historia* and with other translations and redactions of the same reveals that the source of the Icelandic translation could not have been the Latin text known to us today in the several editions. A case in point is a minor detail in the depiction of Arthur's coronation. We are told that archbishops accompanied the queen to her seat and that four kings walked before her who 'báru með sínum höndum fiórar huítar dúfur, sua sem sníorr' (bore in their hands four doves, white as snow) (Jón Sigurdsson edn 1849, 100). Geoffrey's *Historia* has a variant of this detail: not four kings walked before the queen, but rather the wives of these kings (Reeve edn 2007, 213). While one might attribute the deviation in *Breta sögur* to a translator's lapse, the very same variant is found, however, in the metrical version, *Gesta regum Britannie*, where we read: 'Quam precedentes precedunt bis duo reges / Portantes manibus albas de more columbas' (Before her walk four kings, carrying, according to custom, white doves in their hands) (Wright edn and trans. 1991), vv. 429–30). The accord of the readings in the Icelandic translation with the metrical Latin version suggests that the source of *Breta sögur* did indeed contain the deviating reading.

Similarly, in the account of the festivities following Arthur's coronation, Geoffrey summarizes: 'Refecti tandem epulis, diuersi diuersos ludos composituri campos extra ciuitatem adeunt' (Reeve edn 2007, 213) (When at last they had had their fill at the banquets, they separated to visit the fields outside the city and indulge in varied sports) (Wright trans. 2007, 212), whereas *Breta sögur* provides details. Geoffrey's 'diuersi diuersos ludos composituri' are listed: 'þá voru leikar oc taufl oc saugur. Þar var allzkyns streingleikar: fiðlur oc gígiur, bumbur oc pípur oc simphóníam oc haurpur' (there were games of chance and board games and stories; there were all kinds of stringed instruments, fiddles and viols, drums and pipes and hurdy-gurdies and harps) (Jón

Sigurdsson edn 1849, 100–1). That the enumeration in *Breta sögur* is not the work of the translator is attested by the corresponding passage in Wace's *Roman de Brut*, which reports at even greater length on the music and games played on the occasion (Weiss edn 2002, vv. 10,543–60). Comparison with Wace's *Brut* reveals that many of the passages and details in *Breta sögur* that are not found in the *Historia* also occur in French translation, and this suggests that the source of *Breta sögur* was a Latin redaction that had expatiated on the *Historia*, that is, as we know it today, and this was in many respects similar to one of Wace's sources. The example given here is only one of many passages containing additional details in *Breta sögur* that agree with text in Wace's *Brut*. Others occur neither in the *Historia* nor the *Brut*, but taken together they attest that the Latin redaction available to the translator of *Breta sögur* contained a text of the Arthurian legend that deviated in many respects from the *Historia* as we know it.

The divergences occur not only in respect to detail but also the structure of the narrative. One of the more noteworthy structural discrepancies concerns the location in the narrative of Arthur's two encounters with giants, with the giant of Mont-Saint-Michel and the giant Ritho who challenged kings, including finally Arthur, to give him their beards so that he might fashion a cloak from them. In the *Historia* the two episodes relating Arthur's encounters with giants succeed each other (Reeve edn 2007, 224–7). After having slain the giant of Mont-Saint-Michel, Arthur comments that he had never met anyone as strong other than the giant he had killed on Mount Aravius. This had taken place on an earlier occasion, and thus the episode is recounted as a flashback by Geoffrey. This is also the case in the *Roman de Brut*. In *Breta sögur*, however, the encounter with the beard-collecting giant, here called Rikion, occurs at what one redactor must have considered the chronologically more appropriate place, that is, after Arthur's killing of Frollo in single combat. The aptness of having the episode with the giant Rikion follow hard upon Arthur's single combat with Frollo may have been suggested by the manner in which Frollo is depicted in *Breta sögur*, and presumably in its Latin source. Frollo is described as being 'mikill sem risar oc suartr sem iörð, oc var þó meira afl en uauxtr, hann var oc allra manna fimaztr til vapns oc því var trautt menzkra manna at eiga við hann vapnaskipti' (Jón Sigurdsson edn 1849, 96, fn. 1) (large like giants and black as earth, yet this was more due to physical strength than size; he was the most dexterous of all men in wielding weapons and for this reason human beings were reluctant to engage him in combat). Even though Frollo is not identified as a giant, the reference to *menzkra manna* 'human beings' suggests that there is something of the monster in him. Thus, Arthur's slaying of Frollo seems to be a logical preliminary to his encounter with Rikion, who is identified as 'nálega risi at afli ok vexti ok enn mesti berserkr at yfirgángi oc viafnaði, oc bitu hann eigi iárn' (Jón Sigurdsson edn 1849, 96–7) (nearly a giant in strength and size and the greatest *berserkr* in respect to arrogance and injustice, and weapons did not bite him).

The *matière de Bretagne* that was transmitted in the thirteenth century in Iceland and Norway consists of translations of French and Latin texts. The significance of a work like *Breta sögur* resides in its transmitting in Icelandic a version of the Arthurian legend in Geoffrey's *Historia* that may be considered, like Wace's *Roman de Brut*, transitional in the development of romance from historiography. The AM 573 redaction of *Breta sögur*, even while it presumably is a somewhat condensed version of the translation that took place shortly after the year 1200, nevertheless attests a Latin redactor's efforts to augment the story of the life of King Arthur. The source of the translation has not been preserved, or at least is unknown to this day, and hence *Breta sögur* is important for giving us a different perspective on and mode of narrating the biography that is Arthur's. Unfortunately to date no scholarly edition of *Breta sögur* exists – although one is to be published in the Editiones Arnamagnæanæ – but the important manuscript that transmits the longer version of the translation suggests that in all likelihood we possess here a distinct, augmented version of the legend of King Arthur in Geoffrey of Monmouth's *Historia regum Britanniae*. To judge by the extant text, the translator was an exceptional Latinist and the translation permits conjectures as to some of the content of the Latin source.

In the case of *Breta sögur*, which contains the oldest of the Arthurian texts translated in the North, comparison with the extant (edited) manuscripts of Geoffrey of Monmouth's *Historia regum Britanniae* and variant versions and translations thereof, leads to the conclusion that for want of the actual source manuscript there is some but not much basis for determining whether the changes, omissions or additions in *Breta sögur* are to be ascribed to the translator or his Latin source. The situation is both similar and different in the shortest Arthurian text, *Geitarlauf*, one of the lais in the *Strengleikar* collection, which was translated in Norway and is preserved in the oldest and only Norwegian manuscript containing Arthurian narratives, De la Gardie 4–7. The source of *Geitarlauf* is Marie de France's *Chèvrefeuille*, which is 118 verses in length. The brevity of the lai, which is extant in only two French manuscripts, and the fact that the translation contains all but twelve of the lai's verses (Cook and Tveitane edn and trans. 1979, 195) provide insight into both the translator's method and the difficulty of determining whether deviations from the French lai are to be ascribed to the translator or to his source manuscript. Comparison of *Geitarlauf* with Richard O'Gorman's diplomatic transcription of the two manuscripts of *Chèvrefeuille* (1998, 195–7) reveals that neither can have been the source of the translation. One vexing passage exemplifies, however, the kind of crux scholars face when they attempt to determine the usefulness of the translations for either revealing the nature of the French source or judging the translator's ability or method.

The focal point of the lai is the message that Tristan inscribes on a piece of hazelwood to apprise Isolt of his presence. Verses 61–78 of *Chèvrefeuille* have been the object of scholarly speculation as to whether the piece of wood contained only Tristan's name or the text of a message (Cagnon 1970). *Geitarlauf* is unambiguous:

Tristan inscribed not only his name but also a long message – *nu var ristið a stavenom* 'now it was carved on the stick' (Cook and Tveitane edn and trans. 1979, 198–9) – in which he compares his relationship to Isolt to that between the honeysuckle and the hazel tree. The French text cited for the lai has generally been that of British Library, MS Harley 978, which leaves the issue unresolved, and hence the Norse translator would seem to have been the first interpreter, as it were, of the ambiguous French text (Kalinke 1981, 78–9). With O'Gorman's transcription of the text of *Chèvrefeuille* in the manuscript nouv. acq. fr. 1104 (Paris, Bibliothèque Nationale) it is now evident that this manuscript supports the reading in *Geitarlauf*: *Ce fu la somme de l'escrit / qui fu el baston que j'e dit* 'This is the gist of the message / on the stick that I described' (O'Gorman edn. 1998: vv. 61–2).

Geitarlauf is not only extraordinarily brief, compared to the other translations of Arthurian texts, but also preserved in the oldest manuscript containing the *matière de Bretagne* in the North. This may account for the relative 'accuracy' of the translation, if judged by the two extant French manuscripts. Despite the agreement of the above passage in *Geitarlauf* with that in nouv. acq. fr. 1104, at other times the Norse translation sides with Harley 978 (see Cook and Tveitane edn and trans. 1979, 195–9). Hence, neither manuscript can be said to represent the source of the translation.

Whereas *Geitarlauf* is exceptional in the corpus of the Norse *matière de Bretagne* for having been transmitted in the oldest and only Norwegian manuscript, *Tristrams saga ok Ísöndar* is beyond a doubt the most important and invaluable of the translations commissioned by King Hákon Hákonarson. There is scholarly consensus that it was the first of the translations of foreign literature in the North and that it set the tone for the translations that were to follow. More remarkably, *Tristrams saga* is the only complete representative of the Thomas branch of the legend. Thomas's romance is preserved only fragmentarily and Gottfried von Strassburg's adaptation is incomplete. The most thorough and meticulous analysis of the saga in respect to its source was conducted by Álfrún Gunnlaugsdóttir who concluded that there can be no doubt that the saga faithfully transmitted the content of Thomas's romance. Where Brother Robert altered the poem in translation, it was not by way of addition but rather chiefly by omission. The text that is there, the omissions excepted, may properly be called a translation (Álfrún Gunnlaugsdóttir 1978, 332, 350). This has consequences for our assessment of deviations from Thomas's *Tristan* in the saga.

One notable divergence between Thomas's text and the saga has come to light only since the publication of *Tristán en el Norte*, with the discovery of the Carlisle Fragment of the romance (Short edn 1998, 173–83), which contains the wedding-night episode. This differs markedly in one significant point from what we read in *Tristrams saga*. According to the Carlisle Fragment Brangain leaves Mark's bed after he has satisfied his desires; Yseut takes her place, and after the wine has been served (v. 149), Mark sleeps with her. There is no indication that the wine is actually the magic potion that Yseut and Mark were to drink. In the saga, however, when Markis wakes

up at Ísönd's side and asks for some wine, Bringvet gives him the wine that Ísönd's
mother had concocted – but Ísönd, the narrator comments, did not drink any of this
(Jorgensen edn 1999, 120). Some scholars believe that Brother Robert introduced the
change in translation, and this in turn has been interpreted as the translator's attempt
to accommodate the narrative to conditions at the Norwegian court through the creation of a more positive figure in the king: his drinking of the love potion explains King
Mark's inordinate love for Isolt despite her adultery.[1] Such an interpretation is based
on the assumption that the text of the Carlisle Fragment represents the text of Brother
Robert's source. If this is indeed the case and the translator modified the text, then it
is at odds with Brother Robert's otherwise consistent approach to translation: there is
certain evidence that while he may omit text from his source, he does not modify.

One of the most vexing questions concerning the French narratives translated
during the reign of King Hákon Hákonarson of Norway is the reliability of the extant
manuscripts in transmitting the work of the thirteenth-century translators. Scholars
fall into two camps, those who believe the extant manuscripts of the Old Norse
Arthurian narratives represent the work of the thirteenth-century translators[2] and those
who consider them the result of interventions by Icelandic copyists.[3] On the basis of
omissions, additions and changes *vis-à-vis* the sources, the former seek to assess both
the competence of the translator and his motivation for omitting or modifying the
text of his source. The latter view the divergences of the Arthurian narratives from
their sources in the context of indigenous Icelandic literature and the attested penchant
of Icelandic scribes for modifying, in content or style or both, the texts they were
copying. Whatever position one takes, scholars have to keep in mind that the preserved
Latin and French manuscripts of the texts translated in Iceland and Norway are not the
source manuscripts and that not a single preserved manuscript, even the Norwegian
manuscript De la Gardie 4–7 containing the Arthurian lais, accurately reflects the text
that left the translator's pen, as will be seen below.

The manuscript transmission of the *matière de Bretagne* in the North

It is fairly certain that the earliest translation of an Arthurian text in the North,
Merlínússpá, occurred in Iceland around the year 1200. This metrical version of the
'Prophetiae Merlini' was presumably produced at around the same time and in the
same place as *Breta sögur*, the Icelandic version of the *Historia regum Britanniae*.
Unlike these two prophetic and historiographic texts, the courtly narratives, that is,
the Arthurian romances and lais, were presumably translated, with one or possibly
two exceptions, at the court of King Hákon Hákonarson of Norway. This places the
translation of Thomas's *Tristan* and Chrétien de Troyes's *Yvain*, and presumably also
Perceval in the years 1217–63, the period of Hákon's reign. During this same time
three Arthurian lais were translated, Marie de France's *Lanval* and *Chèvrefeuille*,

which are part of the *Strengleikar* compilation, and the anonymous *Lai du cort mantel* (or *Lai du mantel mautaillié*). Yet, with but a single exception – the *Strengleikar* – the Arthurian narratives that are thought to have been translated at and for the Norwegian court of Hákon Hákonarson are extant only in Icelandic manuscripts, produced at a time and in a social milieu quite different from that of early thirteenth-century Norway.

Only two Arthurian narratives are transmitted in a thirteenth-century Norwegian manuscript, namely *Januals ljóð* (a translation of *Lanval*) and *Geitarlauf* (a translation of *Chèvrefeuille*). The two lais are found in the codex De la Gardie 4–7, dated *c*.1270 and produced during the reign of King Magnús *lagabœtir* (Law-mender) of Norway (r.1263–80), son of Hákon Hákonarson. The two lais, along with nineteen others, constitute the *Strengleikar* collection, the translation of which, thus the manuscript, was commissioned by King Hákon Hákonarson.[4] Given that the De la Gardie codex was produced only a short time after the lais were translated, it was long assumed that the texts in the codex represented the translator(s)' work. In fact, Keyser and Unger, the first editors of the collection, thought that the texts in the manuscript represented the first fair copy of the translator's draft (Cook and Tveitane edn 1979, XIX). Comparison of the seventeen narratives in the *Strengleikar* collection known from French sources reveals that the fidelity or the completeness of the Norse translations varies considerably and that the range of abridgment in content vis-à-vis the extant French texts ranges from 5 per cent (*Bisclavret*) to 49.5 per cent (*Milun*) (Budal 2009, 189). The position of scholarship has been that the cuts, and also modifications, represent the work of the translator, and on that basis scholars have attempted to analyse the various *Strengleikar* with a view to understanding the motivation underlying the changes in the Norse translations.

Rudolf Meissner was the first to undertake a systematic study of the Norse translations in relation to their French sources (1902) and he attributed the various omissions and modifications to the translator. Thus, Meissner believed that some of the reduction in the Norse texts reflected the translator's dislike of descriptive detail and retarding moments and a preference for action. Meissner ascribed some changes to the 'national peculiarity' of the translator and the prose form of the translation (p. 263). Modifications of sequence in the presentation of plot and of characterization he interpreted as revealing a different attitude toward characters, for example, the eunuch priest in *Guiamars ljóð* (pp. 258–9) who, according to Meissner, had become a more worthy figure than in Marie de France's *Guigemar*. Unknown to Meissner, however, was an Icelandic copy of the *lai* produced in 1737 and entitled *Gvímars saga* in the manuscript Lbs. 840 4to. The Icelandic redaction of *Guiamars ljóð* has proved beyond any doubt that at least in the case of this one narrative the Norwegian manuscript De la Gardie 4–7 is a copy of an older manuscript and that some of the mistakes and changes Meissner had ascribed to the translator are in fact attributable to a copyist (Kalinke 1979, 106–39).

A comparison of the Norwegian *Guiamars ljóð* and the Icelandic *Gvímars saga* with the source, *Guigemar*, establishes that the thirteenth-century Norwegian redaction, despite its antiquity, is defective by reason of textual attrition, scribal misreadings, and editorial tampering with narrative structure. The Icelandic redaction, at a remove of some five centuries from the translation of *Guigemar* into Norse, contains instances of agreement with the French source where the Norwegian redaction had already incurred loss of text or acquired corrupt readings. The divergences from the original translation occurred in the process of scribal transmission. Unfortunately *Guiamars ljóð* is the only lai to be transmitted in a second manuscript. Nonetheless, the evidence from this one lai permits us to claim that the *Strengleikar* collection in the De la Gardie manuscript does not transmit an unadulterated text of the original translation. Indeed, I. B. Budal has demonstrated that deviations from the extant French sources in the narratives in the De la Gardie collection occurred at various stages, in variants in the French manuscripts themselves, in the translation process, and in the transmission of the Norse translation through modifications introduced by copyists. In other words, the translations of French lais in the only extant Norwegian manuscript represent the cumulative work of a translator and a succession of scribes (Budal 1999, 423).

This affects our understanding of the Arthurian narratives that are transmitted solely in Icelandic manuscripts, in some cases at a remove of at least four centuries. The oldest Icelandic fragment to contain an Arthurian text is one leaf, AM 598 Iβ, from around 1300, that contains the beginning of *Möttuls saga*. The oldest complete text of this narrative is preserved in two seventeenth-century manuscripts, AM 179 fol. and AM 181b fol. These two manuscripts are copies of a redaction from around 1400 that is extant today in only two leaves, AM 598 4to Iα and Sth. Perg. 4to nr 6 (*c*.1400), Royal Library, Stockholm, the latter belonging to a codex of romances that also contains *Ívens saga*, *Parcevals saga* and *Valvens þáttr*. The manuscript AM 179 was produced when the Stockholm codex was still intact and comparison of the seventeenth-century manuscript with the two extant fragments demonstrates that it is an accurate copy and thus actually represents a text from around 1400.

Tristrams saga ok Ísöndar was the first of the translations undertaken at Hákon's court and it is the most problematic text in respect to manuscript transmission. Four leaves from the second half of the fifteenth century are extant, three leaves with the manuscript signature AM 567 4to, XXII (Schach edn 1964, 51) and another leaf, the so-called Reeves Fragment (Schach edn 1969, 298). The complete text of *Tristrams saga* is found only in the Icelandic paper manuscripts AM 543 4to (seventeenth century), ÍB 51 fol. (*c*.1688) and JS 8 fol. (1729). As will be shown, the vellum fragments and paper manuscripts complement each other in transmitting a text that brings us closer to understanding the nature of the translation produced by Brother Robert.

The transmission of *Ívens saga* is also problematic. Like *Möttuls saga* its oldest text is found in the Stockholm 6 codex of romances from around 1400. A variant redaction is transmitted in the manuscript AM 489 4to (fifteenth century), and a greatly condensed version in Sth. Papp. fol. nr 46 (1690). Despite severe reduction of text in this last manuscript, which is a copy of the so-called *Ormsbók* (*c*.1350–1400), which has not been preserved, it nevertheless contains passages not found in the older manuscripts but which indubitably were part of the thirteenth-century translation.

The Stockholm 6 codex also contains a redaction of *Parcevals saga* (with *Valvens þáttr*) and this text is also preserved in two seventeenth-century copies, AM 181a fol. and AM 179 fol. The saga is defective in both the Stockholm 6 codex and its copies. A different branch of the narrative is transmitted in a vellum fragment of one leaf, Ny kgl. saml. 1794b 4to (Royal Library, Copenhagen), which is thought to antedate the Stockholm codex by as much as half a century.

The most poorly transmitted translation is *Erex saga*, which was also one of the narratives in *Ormsbók*, but which is preserved in whole solely in the manuscripts Sth. Papp. fol. nr 46 (1690) and AM 181b fol. (*c*.1650), the latter also containing *Möttuls saga*. There also exists a vellum fragment from around 1500, Lbs. 1230 III, but this consists of a mere two small strips of parchment that had been used in bookbinding in the seventeenth century. Unlike the other two translations of Chrétien's romances, *Ívens saga* and *Parcevals saga*, *Erex saga* transmits what might more accurately be called a recreation of the romance. Not only does it differ drastically in style from the other Old Norse-Icelandic Arthurian texts, but it is also a starkly condensed and restructured version containing interpolated material from *Þiðreks saga*, a non-Arthurian text (Kalinke 1981, 194–8; Kramarz-Bein 2002, 291–303). It is most unlikely that the drastic intervention in the plot of Chrétien's romance occurred at the time of translation.

Although the Arthurian romances and lais – with the likely exception of *Erex saga*[5] – were translated in the first half of the thirteenth century in Norway,[6] only *Januals ljóð* and *Geitarlauf* are extant in a thirteenth-century Norwegian manuscript. The other Arthurian texts are preserved solely in Icelandic copies, the oldest removed by at least a century and a half from the presumed time of translation. The copies diverge in the extent to which they have preserved the original translations; therefore, what can be inferred today about the nature of the thirteenth-century translations varies from text to text. The preserved texts in the aggregate of their manuscripts most likely represent the combined but successive efforts of a translator and one or more copyists, as will be seen. Only where comparison between the translation and its presumed source reveals a clause-for-clause correspondence, can we with any degree of certainty draw conclusions concerning the ability of the translator. Instances of condensation, amplification or rhetorical ornamentation may be the work of either the translator or a copyist or both. Here one can only speculate. What the aggregate of manuscripts of any one saga reveals, however, is that we are dealing with a phenomenon that may be called complementary attrition. Not infrequently, deviating readings in the extant manuscripts do not result from scribal modification, but rather from attrition, be it intentional or accidental. This type of textual loss is at times linked to the style of the original translations, which favoured semantic parallelism and synonymy. Inadvertently or intentionally a scribe, whose copy transmits one branch of the preserved text, left out one member of a synonymous doublet or collocation; another copyist, whose work transmits a different branch, left out its mate. In the aggregate, the texts of two variant redactions may provide a sense of what the original translation must have contained.

Loss of text in transmission

Möttuls saga seems to have suffered least in the Icelandic transmission of the original translation. Yet, even here, a fragment from *c.*1300 (AM 598 4to Iβ) containing the beginning of the saga reveals significant loss of text in the process of transmission. Four lines at the beginning of the *Lai du cort mantel* situate the tale in time and place:

> A la Pentecoste en esté
> tint li rois Artus cort pleniere.
> Onques rois en nule maniere
> nule si tres riche ne tint;
> de maint lointien païs i vint
> maint roi et maint duc et maint conte. (Bennett edn 1987, vv. 6–11)

(At Pentecost in the springtime King Arthur maintained an opulent court. Never did a king in any way maintain as splendid a court. From many distant countries there came many kings and many dukes and many counts.)

If one conflates the texts of the two manuscript branches of *Möttuls saga*, that is, text transmitted in the vellum fragment and the paper manuscripts, it turns out that the translator had indeed rendered the entire passage:

> Á þeiri hátíð, er heilög kirkja kallar Pentecosten, en Norðmenn kalla pikkisdaga, *þá hafði Artúr konungr samansamnat hirðliði sínu öllu at veita þeim margskonar góðgæti svá at engi konungr hélt svá ríkuliga sína hirð.* Ok fyrir því sakir hans frægðar ok hins vinsælazta mikilleiks þá komu til Artús kóngs dýrligir höfðingjar ok kóngar margra landa með hertugum ok öðrum heiðursmönnum. (Kalinke edn 1987, 7)

(During that festive period which the Holy Church calls Pentecost but the Norse call Pikkisdagar, *King Arthur had assembled about him his entire court and offered them all kinds of good fare, so that no king kept as sumptuous a court. And on account of his fame and his most popular largesse*, there came to King Arthur illustrious chieftains and kings of many lands, together with dukes and other honourable men.)

The italicized words are found only in the vellum fragment AM 598 4to Iβ; this provides evidence that considerable textual loss had already occurred by at least *c.*1400, the date of Sth. Perg. 4to nr 6, of which one of the paper manuscripts is a copy. Had this one leaf not been preserved, scholars might have interpreted the abbreviated version in the paper manuscripts upon which editions prior to the publication of the critical edition (Kalinke 1987) were based as revealing the translator's tendency to render only absolutely essential information pertaining to the setting of the tale.

The problem of textual loss is especially acute in *Tristrams saga ok Ísöndar*, since there is a gap of nearly 500 years between the Norwegian translation and the oldest complete Icelandic manuscript of the romance. Here too the felicitous preservation of one vellum leaf from the second half of the fifteenth century, the so-called Reeves Fragment, and corresponding text in the Sneyd[1] Fragment (Oxford, Bodleian Library, MS Fr. d 16) of Thomas's *Tristan* enables one to conclude that earlier scholarly opinion that Brother Robert entertained a rather cavalier attitude towards the text he was translating is not supported by the manuscript evidence. A case in point are the words of a wise man (*li sages* [v. 812]), found in ancient writings (*ancïen escrit* [v. 813]), on the subject of envy and cited by the narrator in the Sneyd[1] Fragment:

> Milz valt ester senz compainie
> Qu'aveir a compainun envie,
> E se[n]z compainun nuit e jor
> Quë aveir tel u n'ait amor.
> Le bien celerat quë il set,
> Le mal dirat quant il le het;
> Se bien fait, ja n'en parlerat,
> Le mal a nul ne celerat,
> Put ço valt milz senz compainun
> Que tel dunt ne vient si mal nun. (Gregory edn 1998, vv. 814–23)

(Better to have no company at all than to have envy for companion, to lack company both night and day than to have a companion lacking in love. For the good he knows of he will conceal, but, since he hates his friend, he will reveal the bad; let him do good, never a word, but let him do ill and everyone will know. That is why it is better to have no companion than a man from whom only evil comes.) (Gregory trans 1998, 49)

Until Paul Schach edited and published the Reeves Fragment (Washington, DC, Library of Congress) in 1969, the paper manuscripts – and the editions based on them – suggested that Brother Robert had translated only the first two lines above (italicized below). The Reeves Fragment shows, however, that the Norwegian translation contained a much fuller rendering of the French discourse on envy:

Betra er at bua einn än felaga enn uera med þeim er hann aufunda. betra er at uera einn nætur ok daga enn j fjaulda þeirra er jllt uilia ok jafnan hata þuiat þeir leyna þui godu er þeir eru uitandi fyrir þui er betri eingi felagsskapur enn hafa þann er jllt kemur af. (Schach edn 1969, 303)

(*It is better to live alone without companions than to be in the company of those who envy you.* Better to be alone night and day than in the company of those who have ill will and always hate, for they conceal the good that they know of. Therefore it is better to have no companionship than to have such from which evil comes.)

Thomas frames the passage with the chiastic *milz valt / valt milz* and Brother Robert mimics this very device with *betra er / er betri*.[7]

The Reeves Fragment contains evidence that Brother Robert had actually translated much more of Thomas's text than the paper manuscripts would suggest. The
above shows that content had not been lost in translation. Another fragment, one of
three vellum leaves from the second half of the fifteenth century, AM 567 4to XXII, 2,
attests that the loss of text in the course of copying affected not only content but also
style. The latter is important since the translations undertaken at the behest of King
Hákon Hákonarson are characterized by a rhythmic alliterative prose. The AM 567
fragment testifies that Brother Robert's translation contained more alliterative collocations than those transmitted in the surviving paper manuscripts. This is the case, for
example, in Roaldr's lament upon hearing that Tristram has been kidnapped. He says:

> 'Tristram', segir hann, 'huggari minn ok herra, hugarró mín *ok hjarta*, ást mín ok yndi, guði gefi ek
> þik, ok í hans vörn *ok varðveizlu* fel ek þik'. (Schach edn 1964, 54–5)

> ('Tristram,' he said, 'my comforter and my lord, solace of my mind *and heart*, my love and delight,
> to God I commend you, and into his care *and keeping* I commit you.')

The additional text in the vellum fragment is italicized above. The fragment attests
that the translation had actually contained four more or less synonymous alliterating
collocations. In conjunction with the alliterating verb and object – *guði gefi ek þik* –
the fragment transmits a highly charged poetic prose text.

Parcevals saga, like *Möttuls saga*, furnishes evidence that textual corruption is
a fairly early phenomenon in the transmission of the Arthurian romances. Scholars
generally assume that *Parcevals saga* was translated, like *Ívens saga*, during the reign
of King Hákon Hákonarson. The saga is transmitted in two vellum manuscripts, the
aforementioned Sth. Perg. 4to nr 6 and Ny kgl. saml. 1794b 4to (*c*.1350), the latter
a fragment of one leaf. The fragment transmits the translation of a long passage in
Perceval (vv. 2456–83) depicting a battle. Throughout this passage, the vellum fragment transmits anywhere from one to four words of the original text that no longer
exist in the Stockholm redaction. Six entire verses are transmitted only in the fragment, the last four translating vv. 2480–3:

> Et cil desus ont abatue
> Une porte sor cels desoz,
> Qui ocist et estainst trestoz
> Ciax qu'ele ataint en son cheoir. (Roach edn 1959)

> (But the defenders dropped the portcullis as they passed under it, crushing and killing all those
> struck in its fall.) (Kibler trans. 1991, 412)

The following translation of these four verses is found solely in the vellum fragment:

> En þeir sem í turninum váru hrundu miklum borgarvegg á hliðit ok drápu hvert manns barn er
> innan borgar var komit. (Kalinke 1981, 70)

> (And those who were in the tower pushed a big piece of castle wall down onto the gateway and
> killed every last person who had come into the castle.)

In the examples above, vellum fragments enable us to reconstruct certain passages of the original translation. The vellum fragments reveal that corruption and loss of text occurred fairly early in the transmission of the translations. But late paper copies, even when they appear on the whole to contain condensed versions of the translations, occasionally transmit an entire episode that had disappeared in the 'better' manuscripts on which older editions were based. *Ívens saga* offers a striking instance of combined textual attrition and retention. Until Blaisdell published his critical edition of 1979, the text available to scholars was that edited by Eugen Kölbing (1872), based on the vellum manuscripts Sth. Perg. 4to nr 6 and AM 489 4to (fifteenth century). In his edition, however, Blaisdell published a third primary manuscript, Sth. Papp. fol. nr 46 (1690), a paper manuscript considered worthless by Kölbing (1872, IX). This paper manuscript is a copy of the now-lost *Ormsbók*, however, a manuscript dating from *c*.1350–1400. Papp. fol. nr 46 contains a condensed version of *Ívens saga*, yet it alone transmits a translation, albeit in reduced form, of vv. 5188–5340 (Roques edn, 1967), which provide the background for the *Pesme aventure* episode. This tells how 300 maidens are held captive and forced to spin and weave and whom Íven is to rescue by engaging in combat with two giants (Kalinke edn 1999, 84–7). Despite extensive condensation in the paper manuscript, it alone transmits a sizeable portion of the original translation of some 150 verses of *Yvain* which, for whatever reason, are omitted in the older vellum manuscripts.

Finally, *Erex saga* needs to be addressed. The manuscript transmission of *Ívens saga* reveals on the one hand that the original rendering of *Yvain* in Old Norse must have been fairly accurate, but on the other hand, on the basis of the manuscript Sth. Papp. fol. nr 46, that an anonymous Icelandic copyist asserted his right to edit and condense the text before him. *Erex saga* is an extreme case of reduction and recreation at the hands of an anonymous Icelandic redactor and of adaptation of a style more in accord with indigenous narrative prose. It is most unlikely that the text as transmitted reflects the substance, style and structure of the original translation, whether that occurred in Norway or Iceland. A comparison of *Erex saga* with *Erec et Enide* reveals that the saga is the result of a systematic and intentional revision of the structure of the romance, including the interpolation of new episodes and the rearrangement of others (Kalinke 1981, 192–8, 247–8; see chapter 6). In some of his changes the 'author' of the extant *Erex saga* was inspired by another work in translation, *Þiðreks saga*, a compilation of tales about Dietrich von Bern (Theoderic) translated from German sources in thirteenth-century Norway.[8] Given the very extensive and substantial revision evident in *Erex saga*, it is paradigmatic for the acculturation that sometimes took place in the transfer of foreign narrative to and in Iceland.

Icelandic copyists could be quite cavalier toward the texts they were copying. They asserted their right to improve a text if they found it wanting. In a number of apologiae introducing or appended to indigenous Icelandic romances as well as translated *riddarasögur* the anonymous scribe explains why the saga in question may be longer than or differ from a version of the same story that listeners or readers are already familiar with. For example, the longer redaction of *Mágus saga jarls*, thought to have been composed around 1350, concludes with such an apologia. It offers an explanation for the penchant of Icelanders to tamper with narratives they might have copied verbatim, but chose not to:

> Nú þó að vér finnim eigi, að þessari sögu beri saman við aðrar sögur, þær er menn hafa til frásagnar, þá má það til bera, að ófróðir menn hafa í fyrstu slíkar eða aðrar frásagnir saman sett, ok skilur því mest á um frásagnir, að þeir, sem rita eða segja þær sögur, er þeim þykir skammt um talað, er orðfærir eru, þá auka þeir með mörgum orðum, svo að þeim, sem skilja kunna, þykir með fögrum orðum fram bornar, sem áður voru sagðar með ónýtum orðum. (Bjarni Vilhjálmsson edn 1953, 428)

> (Now though we realize that this story does not agree with other stories that men have recounted, this may be because ignorant persons have at first composed such stories or others, and these stories differ most inasmuch as those who are eloquent and who write or tell such stories that they consider to be told briefly augment them with many words, so that those who are able to perceive this consider the stories related with beautiful words when before they were told with useless words.)

In only one instance do we know the identity of an Icelandic redactor of an Arthurian text. Between 1301 and 1314 Haukr Erlendsson, a lawman in Iceland and then Norway, produced a large codex, named *Hauksbók* after him. This codex contains historiography, mathematical treatises and philosophical or theological dialogues. Among the historiographic texts we find *Breta sögur*, a translation of the *Historia regum Britanniae*, including *Merlínússpá* 'Merlin's Prophecies'. *Breta sögur* is preserved in one other manuscript, AM 573 4to, which is dated slightly after *Hauksbók*, but which transmits a redaction of the saga that, while assumed to be a somewhat abridged version (Louis-Jensen 1993, 57), nonetheless contains a text approximating that of the original translation, which is thought to have been produced around 1200 in Iceland.

The redaction of *Breta sögur* in *Hauksbók* is important, since it provides significant insight into how Icelanders 'edited' older texts. A comparison of the *Hauksbók* and the AM 573 versions of *Breta sögur* reveals a redactor at work, and in this case one who is identifiable. The most extreme example of Haukr's editing of the Arthurian portion of *Breta sögur* is the depiction of Arthur's coronation. In Geoffrey's *Historia* the report of the festivities extends to nearly one hundred lines in print (Reeve edn 2007, 209–15). Geoffrey names the many notables who attend, describes the coronation ritual, and the order of seating at the banquet. He depicts the entertainment both inside the hall and outside. The AM 573 redaction transmits not only much of Geoffrey's text – it includes the list of guests and the description of the coronation ceremony – but also additional matter not found in the *Historia* (Jón Sigurdsson edn 1849, 100–1). The very long account of Arthur's coronation is reduced in *Hauksbók* to a single sentence:

> Hann bavð til sin at hvita svnv ollvm konvngvm hertogvm ok iorlvm ok ollvm hofþingivm i sinv ʀiki ok var hann þa krvnaðr ok sva drottningin ok er sv veizla viðfrægivz orðin a Nordrlondvm bœði at fornv ok nyiv. (Finnur Jónsson edn 1892–6, 290)

(At Whitsun he invited to his court all the kings, dukes, earls and other chieftains in his realm. And he was crowned and also the queen. And that festival became the most famous in the Northern lands both in old and modern times.)

The AM 573 redaction of *Breta sögur* transmits not only Geoffrey's elaborate depiction of feasting at Arthur's coronation but in a number of instances, for example, in the account of Arthur's conception, a narrativized and fictionalized account of the Arthurian legend that is reminiscent of courtly romance (see chapter 3). Some material not found in Geoffrey's *Historia* exists in Wace's *Roman de Brut*, as noted earlier, and this suggests that, like Wace's work, *Breta sögur* derives from a Latin manuscript of the Variant Version of the *Historia* (Weiss edn 2002, XVIII). The remarkable aspect of the two redactions of *Breta sögur* is that whereas the AM 573 redaction more or less faithfully transmits a Latin version that had undergone substantial narratival augmentation, Haukr Erlendsson's editing of the translation returns the Arthurian narrative to an earlier chronicle form.

Style

In its transmission to the North the *matière de Bretagne* underwent transformation of its formal features. Except for some of the poems of the *Poetic Edda* (or *Elder Edda*), Norse narrative was in prose. The translations of Arthurian literature are on the whole characterized by a style that has been called 'courtly'. Alone *Breta sögur* is a translation of a prose text; the Norse lais and romances are translations of metrical texts in end-rhyming couplets. With the exception of *Erex saga*, the prose of the translations is characterized by a euphonious, rhythmic language, effected largely by synonymous collocations that frequently alliterate. The translations also mimic a Latinate style, replicating ablative absolute and participial constructions that otherwise are foreign to Norse prose.

Tristrams saga ok Ísöndar is the primary example of a text written in the so-called 'courtly' style (Halvorsen 1962; Damsgaard Olsen 1965, 110–11). Indeed, it is thought that the translator, Brother Robert, introduced this style in the North. Comparative study of the Norse translation with the French source is problematic at best, however, since Thomas's romance has been transmitted solely in a few fragments, and the extant text of *Tristrams saga* is removed by several centuries and copyists from the Norwegian translation. Nonetheless, Tristan's dying words can be read against the French text preserved in the Douce fragment. When he is told that Ysolt had not come, Tristan responds:

> Dunc a Tristran si grant dolur
> Unques n'ot në avrat maür,
> E turne sei vers la parei.
> Dunc dit: 'Deus salt Ysolt e mei!

Quant a moi ne volez venir,
Pur vostre amur m'estuet murrir.
Jo ne puis plus tenir ma vie;
Pur vus muer, Ysolt, bele amie.
N'avez pité de ma langur,
Mais de ma mort avrez dolur.
Ço m'est, amie, grant confort
Que pité avrez de ma mort.' (Gregory edn 1998, vv. 3026–37)

(At this Tristran felt such great pain
that never had he known, nor would know, greater.
He turned his face to the wall
and then said: 'May God save Yseut and me!
Since you have no wish to come to me,
I must die for your love.
I can no longer go on living:
I am dying for you, Yseut, my sweet.
You take no pity on me in my languor,
but you will be aggrieved by my death.
Sweet love, it is a great comfort to me
that you will have pity on me in my death'.) (Gregory trans. 1998, 141)

The corresponding passage in *Tristrams saga* is as follows:

Þá var hann svá mjök *syrgjandi*, at aldri beið hann slíkan harm. Ok sneriz hann þegar upp til veggjar ok mælti þá með harmsfullri röddu: 'Nú ertu, Ísönd, mik *hatandi*. Ek em nú *syrgjandi*, er þú vill ekki til mín koma, en ek sakir þín *deyjandi*, er þú vildir ekki miskunna sótt minni. Ek em nú *syrgjandi* sótt mína ok *harmandi*, er þú vildir ekki koma at hugga mik'. (Jorgensen edn 1999, 220)

(He was so grief-stricken that he had never endured such suffering. He immediately turned towards the wall and spoke in an anguished voice: 'Ísönd, you hate me now. My heart aches, because you do not want to come to me, and because of you I will die, for you did not wish to take pity on me in my illness. Now I am suffering from my sickness and grieving, because you do not want to come to comfort me.') (Jorgensen trans. 1999, 221)

This particular passage is noteworthy for its use of the present participle (italicized above), a distinct Latinate feature, with which the translator attempted to capture the state of being and duration of Tristram's emotional turmoil (Krammarz-Bein 2000, 168–9). There can be little question 'that the stylistic and esthetic intention of the translator was to heighten and to intensify the emotional impact' of Tristram's lament above (Schach 1965, 77). The occurrence of the present participle in the translations undertaken at the court of King Hákon is not restricted to *Tristrams saga*. A similar accretion of present participles but combined with a concluding rhymed couplet – the latter a feature restricted to *Parcevals saga* – occurs in the drops-of-blood episode where Parceval's state of mind is depicted:

Ok sem hann sá þessa hluti, nýfallinn snjó ok it rauðasta blóð, þá kom honum í hug at **slíkr litr** var í and**liti** Blankiflúr, unnustu hans, ok var hann þat nú svá mjök *hugsandi*, at hann var öllu öðru *gleymandi*. Hann gáði enskis annars en sjá hér á. Svá var hann þetta mjök *íhugandi*, ok svá tók hann þá mjök at **unna**, at ekki mátti hann þá annat **kunna**. (Wolf edn 1999, 160)

(And when he saw these things, the newly fallen snow and the very red blood, then it came into his mind that such colouring was in the complexion of Blankiflúr, his beloved, and on that so deeply did he reflect that nothing else did he recollect. He cared to do nothing other than to gaze on this. So deeply upon this did he meditate, and so deeply did he then begin to adore, that he was powerless to comprehend anything more.) (Maclean trans. 1999, 161)

Especially through the use of the present participle (italicized above) the translator has succeeded in expressing both state of being and duration, and this is also supported by assonance and a rhyming concluding couplet (both indicated in bold).

A favourite rhetorical device in the translated romances is alliteration. *Geitarlauf*, the translation of *Chèvrefeuille* and the shortest Arthurian text in the North, contains no dialogue. Alliteration occurs rather unobtrusively throughout the lai, but the message to Ísönd that is inscribed by Tristram on a piece of hazel wood is remarkable for alliteratively mimicking the entwining Tristram writes about in the inscription:

'Sva ferr með ocr', kvað hann, 'sem *vi*ð*u*indil sa er **b**innz um hæslivið. Meðan þessir tveir *vi*ðir **b**ua **b**aðer saman, þa *l*iva ok **b**era *l*auf sitt. En sa er þessa *vi*ðe skildi hvarn frá oðrum, þa déyr haslenn oc þui nest *u*idvinndillenn oc **b**err hvarki *l*auf, nema þorna, oc firir *v*erðaz **b**æðe. Hin friða unnasta min. sva ok eftir þeim hætti ero *v*it. Ei ma ec *l*ifa *on þin*, ok ei þu *on min*'. (Cook edn 1999, 4)

('It goes with us', he said, 'as with the honeysuckle that fastens itself around the hazel tree. As long as these two trees are together they live and bear foliage, but if anyone should separate these trees from each other, the hazel will die and then the honeysuckle, and neither of them will bear foliage. Instead, they will both dry up and perish. My beautiful sweetheart, such and in the same way are we. I cannot live without you, nor you without me'.) (Cook trans 1999, 5)

It is remarkable that although the translator uses the word *geitarlauf* (goat leaf) in the opening and closing sentences of the lai to transmit the French *chèvrefeuille*, the loan translation is abandoned in Tristram's message in favour of the native *viðvindill* for the woodbine or honeysuckle. The choice of *viðvindill* is fortuitous, since the very name of the plant evokes what Tristan is trying to say about himself and Ísönd. The Norse name of the honeysuckle, literally 'winding wood', suggests a wrapping around something, and this notion is repeated in the word *binnz* 'wind itself' or 'bind itself'. The notion of *binnz* is then connected to *bua baðer*, literally 'dwell together'. Finally, if the honeysuckle and the hazel are separated, then the two *firir verðaz*, 'perish', and this is once again connected alliteratively to *viðvindill*. Tristram's message ends with an end rhyme, *on þin, on min*, the only such occurrence in the translation. This renders v. 78 of *Chèvrefeuille* – 'ne vos sanz moi, ne ge sanz vos' (neither you without me, nor I without you) (O'Gorman edn 1998) – which does not have internal rhyme, but which rather rhymes with the preceding verse: 'Bele amie, si est de nos' (My beloved, so it is with us).

The alliteration in the above passage is subtle but effective to the native ear. *Ívens saga* offers an example of the manner in which especially emotionally charged passages in end rhyme were transformed into a rhythmic prose governed in large part by alliterative couplets. Yvain's lament in the French romance over having been rejected by his wife extends to 32 verses (Roques edn 1967, 3525–56). Yvain's recognition that he has lost his happiness and comfort through his own fault – 'Qui pert sa joie et son solaz / par son mesfet et par son tort' (vv. 3536–7) – provokes in the Norse version an extended lament culminating in a series of alliterating collocations (see chapter 6). The Norse Íven echoes the French Yvain's question why he should not kill himself – 'Que fais je, las, qui ne m'oci' (v. 3527) – when he asks 'Hvat skal ek útan drepa mik sjálfr?' He responds with a series of antithetic alliterative couplets that are a variation of the French 'Qui pert sa joie et son solaz' (He who through his own fault loses his happiness and his comfort) (Kibler trans. 1991, 339):

> Ek hefi týnt huggan minni ok fagnaði,
> ok um snúit af sjálfs míns glæp virðing minni,
> ok vent tign minni í týning,
>   yndi mitt í angrsemi,
>   líf mitt í leiðindi,
>   hjarta mitt í hugsótt,
>   unnustu mína í óvin,
>   frelsi mitt í friðleysi;
> eða hví dvel ek at drepa mik? (Kalinke edn 1999, 74)

(I have lost my consolation and joy, and through my own fault brought down my honor and turned my reputation into loss, my delight into suffering, my life into loathing, my heart into anxiety, my beloved into my enemy, my freedom into outlawry; why do I delay in killing myself?) (Kalinke trans. 1999, 75)

The passage is of course not set down in the manuscripts or editions as above, but presenting it so as to highlight the rhetorical figures gives some sense of how an audience might have heard the text and been pleased by its rhythmic alliterating repetition. The reversal of Íven's fortunes is acoustically transmitted through the alliterative linking of his former and present state.[9]

Unfortunately Thomas's *Tristan* is extant only fragmentarily and hence the greater part of *Tristrams saga* cannot be compared with its source. The emotional force of Thomas's text is reflected rhetorically, however, throughout the translation. Blensinbil's (that is, Blancheflor) lament upon learning of Kanelangres's (that is, Rivalin) death is exemplary for the manner in which the translators expressed emotional content through repetition and alliteration:

> Aum em ek yfir alla kvennmenn. Hvernig skal ek *lifa* eptir svá dýrligan dreng? Ek var hans *líf* ok huggun, en hann var unnasti minn ok *líf* mitt. Ek var hans yndi, en hann mín gleði. Hversu skal ek *lifa* eptir hann **dauðan**? Hversu skal ek huggaz, er gaman mitt er grafit? Báðum okkr sómir saman at **deyja**. Fyrir því hann má ekki til mín koma, þá verð ek gegnum **dauðann** at ganga, því hans **dauði** drepr á mitt hjarta. Hversu skal ek hér mega lengr *lifa*? Mitt *líf* skal hans *lifi* fylgja! (Jorgensen edn 1999, 46–8)

(There is not a woman alive who is more wretched than I. How could I survive such a glorious, gallant man? I was his life and his comfort, and he was my beloved and my life. I was his delight, and he was my joy. How shall I live on after his death? How shall I be comforted, when my joy is buried? It is fitting for us to die together. Since he cannot come to me, I must walk through death's door, for his death hammers at my heart. How shall I be able to live here any longer? My life should follow his life.) (Jorgensen trans. 1999, 47–9)

The two preceding examples reveal how alliteration and antithesis serve to express emotional states. In the latter case, polyptoton (*líf, lifa; dauðan, deyja, dauði*) emphasizes what is at stake and at the same time serves to stress the contrast between being and non-being. The occurrence of these rhetorical devices in the translations undertaken at the court of King Hákon as well as other stylistic characteristics, such as normal or inverse word order, choice of tense for narration, or the use of certain adverbs of time have been linked to a group of texts considered to belong to a 'Tristram-group'. These include all the Arthurian translations presumed to have occurred in Norway, *Erex saga* excepted (Hallberg 1971).

Möttuls saga furnishes a final example of the amplificatory, alliterative prose of the translations undertaken at the Norwegian court. One should remember, however, that neither the text of the French source nor of the Norwegian translation has been preserved. In the case of both the French and Old Norse-Icelandic versions we are dependent upon the extant manuscripts and editions. Keeping this in mind, a statement by Gawain towards the conclusion of the *Lai du cort mantel* and its rendering in Old Norse provides some sense of how rhymed verse was transformed into rhetorically embellished prose. Towards the conclusion of the lai, when one chaste woman has finally been found whom the mantle fits, Gawain states that the other women would gladly have objected if they could have done so. And then adds, 'Une chose pouez savoir, / que li plusor en sont dolent!' (One thing you may know, that the majority are sorrowful) (Bennett edn 1987, 871–2). In *Möttuls saga* this simple statement is expanded into four antithetic and partly tautological collocations supported by alliteration:

En nú *h*efir at *h*ögum til skipaz at þeira *ö*fund ok *a*ngrsemi er þér fagnaðr, þeira *h*armr þér *h*uggun, þeira sví*v*irðing þér *v*irðing, þeira glæpr mun þitt *l*of í hverju *l*andi *v*axanda. (Kalinke edn 1999, 28)

(But now the situation has undergone a change for the better, as their envy and grief become your joy, their sorrow your consolation, their disgrace your honor, and their misdeeds your praise, which will swell in every land.) (Kalinke trans. 1999, 29)

Parcevals saga has one distinguishing feature that occurs only in isolated instances in the other romances known to have been commissioned by King Hákon, namely end rhyme (see chapter 6). Like *Tristrams saga* and *Möttuls saga* the translation of *Perceval* contains a rhetorically ornamented prose. In addition, it contains rhyme, mostly at the end of chapters, thus functioning as a concluding statement. In vv. 3434–52 of *Perceval*, the eponymous protagonist comes upon a maiden who laments the death of her husband. She apostrophizes death and concludes by asking death to take her life too (Roach edn 1959, v. 3450). In the saga the lament is not quite as extended as in the romance, but the maiden's address of death is balanced by one of her heart, and the passage is rounded out by three rhyming couplets:

'Súrr ert þú, dauði, er þú tókt mitt líf eigi fyrr en bónda míns ok illt verði þér, hjarta, er þú springr
eigi af hans dauða, þvíat ek vilda dauð vera með honum svá sem mitt líf var kært hans lífi.'

> Ólík var ást manna *forðum*,
> sem hún sýndi í sínum *orðum*.
> Þá var *trygt* þat er nú er *hrygt*.
> Þá var *blítt* þat er nú er *strítt*. (Wolf edn 1999, 150)

('Death, you are bitter, that you did not take my life before my husband's; and may evil befall you,
heart, that you did not break at his death, for just as in life I was so dear to him I would dearly like
to be dead with him'. Their love was different in former days, as she has shown by what she says.
What was then plighted now is blighted. What was then fair is now hard to bear.) (Maclean trans.
1999, 151)

The narrator's voice, distinct from the maiden's because in rhymed verse, serves
both to comment on and summarize the lament. It is a lament for times gone by
expressed through rhyming antitheses. Since the rhymed passages in *Parcevals saga*
generally occur at the conclusion of episodes, some scholars have thought that these
might have been added by an Icelandic copyist. That may indeed have been the case,
but there is no reason why the use of rhyme in addition to alliteration might not also
have been the hallmark of one particular, presumably Norwegian, translator.

The most striking formal aspect of the Norse translations is that the verse of the
sources was converted into prose, the normal form of narrative in the North. While it
has been suggested that the alliteratively rich prose of the translations was intended as
a substitute for the end rhyme of the French romances and lais, this is not necessarily
the case. Alliteration as a means of emphasis in prose texts predates the translations undertaken at Hákon's court and was a common rhetorical device in Icelandic
literature. *Breta sögur* is a translation from Latin prose into Icelandic prose, and this
translation too is characterized by the use of alliteration as a means of emphasis. This
is found, for example, in the portrait of King Arthur aged fifteen.

> hann var þa .xv. vettra gamall. hann var mikill a *v*oxt, *v*enn at aliti spekingr at *v*iti a*v*ʀ af fe sterkr
> harðr ok *v*apndjarfr *g*laðr ok *g*oðr *v*invm en *g*rimr *v*vinvm *f*astnæmr ok *f*orsiall siðlatr ok sigrsæll
> *v*íðfrægr ok at ollv *v*el menntr. (Finnur Jónsson edn 1892–6, 287)

(He was then fifteen years of age. He was tall of stature, handsome in appearance, a wise man in
reasoning, generous with his riches, stern and dauntless, cheerful and kind to his friends but pitiless
to his enemies, trusty and prudent, well mannered and victorious, far renowned and in everything
very accomplished.)

Geoffrey's depiction is comparatively terse:

> Erat autem Arturus quindecim annorum iuuenis inauditae uirtutis atque largitatis, in quo tantam
> gratiam innata bonitas praestiterat ut a cunctis fere populis amaretur. (Reeve edn 2007, 193)

(He was a youth of fifteen, of great promise and generosity, whose innate goodness ensured that he
was loved by almost everybody.) (Wright trans. 2007, 192)

Wace, however, offers a longer portrait in his *Roman de Brut* (vv. 9013–32) than
does the *Historia*, and some of Arthur's qualities in the French translation, but not

mentioned by Geoffrey, correspond to those listed in *Breta sögur*: Arthur was 'de sun eage fors e granz' (tall and strong for his age); 'forz e hardiz e conqueranz' (strong, bold and invincible); 'cuntre orguillus fu orguillus / E cuntre humles dulz e pitus' (proud to the haughty and gentle and compassionate to the humble) (Weiss edn and trans. 2002, vv. 9014, 9021, 9019–20). The *Roman de Brut* was not the source of *Breta sögur*, but the similarity of the portrayal of King Arthur in the Icelandic and French translations suggests that the Latin redaction of the *Historia* that was the source of *Breta sögur* contained a fuller portrait than that transmitted by Geoffrey. The passage above is of interest because it shows that the alliteration so prevalent in the translations undertaken at the Norwegian court was already employed earlier by Icelandic translators of prose texts.

The alliteration that is used to such good effect in the portrayal of King Arthur occurs also in an exhortatory speech by Bishop Dubric of Caerleon, given just before King Arthur's combat with the heathen Saxons. Dubric says:

Þèr góðer dreingir, er prýddir erut *t*áknum kristiligrar *t*rúar oc ágætir at góðum siðum, *r*eyndir at *r*áðuendi oc *r*auskuer í framgaungum! *m*innumz á *m*anndóm oc *m*illdi þá sem erut skyllder at *v*eita *v*inum yðrum oc fèlugum, er nú ero miog þraungðer af heiðnum mönnum, kostið nú oc dugit oc beriz hraustliga fyri yðru *fè* oc *f*relsi, því at á yðr mun liggia eilíft brigzli ef þèr standit eigi í mót af öllu megni yðrum *v*uinum. gángit fram *v*hrædiliga oc *þ*olit *þ*rekmannliga dauðann, þótt hann komi fram, því at sá dauði er sigr oc lausn alldarinnar, er maðr tekr sakar brædra sinna. Nú látið yðr eigi í augu vaxa í þessa mannraun at gánga, því at hverr er til skripta gengr oc *s*ýnir guði *s*anna iðran sinna *s*ynda, þá mun hann hólpinn auruggliga í sínum dauða. (Jón Sigurdsson edn 1851, 90–1)

(Good men, you who are adorned with the sign of the Christian faith and are outstanding in good conduct, proven in probity and valiant in battle! Let us remember the kindness and mercy that you should grant your friends and comrades who are now pressed hard by heathen men, exert yourselves and do your best and fight valiantly for your faith and freedom, for you will earn eternal shame if you do not oppose your enemies with all your might. Step forward unafraid and endure death stoutly, should it approach, for that death which a man accepts for his brethren is victory and eternal redemption. Now do not want for courage to put yourselves in peril because whoever confesses and shows God true contrition for his sins, will unfailingly be helped when he dies.)

Of particular interest in the speech above are its rhythm, euphony and the use of verbal collocations and alliteration for emphasis and rhetorical effect. There is a compelling auditory component in the bishop's speech. Alliterative rhythmic prose is of course one of the hallmarks of the romances translated at the court of King Hákon Hákonarson, which are said to employ a 'court style' (Damsgaard Olsen 1965, 110–11). This very same style existed, however, even earlier in Iceland, as the above speech attests. Indeed, the style of the Arthurian legend in *Breta sögur* conforms to that found in other historiographic works produced in the Þingeyrar monastery, notably *Sverris saga*, composed by Karl Jónsson, abbot of the monastery in the years 1169–81 and 1190–1207 (Turville-Petre 1953, 214–15). The biography of King Sverrir of Norway (r.1177–1202) concludes with a remarkable characterization of Sverrir and his father King Sigurðr Munnr (d.1155):

Sigurðr var *léttl*átr ok ákaflyndr, en Sverrir var *sta*ðfastr ok *st*illtr vel, Sigurðr auð*t*ryggr ok *t*al-
hlýðinn, Sverrir *v*arúðigr ok *v*invandr, Sigurðr hverfráðr ok mis*l*yndr, Sverrir fastúðigr ok jafn*l*yndr,
Sigurðr *óð*látr ok *o*pinspjallr, Sverrir *f*astorðr ok *f*ályndr, Sigurðr *f*áfróðr ok *f*j*ǫ*lráðr, Sverrir *r*áðugr
ok *r*áðvandr. (*Sverris saga* edn 2007, 280)

(Sigurðr was light-hearted and impetuous, while Sverrir was steadfast and temperate; Sigurðr was
credulous and easily swayed, Sverrir was wary and choosy as to friends; Sigurðr was fickle and
vacillating, Sverrir was firm and even-tempered; Sigurðr was impatient and outspoken, Sverrir was
true to his word and reserved; Sigurðr was ignorant and fickle, Sverrir was sagacious and upright.)

The portrayal of father and son above is based on tautological and antithetical collocations that are reinforced by alliteration. The translations of the metrical rhymed
Arthurian romances and lais in Norway occurred in a culture that chose prose as the
normal vehicle for narrative, and alliteration as the chief poetic device. In their transfer
to the North, the French Arthurian romances and lais underwent a formal acculturation
when they were rendered in the rhetorically ornamented prose that was the hallmark
of Old Norse-Icelandic narrative.

Notes

[1] Alison Finlay does not believe that the wine in the Carlisle fragment is the love potion and claims that
'Thomas is eliminated as the source for the detail' (2004, 211). Similarly, Vera Johanterwage considers
this an independent addition in the saga and asserts that Brother Robert 'wollte seinem Auftraggeber
Hákon eine positivere Königsfigur präsentieren und er erreichte dies durch die Minnetrankszene in der
Hochzeitsnacht' (wanted to present to his patron Hákon a more positive figure of the king and he achieved
this through the love-potion scene in the wedding night) (2007, 217). Furthermore, she believes that
'Bruder Róbert die Geschichte speziell auf die Verhältnisse am norwegischen Königshof zugeschnitten
hat. Wenn die erste Einnahme des Minnetranks die Begründung dafür liefert, daß Ísǫnd nicht – wie es
sich für eine Königin ziemt – ihren Mann, sondern Tristram liebt, so erklärt die zweite Einnahme durch
Markis *alleine*, warum dieser seiner Frau dennoch in Liebe verbunden bleibt, obwohl sie ihn fortge-
setzt mit einem anderen hintergeht' (Brother Robert tailored the story specifically to the conditions at
the Norwegian royal court: While the first drinking of the love potion provides the reason why Ísǫnd
does not love – as is appropriate for a queen – her husband but rather Tristram, the second drinking by
Markis *alone* explains why the latter nonetheless continues to love his wife, even though she persists in
deceiving him with another man) (p. 217).

[2] Some thirty years ago Geraldine Barnes wrote: 'For purposes of literary and historical analysis,
at least, it seems safe to assume that in their present state the riddarasögur MSS accurately represent
the material translated, abbreviated or amplified by Brother Robert and his nameless colleagues' (1977,
438). The same assumption *vis-à-vis* the preserved Arthurian translations is expressed by Nicola Jordan
when she writes about *Ívens saga* that 'Längere Exkurse . . . hat der Sagaverfasser seinem Publikum, das
derlei aus der einheimischen erzählenden Literatur nicht gewöhnt war, nicht zugemutet' (the author of
the saga deemed longer excursuses not acceptable to his public, which was not accustomed to such from
indigenous narratives) (2007, 152), and 'Die Tatsache, daß Artus in der *Ívents saga* ebenso wie in anderen
Riddarasögur auch als selbstbewußter, mit Macht und Autorität ausgestatteter Herrscher erscheint,
muß im Zusammenhang mit der Entstehungsgeschichte des Werks gesehen werden: die Riddarasögur
entstanden am norwegischen Königshof, und in der Gestaltung einer starken, souveränen Herrscherfigur
spiegeln sich die Interessen des königlichen Auftraggebers wider' (The fact that Arthur appears in *Ívents
saga* as well as in other Riddarasögur as a self-conscious ruler who is vested with power and authority,

should be understood in connection with the origin of the work: the Riddarasögur originated at the Norwegian royal court, and the presentation of the ruler as a strong, sovereign figure reflects the interests of the royal patron) (p. 159). And finally: 'Die straffe Handlungsführung und das aus der Reduzierung bzw. Eliminierung von Exkursen und Erzählerkommentaren resultierende Zurücktreten der Erzählerfigur hinter die Figuren der erzählten Welt bedeuten eine Annäherung an altwestnordische Erzähltraditionen und damit eine Rezeptionserleichterung für die norwegischen Hörer' (the tight plot and the withdrawal of the figure of the narrator in favour of those peopling the narrative world, a result of the reduction or elimination of excursuses and narrator commentaries, indicates an approximation to Old West Norse narrative traditions and thereby an easier reception by the Norwegian listeners) (p. 165).

[3] Kjær (1992, 131) writes: 'Having chosen to analyze them [*Erex saga* and *Ívens saga*] starting from the hypothesis that they represented more or less faithful witnesses to the same center of activity that arose at the court of King Hákon of Norway, I now conclude that these late Icelandic manuscripts in fact contain recastings made in Iceland at a later date, and closer to the Reformation, than *Tristrams saga*. Whatever the case may be, it has to be admitted that there no longer exist Norwegian versions of these two texts.'

[4] Two leaves of this Norwegian manuscript became separated at some point and were discovered in 1703 in the lining of a bishop's mitre at Skálholt in Iceland. They are preserved today in the Arnamagnæan Collection in Copenhagen under the signature AM 666b 4to. The two leaves, in the form of a mitre, contain fragments of *Tveggja elskanda strengleikr* ('Lai of Two Lovers'), for which no French source is extant, and *Grelent*, the Norse translation of *Lai de Grelent*.

[5] Some scholars believe *Erex saga* was translated after 1250, towards the end of Hákon's reign, for example, Kramarz-Bein (2002, 107, 291).

[6] Scholars have assumed that the translations commissioned by King Hákon were undertaken in the environs of the Norwegian court. In her doctoral dissertation I. B. Budal (2009) argues persuasively, however, that the lais – including the two Arthurian narratives – were translated in Anglo-Norman England rather than in Norway (I:415–26).

[7] Peter Jorgensen's edition and translation of *Tristrams saga ok Ísöndar* (1999) is based on the oldest complete manuscript, AM 543 4to (seventeenth century), which contains only the first, italicized, sentence above.

[8] *Þiðreks saga af Bern*, I–II, ed. Guðni Jónsson, [Reykjavík], 1954.

[9] The use of extended alliteration to convey emotions is also evident in other translations of French literature. As striking an example as that in *Ívens saga* is found in the Norse translation of the anonymous lai *Desiré* in the *Strengleikar* compilation. The two antitheses in the couplet 'sa grant joie met en tristur, / e sis chanz est turnez a plur' (vv. 344–5) (his great joy becomes sadness, and his songs turn into tears) is rendered in the Norse version by eight antithetic alliterative collocations: 'Mioc þyntize hann oc gerðize mioc sivcr. með þessvm hætti snœriz *huggan* hans i *harm*. *Gleðe* hans i *grat*. *leicr* hans i mi*slican*. *ast* hans i *angr*. *sœmd* hans i *sorg*. *atgerð* hans til *enskis*. *afl* hans i *vmát*. Sialfr hann i sottar *kvol* og *kvein* (ed. Cook and Tveitane 1979, 120). R. Cook translates this rather freely in order to preserve the alliteration: 'He became thin and very sick, and in this fashion his comfort turned to care, his gladness into groans, his play into displeasure, his love into longing, his dignity into dejection, his accomplishments to emptiness, his power into puniness, his very self into the tortures and trials of sickness' (p. 121).

Reference List

Texts and Translations

Breta sögur, ed. Jón Sigurdsson, in *Annaler for nordisk Oldkyndighed og Historie* (Copenhagen, 1849), pp. 3–145.

'The Carlisle fragment of Thomas's *Tristran*', ed. and trans. I. Short, in *Early French Tristan Poems*, 2, ed. N. J. Lacy (Cambridge, 1998), pp. 173–83.

Le Chevalier au lion (Yvain), ed. M. Roques, *Les Romans de Chrétien de Troyes édités d'aprés la copie de Guiot* (Bibl. Nat. fr. 794), 4 (Paris, 1965).

Chrétien de Troyes. Le Roman de Perceval ou Le Conte du Graal, ed. W. Roach, 2nd rev. edn (Geneva, 1959).

Geoffrey of Monmouth, *The History of the Kings of Britain: An Edition and Translation of* De gestis Britonum [Historia Regum Britanniae], ed. M. D. Reeve, trans. N. Wright (Woodbridge, 2007).

'Gvímars saga', ed. M. E. Kalinke, *Opuscula*, 7, Bibliotheca Arnamagnæana, 34 (Copenhagen, 1979), pp. 106–39.

The Historia Regum Britannie of Geoffrey of Monmouth. V: Gesta Regum Britannie, ed. and trans. N. Wright (Cambridge, 1991).

Ívens saga, ed. F. W. Blaisdell, Editiones Arnamagnæanæ, B, 18 (Copenhagen, 1979).

Ívens saga, ed. M. E. Kalinke, in *Norse Romance*, II: *The Knights of the Round Table*, ed. M. E. Kalinke (Cambridge, 1999), pp. 33–102.

Ívents saga, ed. E. Kölbing, in *Riddarasögur* (Strassburg, 1872), pp. 73–136.

The Knight with the Lion (Yvain), trans. W. W. Kibler, in *Chrétien de Troyes: Arthurian Romances* (London, 1991), pp. 295–380.

Le Lai du cort mantel, ed. P. E. Bennett, in *Mǫttuls saga*, ed. M. E. Kalinke, Editiones Arnamagnæanæ, B, 30 (Copenhagen, 1987), pp. 4–68.

Mágus saga jarls hin meiri, ed. Bjarni Vilhjálmsson, in *Riddarasögur*, II ([Reykjavík], 1953), pp. 135–429.

'Marie de France, *Chèvrefeuille*', ed. and trans. R. O'Gorman, in *Early French Tristan Poems*, II, ed. N. J. Lacy (Cambridge, 1998), pp. 185–97.

Mǫttuls saga, ed. M. E. Kalinke. With an edition of *Le Lai du cort mantel* by Philip E. Bennett, Editiones Arnamagnæanæ, B, 30 (Copenhagen, 1987).

Möttuls saga, ed. M. E. Kalinke, in *Norse Romance*, II: *The Knights of the Round Table*, ed. M. E. Kalinke (Cambridge, 1999), pp. 1–31.

Parcevals saga. Valvens þáttr, ed. K. Wolf, trans. H. Maclean, in *Norse Romance. II. The Knights of the Round Table*, ed. M. E. Kalinke (Cambridge, 1999), pp. 103–216.

Schach, P. 'The Reeves Fragment of *Tristrams saga ok Ísöndar*', in *Einarsbók. Afmæliskveðja til Einars Ól. Sveinssonar. 12. Desember 1969*, ed. Bjarni Guðnason, Halldór Halldórsson, Jónas Kristjánsson (Reykjavík, 1969), pp. 296–308.

Schach, P. 'An unpublished leaf of *Tristrams saga*: AM 567 Quarto, XXII, 2', *Research Studies* (Washington State University), 32 (1964), 50–62.

The Story of the Grail (Perceval), trans. W. W. Kibler, in *Chrétien de Troyes: Arthurian Romances* (London, 1991), pp. 381–494.

Strengleikar. An Old Norse Translation of Twenty-one Old French Lais, edited from the manuscript Uppsala De la Gardie 4–7 – AM 666 b, 4o, ed. and trans. Robert Cook and Mattias Tveitane, Norrøne tekster, 3 (Oslo, 1979).

Strengleikar eða Lioðabok. En Samling af romantiske Fortællinger efter bretoniske Folkesange (Lais), oversat fra fransk paa norsk ved Midten af det trettende Aarhundred efter Foranstaltning af Kong Haakon Haakonssøn, ed. R. Keyser and C. R. Unger (Christiania, 1850).

Sverris saga, ed. Þorleifur Hauksson, Íslenzk fornrit, 30 (Reykjavík, 2007).

'Thomas's *Tristran*', ed. and trans. S. Gregory, in *Early French Tristan Poems*, 2, ed. N. J. Lacy (Cambridge, 1998), pp. 1–172.

Tristrams saga ok Ísöndar, ed. and trans. P. Jorgensen, in *Norse Romance. I: The Tristan Legend*, ed. M. E. Kalinke (Cambridge, 1999), pp. 23–226.

Wace's Roman de Brut: A History of the British, ed. and trans. Judith Weiss (Exeter, 1999; 2nd edn 2002).

Studies

Álfrún Gunnlaugsdóttir (1978). *Tristán en el Norte*, Reykjavík.

Barnes, G. (1977). 'The riddarasögur, a medieval exercise in translation', *Saga-Book*, 19, 4, 403–46.

Budal, I. B. (2009). '*Strengleikar* og *Lais*. Høviske noveller i omsetjing frå gammalfransk til gammalnorsk. I. Tekstanalyse. II. Synoptisk utgåve' (unpublished Ph.D. thesis, University of Bergen).

Cagnon, M. (1970). '*Chievrefueil* and the Ogamic Tradition', *Romania*, 91, 238–55.

Damsgaard Olsen, T. (1965). 'Den høviske litteratur', in H. Bekker-Nielsen, T. Damsgaard Olsen and O. Widding (eds), *Norrøn fortællekunst. Kapitler af den norsk-islandske middelalderlitteraturs historie*, Copenhagen, pp. 92–117.

Finlay, A. (2004). '"Intolerable Love": Tristrams saga and the Carlisle Tristan fragment', *Medium Ævum*, 73.2, 205–24.

Gibbs, M. E. and Johnson, S. (1997). *Medieval German Literature*, New York and London.

Hallberg, P. (1971). 'Norröna språkdrag. Några språkdrag', *Arkiv för nordisk filologi*, 86, 114–38.

Halvorsen, E. F. (1962). 'Høvisk stil', in *Kulturhistorisk leksikon for nordisk middelalder*, 7, Copenhagen, cols 315–18.

Johanterwage, V. (2007). 'Minnetrank und Brautunterschub in der *Tristrams saga ok Isǫndar*. Ein Vergleich mit dem Text des Carlisle-Fragments', in V. Johanterwage and S. Würth (eds), *Übersetzen im skandinavischen Mittelalter*, Studia Medievalia Septentrionalia, 14, Vienna, pp. 177–222.

Jordan, N. (2007). 'Eine alte und doch immer neue Geschichte. Die *Ívents saga Artúskappa* und der *Iwein* Hartmanns von Aue als Bearbeitungen von Chrétiens *Yvain*', in V. Johanterwage and S. Würth (eds), *Übersetzen im skandinavischen Mittelalter*, Studia Medievalia Septentrionalia, 14, Vienna, pp. 123–39.

Kalinke, M. E. (1981). *King Arthur, North-by-Northwest: The matière de Bretagne in Old Norse-Icelandic Romances*, Bibliotheca Arnamagnæana, 37, Copenhagen.

Kalinke, M. (2009). 'The Arthurian legend in *Breta sögur*: historiography on the cusp of romance', in Margrét Eggertsdóttir et al. (eds), *Greppaminni*, Reykjavík, pp. 217–30.

Kjær, J. (1992). 'Franco-Scandinavian literary transmission in the Middle Ages: two Old Norse translations of Chrétien de Troyes – *Ívens saga* and *Erex saga*', in K. Busby (ed.), *The Arthurian Yearbook*, New York and London, pp. 113–34.

Kramarz-Bein, S. (2000). 'Der *Spesar Þáttr* der *Grettis saga*. Tristan-Spuren in der Isländersaga', in *Studien zur Isländersaga. Festschrift für Rolf Heller*, Berlin and New York, pp. 152–81.

Kramarz-Bein, S. (2002). *Die Þiðreks saga im Kontext der altnorwegischen Literatur*, Beiträge zur Nordischen Philologie, 33, Tübingen and Basel.

Louis-Jensen, J. (1993). 'Breta sǫgur', in P. Pulsiano and K. Wolf (eds), *Medieval Scandinavia: An Encyclopedia*, New York and London, pp. 57–8.

Meissner, R. (1902). *Die Strengleikar. Ein Beitrag zur Geschichte der altnordischen Prosalitteratur*, Halle a. S.

Schach, P. (1965). 'The style and structure of *Tristrams saga*', in C. F. Bayerschmidt and E. J. Friis (eds), *Scandinavian Studies: Essays Presented to Dr. Henry Goddard Leach on the Occasion of his Eighty-fifth Birthday*, Seattle, pp. 63–86.

Skårup, P. (1984). 'Tre marginalnoter om Erex saga', *Gripla*, 6, Reykjavík, pp. 49–63.

Turville-Petre, G. (1953). *Origins of Icelandic Literature*, Oxford.

3

BRETA SÖGUR AND *MERLÍNÚSSPÁ*

Stefanie Gropper

Breta sögur (The Sagas of the Britons) is the Old Icelandic translation of Geoffrey of Monmouth's *Historia regum Britanniae*. *Breta sögur* also contains *Merlínússpá*, the Old Icelandic translation of the *Prophetiae Merlini*. *Merlínússpá* is the only translation into verse and thus has a unique position among the translations of foreign literature undertaken in Norway and Iceland. According to two manuscripts (AM 544 4to, the so-called *Hauksbók*, and AM 573 4to) the poem was translated by Gunnlaugr Leifsson, a monk and well-known author of Kings' Sagas in the Benedictine monastery of Þingeyrar in northern Iceland, a centre of literary production in the Scandinavian Middle Ages. Although it seems probable, it cannot be proved that the *Prophetiae Merlini* and the *Historia regum Britanniae* were both translated by Gunnlaugr Leifsson around 1200. Since later manuscripts contain the poem independently of the prose context, proving thus that it could stand alone, Philip Lavender has suggested that Gunnlaugr originally wrote the poem as a stand-alone piece and that *Merlínússpá* was later inserted into the *Breta sögur* (Lavender 2006, 135). Simone Horst (2006) has claimed, however, that differences in metre, style and narrative structure permit one to conclude that the two sections of the poem, which is clearly divided into two parts in *Hauksbók*, might have had different authors. Based on internal evidence, she suggests that the second part of the poem – probably by Gunnlaugr as the manuscripts claim – was composed between 1210 and 1219, whereas the first part of the poem was composed between 1220 and 1270.

Scholars agree that *Breta sögur* together with *Rómverja saga* (The Saga of the Romans), *Veraldar saga* (The Saga of the World) and *Trójumanna saga* (The Saga of the Trojans) belongs to the oldest layer of translations of secular literature into Old Norse-Icelandic. *Breta sögur* is thus the oldest translation of Arthurian matter in the North. The saga is preserved in two redactions of the fourteenth century, one concentrating on the historic information (*Hauksbók*) and one focusing on the courtly material (AM 573 4to). Since the transmission of *Breta sögur* is rather poor, a comparison between the saga and the Latin exemplar, which is unknown, as well as between the two redactions of the saga and the original translation, which does not exist, is problematic at best. It is clear, however, that the preserved text is a reworking of an older translation. Despite its poor transmission, *Breta sögur* must have been known quite well, since its contents were used or excerpted in several later works.

In all manuscripts *Breta sögur* appears as the continuation of the so-called version β of *Trójumanna saga* (The Saga of the Trojans), that is, the Old Norse translation of

Dares Phrygius' *De excidio Troiae historia* (Louis-Jensen edn 1981). The combining of Dares's text with Geoffrey's *Historia* was quite common in the Middle Ages (D'Arcier 2005; Crick 1991). As is the case with this version of *Trójumanna saga*, *Breta sögur* is preserved in a longer and in a shorter version. There are only two, incomplete, manuscripts of the longer version:

(a) AM 573 4to, a vellum manuscript, which has been dated to the fourteenth century. Besides *Trójumanna saga* and the longer version of *Breta sögur*, it also contains the beginning of *Valvens þáttr* (The Story of Valven), a translation of the concluding Gawain section of Chrétien de Troyes's *Perceval*. In this manuscript the text of *Breta sögur* ends with King Arthur's death, thus linking it to the story of the grail. Since the text of *Breta sögur* starts in a new gathering, Jonna Louis-Jensen (1963, XXII) concluded that the saga was originally intended for a separate codex. This does not seem probable, however, since the first part of *Breta sögur* is written in the same hand as the preceding *Trójumanna saga*. In addition, there is a reference to *Breta sögur* at the conclusion of *Trójumanna saga* (Würth 1998, 57). The second part of *Breta sögur*, which was written in a different hand seems to be based on a different exemplar than the first part. This is distinguished by a more verbose style and by several additions. Although some of these additions may have been the invention of an Icelandic redactor, others must have already existed in the Latin exemplar, which can be seen from a comparison with Wace's *Roman de Brut* (Würth 1998, 58).

(b) Sth. Papp. fol. nr 58, a paper manuscript copied in the seventeenth century from *Ormsbók*, a now lost manuscript from the fourteenth century. Sth. Papp. fol. nr 58 only contains the first part of *Breta sögur*, which ends before the story of King Arthur begins. Verbal correspondences with AM 573 4to let us conclude that both manuscripts are copies of the same exemplar.

The shorter version of *Breta sögur* is preserved only in AM 544 4to, one of the parts of the vellum manuscript called *Hauksbók*. This voluminous manuscript was written between 1301 and 1314 on behalf of Haukr Erlendsson, an Icelandic lawman living in Norway, who also wrote parts of the manuscript himself. *Hauksbók* is the only manuscript preserving a complete text of *Breta sögur*, including *Merlínússpá*, and a catalogue of West-Saxon kings from Cædvalla to Æthelstan. Several copies and excerpts of *Breta sögur* are based on this manuscript. *Hauksbók* contains a large number of texts with very different contents. Although *Trójumanna saga* and *Breta sögur* today are separated by two leaves, they nonetheless form a textual unit.[1] This can be deduced from the fact that *Trójumanna saga* refers to the following *Breta sögur* which, from a chronological point of view, is the continuation of *Trójumanna saga* by reporting on the foundation of Rome by Aeneas.

The manuscript AM 764 4to, which was written 1376–86 in Skagafjörður (North Iceland) and which was intended as a history of the world, contains an excerpt of

Breta sögur. Several passages agree almost word for word with the saga whereas other passages are summarized quite succinctly. Verbal correspondences as well as mistakes in names indicate that the exemplar for this excerpt was either a manuscript closely affiliated with AM 573 4to or even this manuscript itself (Würth 1998, 179).

The impulse for the composition of *Breta sögur* may have been provided by the information given by Geoffrey in his *Historia* about Icelandic and Scandinavian prehistory. He reports that the king of Thule fought on King Arthur's side and that the Orkneys, Norway, Gotland and Denmark had been obliged to pay taxes to King Arthur (Reeve edn 2007, 205, 221). The *Historia* also included the possibility to connect the Norwegian dynasty – and thus also the leading Icelandic families – to the Trojan dynasty. One of the first Norwegian kings, Hákon, the son of Harald Fairhair (d. *c*.932), was fostered at King Æthelstan's court. *Breta sögur* follows the outlines of Geoffrey's *Historia* very closely, but the first five paragraphs of the *Historia*, containing the dedication, a prologue and the description of the British Isles, are replaced by a summary of Virgil's *Aeneid*, reporting about the period between the end of the Trojan War until Aeneas' arrival in Italy and thus closing the gap between the end of *Trójumanna saga* and the beginning of the action in the *Historia* with the settlement of the British Isles. In the preserved manuscripts *Trójumanna saga* and *Breta sögur* are thus connected to a continuous narrative from the mythical ancestors of King Priamus in Troy to King Arthur (in *Ormsbók* and AM 573) to King Hákon Haraldsson (r. 934–60) in Norway (in *Hauksbók*).

In respect to plot and structure, *Breta sögur* follows its exemplar closely, albeit with a tendency to abridgement. Passages that have been translated almost verbatim alternate with very free renderings of the Latin text. Compared to Geoffrey's *Historia* the narrative in *Breta sögur* is more balanced, since all kings receive more or less the same space. This is also true for King Arthur, although the description of his person is longer and more detailed than in the *Historia* (Würth 1998, 73–4, fn. 292). Passages from the *Historia* are lacking in *Breta sögur* that needed specific knowledge about British conditions, such as details about the construction of streets, or that offer parallels between the plot of the *Historia* and contemporary British history. Passages with a pronounced nationalistic tone or that contain negative statements about Scandinavia and its inhabitants are also left out. The structure of the passages concerning each British king has parallels in Norwegian chronicles, such as *Ágrip af Nóregs konunga sögum* (Summary of the Sagas of the Kings of Norway), the oldest preserved history of the Norwegian kings in the vernacular; the *Historia Norwegiae*, one of the most ancient documents of Norwegian history; and the late twelfth-century *Historia de antiquitate regum Norwagiensium* by Theodoricus Monachus. These Norwegian synoptics may have functioned as models for the presentation of the British kings, but *Breta sögur* may have in turn influenced the indigenous portrayals of kings, such as in Snorri Sturluson's *Ynglinga saga*, the first of the sagas in his monumental compilation *Heimskringla*.

Merlínússpá is problematic not only because of the dating but also because of its structure. Since it is preserved only in a single manuscript it is difficult to decide whether it still reflects the translation ascribed to Gunnlaugr Leifsson. In *Hauksbók* the name *Merlínússpá* is given to two poems, which together render the *Prophetiae Merlini*, albeit in reversed order, that is, the second poem corresponds to the first part of the *Prophetiae* and the first poem to the second part.[2] Since *Hauksbók* also contains *Völuspá*, an eddic poem in the same metre as *Merlínússpá* and also a prophetic poem, it could be that the order of stanzas in *Merlínússpá* might have been intended to emphasize the parallels with *Völuspá* in respect to content (Würth 1998, 81). Instead of the *Prophetiae*'s prologue, *Merlínússpá* starts with four introductory stanzas about its own production and author. At the end of the poem (stanzas 93–103) the author comments on poetry and a Christian interpretation of the prophecies. In general *Merlínússpá* reflects the Latin text very closely at the same time that it uses metaphors and images from indigenous poetry, thereby giving the translation the semblance of an Eddic poem.

The combination of stories of the Trojan War and the history of the British was quite common in Europe during the Middle Ages. Although the Latin exemplars of both texts came independently to Iceland it seems that the translations were rather soon combined in manuscripts, transmitted together and regarded as two parts of one story. Version β of *Trójumanna saga* differs from version α mainly by its additional sources. As Jonna Louis-Jensen has demonstrated, the original translation of *Trójumanna saga* was interpolated with excerpts from the *Ilias Latina* (Louis-Jensen 1981, XXX), which was regarded as a text from classical antiquity and was part of the school canon (Glauche 1970, 70f. and 110). The reworking as well as the interpolations of *Trójumanna saga* were possibly motivated by its connection to *Breta sögur*.

Although the two preserved redactions of *Breta sögur* derive from a common archetype they differ from each other in respect to style and focus. Whereas the *Hauksbók* redaction of *Breta sögur* obviously functions as part of a historic encyclopaedia, in *Ormsbók* and AM 573 4to *Breta sögur* was read as an Arthurian narrative. This can be clearly deduced from the context of the manuscripts: The first part of *Hauksbók* (AM 371 4to)[3] contains texts dealing with the history of Iceland: *Landnámabók* (The Book of Settlement) and *Kristni saga* (The Saga of Christianization). At the end of *Landnámabók*, Haukr Erlendsson declares that in his version of *Landnámabók* he combined two older redactions of the text.[4]

Among others, the second part of *Hauksbók* (AM 544 4to) contains a text that Finnur Jónsson called *Heimslýsing ok helgifræði* (Cosmography and Theology) in his edition and which consists of several passages about geography, calendars and theology. Most of these passages derive from Latin or Old English texts. Since some of these passages are also preserved in other Icelandic manuscripts, it is unlikely that Haukr commissioned the translations.[5] The following passages, which Finnur Jónsson combined under the heading *Heimspeki ok helgifræði* (Philosophy and Theology), are most certainly also based on exemplars in foreign languages, although in most instances the sources have not yet been identified (Finnur Jónsson 1892–96, CXXIII–CXXV).

Following this group of encyclopaedic texts we find the eddic poem *Völuspá* in a version differing somewhat from the poem in the Codex Regius of the *Poetic Edda* and Snorri Sturluson's use of the poem as a framework for his account of Norse mythology in the so-called *Prose* or *Younger Edda*. *Völuspá* is then followed by *Trójumanna saga* and *Breta sögur*, and these by *Viðrœða líkams ok sálar* (Dialogue between body and soul). This last is a combined text of two exemplars with an introduction and connecting elements (Finnur Jónsson 1892–96, CXXV–CXXVI).

Three *Íslendingasögur*, Sagas of Icelanders, follow this large group of translations in the manuscript: *Hemings þáttr* (The Story of Hemingr), the beginning of which is lost on account of a large lacuna; *Heiðreks saga ok Hervarar* (The Saga of Heidrek and Hervör), which is also fragmentary, but which can be completed from younger paper copies of *Hauksbók*;[6] *Fóstbrœðra saga* (The Saga of the Sworn Brothers) in a substantially abridged version. Then follows a short introduction to calculation (Christoffersen and Bekken 1985, 131–50). The next four texts deal with Norwegian history: *Eiríks saga rauða* (The Saga of Eirik the Red), which, like all other texts that have been reworked by Haukr Erlendsson, has a tendency toward *brevitas* and a simple style; *Skálda saga* (The Saga of Skalds), which has been preserved only in *Hauksbók* and its copies; *Þáttr af Upplendinga konungum* (The Story of the Kings of Uppland), which too has only been preserved in *Hauksbók* and which is connected to the last paragraph of *Ynglinga saga* (The Saga of the Ynglings); *Ragnars sona þáttr* (The Story of Ragnar's Sons), which also has been preserved only in *Hauksbók*. This second part of *Hauksbók* ends with a text called *Prognostica Temporum*, known also from other Icelandic and Norwegian manuscripts. The third and last part of *Hauksbók* (AM 675 4to) contains only a fragment of the Icelandic translation of the *Elucidarium*. In Finnur Jónsson's edition this text is followed by genealogies that have been preserved only in younger paper copies.

Some scholars have argued that the diverse material of *Hauksbók* is neither coherent nor presented systematically (Jón Helgason 1960, XVIII; Finnur Jónsson 1892–96, LXIII, fn.). But this opinion does not take into consideration that the manuscript is not complete and that we therefore do not know whether the order of texts is correct (Stefán Karlsson 1964, 117f.). But at least we can be certain that *Hauksbók* originally was an impressive and rather voluminous codex, albeit presumably never a richly decorated manuscript for representative purposes but rather for everyday usage. When considered as a whole, *Hauksbók* is a comprehensive encyclopaedia. Although the focus is on history, the four parts characteristic of medieval encyclopaedias are represented: cosmology, history, natural sciences and ethics. As an encyclopaedia *Hauksbók* functioned as a library because it contains the *materia* of many books covering a broad range of knowledge. Within this context *Breta sögur* – together with *Trójumanna saga* – has to be regarded as a historic text that was used by Icelanders and Norwegians to trace their origins to Troy and thus to integrate Icelandic and Norwegian history into world history.

Compared to their redactions in *Hauksbók*, *Trójumanna* saga and *Breta sögur* were transmitted in a quite different context in the other two manuscripts. Although *Ormsbók* is lost, its contents can be reconstructed with the help of an index written in the seventeenth century:

> Orms Snorrasons Book | Continet Troijomanna Saga. Anundar Jarls Sona Saga; & alia varia, nempe Magus Jarls Saga | Lais Floretz | Berings | Remundars | Eriks Iwenis | Bewis | Myrmans | Parhalops | Enohs & Partiwals Sagor.

> (Orms Snorrason's book contains Trójumanna saga, the Saga of Önundr jarl's sons and several others, i.e., the Saga of Magus jarl, the Lais of Flores as well as the Saga of Beringr, the Saga of Remundr, the Saga of Erex, the Saga of Iven, the Saga of Bever, the Saga of Myrman, the Saga of Partalopi, the Saga of Enok and the Saga of Parceval.)[7]

Although there has been some debate about the information conveyed above, scholars have agreed that 'Troijomanna saga' also included *Breta sögur*.[8] The other sagas that can be identified, but whose order is probably not the same in the index as it was in the manuscript (Sanders 1979, 141), were translations of French *lais*, Arthurian romances and Icelandic *riddarasögur* (Sagas of Knights), that is, indigenous romances. This means that *Trójumanna saga* and *Breta sögur* were included in a context of courtly literature. Therefore the focus of the works in *Ormsbók* was probably *delectare* (entertainment) rather than that of *Hauksbók*, *prodesse* (learning).

The same is true for the related, albeit fragmentary manuscript AM 573 4to, where *Trójumanna saga* and *Breta sögur* obviously were also presented in a context of courtly literature. The text of *Breta sögur* ends after King Arthur's death and is immediately followed by *Valvens þáttr* (The Story of Valven), the concluding Gawain section of *Parcevals saga* (The Saga of Parceval). Since the preserved copies of *Ormsbók* and the text of AM 573 4to only partially overlap, we cannot be certain whether *Breta sögur* in *Ormsbók* also ended with King Arthur's death and was then continued by *Valvens þáttr*. Nonetheless, it is certain that both manuscripts contained mostly courtly literature.

A comparison of the two redactions of *Breta sögur* reveals that their content and style correspond to the context of the manuscripts in which they are found. In *Hauksbók* the language of the text as well as the selection of narrative elements correspond to the historical focus of an encyclopaedia. In *Ormsbók* and AM 573, however, more attention is devoted to fantastic and entertaining elements, so that in content and style this redaction is more reminiscent of the surrounding *riddarasögur* (Würth 1998, 168–9). This becomes especially clear in the love scenes. Whereas in *Hauksbók* love or the emotions in general are mentioned only when they are essential for an understanding of the plot, in *Ormsbók* and AM 573 they are emphasized. The narrative and its entertaining aspects predominate at the expense of the chronological order of events and their inner logic. Thus the redaction of *Breta sögur* in *Ormsbók* and AM 573 corresponds to the accepted understanding of the nature of the translated and indigenous *riddarasögur* (Kalinke 1985, 317). In these manuscripts *Breta sögur* is a medieval, courtly romance with an emphasis on human relationships and composed in the so-called 'courtly style' (see chapter 2).

The first major event in the Arthurian portion of *Breta sögur* and following *Merlínússpá*, to which the AM 573 redaction refers but does not include, is the story of Uther's seduction of Igerna, who gives birth to King Arthur. As Geoffrey tells it, Uther falls passionately in love with the wife of Duke Gorlois of Cornwall when he meets her at a banquet. Aware of Uther's flirtation, Gorlois abruptly leaves the court and secludes Igerna in the castle of Tintagel. Uther retaliates by declaring war on the duke. At the same time he is so smitten with Igerna that he engages Merlin to help him gain access to her. With Merlin's help, Uther takes on the appearance of Gorlois, goes to Tintagel and spends the night with Igerna, who believes him to be her husband, and Arthur is conceived. Gorlois is subsequently killed, and Geoffrey summarizes the aftermath:

> Cumque omnem euentum didicisset, ob caedem Gorlois doluit sed ob Igernam a maritali copula solutam gauisus est. Reuersus itaque ad oppidum Tintagol, cepit illud cepitque Igernam et uoto suo potitus est. Commanserunt deinde pariter non minimo amore ligati progenueruntque filium et filiam. Fuit autem nomen filii Arturus, filiae uero Anna. (Reeve edn 2007, 189)

> (When he had learned the whole story, he regretted Gorlois' death, but rejoiced that Igerna was now free from the bond of marriage; so he returned to the castle of Tintagel, took it and Igerna and fulfilled his desire. They remained together thereafter, united by no little passion, and had a son and daughter. Their son was called Arthur, their daughter Anna.) (Wright trans. 2007, 188)

Unlike the very matter-of-fact resolution of the Uther-Igerna tale in the *Historia*, the AM 573 redaction of *Breta sögur* dramatizes the consequences of Gorlois's death. The author has Uther, here called Yðir, confess to Igerne with what trickery (*með huerium brögðum*) he had deceived her, and he promises to compensate her:

> oc þó at þú þikiz nú mikinn skaða beðit hafa í drápi bónda þíns, þá munu skiótt ráðaz bætr á því fyri þá grein, at nú skaltu vera mín drotníng oc skal ek í ockarri samuist allt þat bæta sem ek hefir áðr brotið við þig. (Jón Sigurðsson edn 1849, 86, fn. 1)

> (And even though you think that you have suffered great damage through the death of your husband, you will quickly be compensated for this, for you shall now be my queen and in our marriage I shall compensate you for all my previous transgression against you.)

Her response, *með miklum harmi*, 'with great grief', is an extended lament:

> nú er ek sárliga suikin oc hörmuliga gint; hó, hó! segir hon, mikil óskaup ero vorðin, sua er sem ek sè vorðin banamaðr bónda míns, sua ágætz, honum unna ek (sem) líkama siálfrar minnar oc sua sem lífi mínu, hann villdi mèr allt gott oc þat skal verða alldri at ek gángi lostig í sama sæng þeim manni, er minn bónda hefir suikit, ok fyrr skal ek láta mitt líf en þat verði. Hon grætr nú sárliga oc berr sua mikinn harm, at engi maðr mátti hugga hana. (Jón Sigurðsson edn 1849, 86, fn. 1)

> ('I have now been sorely betrayed and grievously deceived. Woe,' she says, 'a terrible fate has now occurred since I have brought about the death of my husband, who was so excellent. I loved him as my own self and my life. He wanted nothing but good for me and it shall never happen that I shall of my own free will share the same bed with the man who has betrayed my husband. I would rather

lose my life than have that happen.' She now cried woefully and was in such great distress that no one could comfort her.)

Yðir has to have recourse to Merlin once more. The sorcerer gives Igerne a magic potion 'at hon kastar þegar öllum ecka oc ángri, oc samþyckir konúnginum, oc fær hann hennar' (Jón Sigurðsson edn 1849, 87, fn. 1) (so that she casts off all her sorrow and grief, and gives her consent to the king and he receives her in marriage).

Geoffrey wrote as a chronicler in relating the Uther–Igerna story; he was solely interested in establishing how King Arthur came to be conceived. And that is also the case in *Hauksbók*, where what is related in the passage corresponding to the above is reduced to the following: 'hann gengr siþan til kastalans, ok segir Igerne allt eð sanna. hon samþyckir þa við konvng ok feck hann þa hennar' (Finnur Jónsson edn 1892–96, 286) (then he goes to the castle and tells Igerne the whole truth. She gives her consent to the king and he receives her in marriage). In the AM 573 redaction, however, Igerne's lament in response to having learned the truth from Yðir is the stuff of romance. It is comparable, for example, to Blensinbil's lament in *Tristrams saga ok Ísöndar*, when she learns of the death of Kanelangres:

> Aum em ek yfir alla kvennmenn. Hvernig skal ek lifa eptir svá dýrligan dreng? Ek var hans líf ok huggun, en hann var unnasti minn ok líf mitt. Ek var hans yndi, en hann mín gleði. Hversu skal ek lifa eptir hann dauðan? Hversu skal ek huggaz, er gaman mitt er grafit? Báðum okkr sómir saman at deyja. (Jorgensen edn 1999, 46–8)

> (There is not a woman alive who is more wretched than I. How could I survive such a glorious, gallant man? I was his life and his comfort, and he was my beloved and my life. I was his delight, and he was my joy. How shall I live on after his death? How shall I be comforted, when my joy is buried? It is fitting for us both to die together.) (Jorgensen trans. 199, 47–9)

The author of Igerne's monologue in *Breta sögur* was writing not as a chronicler but rather as a romancier, like Thomas de Bretagne, as known from the Norwegian translation, in his *Tristan*. He wished to transmit more than the facts of Arthur's conception; his interest also lay in characterization and motivation. He went beyond the sober facts to include emotional response, and thus he stepped over the threshold of historiography and entered the realm of romance.

Igerne's monologue is found only in the AM 573 redaction of *Breta sögur*. Haukr Erlendsson was not interested in the depiction of emotion nor in motifs characteristic of courtly literature, such as feasts (Würth 1998, 167). His redaction was intended less as an entertaining narrative than a historiographical work. If one compares the Yðir–Igerne episode in AM 573 with that in *Hauksbók*, we are in fact confronted by distinct types of narrative, romance if you will, in the former and chronicle in the latter. In AM 573 the lacunae in Geoffrey's *Historia* were filled with narrative matter produced by one redactor's imagination when he confronted Geoffrey's at times laconic version.

The passages above reveal that, when compared with Geoffrey's *Historia*, the Arthurian legend in the AM 573 redaction of *Breta sögur* favours dramatization and the exploration of emotions. This redaction also transmits details associated with courtly ritual, for example, in the depiction of Arthur's coronation festivities at Whitsun. Geoffrey too lavishes extraordinary attention in the *Historia* on this important event in Arthur's life. Geoffrey names the many notables who attend, describes the coronation ritual and the order of seating at the banquet. Geoffrey's very long account of Arthur's coronation (Reeve edn 2007, 209–15) is reduced in *Hauksbók* to a single sentence:

> hann bavð til sin at hvita svnv ollvm konvngvm hertogvm ok iorlvm ok ollvm hofþingivm i sinv ʀiki ok var hann þa krvnaðr ok sva drottningin ok er (sv) veizla viðfrægivz orðin a Nordrlondvm bœði at fornv ok nyiv. (Finnur Jónsson edn 1892–96, 290)

> (He invited all kings, dukes and earls and all the chieftains in his realm to come to him at Whitsun, and he was then crowned and also the queen. And that festivity has become the most famous in the Northern lands both in days of old and in our own times.)

The AM 573 redaction diverges from *Hauksbók* by transmitting not only much of Geoffrey's text – it includes the list of guests and the description of the coronation ceremony – but also additional matter not found in the *Historia*. Geoffrey restrains himself in the account of the banquet by commenting: 'quem si omnino describere pergerem, nimiam prolixitatem historiae generarem' (Reeve edn 2007, 213) (if I were to describe it all in detail, my history would become too wordy) (Wright trans. 2007, 212). This did not deter *Breta sögur*, that is, the redactor of its Latin source, from informing us:

> Krásadiskar aller voru af rauða gulli geruir, eða silfri oc settir gimsteinum . . . Aull ker oc bollar oc skáler voru af gulli eða brendu silfri . . . allt var tialldat vefium enum dýrstum eða guðuef, oc gengu náliga aller menn í gullofnum klæðum. (Jón Sigurðsson edn 1849, 100)

> (The dishes for the appetizers were all made of red gold or silver and decorated with gems . . . All the goblets and cups and bowls were of gold or burnished silver . . . everywhere hung tapestries of the most precious cloth or velvet, and nearly everyone wore garments shot through with gold.)

And then, when Geoffrey summarizes: 'Refecti tandem epulis, diuersi diuersos ludos composituri campos extra ciuitatem adeunt' (Reeve edn 2007, 213) (When at last they had had their fill at the banquets, they separated to visit the fields outside the city and indulge in varied sports) (Wright trans. 2007, 212), *Breta sögur* expatiates:

> Þá er dryckiu var lokit oc hennar varð í milli, þá voru leikar oc taufl oc saugur. Þar var allzkyns streingleikar: fiðlur oc gígiur, bumbur oc pípur oc simphóníam oc haurpur. (Jón Sigurðsson edn 1849, 100–1)

> (During the drinking and afterwards, there were games of chance and board games and stories; there were all kinds of stringed instruments, fiddles and viols, drums and pipes and hurdy-gurdies and harps.)

Whereas the board games, storytelling and music during the festivities at Arthur's coronation are not mentioned in the *Historia*, they are found in Wace's *Roman de Brut*, who reports at great length on the kinds of music played and the instruments used, including fiddles, rotes, harps, flutes, lyres, drums, shawms, bagpipes, psalteries, monochords, tambourines and choruns (Weiss edn 2002, vv. 10,543–60). To judge by the *Brut*, neither the account of storytelling nor that of the music enjoyed at Arthur's court is original in *Breta sögur*.

The courtly entertainment is not limited to the hall, however, for the knights continue their activities outside. Like the *Historia*, *Breta sögur* reports that the knights entertained the men and women watching from the battlements – Geoffrey refers only to the womenfolk – with such activities as tilting and hurling heavy stones. Moreover, according to *Breta sögur*, Arthur had also assembled there his wise men and scholars whose task was to entertain the older folks and all those assembled at the games. While the ultimate source of the above is the *Historia* (Reeve edn 2007, 215), *Breta sögur* contains additional and diverging information, for example, concerning Arthur's generosity to his guests:

> Þessi gleði stóð yfir .iij. daga hina fyrstu þessarrar veizlu oc maurg aunnur, sú at hèr er eigi getið. Hinn fiórða dag veizlunnar skipti Artus konúngr giöfum með mönnum, oc lèt þat huern af sèr þiggia sem hann var fúsaztr til: gull eða silfr, eða gersemar, vàpn eða klæði dýrlig, borgir eða kastala, eða iók tign manna, er leituðu gaufugra kuanfánga. Biskupum oc ábótum oc öðrum lærðum mönnum veitti hann mikil gæðe, oc náliga gædde hann alla nockurri virðíngu, þá sem hann hafði þángat boðit. (Jón Sigurðsson edn 1849, 101)

> (This merriment lasted for three days at this first festival and many others that are not reported here. On the fourth day of the feasting King Arthur distributed gifts to men and he permitted each to take what he most desired: gold or silver, or precious objects, weapons or precious garments, towns or castles, and the reputation of those men increased who got themselves noble wives. To bishops and abbots and other learned men he granted boons and on nearly everyone whom he had invited there he bestowed some honour.)

The corresponding passage in Geoffrey of Monmouth's account is here brief. We are simply told:

> Consumptis autem primis in hunc modum diebus tribus, instante quarta uocantur cuncti qui ei propter honores obsequium praestabant et singuli singulis possessionibus, ciuitatibus uidelicet atque castellis, archiepiscopatibus, episcopatibus, abbatiis, ceterisque honoribus donantur. (Reeve edn 2007, 215)

> (After they had devoted the first three days to these pursuits, on the fourth all those who were serving the king in expectation of some title were summoned and each was rewarded with a city or castle, with archbishoprics, bishoprics, abbeys or some other honour.) (Wright trans. 2007, 214)

The account in the *Roman de Brut* reveals that the additional material in *Breta sögur* did not originate with the Icelandic translator. Wace's King Arthur, like the king of *Breta sögur*, is depicted as extraordinarily generous to those who have visited his court from abroad: he bestows jewels, greyhounds, birds, furs, cloth, cups, goblets, brocades, rings, tunics, cloaks and more (Weiss edn 2002, vv. 10,599–616).[9]

We do not know the Latin source of the translation reflected in the AM 573 redaction of *Breta sögur*. To judge by the additions in *Breta sögur* that the Icelandic translation shares with Wace's *Roman de Brut* (see chapter 2), it is most likely that what we read in the AM 573 redaction corresponds to the original translation which transmitted more or less faithfully the text of the Latin source, in which Geoffrey's Arthurian legend had already been fictionalized and augmented.

Two different redactions of *Breta sögur* were circulating in Iceland at the same time, that is, at least during the thirteenth and fourteenth centuries, but it is still an open question what the original translation looked like and what effect a later reworking had on the existing redactions. Until recently *Breta sögur* had been regarded chiefly as a historiographic work that had been refashioned into what might be considered a *riddarasaga*, that is, a romance. But since both redactions are preserved in manuscripts from the same time, we cannot be certain that the historiographic redaction predates the redaction as a *riddarasaga*. Moreover, it seems likely that the Icelandic translator used a Latin exemplar closely related to that used by Wace for his *Roman de Brut*. Some of the features that argue for the transformation of the translation of the *Historia regum Britanniae* in *Breta sögur* into what might be considered a romance may therefore have already existed in the Latin exemplar (Würth 1998, 58, fn. 228).

Notes

[1] Fols 34 and 35 were inserted at a later time between *Trójumanna saga* and *Breta sögur* to complete a gathering (Stefán Karlsson 1964, 117).

[2] Stanzas 5–68 of *Merlínússpá* correspond to stanzas 31–74 of *Prophetiae Merlini*, and stanzas 69–92 of *Merlínússpá* correspond to stanzas 1–30 of the *Prophetiae*.

[3] This part of the manuscript is defective, but the lacuna can be filled from a copy of the seventeenth century (Jón Helgason 1960, xii).

[4] 'Enn þersa bok ritada (ek) Haukr Ellinz svn. epter þeiri bók sem ritad hafdi herra Sturla logmadr hinn frodazti madr ok eptir þeiri bok annarri er ritad hafdi Styrmir hinn fródi. ok hafda ek þat or hvari sem framar greindi. enn mikill þori var þat er þær sogdu eins badar' (And this book wrote (I), Haukr Erlendsson, according to that book which the lawspeaker Herra Sturla, a very prudent man, had written, and according to another book, which Styrmir the Wise had written. And I took from each as I explained before. But it was a large part where both agreed in their report.) (Finnur Jónsson edn 1892–96, 124, ll. 19–23).

[5] The sources are listed in detail in Finnur Jónsson edn, 1892–96: CXVI–CXXIII.

[6] In this text, too, Haukr tried to harmonize several exemplars. Jón Helgason edn 1960, xvi–xvii.

[7] Quoted from Broberg 1908, 56f.

[8] This can be seen from an entry in Johannes Thomae Bureus's catalogue from 1651: 'Ormer Snorresson, på Pergament, in folio, rätt gammal Suänska, och mächta tätt styl, om Troiæ förstöring, och Ängelands första bebygning, samt een hoop andra Historier, angående Frankerike och Tyskland' (Ormr Snorrason, on Parchment, in folio, rather old Swedish and quite dense style, about the destruction of Troy and the earliest settlement in England together with a group of other stories concerning France and Germany). Quoted from Gödel 1904, 357.

[9] The foregoing discussion of courtly elements in the AM 573 redaction of *Breta sögur* is based on Kalinke, 2009.

Reference List

Texts and Translations

Breta sögur

The Arnamagnæan Manuscripts 371, 4to; 544, 4to; and 675, 4to, ed. Jón Helgason (Copenhagen, 1960).

Breta sögur, ed. Jón Sigurðsson, in 'Trójumanna saga and Breta sögur, efter Hauksbók med dansk Oversættelse', *Annaler for Nordisk Oldkyndighed og Historie* (Copenhagen, 1849), pp. 3–145.

Hauksbók, ed. Finnur Jónsson (Copenhagen, 1892–96).

Die Saga von den britischen Königen, trans. S. Würth, in *Isländische Antikensagas*, ed. and trans. S. Würth (Munich, 1996), I, 51–142.

Merlínússpá

Merlínússpá, ed. Finnur Jónsson, in *Hauksbók* (Copenhagen, 1892–96), pp. 272–83.

Merlins Prophezeiung, trans. S. Würth, in *Isländische Antikensagas*, ed. and trans. S. Würth (Munich, 1996), I, 98–120.

Other Editions and Translations

Geoffrey of Monmouth, The History of the Kings of Britain: An Edition and Translation of De gestis Britonum [Historia Regum Britanniae], ed. M. D. Reeve, trans. N. Wright (Woodbridge, 2007).

Tristrams saga ok Ísöndar, ed. and trans. P. Jorgensen, in *Norse Romance*, I: *The Tristan Legend*, ed. M. E. Kalinke (Cambridge, 1999), pp. 23–226.

Trójumanna saga, ed. J. Louis-Jensen, Editiones Arnamagnæanæ, 8 (Copenhagen, 1963).

Trójumanna saga: The Dares Phrygius Version, ed. Jonna Louis-Jensen, Editiones Arnamagnæanæ, 9 (Copenhagen, 1981).

Wace's Roman de Brut: A History of the British, ed. and trans. J. Weiss (Exeter, 1999; 2nd edn 2002).

Studies

Broberg, G. (1908). 'Ormr Snorrasons bok', *Arkiv för nordisk filologi*, 24, 42–66.

Crick, J. (1991). *The Historia Regum Britannie of Geoffrey of Monmouth*, IV: *Dissemination and Reception in the Later Middle Ages*, Cambridge.

Christoffersen, M. and Bekken, O. B. (1985). 'Algorismus i Hauksbók i europeisk perspektiv', *The Sixth International Saga Conference 28.7.–2.8.1985, Workshop Papers*, I, Copenhagen, pp. 131–50.

D'Arcier, L. F. (2006). *Histoire et géographie d'un mythe. La circulation des manuscripts du* De Excidio Troiae *de Darès le Phrygien*, Paris.

Glauche, G. (1970). *Schullektüre im Mittelalter. Entstehungen und Wandlungen des Lektürekanons bis 1200 nach den Quellen dargestellt*, Munich.

Gödel, V. (1904). 'Ormr Snorrasons bok', in *Nordiska Studier tilegnade Adolf Noreen*, Uppsala, pp. 357–74.

Gropper, S. (2014). 'Die Transmission der *Breta sögur* als Beispiel für verschiedene Formen der *translatio* innerhalb der mittelalterlichen isländischen Literatur', in J. Glauser and S. Kramarz-Bein (eds), *Rittersagas. Übersetzung – Überlieferung – Transmission*, Tübingen, pp. 219–37.

Horst, S. (2006). 'Die *Merlínússpá – ein* Gedicht von Gunnlaugr Leifsson?', *skandinavistik*, 36, 22–31.

Kalinke, M. (1985). 'Norse Romance (*Riddarasögur*)', in C. J. Clover and J. Lindow (eds), *Old Norse-Icelandic Literature: A Critical Guide*, Ithaca and London, pp. 316–63.

Kalinke, M. (2009). 'The Arthurian legend in *Breta sögur*: historiography on the cusp of romance', in Margrét Eggertsdóttir et al. (eds), *Greppaminni: Essays in Honour of Vésteinn Ólason*, Reykjavík, pp. 217–30.

Lavender, P. (2006). 'Merlin and the Völva', *Viking and Medieval Scandinavia*, 2, 111–39.

Sanders, C. (1979). 'The Order of Knights in Ormsbók', *Opuscula*, 7, Bibliotheca Arnamagnæana, 34, Copenhagen, pp. 140–56.

Stefán Karlsson. (1964). 'Aldur Hauksbókar', *Fróðskaparrit. Annales Societatis Scientiarium Færoensis*, 13, 114–21.

Würth, S. (1998). *Der 'Antikenroman' in der isländischen Literatur des Mittelalters. Eine Untersuchung zur Übersetzung und Rezeption lateinischer Literatur im Norden*, Basel and Frankfurt/Main.

4

THE TRISTAN LEGEND

Geraldine Barnes

According to tradition, *Tristrams saga ok Ísöndar*, the Old Norse version of Thomas of England's *Tristan* (*c*.1180), was the first of the Matter of Britain *riddarasögur*: romances translated and adapted from Old French and Anglo-Norman verse into Old Norse prose during the reign of the Norwegian king, Hákon Hákonarson (r.1217–63). Although the authenticity of the statement that prefaces the only two complete *Tristrams saga* manuscripts (AM 543 4to and ÍB 51 fol.) has been disputed (Sverrir Tómasson 1977), it offers specific details about the production of the work:

> Hér skrifaz sagan af Tristram ok Ísönd dróttningu, í hverri talat verðr um óbæriliga ást, er þau höfðu sín á milli. Var þá liðit frá hingatburði Christi 1226 ár, er þessi saga var á norrænu skrifuð eptir befalningu ok skipan virðuligs herra Hákonar kóngs. En Bróðir Robert efnaði ok upp skrifaði eptir sinni kunnáttu með þessum orðtökum, sem eptir fylgir í sögunni ok nú skal frá segja. (Jorgensen edn 1999, 28)

> Written down here is the story of Tristram and Queen Ísönd and of the heartrending love that they shared. This saga was translated into the Norse tongue at the behest and decree of King Hákon when 1226 years had passed since the birth of Christ. Brother Robert ably prepared the text and wrote it down in the words appearing in this saga. And now it shall be told. (Jorgensen trans. 1999, 29)[1]

In his seminal work on Anglo-Norman and Scandinavian cultural relations, *Angevin Britain and Scandinavia* (1921), Henry Goddard Leach averred that *Tristrams saga* may have been commissioned to celebrate Hákon's marriage to Margrét Skúladóttir, daughter of his uncle and political rival Skúli Barðarson (1921, 183–4), although this unhappy story of adulterous passion, pervaded from beginning to end by sadness, sorrow and forebodings of death, seems curiously at odds with the occasion. The identity of 'Brother Robert' is unknown, but the name is suggestive of Anglo-Norman origins. Also produced at Hákon's court was *Geitarlauf* ('Honeysuckle'), a translation of Marie de France's *lai* of *Chèvrefeuille*, which relates a single episode from the legend in which the lovers contrive a secret meeting.

Tristrams saga has always enjoyed special status in the Tristan-corpus because it is the only extant complete rendition of the so-called 'courtly' (as opposed to 'popular') branch of the legend, although Thomas's pessimistic view of love has caused that epithet to be disputed by a number of scholars (Hunt 1981; Grimbert 1995; Adams 1999; Finlay 2004). Moreover, as the product of a process of medieval *translatio* rather than 'translation' in the modern sense (Copeland, 1987), *Tristrams saga* can be read, independently, as an interpretation of Thomas's poem.

Tristrams saga scholarship has in the main focused on comparative and source studies (Schach 1964, 1969; Álfrún Gunnlaugsdóttir 1978). More recently, the saga's ethos has been examined by Jonna Kjær (1990) and Alison Finlay (2004). Kjær sees it as an attempt to reconcile *courtoisie* and chivalry: one of the saga's rare additions to Thomas's poem, for example, is a prayer by the dying Ísönd, in which she asks for the remission of sins originally granted to Mary Magdalen. In her close analysis and comparison of the Carlisle Fragment of *Tristan* with the corresponding passages in *Tristrams saga* – which relate the accidental consumption of the love potion, the consummation of the love affair and Markis and Ísönd's wedding night – Alison Finlay postulates possible clerical bias on the part of the saga-writer for some discernible displacement of 'blame' on to Ísönd, since it is she who initiates the manoeuvre to substitute her virgin attendant, Bringvet, in the bridal bed (Finlay 2004, 208).

The saga's consistent reduction of dialogue and of the interior monologues that detail the tormented inner lives of the lovers and, to quote Stewart Gregory, render the events of Thomas's poem '[s]ubordinate to the logic-chopping analyses to which they give rise' (Gregory edn 1998, 8) gears it towards a more 'heroic' ethos, in which Tristan struggles against the forces of fate and chaos. Instead, for example, of the delight in the satisfaction of their desire which Thomas attributes to Tristan and Isolt after they unwittingly slake their thirst on the voyage from Ireland to England with the love potion intended for Mark (Carlisle Fragment, Short edn 1998, 74–93), the emphasis in *Tristrams saga* is on their reluctance to surrender to the irresistible force of passion and its likely unhappy result: a 'harmfullt líf ok meinlæti ok langa hugsótt með líkams girnd ok tilfýsiligum hætti' (120) (a life of sorrow and trouble and anxiety caused by carnal desire and constant longing) (121; Finlay 2004, 214–15). Markis, too, in a noteworthy deviation from Thomas's and other versions of the legend, drinks the potion.

Tristrams saga brings to the fore two episodes in which Arthur of Britain plays a leading role, and which are key to the reading of the saga in the following discussion. In each case, Arthur is not the figurehead of Chrétien de Troyes but the giant-killing warrior king of Geoffrey of Monmouth's *Historia regum Britanniae* (c.1138) and Wace's *Roman de Brut* (c.1155), the latter the apparent source of Thomas's Arthurian material. Both episodes are related in the last quarter of *Tristrams saga* but take place prior to the action of the main narrative.[2] In the first, Arthur slays a giant who makes a cloak from the beards of kings whom he has slain or captured and invites Arthur to contribute his own in pride of place; in the second, he kills the giant of Mont-Saint-Michel. Although interconnected in Wace's *Brut*, where the story of the beard-collecting giant is incorporated into the larger narrative of the giant of Mont-Saint-Michel as a feat of near comparability (vv. 11,562–92), these two exploits are related separately in the saga (chapters 71, 78).[3]

Indirect reminders of Arthur permeate *Tristrams saga* from the beginning. Markis, 'yfir öllum enskum mönnum ok Kornbretum einvaldsherra ok höfðingi' (30) (sole chief and ruler of all the English and the men of Cornwall) (31), has his capital in

Tintagel, the place of Arthur's conception in Geoffrey's *Historia* and Wace's *Brut*. Locations famously associated with Arthur are mentioned again, when the first people encountered by the youthful Tristram after his kidnapping from Brittany by Norwegian pirates and abandonment on what turns out to be the coast of Cornwall, are identified as two pilgrims on their way to Tintagel on the return trip from Mont-Saint-Michel (chapter 20). The earliest section of the narrative, which recounts events leading up to Tristram's birth, is, moreover, bathed in what appears to be the afterglow of Arthur's Britain. The first four chapters present an idyllic picture of a prosperous and secure domain – a veritable replica of the golden age of Arthur, ruled by a king of similar renown and power. All is peaceful, ordered, governed by chivalric ritual, and apparently impregnable.

When Kanelangres, ruler of Brittany, arrives in Tintagel in order to enhance his own reputation, broaden his experience, hone his knowledge of courtly manners, and generally enjoy himself, the lexis is of custom, courtesy and what is befitting. Kanelangres and his company are 'sæmiliga gætandi tign ok virðing hirðligrar siðvenju' (30) (suitably mindful of the pomp and magnificence of courtly custom) (31). Markis is greeted with due propriety and responds in kind. In a spectacular display of munificence, he stages a feast and tournament in a *locus amœnus* of natural and crafted beauty, reminiscent of Caerleon's beautiful meadows and fertile fields and on a scale to match the splendour of the festivities which mark Arthur's coronation there in Wace's *Brut* (Weiss edn 2002, 10,217–20):

> Þar váru fagrir vellir ok víðir, sléttir, prýddir fögrum grösum ok blómasamligum. En fyrir sakir þess, at staðr þessi var hinn lystiligasti sakir margfaldrar skemtanar, þá lét Markis kóngr á þeim völlum þar setja ok skipa stórum landtjöldum, gulum ok grænum, blám ok rauðum, ok ríkuliga búnum, gylldum ok gullsaumuðum, undir ilmöndum laufum ok nýsprungnum blómstrum. (32)

> (There were beautiful fields, spacious and flat, adorned with fine herbs in bloom. Because this place was the most delightful due to its many pleasures, King Markis had large tents set up and furnished in yellow and green, blue and red – and richly decorated, gilded and embroidered with golden thread – under fragrant foliage and bursting blossoms.) (33)

The tournament itself is choreographed with similarly idealized ceremony. Knights joust 'fyrir útan öfund ok hégóma' (without jealousy or deceit) and win the 'ást ok yndi' (32) (fondness and love) (33) of maidens and ladies, while husbands and lovers mingle in a scene which, to quote Jeffrey Jerome Cohen, exemplifies chivalric ritual as 'public theater of good conduct, extravagant gesture, and bodily control' (1999, 79). Equally, Markis's reported satisfaction when he surveys the scene is a demonstration of chivalry's function as 'spectacle useful, even essential, for a monarch to materialize his power over his subjects by performing a well-regulated, microcosmic vision of macrocosmic harmony' (Cohen 1999, 79):

> Ok sem Markis kóngr er á lítandi sitt heiðarligt herlið, þá vex honum mikil gleði ok hyggr at hann skyldi vera einn höfðingi yfir því landi, sem svá var ríkt ok auðugt af jafnmiklu fólki hæverskra manna ok kurteisra kvenna. (32)

(When King Markis looked upon his worthy troops, great joy and comfort welled up in him that he alone should be the chieftain over this realm that was so rich and powerful with such a large population of well-mannered men and courtly ladies.) (33)

But when individual achievement distinguishes itself from stylized ritual, and Kanelangres emerges as the outstanding performer, the 'fondness and love' conventionally demanded of its female spectators by the theatre of chivalry give way to concupiscence, 'allar girntuz hann' (34) (they all desired him) (35), evocative of Dido's for Aeneas, 'er svá mjök unni, at hún brendi sik inni, þá er unnasti hennar fór frá henni' (34) (who loved so deeply that she immolated herself when deserted by her lover) (35), and ominously prophetic of the destructive power of sexual craving.

Dido's *alter ego* here is Markis's sister, Blensinbil, whose reciprocated desire for this young, unknown knight ends in her death after she delivers their son, Tristram, on the same day that Kanelangres himself is killed in battle. The sorrowful love story of his parents, which entails fear of discovery, deception of Markis and his court and elopement, foreshadows the dire consequences of the fatal passion to which Tristram himself will become subject. In the meantime, the 'play' of chivalry (*leik riddaranna*) offers Blensinbil temporary respite from the mental torment of fleshly attraction:

Nú sem hún sá á leik riddaranna, þá minnkaði bruna hennar, því ásýnd þess hins fagra staðar ok gagnsamligrar atreiðar hæverskra riddara stöðvaði ástareld hennar ok gerði henni kælu af mikils hita. Ok sem hún sá leikinn, huggaðiz hún nokkut ok gleymdi mjök fyrra skapi sínu, því þat er ástar siðvenja, þó at einhverr sé hugstolinn í ástar æði ok ef hann er á gamansgangi ok nokkut starfandi, þá er þá ást miklu hægra at bera. (36)

(As she was looking upon the knights jousting, her fever diminished because the sight of that beautiful place and the beneficial effects of chivalrous knights jousting quenched the fire of her love and granted her coolness from great passion. As she watched the games she calmed down somewhat and forgot her previous state of mind, for that is the way with love, that when someone is distraught because of love's fury, it is much easier to bear that love if one works a bit or is pleasurably distracted.) (37)

Having acquitted himself admirably at Markis's court for the three years following his inauspicious arrival there, Tristram goes back to Brittany to liberate his native land from Duke Morgan, the Irish usurper who killed Kanelangres. On his return to Tintagel, he confronts a radically different image of England as a land in servitude, with a royal court in disarray. The brilliantly staged rituals of chivalry which shot Kanelangres to prominence and soothed Blensibil have been displaced by riot and confusion, in which self-interest is the order of the day. England is, in short, a shambles. The apparent prosperity, security and harmony of Markis's reign were, it appears, no more than a flimsy façade. Concealed to this point by the pageantry of chivalry comes the shocking revelation that, outside the theatre of the joust, England is bereft of knightly capability.

The kingdom has, we now learn, long been a tributary to Ireland and meek servant to its king's increasingly outrageous demands. In the first year of an ongoing tributary cycle, the request was for brass and copper; in the second, pure silver; in the third, refined gold; in the fourth year, Markis and his nobles were ordered to present themselves in Ireland; and, in this fifth year, the order is for sixty handsome men to serve as slaves to the Irish king. Markis is impotent in the face of the oppressor, and his knights are equally ineffectual: not a single one will volunteer to challenge the Irish king's giant-like emissary, Morhold, in single combat. All pretensions to dignity and chivalric honour have been abandoned in the uproar which greets Tristram: women wail; children scream; and strong men weep. The weeping knights of England appear to have surrendered all capacity for action; and, with imprecations, accusations and recriminations, the victims are chosen by lot:

> Ríkir menn grétu. Konurnar kveinuðu ok illa létu. Börnin æptu. Mæðrnar bölvuðu feðrum barnanna, er ekki þora sín börn fyrir vesöld at verja móti þeim, er börnin taka – kalla feðrna hrædda, svívirða, sigraða ok yfirkomna, er þeir þori ekki at berjaz við Morhold, er skattinn krafði. (74)

> (Strong men cried. Women wailed and lamented. Children screamed. Mothers cursed the children's fathers, who dared not protect their children from suffering at the hands of those who carry off children. They called the fathers cowards, dishonored, defeated, and vanquished, because they dared not fight against Morhold, who demanded the tribute.) (75)

The highest-ranking nobles distinguish themselves only by their utter cowardice. It is every man for himself: 'ok bað hverr guð sér miskunnar, at hann skyldi verja þá fyrir hlutfalli' (74) (each one imploring God to show mercy by protecting them in the casting of lots) (75).

The glittering ceremony of Markis's court has, in other words, proved to be an entirely false simulacrum of the Round Table. Markis's epithet, *hinn frægi* (the famous) or *hinn frægi ok ríki* (the famous and powerful), is exposed as equally ironic. Surrounded by his chosen warriors (*vildarlið*), he may live in the strongest castle in the land, but he is, unequivocally, an impotent king, and his feebleness is the direct cause of England's predicament: 'Engliskóngr . . . kunni ekki at verja sik verjandi, ok fyrir því var England langa tíma skattgilt Írlandi' (72) (the English king . . . was unable to defend himself, so England was a tributary to Ireland for a long time) (73). Markis's England, as Tristram now finds it, is the very antithesis of Arthur's triumphantly expansionist kingdom in Geoffrey and Wace; and it recalls Wace's ominous allusion, at the time of Arthur's coronation, to the subsequent deterioration of Caerleon: 'Bon ert a cel tens Karlion, / Ne fist puis se empeirer non' (vv. 10,235–6) (Caerleon was a good place then; it has deteriorated since) (257).

Although for the most part narratively absent, Arthur's role is an important one. As Adrian Stevens has argued, on the assumption that Thomas's audience would have been familiar with the histories of Britain by Geoffrey and Wace, '[t]he true significance of Mark's reign as Thomas defines it is that it is inferior because it is post-Arthurian: the age of Mark, in stark contrast to the age of Arthur, is an unheroic age presided over by an unworthy king' (Stevens 2003, 225), and it is likely that the *Tristrams saga* writer and his audience may also have been acquainted with the glories of Arthur's reign through the *Breta sögur* (Sagas of the Britons), the Norse version of

Geoffrey's *Historia* (Eysteinsson 1953–57). Arthur's giant-killing exploits underline not only Mark's feebleness but also that of other rulers (Stevens 2003, 226). The beard-collecting giant episode in *Tristrams saga*, for example, ends with the telling detail, absent in Wace, that by killing the monster, Arthur is saving the lands of other, less capable kings and nobles from his assaults (chapter 71).

As the only knight equal to similar challenges, Tristram proves himself to be not only Markis's legal successor – as he is by birth, and as Markis promised he would be, should he defeat Morhold (chapter 27) – but also Arthur's spiritual heir (Stevens 2003, 224–6). Appalled at the collective capitulation to tyranny that he witnesses in England, Tristram takes on and defeats Morhold in single combat. In raking off his opponent's beard and hair as his sword plunges into Morhold's skull, he prefigures Arthur's killing of the arrogant, beard-collecting giant, named Orguillus (Proud) in Thomas's poem (Gregory edn 1998, v. 720) but anonymous in *Tristrams saga* (chapter 76). In a further manifestation of the chivalric sham that is Markis's court, Tristram becomes the object of plotting and calumny by those same knights who were earlier said to joust 'without jealousy or deceit', but who now actively resent his goodness and designation as the king's successor and fear retribution for their own cowardice. It is, as Adrian Stevens has argued, a further measure of the inferiority of post-Arthurian Britain that it is the fate of Tristan 'the heroic double of Arthur . . . to be maligned and denigrated at the court of Arthur's nominal successor' (Stevens 2000, 415).

The giant fights of Wace's *Brut* are myths of foundation and imperial conquest. The Trojans purge Albion of the terrifying giants whom they find there. Corineus wrestles their leader, Gomagog, to death, and the Trojans collectively slaughter the rest of his company and claim the land as their own (vv. 1063–169). Arthur's victory over Dinabuc, the giant of Mont-Saint-Michel, who has laid waste to Brittany and abducted and killed Elena, the daughter of his kinsman Hoel, king of Brittany, prefigures his victory over the Roman emperor Lucius, whose unjust demand for tribute from Britain he is *en route* to challenge when he arrives in Brittany to learn of the giant's pillaging spree. In slaying Dinabuc, Arthur 'signals his political coming of age, his readiness to assume the heavy mantle of world-class heroism and be numbered among the Nine Worthies' (Cohen 1999, 71).

Detached from the wider concerns of British history central to the *Roman de Brut*, giant aggression in *Tristrams saga* is clearly aligned with the devastating repercussions of unsanctioned sexual desire. As elsewhere in romance, giants are not only disruptors of the social and political order but also the embodiment of uncontrollable, and perverse, sexual appetite (Cohen 1999, 77). In ripping off the beards of the kings and noblemen he has overcome, for example, Orguillus commits symbolic acts of castration. Both giants slain by Arthur in *Tristrams saga* are, moreover, said to come from Africa and are thus explicitly stamped with the sexual threat of the Saracen body which runs through medieval thought (Cohen 1999, 180). From this perspective, Tristram's destruction of an interrelated network of giants across Europe – in Poland, Brittany and Spain – can be viewed as emblematic of his constant quest to quell the torment of carnal desire to which the love potion has condemned him. Morhold is giant-like, and Tristram kills a dragon in Ireland in order to deliver that kingdom from abject submission to tyranny, but his full-scale giant-killings follow the consumption of the potion and his first period of exile (chapter 61) from Britain. Further, in the amputatory savagery with which he treats these foes – he hacks off one giant's right hand and severs the leg of another – Tristram symbolically dismembers his own bodily demons.

Twin slayings of beard-collecting giants by Arthur and Tristram come at a point of intense sexual frustration for both Tristram and Ísönd in the saga. Thoughts of Ísönd make it impossible for Tristram to consummate the marriage that he has contracted to Ísodd, daughter of the Duke of Brittany and sister of his best friend, Kardín, in the hope of finding distraction from his obsession with Ísönd and a measure of legitimate contentment. Back in England, Ísönd is also gripped by sexual yearning. In a scene which follows and forms a parallel to Tristram's miserable wedding night, she lies in her bedroom and longs for love-making with him as the only means which 'vilja hennar mætti hugga ok harm hennar bæta' (170) (might comfort her desires and alleviate her sorrow) (171), her misery exacerbated by her ignorance of his whereabouts and welfare. The narrative abruptly switches at this moment to accounts of Arthur's defeat of the beard-collecting giant and Tristram's killing of the nephew of the same giant on behalf of the king of Spain, which is said to have taken place at an earlier point in the narrative (chapter 68). The Spanish king faced the same insulting challenge as Arthur but was terrified of the giant and bereft of kinsman or any other knight willing and able to come to his defence. According to Thomas and the *Tristrams saga* narrator, Arthur's feat is related simply because Tristram has emulated it:

> Nú þó at þetta falli ekki við söguna, þá vil ek þetta vita láta, þvíat sá jötunn, er Tristram drap, var systurson þessa jötuns, er skeggjanna krafði. (172)

> (Even though this event is outside the scope of this saga, I wanted to tell about it, because Tristram also killed a giant who was the nephew of this giant who had demanded the beards.) (173)

Blakeslee suggests (1989: 103–4) that the episode, as Thomas relates it (Gregory edn 1998, vv. 720–805), is an oblique explanation of why Tristan cannot consummate his marriage. In both *Tristan* and *Tristrams saga* he is said to have been severely wounded in battle with the giant, and in both narratives he attributes his wedding-night impotence to the pain of an old wound on the right hand side of his body. That wound, he confides to his bride in *Tristan*, is close to his liver (Gregory edn 1998, v. 689), the site of the libido, according to the thirteenth-century encyclopaedist Bartholomaeus Anglicus (Blakeslee 1989, 103). The inference to be drawn, as Blakeslee reads it, is that Tristan sustained this sexually debilitating wound in the battle with the giant in Spain. *Tristrams saga* locates the wound to the lower right side of Tristram's body but negates any implication that it is directly connected with Tristram's impotence with the explicit statement that his infirmity is not physical: 'Ekki var önnr sótt Tristrams en um aðra Ísönd dróttningu' (170) (Tristram's illness was nothing but the other Queen Ísönd) (171).

In defeating Orguillus, Arthur defends his kingdom and overcomes a direct and insulting threat to his masculinity. In taking on the same giant's nephew, Tristram defeats a challenge to the masculinity of a king incapable of defending himself. His actions serve as a reminder that, although he may be sexually incapacitated with Ísódd, he is capable of defending and destroying challenges to the virility of impotent rulers.

Arthur's killing of the giant of Mont-Saint-Michel is more closely integrated into the narrative and, in this reading of the saga, central to it. Despite the narratorial disclaimer that the giant whom Arthur killed 'heyrir ekki til þessari sögu nema þat eitt, at hann gerði þetta hit fagra hválfhús' (184) (doesn't belong to this saga except that this was the giant who constructed the beautiful, vaulted chamber) (185), it is the essential precursor to Tristram's greatest triumph: his subjugation of the giant, Moldagog, in the course of which he completes business which Arthur himself might be said to have left unfinished after his victory at Mont-Saint-Michel.

Moldagog (the name is perhaps deliberately reminiscent of Wace's Gomagog) occupies territory on the border (í landamæri) of Brittany, bounded on one side by the sea. He has in the past driven Kardín from his own land, but the two have since concluded a treaty which acknowledges a river as the point of demarcation between their territories. Tristram admires the great beauty and variety of trees in Moldagog's forest – 'hann hafði hinn fríðasta við, hávan ok réttan ok digran, með alls kyns við, þann er hann hafði sét ok heyrt nefndan' (176) (it contained the most beautiful trees, tall and straight and stout, with all the kinds of wood that he had ever seen or heard about) (177) – he disobeys Kardin's injunction not to cross the river and challenges Moldagog to a fight for control of his forest. When the giant ducks as Tristram strikes at his neck, and the blow severs his leg instead, he pleads for his life in exchange for all his land and gold; but it is not the acquisition of Moldagog's wealth for its own sake that motivates Tristram but the use to which he can put the natural riches of his forest. With a touch of the comic grotesque that attends giant casualties elsewhere in romance (Cohen 1999, 157), Tristram fashions a wooden leg for his vanquished foe and presses him into service as a builder's labourer.

Within the densest part of Moldagog's forest, the narrator observes, is a semi-underground rock, accessible only at low tide; its hollowed-out chamber, architecturally similar to a church crypt, has a skilfully carved, vaulted ceiling and an elaborately decorated central stone arch. This topographical information serves as a self-prompt for the narrator to recount Arthur's defeat of the giant of Mont-Saint-Michel, because, he says, that same giant made and for a long time lived in the vault. This was, moreover, the place to which he took Elena, daughter of Duke Orsl in the saga – 'hann helt hana með sér í hellinum' (182) (he kept her with him in the cave) (185) – and, thwarted by his very monstrousness in his attempt to ravish her, crushed her to death 'sakir mikilleiks hans ok þunga, þá kafnaði hún undir honom ok sprakk'

(184) ([d]ue to his size and weight, she suffocated and burst beneath him) (185). (Tristram's inability to consummate his union with Isódd a few chapters earlier is the reverse image of the giant's murderous hypersexuality and, ironically, as destructive of the possibility of legal heirs.) Tristram's harnessing of Moldagog's riches and labour to the transformation of this house of sexual horror into a sanctuary of perfect love becomes a more glorious conclusion to the Mont-Saint-Michel episode than Wace's brief afterword (vv. 11, 599–608) about Hoel's building of a chapel to the Virgin Mary there, in memory of Elena.

Tristrams saga draws upon other facets of giant lore here: Norse myths in which the bodies of giants are the building material of the universe (Clunies Ross 1994, I, 152–6) and Old English poetry, where ancient stone ruins are attributed to *enta geweorc* 'the work of giants' (Cohen 1999, 9–10). The chamber in which the giant imprisoned and killed Elena is a construction of such beauty that it pleases Tristram 'sem sjálfr hann kunni at vera æskjandi' (184) (as much as he himself could have wished) (185). It is the paradoxical nature of giants to be builders and craftsmen as well as ravagers and destroyers. The same tradition underlies the description earlier in the narrative of the finely crafted underground chamber, hollowed out from a cliff in sweet-smelling, fertile surrounds evocative of the earthly paradise (Harris 1977, 307–11), which provides shelter for the lovers during their period of banishment from Markis's court:

> . . . leyniligan stað hjá vatni nokkuru ok í bergi því, er heiðnir menn létu höggva ok búa í fyrnsku með miklum hagleik ok fagri smíð. Ok var þetta allt hvelft ok í jörðu til at ganga, djúpt höggvit. (160)

> (. . . a secret place near the water in a cliff that heathen men in ancient times had hollowed out and crafted with great skill and fine workmanship. It was high and vaulted, but the entrance was deeply hewn into the ground.) (161)

In contrast to its original stonework, the refurbishment that Tristram orders for the cave in Moldagog's forest is entirely in wood. The vaulted chamber is fully panelled within and waterproofed with the finest wood; the beautiful wooden hall which he has built outside and decorated by goldsmiths, who make it 'svá ljós innan sem útan' (184) (as bright inside there as it was outside) (185), serves as their studio and joinery. In Northern tradition, giants work in stone; humans work in wood, 'a living substance to be carved and joined . . . stone was recalcitrant and dead' (Cohen 1999, 5). Wood, in other words, beats stone; human artistry transforms elemental harshness into fount of solace. Brute lust is sublimated into idealized expression of sculptural and decorative beauty.

When the products of the painting, gilding and woodwork are ready for assembly, Tristram despatches Moldagog's carpenters and goldsmiths, and, in a literal projection of the image of the giant as the 'primal enemy of the human, and humanity's most constant companion' (Cohen 1999, xii), the two of them set to work on the final part of the project, the nature of which Tristram has kept secret from the craftsmen, and the narrator from his audience. Its magnificent centrepiece is an exquisite, lifelike representation of Ísönd: a beautifully crafted, gilded, and richly attired statue, crowned with gold and gems and positioned directly under the centre of the chamber's arch. Although not explicitly stated, the indications are that this is a wooden sculpture, after the style of interior devotional statues which survive in France, Germany and Italy from the twelfth to the fifteenth century (Rorimer 1929; Forsyth 1972). Through delicate gold tubing, which Tristram has ingeniously connected to the breast and neck, the statue emits a perfume of gold dust mixed with sweet herbs, redolent of the odour of sanctity. The figure is, in some respects, reminiscent of French Romanesque statues of 'Madonnas in Majesty' from the latter part of the twelfth century: free-standing wooden statues, gilded, sometimes encrusted with jewels, a few of them 140 cm (55 inches) or a little more in height (Forsyth 1972, 134–55).

Like a gargoyle serving as a reminder of the demonic origins of this place of worship is the huge statue of Moldagog, which, with gnashing teeth, fierce gaze, shaggy goatskin and iron staff, stands as guardian at the entrance to the chamber, projecting homicidal menace and crude sexuality: 'tók kyrtillinn honum skammt ofan, ok var hann nakinn niðr frá nafla' (186) (his tunic didn't come down very far, so he was naked from the navel down) (187). So lifelike is this statue that the sight of it causes Kardín to faint with terror (chapter 85).

As well as artistic homage to love, the refurbished chamber also serves as performance space for Tristram's acting out and rewriting of the script of his passion and devotion. Inscribed on the gold ring on the finger of the statue of Ísönd, which appears to be the one that she gave him at their parting, are words which she spoke to him then about their hardships and misfortunes (chapter 68). On that occasion, Ísönd called the ring the *bréf ok innsigli* (166) 'written deed and its seal' (167) of their love; now it serves as a medium for a silent reprise of those words. At odds with the saga's earlier account of the circumstances in which they drank the love potion, a small and finely dressed statue of Bringvet holds out a vessel to Ísönd on which are written the words which she is said to have spoken to her at that fatal moment: 'Ísönd dróttning, tak drykk þenna, er ger var á Írlandi Markis kóngi' (186) (Queen Isönd, take of this drink, which was prepared in Ireland for King Markis) (187). Beside Ísönd is a golden replica of the magic dog which Tristram demanded as a gift for her from a Polish duke when he despatched a giant named Urgan, who demanded one-tenth of the duke's livestock as annual tribute (chapter 62), which shakes its head and rings its bell. There is active engagement, too, between the performers of this drama in which the villains are crushed and Tristram and Ísönd ascendant. As if to trample her weeping, fallen enemy, the statue of Ísönd stands upon a copper likeness of a malicious dwarf who denounced the lovers to Markis (chapter 67): 'Líkneskjan stóð á brjósti honum, því líkast sem hún skipaði honum undir fætr sér, en hann lá opinn undir fótum hennar, því líkt sem hann væri grátandi' (186) (The statue stood on his breast as if Ísönd were trampling him under foot, and he lay prostrate under her feet as if crying) (187). On subsequent visits to the chamber, Tristram not only embraces the statue of Ísönd but also vents his anguish at the trials and tribulations that he has suffered at the hands of slanderers to the figure of Markis's counsellor (chapter 81), now rendered helpless in the grip of a copper lion rampant (chapter 80).[4]

One or two indirect echoes of past exploits by Arthur and Tristram hover around the closing stages of *Tristrams saga*. In Geoffrey, Wace and *Breta sögur* Arthur meets his end in the battle that follows Mordred's usurpation of Britain and bigamous marriage to Guinevere while he has been in Burgundy, preparing for the assault on Rome. Tristram's death is brought about when he accedes to a mysterious knight's request to rescue his abducted wife (*frú, húsfrú*) and is fatally wounded in the resulting battle (chapters 94, 95). The knight in question introduces himself as 'Tristram dvergr' (Tristram the Dwarf), but, contrary to his epithet, he is, as both he and the narrator remark, a very large man (*manna mestr*). Tristram the Dwarf has other giant-like attributes. Like Moldagog, he lives on the border (*í landamæri*) of Brittany; and although he is anonymous in the saga, his name in Thomas's *Tristan*, Estult l'Orgillius (Gregory edn 1998, v. 2,212), makes him the 'symbolic double' (Stevens 2000, 414) of Arthur's beard-collecting foe, Orgillus. After the battle with Mordred and his forces in Wace's *Brut*, the mortally wounded Arthur is taken to Avalon, and the Britons wait in vain for his return (vv. 13,275–94). In Thomas and *Tristrams saga*, the severely injured Tristram makes it back to his castle after he and his company win the battle with the lady's abductor, his seven brothers, and their hundred-strong army. He waits for the healing hands of Ísönd but dies before she reaches him. Overcome with grief at the sight of his lifeless body, she dies of sorrow.

In a final gesture of bitterness, Tristram's wife, Ísódd, has the lovers buried on separate sides of a church to prevent any future union, but eventually the branches of the trees that spring from their graves meet and knit together in the last lines of the narrative. Of Markis and the subsequent history of Britain we hear no more.

Later versions

Although the Matter of Britain *riddarasögur* continued to circulate in Iceland, Arthur and his knights largely disappear from the corpus of late medieval Icelandic prose romance. The Tristan legend is nevertheless represented across various literary modes in medieval Scandinavia: Icelandic romance and Danish, Faroese and Icelandic ballad and folktale (Schach, 1964). Among this Scandinavian Tristan corpus is the fourteenth-century Icelandic romance, the *Saga af Tristram ok Ísodd*, which, particularly in the matter of its relationship to *Tristrams saga*, has attracted considerably more critical attention than the earlier work and become something of a focal point for analysis of the assimilation of chivalric romance into the indigenous literary models of late medieval Iceland (Kalinke 2008). Discussion hinges on the question of whether the *Saga af Tristram ok*

Ísodd should (Schach 1960, 1987) or should not (Thomas 1983; Van Dijk 2008) be read as burlesque, parody or 'reply' to *Tristrams saga*; as a 'humorous commentary' on the romances with direct French sources and Arthurian romance in general (Kalinke 1981, 199, 201–2); or as a narrative which can be read, independently, as representative of late medieval Icelandic romance (Barnes 1999; Francini 2007).

The only trace of specifically Arthurian association in the *Saga af Tristram ok Ísodd* is the name of a bad and dishonest counsellor at the court of the king of Ireland, apparently inspired by the irascible (but otherwise worthy) knight of the Round Table, Sir Kay: Kæi *hinn kurteisi* (the Courteous) (Jorgensen and Hill edn and trans. 1999, 264, 265).[5] Challenges to Tristram's military prowess and threats to vulnerable rulers come in this saga not from giants but from raider kings: Engres of Ireland and the Saracen Fúlsus, both of whom attack England, and Amilías, who makes incursions into Saxland. Tristram's father, Kalegras, is the son of a Spanish knight, and Spain becomes his homeland. After his victory over Fúlsus, Tristram returns there and delivers the kingdom from the occupying forces of a king by the name of Beniðsus.

The overwhelming power of fate and the voraciousness of giants in *Tristrams saga* are replaced in the *Saga af Tristram ok Ísodd* by the hand of Providence and the rapaciousness of foreign rulers. After Tristram kills a dragon in Ireland, refuses the hand of Engres's daughter, Ísódd the Fair, as his reward and brings her to England as the intended bride of King Mórodd, Mórodd altruistically declares Tristram to be the better match and offers him both Ísodd and his kingdom. Although Tristram and Isódd have consumed the love potion on the voyage to England and their affair is well underway, he declines Mórodd's offer. Later, however, he makes a promise to God that he will end the liaison if he is victorious against Fúlsus. Tristram honours his pledge and returns to Spain, where he marries a Spanish noblewoman named Ísodd the Dark. Although Isódd the Fair is said to be much on Tristram's mind, and it appears to be three years before the marriage is consummated, the couple beget a son, Kalegras Tristramsson. The notion of fateful passion is reduced to a single narratorial observation after Tristram's death that 'mátti hann þó fyrir engan mun við sköpunum vinna' (288) (yet he was by no means able to withstand the fates) (289), an assertion somewhat contrary to the immediately preceding attribution of the love affair to God's purpose: 'sjálfr guð hafði þeim skipat saman af sinni samvizku' (288) (God himself in his wisdom had destined them for each other) (289). Tristram's pledge to God before the battle with Fúlsus and his victories over aggressively heathen opponents – Fúlsus, for example, is condemned by the narrator as *heiðinn sem hundr* (280) (heathen as a dog) (281), his forces invoke Mahomet, and his soul goes to hell – endow him with some Crusader qualities. Although they are not explicitly said to be Saracens, the names of two of the seven brothers who have driven a knight called 'Tristram the Stranger' from his kingdom of Jakobsland (Galicia, in north-west Spain), Ayad and Dormadat, in combat with whom Tristram sustains his fatal wound, suggest that they are.

The burials of Tristram and Isódd the Fair are conducted with due reverence and Christian rite in the greatest cathedral in the land. The trees bearing beautiful fruit that spring from their separate tombs and enlace serve as a sign of divine endorsement of their union. Tristram is further celebrated in the last chapter of the saga as a dynastic founder, and Mórodd as a courageous and pious monarch who mourns his nephew's death, summons his great-nephew, Kalegras Tristramsson, to the English throne, and ends his days as a holy hermit in Jerusalem. Kalegras is a model king. He marries the daughter of the emperor of Saxland and sires two sons and a daughter, the former said to be the subject of a great saga. Subsumed into this concluding narrative of subsequent generations and dynastic alliance, the story of Tristram and Isódd becomes merely an episode, although the most important one, in an ongoing history of familial success.[6]

Elsewhere in saga literature, motifs from *Tristrams saga* and other versions of the Tristan legend have been identified in the 'Spes' episode of the late classical saga, *Grettis saga* (Kramarz-Bein 2000; Kalinke 2008); in *Kormáks saga*, one of a group of sagas about famous poets known as *skáldasögur* (sagas of poets) (Bjarni Einarsson, 1961); and in other Icelandic romances of the fourteenth and fifteenth century (see chapter 8). In what appears to be a direct borrowing from *Tristrams saga*, the hero of the mid-fourteenth-century *Rémundar saga keisarasonar*, for example, embraces a statue in the likeness of a beautiful woman who has appeared to him in a dream (Schach 1969, 88–91). In her recent testing of Bjarni Einarsson's argument (1961) that *Tristrams saga* directly inspired the composition of *Kormáks saga*, the hero of which loves another man's wife, Alison Finlay has postulated instead a more nuanced genealogy of influence, by *Tristrams saga* and by native traditions, in the articulation of emotional states in saga narrative (Finlay 2004, 215–21).[7]

The only work in the Scandinavian ballad and folktale tradition of Tristan and Ísönd (Schach 1964; Jonsson 1978, 183–4) which appears to derive directly from *Tristrams saga*, and possibly also borrows from the *Saga af Tristram ok Ísodd*, is the fourteenth- or fifteenth-century Icelandic ballad, *Tristrams kvæði*. The poem tells of Tristram's mortal wounding in battle with a 'heiðinn hund' (perhaps an echo of Fúlsus in the *Saga af Tristram ok Ísodd*) – on London Bridge in one version of the poem (Cook edn 1999, 229) – the death of the lovers, their funeral rites and burial and the joining of the trees that grow from their tombs. More in the spirit of Thomas's *Tristran* than either *Tristrams saga ok Ísöndar* or the *Saga af Tristram ok Ísodd*, the emphasis in *Tristrams kvæði*, distilled in the poem's refrain – 'Þeim var ekki skapat nema skilja' (They had no other fate than to be parted) (Cook edn and trans. 1999) – is on fate, sadness and separation. Otherwise, the popular tradition of the Tristan legend in Scandinavia is primarily concerned with the outwitting of their evil elders by young lovers. In Danish ballads, Ísönd (Isold/Ísin) is the daughter or foster-daughter of an emperor served by Tristram (Tistram); in some, the lovers eventually marry or entertain the prospect of reunion (Barnes 1999, 391–3).[8]

The Tristan legend was fully drawn into the French and English Arthurian orbit in the thirteenth-century French prose *Tristan* and Thomas Malory's 'Book of Sir Tristram de Lyones' in *Le Morte Darthur* (1485), where Tristan becomes a member of the Round Table and the consequences of the love potion are subordinate to his dedication to chivalry. There is, however, no evidence that Arthurian prose romance was known in Iceland or elsewhere in Scandinavia. By the time of the composition of the *Saga af Tristram ok Ísodd* and *Tristrams kvæði*, all trace of Arthur had vanished from the Tristan legend in the North.

Notes

[1] Subsequent references to *Tristrams saga ok Ísöndar* are to Jorgensen's edition and translation.

[2] The time frame in the case of Arthur's killing of the beard-collecting giant is not made explicitly clear in the saga. The episode is introduced with the words *Nú var einn jötunn* (p. 170), which Jorgensen translates as 'at that time there was a giant' (p. 171), and which might be read with a sense of pastness as 'once there was a giant'.

[3] Subsequent references to Wace's *Brut* are to Weiss's edition and translation.

[4] See also M. Kalinke (2009) on the sculptural group in *Tristrams saga ok Ísöndar*.

[5] Subsequent references to the *Saga af Tristram ok Ísodd* are to Jorgensen's edition and Hill's translation.

[6] See chapter 8 for a discussion of the *Saga af Tristram ok Ísodd* in the context of the Sagas of Icelanders.

[7] See chapter 8 for a further discussion of Tristan motifs in the Sagas of Icelanders and the indigenous Icelandic romances.

[8] See chapter 9 for further discussion of the Tristan legend in Icelandic, Danish and Norwegian poetry.

Reference List

Texts and Translations

Saga af Tristram ok Ísodd

Saga af Tristram ok Ísodd, ed. P. Jorgensen, trans. J. Hill, in *Norse Romance,* I: *The Tristan Legend*, ed. M. E. Kalinke (Cambridge, 1999), pp. 249–92.

'The Icelandic Saga of Tristan and Isolt (*Saga af Tristram ok Ísodd*)', trans. J. Hill, in *The Tristan Legend: Texts from Northern and Eastern Europe in Modern English Translation*, ed. J. Hill (Leeds, 1977), pp. 6–28.

Thomas's *Tristan*

Thomas's Tristran, ed. and trans. S. Gregory, in *Early French Tristran Poems*, ed. N. J. Lacy (Cambridge, 1998), pp. 1–172.

'The Carlisle Fragment of Thomas's *Tristran*', ed. and trans. I. Short, in *Early French Tristran Poems*, ed. N. J. Lacy (Cambridge, 1998), pp. 173–83.

Tristrams kvæði

Tristrams kvæði, ed. and trans. R. Cook, in *Norse Romance,* I: *The Tristan Legend*, ed. M. E. Kalinke (Cambridge, 1999), pp. 227–39.

'The Icelandic Ballad of Tristan (*Tristrams kvæði*)', trans. J. Hill, in *The Tristan Legend: Texts from Northern and Eastern Europe in Modern English Translation*, ed. J. Hill (Leeds, 1977), pp. 29–38.

Tristrams saga ok Ísöndar

Tristrams saga ok Ísöndar, ed. and trans. P. Jorgensen, in *Norse Romance*, I: *The Tristan Legend*, ed. M. E. Kalinke (Cambridge, 1999), pp. 23–226.
The Saga of Tristram and Ísönd, trans. P. Schach (Lincoln, NE, 1973).

Wace's *Roman de Brut*

Wace's Roman de Brut: A History of the British, ed. and trans. J. Weiss (Exeter, 1999; rev. edn 2002).

Studies

Adams, T. (1990). 'Archetypes and copies in Thomas's *Tristran*: a re-examination of the *Salle aux Images* scenes', *The Romanic Review*, 90, 317–31.
Adams, T. (1999). '"Pur vostr cor su jo em paine": the Augustinian subtext of Thomas's *Tristan*', *Medium Ævum*, 68, 278–91.
Álfrún Gunnlaugsdóttir (1978). *Tristán en el Norte*, Reykjavík.
Barnes, G. (1999). 'Tristan in late medieval Norse literature: saga and ballad,' in Xenja von Ertzdorff (ed.), *Tristan und Isolt im Spätmittelalter. Vorträge eines interdisziplinären Symposiums vom 3. bis 8. Juni 1996 an der Justus-Liebig-Universität Gießen*, Amsterdam and Atlanta, pp. 373–96.
Bjarni Einarsson (1961). *Skáldasögur. Um uppruna og eðli ástaskáldasagnanna fornu*, Reykjavík.
Blakeslee, M. R. (1989). *Love's Masks: Identity, Intertextuality, and Meaning in the Old French Tristan Poems*, Cambridge.
Clunies Ross, M. (1994). *Prolonged Echoes: Old Norse Myths in Medieval Northern Society*, 2 vols, Odense.
Cohen, J. J. (1999). *Of Giants: Sex, Monsters, and the Middle Ages*, Minneapolis and London.
Copeland, R. (1987). 'Rhetoric and vernacular translation in the Middle Ages', *Studies in the Age of Chaucer*, 9, 41–75.
Eysteinsson, J. S. (1953–57). 'The relationship of *Merlínússpá* and Geoffrey of Monmouth's *Historia*', *Saga-Book of the Viking Society*, XIV, 1–2, 95–112.
Finlay, A. (2004). '"Intolerable Love": *Tristrams saga* and the Carlisle *Tristan* fragment', *Medium Ævum*, 73, 205–24.
Forsyth, I. (1972). *The Throne of Wisdom: Wood Sculptures of the Madonna in Romanesque France*, Princeton.
Francini, M. (2007). 'The 'Saga af Tristram ok Ísodd': an Icelandic reworking of 'Tristrams saga', in M. Buzzoni and M. Bampi (eds), *The Garden of Crossing Paths: The Manipulation and Rewriting of Medieval Texts*, rev. edn, Venice, pp. 249–71.
Grimbert, J. T. (1990). '*Voleir* v. *Poeir*: frustrated desire in Thomas's *Roman de Tristan*', *Philological Quarterly*, 69, 153–65.
Grimbert, J. T. (1995). 'Introduction', in J. T. Grimbert (ed.), *Tristan and Isolde: A Casebook*, New York, pp. xiii–xlix.
Harris, S. (1977). 'The cave of lovers in the "Tristramssaga" and related Tristan romances', *Romania*, 98, 306–30 and 460–500.
Hunt, T. (1981). 'The significance of Thomas's *Tristan*', *Reading Medieval Studies*, 7, 41–61.
Hunt, T. and Bromiley, G. (2006). 'The Tristan legend in Old French verse', in G. S. Burgess and K. Pratt (eds), *The Arthur of the French: The Arthurian Legend in Medieval French and Occitan Literature*, Arthurian Literature in the Middle Ages, IV, Cardiff, pp. 112–34.
Jonsson, B. R. (1978). 'The ballad in Scandinavia: its age, prehistory and earliest history,' in O. Holzapfel (ed.), *The European Medieval Ballad: A Symposium*, Odense, pp. 9–15.

Kalinke, M. E. (1981). *King Arthur, North-by-Northwest: The* matière de Bretagne *in Old Norse-Icelandic Romances*, Bibliotheca Arnamagnæana, 37, Copenhagen.

Kalinke, M. E. (2006). 'Scandinavian Arthurian literature', in N. J. Lacy (ed.), *A History of Arthurian Scholarship*, Cambridge, pp. 169–78.

Kalinke, M. (2008). 'Female desire and the quest in the Icelandic legend of Tristram and Ísodd', in N. J. Lacy (ed.), *The Grail, the Quest, and the World of Arthur*, Cambridge, pp. 76–91.

Kalinke, M. (2009). '*Tristrams saga ok Ísöndar*, ch. 80: ekphrasis as recapitulation and interpretation', in *Analecta Septentrionalia*, Ergänzungsbände zum Reallexikon der Germanischen Altertumskunde, 65, Berlin, pp. 221–37.

Kjær, J. (1990). '*Tristrams saga ok Ísöndar.* Une version christianisée de la branche dite courtoise du "Tristran"', in K. Busby and E. Kooper (eds), *Courtly Literature: Culture and Context. Selected papers from the 5ᵗʰ Triennial Congress of the International Courtly Literature Society, Dalfsen, The Netherlands, 9–16 August, 1986*, Amsterdam and Philadelphia, pp. 367–77.

Kramarz-Bein, S. (2000). 'Der Spesar Þáttr der *Grettis saga.* Tristan-Spuren in der Isländersaga', in H. Beck and E. Ebel (eds), *Studien zur Isländersaga*, Ergänzungsbände zum Reallexikon der Germanischen Altertumskunde, 24, Berlin and New York, pp. 152–81.

Leach, H. G. (1921). *Angevin Britain and Scandinavia*, Harvard Studies in Comparative Literature, VI, Cambridge, MA; rpt 1975.

Polak, L. (1970). 'The two caves of love in the *Tristan* by Thomas', *Journal of the Warburg and Courtauld Institutes*, 33, 52–69.

Rorimer, J. (1929). 'A monumental German wood statue of the thirteenth century', *Metropolitan Museum Studies*, 1, 2, 159–75.

Schach, P. (1957–61). 'Some observations on *Tristrams saga*', *Saga-Book of the Viking Society*, 15, 102–29.

Schach, P. (1960). 'The *Saga af Tristram ok Ísodd*: summary or satire?', *Modern Language Quarterly*, 21, 336–52.

Schach, P. (1964). 'Tristan and Isolde in Scandinavian ballad and folktale', *Scandinavian Studies*, 36, 281–97.

Schach, P. (1965). 'The style and structure of *Tristrams saga*', in C. Bayerschmidt and E. J. Friis (eds), *Essays Presented to H. G. Leach*, Seattle, pp. 63–86.

Schach, P. (1969). 'Some observations on the influence of *Tristrams saga ok Ísöndar* on Old Icelandic Literature', in E. C. Polomé (ed.), *Old Norse Literature and Mythology: A Symposium,* Austin and London, pp. 81–129.

Schach, P. (1987). '*Tristrams Saga ok Ýsoddar* as burlesque', *Scandinavian Studies*, 59, 86–100.

Stevens, A. (2000). 'Killing giants and translating empires: the history of Britain and the Tristan romances of Thomas and Gottfried', in M. Chinca, J. Heinzle and C. Young (eds), *Blütezeit. Festchrift für L. Peter Johnson*, Tübingen, pp. 409–26.

Stevens, A. (2003). 'History, fable and love: Gottfried, Thomas, and the Matter of Britain', in Will Hasty (ed.), *A Companion to Gottfried von Strassburg's 'Tristan'*, Rochester, NY and Woodbridge, pp. 223–56.

Sverrir Tómasson. (1977). 'Hvenær var Tristrams sögu snúið?', *Gripla*, 2, pp. 47–78.

Thomas, M. F. (1983). 'The briar and the vine: Tristan goes north', *Arthurian Literature*, 3, 53–90.

Van Dijk, C. (2008). 'Amused by death: humour in *Tristrams saga ok Ísoddar*', *Saga-Book of the Viking Society*, 32, 69–84.

5

THE TRANSLATED *LAIS*

Carolyne Larrington

Among the French texts translated into Old Norse for Hákon IV Hákonarson of Norway (r.1217–63) and his court is a collection of Marie de France's *lais* and a number of *lais* by anonymous authors, known as *Strengleikar* (Cook and Tveitane edn 1979), and *Möttuls saga* (Kalinke edn 1987; Kalinke edn 1999), a translation into prose of the French poem *Le lai du cort mantel*, a chastity-test tale involving a magic cloak. *Möttuls saga* later became the basis for a set of Icelandic *rímur*, a metrical version of the same story, *Skikkjurímur* (Driscoll edn 1999), somewhat expanded in scope and rather more fantastic in its view of court life. The translations of the *lais* ascribed to Marie include a version of *Chèvrefeuille*, the delicate lyric of Tristan's parting from and brief meeting with his lady Isolt. *Geitarlauf*, the Norse translation, retains some of the tenderness of feeling mediated both by Marie's poem and by Tristan's own lyric commemorating his time with the queen in the forest. The only strictly Arthurian text in *Strengleikar* is *Januals ljóð*, the translation of Marie's *Lanval*, the first part of which is missing, thanks to a lacuna in the sole manuscript. Nothing is known of the authors of these texts, though the translators of *Strengleikar* and of *Möttuls saga* were clearly competent in Anglo-Norman and French. The Norwegian texts were doubtless intended for a courtly audience, producing what Lars Lönnroth (1978) has called the 'double scene effect'; the courts described in *Möttuls saga* and *Januals ljóð* might be compared – and contrasted – with the court of Hákon IV by the courtiers who are likely to have formed their first audience (Kalinke 1981, 1–9). *Möttuls saga* probably had a wider appeal, judging from the fact that its surviving textual witnesses are actually from Iceland; here the shift away from identification with a courtly culture is completed by the production of the *Skikkjurímur*, 'Mantle Rhymes'.

Sources and date

Strengleikar translates a collection of *lais*, four of which have no surviving French originals. All but one of the *lais* attributed to Marie de France, preserved in the well-known manuscript BL Harley 978 written at around the same date (see Bruckner and Burgess 2006), are to be found in the single manuscript of *Strengleikar*, Uppsala, De la Gardie 4–7, written between 1250 and 1270. This also contains versions of another six *lais* found elsewhere, and translations of the four otherwise unknown *lais*. Five of the six are preserved in Paris, BNF, nouv. acq. fr. 1104, dating from around 1300; this manuscript contains in total fourteen of the *lais* found in *Strengleikar* and a version of the *Lai du cort mantel* (Cook and Tveitane edn 1979, ix–xxii). Despite this suggestive pairing, no surviving French manuscript could have been the exemplar of *Strengleikar* or *Möttuls saga*. Cook and Tveitane (xxiv) note that certain versions, including *Geitarlauf*, show traces of East Norse orthography, suggesting an East Norse exemplar. The editors argue (xxvi–xxviii) that the subject matter, and indeed the coarseness of some of the *lais*, make it likely that they were translated by clerks at the court rather than by a team of monks. It is even more likely that the translation of the more risqué *Möttuls saga* was produced in a non-monastic context. The translator(s) of *Strengleikar* had a good knowledge of Anglo-Norman; the *lais* of the first half of the collection (including *Geitarlauf*) are closely rendered. Aebischer (Rychner edn 1958, 99) has argued that the translator of *Januals ljóð* curtails some of the longer speeches because he does not understand them. There *is* an obvious misunderstanding of Anglo-Norman *departir* in ll. 471 and 547, but otherwise the abbreviation of the legal arguments at Janual's trial may well be for stylistic reasons; the description of the fairy mistress arriving at Arthur's court is also heavily reduced, probably to avoid duplication (Kalinke 1985, 345).

The *Forræða* (Prologue) of *Strengleikar* and the preamble to *Möttuls saga* place these works in Hákon's reign, but the chronology of the translations attributed to the king's patronage is unknown. Kalinke (edn 1987, lix) proposes that *Möttuls saga* may be among the earliest of the translations, since the names of some of the knights, and the affiliations of others are confused; that Perceval is rendered as *Paternas* argues that *Parcevals saga* was not already familiar to *Möttuls saga*'s translator and audience. Jürg Glauser (2005, 375) warns that references to Hákon IV's patronage occur in seventeenth-century manuscripts, and may be conventional; however, the thirteenth-century dating of De la Gardie 4–7 suggests that this is a genuine attribution, as does the encomiastic portrait of the ideal king with which the author of *Möttuls saga* introduces his tale. The *Skikkjurímur* are likely to be fifteenth-century in origin, judging from manuscript orthography (Driscoll 1991, 130, n. 38).

Möttuls saga (or *Skikkju saga* as it is sometimes known; *skikkja* is a synonym for 'cloak') is a translation of the French *Lai du cort mantel* (also known as *Le mantel mautaillié*). The French exemplar dates from the beginning of the thirteenth century and is preserved in four thirteenth-century manuscripts and one fourteenth-century manuscript. There is also a sixteenth-century prose redaction of the tale (Kalinke edn 1987, xxxiv–lvi). Kalinke shows that the saga contains a number of readings which are more likely to be correct than the readings preserved in the extant French versions, and, moreover, that the prose redaction and the saga share some features which suggest a close relationship; in particular the cloak is described at length in the saga and prose redaction, but not in the poetic versions (Kalinke edn 1987, liv–lvi). The cloak is one of a number of magical objects which function as chastity tests in medieval literature;

most closely related is the horn, first found in Robert Biket's *Lai du cor*, which is probably earlier than *Lai du cort mantel* (Kalinke 1991). The *Skikkjurímur* rework *Möttuls saga* as a ballad; the poem also incorporates some independent knowledge of Arthurian tradition from *Erex saga* and retains a confused memory of the Round Table (Reichert 1986). *Rímur* (literally, 'rhymes') are metrical romances, composed in a ballad-like metre known as *ferskeytt* or 'square metre'. Any one romance consists of several sets of *ríma*, each one roughly equivalent to the fit in Middle English romance (Driscoll 1991, 107–8).

Manuscript transmission

The popularity of the translated *lais* in Norway is difficult to gauge. *Strengleikar* survives only in De la Gardie 4–7, written in Bergen or elsewhere in south-western Norway, with a distinctive Old Norwegian orthography. De la Gardie 4–7 also contains *Pamphilus*, a fragment of a dialogue between Courage and Fear, and *Elis saga ok Rósamundu*, all of which precede *Strengleikar*. The last are written in two different hands; a third hand is responsible for the other works in the manuscript. The change of hands occurs in the middle of a folio, and indeed in the case of the two hands of *Strengleikar*, in the middle of a sentence, suggesting that all three scribes were working together in the same place at the same time; there is no reason to assume that the scribes of De la Gardie 4–7 were also responsible for the translation (Kalinke 1985, 334). An eighteenth-century manuscript, Reykjavík, Lbs. 840 4to, contains a copy of *Guiamars ljóð*, a translation of *Guigemar*, but no other complete copies of any of the *lais* in the *Strengleikar* collection survive elsewhere. Some fragments of *Strengleikar* texts have come to light; these were used as the lining for a bishop's mitre in the Icelandic see of Skálholt and are now preserved as Copenhagen, AM 666b 4to. The fragments contain no material germane to *Geitarlauf* or *Januals ljóð* (Cook and Tveitane edn 1979, ix–xi).

The manuscript tradition of *Möttuls saga* is more complex than that of *Strengleikar*; the medieval witnesses are fragmentary and are augmented by a number of paper copies. A full account of the manuscripts is given in Kalinke's edition (1987, lxxxv–cxlii). In summary, there are two Icelandic manuscript branches, one of which is represented by a single leaf, Copenhagen, AM 598 Iβ 4to, containing the beginning of the saga. The other branch is preserved in Stockholm, Perg. 4to nr 6, from around 1400, to which AM 598 Iα 4to, another fragment, originally belonged. Only two leaves of *Möttuls saga* are preserved in the Stockholm codex, but seventeenth-century paper copies, made when the manuscript was still whole, give the best witness to the saga; Kalinke's edition is based on AM 179 fol., augmented by the medieval vellums. The *Skikkjurímur* are preserved in three manuscripts: Wolfenbüttel, Codex Guelferbytanus 42.7 Augusteus 4to, written between 1470–80; Reykjavík, AM Acc.

22, written probably in 1695, where the text is accompanied by a note that this version is copied from an Icelandic vellum; and the seventeenth-century Stockholm, Papp. 4to nr 15, a radically curtailed and somewhat garbled version of the poem. A fourth text, in AM 603 4to, no longer survives (Driscoll edn 1999, 270). Driscoll's edition uses AM Acc. 22 as its base manuscript.

Style and form

The translators stand on the cusp of literary and oral tradition. They emphasize the truth-value of their works, *sanna sögur*, which contain much useful knowledge, *margskonar góð fræði*, guaranteed by the fact that the works originate in reliable books, certified by notable clerks, *dýrum klerkum*, according to the author of *Möttuls saga*. The works are said to be delivered orally however: to *áheyrendr* (listeners). *Geitarlauf* (Cook and Tveitane edn 1979, 196) stresses the background of the *lai* in written tradition: 'þat heui ec a boc leset þat sem margir segia ok sanna um tristram ok um drotneng' (I have read in a book those things which many tell and testify about Tristram and the queen); this may refer to the *lai* itself, or the larger story of Tristram. Though literacy, on the part of Tristram and the queen, is key to the slender narrative, the poem's conclusion stresses both orality and performance: Tristram composes (or recomposes) his lay for the harp. *Januals ljóð* too thanks those who listened: 'haui þackir þeir er heyrðu' (Cook and Tveitane edn 1979, 226). *Skikkjurímur* deftly manages the claims of the oral and the literary. The poet identifies his work as a new poem from the south, *Suðra söngurinn nýr* (Driscoll edn 1999, I, 8), but classifies it as of the type that commonly circulates (orally) among young men. The source, however, is signalled as literary: wise men put down in writing, *sett í letur*, the king's proclamation of the Pentecost feast (I, 27). The *Skikkjurímur* audience is envisaged as listening to the verses, for every woman who laughs when she hears them, the narrator alleges, demonstrates her infidelity.

Prose had begun to emerge as the form of choice for narrative in the twelfth century in Scandinavia; in Iceland, authors were beginning to compose history, saga and poetic treatises in prose or prosimetrum. The dominant poetic forms, eddic metres and skaldic verse, both offered difficulties for the translator. Eddic metres may have been associated with pagan native tradition, while the verbal complexity of skaldic metres renders them 'terse and obscure, unsuited to extended and lucid narration' (Cook and Tveitane edn 1979, xxxi). Whether the French *lais* were ever performed in their original language, perhaps to a musical accompaniment, at court, with the Norse prose version used to relay something like a simultaneous gloss, as Cook and Tveitane (xxvi), following Holtsmark (1959, 1960), moot, is now impossible to determine, since the only information about performance conditions and motivation for translation is that contained within the works themselves.

The two Norwegian works are largely composed in a style shared with the other translations: 'a tendency to rhythmical structure, a straining after parallelism, and a love of alliteration', as Einar Óláfur Sveinsson notes, somewhat critically (1964: cc). Kalinke identifies a tendency towards elaboration and euphony (Kalinke 1979; more generally Kalinke 1981, 133–77). The translations make heavy use of doublets to amplify the original text; alliterative clusters are also employed, though Kalinke (1981, 176) notes that while *Januals ljóð* shows these, *Geitarlauf* does not. *Skikkjurímur* is typical of Icelandic ballad style; simple kennings are used to denote women, while the text is notable for a number of obscure, probably obscene, idioms (Driscoll 1991).

Social and literary context

The two Norwegian translations were intended for Hákon's court; the texts are set in the Arthurian court or express the anxiety of exile from the court of Cornwall, but the originals are, as Driscoll suggests, 'translated primarily because [they were] French, and what was French was fashionable' (1991, 111). Both *Strengleikar* and *Möttuls saga* note that *gaman* or *skemmtan* (entertainment) is the motive for the translation, and there is no explicit suggestion that *kurteisi* or other improving behaviours are imparted by them. In all likelihood, as with most medieval texts, the different audiences of the *Strengleikar*, *Möttuls saga* and *Skikkjurímur* would have understood not only each text, but each performance or reading as differently positioned and differently intended, along a gamut running from pure entertainment to instruction about courtly etiquette to Christian didactic purpose. Even as Hákon's court chuckled at the shaming of the courtly women in *Möttuls saga*, they were noting the courteous behaviour of Valven (Gawain), the splendour of the romance court, the wisdom (or folly) of the king and the deft way in which the queen handles social embarrassment. From *Strengleikar* they learned a vocabulary of emotion and sensibility, absent from the robustly objective prose of Icelandic saga authors, such as Snorri Sturluson (Glauser 2006, 33). Though *Skikkjurímur* is, as Matthew Driscoll suggests, closer to 'Trivialliteratur' than its exemplar, it is still freighted with ideological import (1991, 126).

Reception

Transmission of the translated *lais* seems to have been limited. The Norwegian commissions clearly travelled to Iceland where they were copied, and where *Möttuls saga* gave rise to *Skikkjurímur*. The courtly sensibilities displayed in the texts had an indirect influence on the *riddarasögur* or indigenous stories about knights, composed in imitation of the imported literature. Their influence may also be seen in *Hákonar saga Hákonarsonar*, written by Sturla Þórðarson just after Hákon's death; alongside detailed political history, Sturla narrates set-piece events such as Hákon's coronation and the wedding journey of Kristín Hákonardóttir to Spain, in a prose which is partly inflected by the language and ambience of the French translations (Larrington 2009).

Plot

Geitarlauf

A close translation of *Chèvrefeuille*, with a few omissions and amplifications, *Geitarlauf* introduces Tristram and the queen, their great love and how they died on the same day. Mark has angrily exiled Tristram from Cornwall; the unhappy lover retreats to south Wales, his native land. Then he surreptitiously makes his way back to Cornwall where he hides in the forest. We should not be surprised, the narrator tells us, that he risks his life so, for the one who loves faithfully is grief-stricken when he cannot get his desire. Tristram learns that the queen will shortly be making her way to Tintagel for the Pentecost feast. Anticipating the route she will take, Tristan makes his way to the roadside, where he cuts a hazel bough, squares off the sides and carves his name on the stick. Tristram also writes that he is nearby, and longs to see the queen. A section in direct speech follows, likening the lovers to the honeysuckle and the hazel, who die if separated: 'Ei ma ec lifa on þin. ok ei þu on min' (I cannot live without you, nor you without me) (Cook and Tveitane edn 1979, 198), translating the Anglo-Norman, 'ne vus sanz mei ne jeo senz vus' (Rychner edn 1966, 153, ll. 77–8). *Geitarlauf* makes clear, as *Chèvrefeuille* does not,[1] that Tristram's name, the information that he is nearby, the extended comparison with the hazel and honeysuckle, and the plaintive refrain cited above, are all inscribed on the bough (Kalinke 1985, 346).

The queen notices the stick, and accompanied only by the faithful Brengveinn, she goes into the forest to meet Tristram. They joyfully tell each other of their feelings. The queen advises Tristram how to regain Mark's favour and that the king regrets his anger. Subsequently he is summoned back to court. Tristram, who is perfect in his knowledge of *lais* for the harp, 'fullkominn … allzskonar strengleica er i horpu gerazc' (Cook and Tveitane edn 1979, 198), composes a new lay, called by the British *gotulæf*, by the French *chæfrefuill*, and which in Norse is called *Geitarlauf*. Thus the poem names itself at its close, and the author ends by stressing the truth of the story he has relayed for entertainment (*skemtan*) (see Kalinke 1981, 22).

Januals ljóð

As noted above, the first section of *Januals ljóð* is missing in De la Gardie 4–7, where a leaf has been lost. It must be assumed that the lost lines contained the story of how Janual was neglected by Arthur when he distributed gifts at a Pentecost feast in Carlisle. Disconsolate and short of money, Janual rides out from town and encounters two damsels who summon him to meet their mistress, reclining nearby in a sumptuous tent. The lady offers Janual her love and endless quantities of money, but stipulates that he must never mention her existence to anyone. Janual agrees, and they spend the rest of the day in bed. That *Januals ljóð* in some version originally contained at least part of this missing material is evidenced by the fourteenth-century text *Helga þáttr Þórissonar* in which the hero Helgi, travelling in the far north of Norway, encounters a supernatural woman whose damsels, tent and basins for washing clearly derive from a version of *Lanval* (Power 1985). When the *Januals ljóð* text resumes, the lady sends Janual on his way telling him that they can continue to meet if he goes to a private place and thinks of her. Janual quickly adapts to his new moneyed style of living, feasting his friends, freeing prisoners, giving money to *leicarar* (jongleurs), and he sees his sweetheart frequently. On St John's Eve, a group of knights including Valuein (Gawein) and Iven (Yvain) are amusing themselves in the garden below the queen's tower, and ask Janual to accompany them. The queen and her maidens join the knights, but Janual sits apart, longing for his lady. The queen tells him that she loves and desires him. Janual politely rebuffs her, declaring that he will not be a traitor to his lord. Angered, the queen accuses him of preferring to *eiga við unga sveina* (have dealings with young boys) (Cook and Tveitane edn 1979, 216). Janual strongly denies this, claiming that he loves the only woman alive worthy of praise and renown, and that her most wretched (*fatækazta*) maiden is more beautiful than the queen. Furious and weeping, the queen takes to her bed; when the king returns from hunting she charges Janual with having disparaged her (*mismællti henni*). He had asked for her love and when she refused him, he had praised his own mistress and denigrated the queen by comparing her with the most wretched maiden.

The king is enraged, swearing to charge and execute Janual. Janual discovers that he can no longer call upon his lady, and is distraught. Summoned to appear before the king, Janual denies the charge that he has disgraced the king, but offers a defence of truth as to his remarks about the queen. Valuein and his friends pledge themselves as guarantors that Janual will appear for his trial. The Norse omits a long passage in which the Count of Cornwall offers a legalistic analysis of the charges against Janual, since the king seems tacitly ready to overlook the issue of whether Janual propositioned his wife. As the trial reaches its climax, a series of beautiful maidens appear, asking that a room be prepared for their mistress. Finally the lady herself appears, riding a splendid horse and accompanied by the aristocratic signifiers of hound and sparrowhawk. The fairy declares, boldly but tactfully, to the king that the queen's initial charge, that Janual had solicited her love, was false, and that Janual's boast about her own beauty may now be vindicated by her appearance. The barons agree, and Janual is acquitted. Leaping up behind the lady, the couple ride away to Avalon, and have never been heard of again.

Geitarlauf demonstrates to its audience how a traditional Norse lexis of emotion, employed in native eddic poetry to express women's grief and longing, can also be used to describe men's emotion. The translator uses such native terms as *tryggazto ast* (most loyal love), *ann trygglega* (loved faithfully), *vilia* (will), *fyst* (desire), *ryggr* (sad), and even the tautological *harmulegan harm* (tragic grief), to render the Anglo-Norman *amer leialement, dolenz* and *volentez*. What would go unexpressed or be attributed to general opinion in saga prose, is laid bare in a depiction of male interiority until now alien to Norse literature. *Geitarlauf* also gives poetic voice – or at least a poetic paraphrase – to male love-lyric; although *mansöngr* (literally songs for maidens) are alluded to in saga, they are rarely recorded; skaldic verses dedicated to women praise a girl's beauty but say little of the feeling of the poet himself. The art of courtly conversation, of speaking about one's love and gaining emotional release from that articulation, is also emphasized in *Geitarlauf*, while native tradition is reticent about open discussion of feelings. Thus the queen is able to speak privately to Tristram in terms that please her, *henne licaðe* (Kalinke 1981, 147–8), and, in the sentiments of the lyric carved on the hazel bough and in person, Tristram reciprocates (Bruckner and Burgess 2006, 196). A similar interest in masculine feeling is evident in *Januals ljóð*; Janual suffers greatly when his lady no longer appears to him: he is *ahyggio fullr, ryggr, mioc angraðr* (full of concern, sad, much grieved). Unlike his French counterpart, he does not sigh or swoon, but Janual comes close to suicide, the narrator avers, because of his *harm*. When first summoned to the king he is already in the depths of despair, *hugsiucr ok harms fullr litlaus ok hryggr* (distressed and dejected, colourless and sad) (Cook and Tveitane edn 1979, 218). Janual's friends curse his *fol amur*, a standard courtly phrase rendered in Norse as *uhofsamlegvm astum* (immoderate love). The king himself is angry (*reiðr*): his speech shows a limited range of expressions for translating the humiliation and shame of the French; *mesfaire, hunir, avillier* are all rendered by variants of *svivirða* (shame). The missing leaf in De la Gardie 4–7 unfortunately makes it impossible to see how the Norse translator rendered the chagrin of Lanval/Janual when Arthur fails to honour him at the Pentecost feast, or how he handled the lady's wooing of the knight, and his response.

The court audience would note the unfavourable portrait that the text gives of King Arthur in *Januals ljóð*. Capricious in his gift-giving, failing to recognize merit, unable to control his wife's sexual behaviour, allowing himself to be deceived by her, and showing himself eager to punish Janual, despite the support offered by major court figures to the calumniated knight, Arthur does not appear to advantage in this text. When he tries to hurry sentencing in Janual's case because the queen is anxious for a decision – a slight amelioration of the French where the queen wants a speedy verdict because she is hungry: *trop leungement jeünot* (Rychner edn 1958, v. 552) – the king fails to judge the mood of the court, who rejoice at the sight of the approaching maidens, sure that they have come to help Janual. His excellent qualities are clear to all; the French *hardi et preux* is expanded into a series of adjectives *vaskr, vapndiarfr, kurteis, milldr, konunglega tigurlega* (valiant, bold with weapons, courteous and agreeable, and of royal blood) (Cook and Tveitane edn 1979, 222). The king's

failure to appreciate Janual, both before and after the accusation, loses him the serv-
ices of a superlative knight.

   Januals ljóð reduces the emotionality of the original. As noted above, though
Janual responds with great feeling to the loss of his lady, somatic reactions – fainting,
sighing, and blushing – are all omitted. The Norse reduces the repetitions of the
queen's charges against Janual, toning down the passion with which she denounces
him to the king. Some courtly and learned detail is also removed: the concern of
Janual's friends as to whether he is eating or drinking sufficiently in his misery, the
silk accoutrements and Spanish mules which signal the status of the second set of
damsels, classical comparisons to Venus, Dido and Lavinia, and the detailed physical
description of the lady's body. Here the translator is content with noting the external
trappings of rank: the hawk, the hound and the excellent horse. Janual's lady seems to
make a deliberate effort not to implicate the queen. Against the blunt Anglo-Norman
la reïne a tort eü (the queen was wrong) (Rychner edn 1958, v. 621) and the fear that
Lanval might suffer for his words (*ceo qu'il dist*), the Norse fairy asks that no one
suffer on account of *her* words (*engum se orð min til meina*), suggesting pointedly in
technical terms that the queen has brought false charges (*ranga soc*) against Janual,
'þui at alldri bað hann hennar' (because he never wooed her) (Cook and Tveitane edn
1979, 226). The king is characterized as most courteous when he stands to greet the
fairy, but this action comes too late; though Arthur agrees to her request, it is the court
that acquits Janual of the charge against him. In contrast with the praise heaped upon
Arthur and thus indirectly on King Hákon in *Möttuls saga*, the depiction of the king
and his relations with his great knights in *Januals ljóð* must have been disquieting for
the poem's courtly audience. As Kalinke observes, 'At stake is no profound injury; no
ethical consideration is involved; only the vanity of a woman – and indirectly that of
her husband or lover – has been assailed' (1981, 38).

Möttuls saga

Möttuls saga opens with a chapter that has no counterpart in the source, an 'extensive and encomiastic' portrait of King Arthur (Kalinke edn 1987, xv; Kalinke 1981,
29–31). A series of superlatives designates him as an epitome of kingly virtue, harsh to
the wicked and clever in his schemes, but also as illustrious, manly, generous, kindly,
charitable, godfearing and hospitable, qualities which must be understood as shared
with the *virðuligr Hákon kongr* (worthy king Hákon) (Kalinke edn 1999, 6).[2] Beyond
this graceful reference to *Möttuls saga*'s patron, the portrait emphasizes generosity,
evidenced by Arthur's decision to hold a great feast and to give splendid presents to
all who attend.

   Arthur is 'hinn forvitnasti maðr ok vildi verða víss um allra tíðinda er gerðuz í
ríki hans ok svá í öðrum löndum' (6) (the most inquisitive of men and wanted to be
apprised of all news of events that took place within his realm as well as in other
lands) (7). The invitation attracts not only prominent knights, but also each man's

fríða unnustu (lady love). The queen takes personal charge of the female guests, giving them splendid garments, edged with grey and white fur. She is praised less highly than the king; though her qualities of munificence (*mildleik*) and noble bearing (*skörungskap*) are mentioned, the nature of her generosity will shortly be called into question. The magnificent feast may not be enjoyed until some 'ný tiðindi um einhvern atburð' (10) (news about some event or other) (11) arrives. A young squire gallops up; greeting Arthur, he requests a boon, undertaking that the request will be damaging neither to the king's honour nor to his kingdom, an assurance which is somewhat misleading. The king agrees and the young man produces from a purse a finely woven cloak, made by an elf-woman (*álfkona*), shot through with silk and (in an apparent addition to the source) a pattern of embroidered leaves (Kalinke edn 1987, l–liii). The narrator explains that the cloak will reveal through its fit the misdeeds of every maiden who had been intimate with her beloved. The *Lai du cort mantel*'s claim is broader: that the cloak reveals whether a woman has *mespris en nul endroit* (misbehaved somewhere) (Bennett edn 1987, v. 209) with regard to her lover or has practised some sort of *vilenie* (v. 322). The *Möttuls saga* cloak, additionally, is said to reveal loss of virginity, a rather different matter.

The queen is summoned by Valven, Kæi and Meon (Yvain), and she tries the cloak on, having been told that, if it fits, the magnificent red garment will be hers. The narrator comments that, had the ladies known the true quality of the cloak they would not have tried it on 'fyrir allt þat gull er í Arabíalandi er' (14) (for all the gold in Araby) (15). The cloak is much too short, however, and the queen blushes with shame. Meon exaggerates the lack of fit, but discreetly draws no conclusion, recommending that another lady, the beloved of Aristes (a mistranslation of Tor, son of Arès) should try the cloak. Now the cloak is even shorter, and the court's reaction arouses the queen's suspicions. Valven gives the game away by remarking that there is less *svik* (falsehood) in the queen than in Aristes's beloved. Once the power (*kraptr*) of the cloak is explained, the queen decides to make a joke of it; the French *jenglois* is expanded into 'gamans ok skemtanar, hlátrs ok leiks ok hlægiligra orða' (16) (entertainment and diversion, into laughter, jest and ridicule) (17). The queen's response chimes with the author's claim that *gaman* (entertainment) is the sole intention behind his work. Kæi reinterprets the meaning of the test as revealing fidelity and steadfastness in love, *trúleikr* and 'trúnaðr ástar yðvarrar' (16), a faithfulness which has encouraged the knights to respect the women's virginity, but, Kæi opines, they have only pretended to be pure.

The king realizes the shame that the women of the court seem likely to face and tries to return the cloak to the squire, but he refuses, emphasizing that it is unkingly to attempt to rescind a promise. The reluctant women of the court are constrained in turn to try on the cloak. Kæi volunteers his lady for the test, confident in her virtue. Both are shamed by the cloak's poor fit; she is openly taunted and Ideus (Yder) reminds Kæi that his scornful treatment of others merits his disgrace. A succession of ladies follows, Kæi and Geres (Guivrez) adding a lubricious commentary. Gerflet, the king's fool, displaying more common sense than the others, cites some familiar Norse proverbs (see below). Other women are humiliated in turn, both by the ill-fitting cloak and Kæi's comments. Finally every woman present has failed, causing their lovers *angr ok hryggleikr* (distress and sorrow) and a search is instigated to make sure no woman has been overlooked. Gerflet locates a maiden who, feeling unwell, had not come down to the hall; her lover Karadín (Carados Briébras) advises her forcefully not to take the test. Although she is well aware of what is at stake, the maiden responds in an exemplary fashion, in marked contrast to the other ladies, saying that she is willing to take the test if her lover gives permission. When this is granted, she puts on the cloak which fits perfectly and is awarded to her as prize. The squire who brought the cloak now reveals that he has visited many courts with it, exposing the hypocrisies of more than a thousand maidens. The *meydóms hreinlífi* (purity of maidenhood) of Karadín's beloved is unexampled (28). Valven takes up both the general praise for the girl and the allusion to virginity. The squire departs and the court falls to feasting. When the feast is over Karadín and his lady leave the court, and the mantle is deposited in a monastery. Recently, the narrator warns, the keeper of the mantle has threatened to send it out to test the women of various courts. The narrator opines that he would not wish to be bearer of the cloak, incurring the wrath – not of the unmasked ladies – but of their powerful menfolk. No one should say anything but good about women, 'ræði engi annat til þeira en gott' (28), he concludes, for it is better to conceal than reveal their misdeeds. Nevertheless the revelation of the cloak's continued existence operates as a veiled, if broadly comic, threat to the ladies in the audience.

The author of *Möttuls saga* makes only a limited effort to localize his material; the manufacturer of the cloak is an elf-woman (*álfkona*) rather than a fairy, and some native proverbs are assigned to Gerflet, fool and truth-teller. The first of these is: 'at kveldi er dagr lofandi' (22) (the day is to be praised at evening) (23), best known from the wisdom poem *Hávamál*, st. 81. In this context it is followed by the adjuration that a woman should only be praised when she is burnt (on her funeral pyre) and a maid when she is married; the audience would surely have relished the tact and wit in Gerflet's evocation of unreliable things. Gerflet's second proverb, 'mart kann öðruvís til at bera en menn hyggja' (22) (many a thing can turn out otherwise than one expects) (23) is a variant of a proverb found in *Jómsvíkinga saga*, chapter 37, where the speaker is about to be executed (Kalinke edn 1987, 76). Continuing the enthusiastic and admiring tone of the description of Arthur himself, the account deploys a great many superlatives to describe the court: nowhere in the world is a court more splendid, nor can lovelier women be found, they are *fríðast í heiminum*; the superlatives drop away once the women's shame is revealed. The adventure, with its humiliating outcome both for the women and their lovers, and indeed the whole custom of waiting for a marvel before feasting, is driven by curiosity, interest in the wider world, a reflection perhaps of the openness to the new which motivated the translation of the French *lais*.

The king's desire for novelty and for information ends with shame for the court, but his curiosity about the larger world mirrors Hákon's own contacts with Europe, his diplomatic initiatives and of course his translation programme. For example, the first *blámenn* (black men) ever seen in Norway at Hákon's court came with a deputation from Emperor Frederick of Germany (Kjaer and Holm-Olsen edn 1986, 582).

In comparison with the source, *Möttuls saga* elaborates on the importance of gift-giving. Ostentatious gift-giving on the part of the king, rewarding service in the court, is an essential part of Norse cultural tradition; here the king's generosity unites the standards of European *kurteisi* with northern ideas of gift-exchange as cementing emotional and political bonds. New, however, is the idea of the boon; the granting of a request which is not necessarily material. Although eddic wisdom poetry warns that gifts may sometimes have a sting in the tail, the rash boon at the heart of the plot belongs to chivalric tradition. The young man's response when the king first tries to terminate the contest emphasizes the impossibility of the king retracting a gift – even a verbal gift – once given. Comedy also drives the elaboration; Kæi's lady shows herself less courtly than in the *Lai du cort mantel* when she bluntly suggests that there are a hundred high-ranking ladies shrinking from the mantle who might easily precede her. Similarly Valven's lady finds that the cloak stretches to an excessive four and a half ells at the back, while in front it barely comes down to her knees and is shorter still on the left side.

The Norse author confuses the stakes in this version of the mantle test. When the cloak is first produced, it is said to test whether young women are virgins or not, indicating 'hver sú mær sem spilz hafði af unnasta sínum' (12) (every maiden who had been intimate with her lover) (13). The cloak's diagnostic power is later modified in line with the *Lai du cort mantel*, so that the test is said to indicate more generally whether the women have been faithful to their lovers: 'hve trúliga þær hafa búit við bændur sína' (14) (how faithfully each has conducted herself toward her husband (15) and 'sína trúlyndi haldit við unnasta sína' (14) (how faithful she has been to her beloved) (15). By the end of the tale, however, *meydoms hreinlífi* (purity of virginity) (28), pronounced by the squire and reiterated by Valven, is what wins the mantle for Karadín's lady; the young man maintains that the cloak has exposed thousands who falsely claim to be virgins at other courts. Thus an emotional state, faithful love, is confounded with a physical state, virginity. What is written on the female body becomes readable through the cloak's interpretive power; the queen reacts bodily, blushing with shame and paling with rage, even before she knows the secret of the cloak. Yet the narrator's probably clerical interest in virginity muddles the logic of the test. Clearly the queen cannot be a virgin, since she is married; equally clearly the other ladies have engaged in sexual activity. Whether this was with their acknowledged lovers or with other knights cannot be investigated, for this would throw an unwelcome spotlight on male sexual mores.

Nor can the sexual honour of the women be disentangled from the social honour of their men. Respect for the women's virginity, Kæi claims initially, drives knights to undertake adventures: 'ok svá sú ást er riddarar hafa á yðrum meydóm, ok leggja sik í lífsháska ok margskonar ábyrgð fyrir yðrar sakir' (16) (because of the love that the knights have for your virginity, they hazard mortal danger and take many risks for your sakes) (17), a change from the French which represents *la lëauté des amors* (the loyalty of love) which the ladies bear their men as motivating the quest for honour. If their virginity no longer exists, how might this lack impact on the honour acquired on its account? Comment is cautious at the first tryings-on of the cloak, since the court fears to insult the queen – and by extension the king – and because the women have not yet realised what the cloak does. Kæi's lady is subjected to cruel public insult; her sexual conduct and his habitual mockery are run together, so that she is effectively punished for his sharp tongue (Kalinke 1981, 114). The pattern of trial and failure settles into a courteous invitation from the king, sardonic commentary from Kæi or others and silence from the women and their embarrassed lovers. By the end of the tale the king's temper begins to fray and his courtesy diminish as the remaining women hesitate, 'Vér föstum of lengi . . . Hvat er konum þessum? Hví dveljum vér at láta þær klæðast skikkjunni?' (22) (We are fasting too long . . . What is the matter with these women? Why do we delay in having them put on the mantle?) (23). Kæi's final claim that all the men are in the same position, and that no one can *ámæla* (blame) another lays aside his customary mocking mode of speech in order to assert masculine solidarity through shared humiliation (Kelly 2000, 65). Valven swiftly rebuts the idea that a good man becomes *dáligr* (reprehensible) if his lady besmirches herself (*spilla*) with another (24), but, despite Karadín's triumph, Kæi's assertion retains its truth-value.

Male honour is, *Möttuls saga* maintains, imbricated in female honour; courtly sexual mores have been scrutinized and found wanting, and the relationship between the panegyric at the start of the text and the saga's outcome ironized (Kalinke 1981, 30, 126). The discourse of virginity is invoked at beginning and end in an attempt to bring the text's morality into line with religious teaching, but, as often in chivalric texts, the foregrounding of the erotic as motivation for the competition for honour trumps the didactic intention. In complicating the examination of courtly sexualities, the text moves beyond the obvious misogyny that governs *Skikkjurímur*, raising vital questions about male and female agency, about sexual guilt and personal honour. The coercion to which the women are subjected in the name of a male-driven honour competition – though at first they collude in their humiliation, driven by a materialist desire for the luxurious mantle – rebounds to bring shame on them, the king and his court. The victory of Karadín's lady scarcely matters; the couple leave the court immediately since she does not belong in this company, and the mantle, concrete token of female failure, is hardly sanctified by being lodged in a monastery. The narrator's conclusion 'betr sómir at leyna en upp at segja' (28) (it is better to conceal than to reveal) (29) is vindicated by the shameful outcome, even if – as he has consistently claimed – what he knows and has related is the truth.

Skikkjurímur

Composed in Iceland, probably in the fifteenth century, *Skikkjurímur* betrays a much less courtly sensibility at work than that of *Möttuls saga*'s author (Kalinke 1981, 216–19; Driscoll 1991). The *Skikkjurímur* author knows more about Arthur than the tale he finds in *Möttuls saga*, his main source, adding information drawn from *Erex saga* (Kalinke 1981, 217) and explaining that, for reasons of egalitarianism, Arthur has a *kringlótt sess*, a 'round seat', engineered so that each knight is seated equally close to the king, which appears to swivel and to be positioned half-way between floor and ceiling (Driscoll edn 1999, 270; I, 20–1).[3] This is doubtless a confused, and somewhat impracticable, recollection of the Round Table (Reichert 1986). As is typical of *rímur*, each of the poem's three fits includes prefatory material (*mansöngvar*, see Driscoll 1991, 112–13) in which the poet reflects on his own experience of love; his observations about women's fidelity form an appropriate introduction to his narrative. The poem is intended to be *kátleg* (amusing), the poet explains; it is typical of the poetry enjoyed by young men, composed, he misleadingly states, in order to *lofa hinn unga svanna* (to praise young ladies) (272; I, 1). A comparison between love and sailing follows; getting a fair wind is likened to gaining female favour, but the wind – like women's faithfulness – can change.

As he embarks on the story, the poet substantially edits *Möttuls saga*'s encomium about Arthur, asserting merely that the king is brave and generous and attracts honourable men to his court, while praise for the queen is even more abbreviated. The scene is set in England, in Yarmouth, not normally an Arthurian site, but a trading port well known in Iceland. Famous Arthurian knights are listed as present for Arthur's feast; in contrast with *Möttuls saga* most of the names are rendered recognizably. Descriptions of courtly display are also reduced; in a native touch Estor and Idús (Ector and Yder) are said to carry spears rather than lances (274; I, 16). The solidarity of the knights is emphasized: in the egalitarian spirit of the *kringlott sess* each man takes it personally if another noble is criticized, a solidarity which will soon be put to the test. The custom of fasting until news of some *ævintýri* (adventure) is heard means that men are encouraged to pursue great endeavours (*mikla þraut*) in order to generate news for the king. Arthur's feast is proclaimed far and wide; not only the usual array of knights, but a series of marvellous figures – the king of Dwarfland, a three-hundred-year-old king, a very young, beardless king, and the queen of Small-Maidenland, all with appropriate retinues – are among the guests drawn from *Erex saga* (Kalinke 1981, 217). The jousting and courtly entertainment of *Möttuls saga* is replaced by music; the guests drink wine, mead and malmsey, not beer, and exert themselves in a mixture of courtly and non-courtly pastimes: throwing lances and heavy stones jostle with wrestling, chess-playing and dancing. Next the company go to table, in expectation apparently of eating cabbage soup (*súpa kál*), surely here an idiom for nourishing fare. The king and queen sit separately; the queen hungrily interrogates Valvent (Gawain) about the delay in serving, and is reminded of the custom of waiting for an adventure, even though 'kappa tekur að svengja' (the men grow hungry) (284; I, 57). Just then, a large man rides into view. Fit I thus ends in suspense – is the desired adventure about to occur?

Fit II commences with another lyrical section, this time referring to the Norse myth of the mead of poetry. Gunnlöð, a giant's daughter, guarded this mead until the god Óðinn deceived her and stole the mead for the gods and for humans. No poet now can win a woman's love through poetry without grief, the poet laments; he has not had much luck in that direction. The poet deftly transforms a mythic allusion in which a man deceives a woman into a complaint about women's mutability and warns that women should cultivate *Friggjar barð* (Frigg's hill), an obscure reference which, with its allusion to the Norse goddess normally regarded as the counterpart of Venus, may be a reference to the *mons Veneris* (see Driscoll 1999, 323–5 for discussion of the putative obscenities in the poem). Now the visitor arrives at the feast; blond and dressed in white he greets Arthur in courtly fashion and asks for his boon. A painted chest – a more usual container for garments in Iceland than the wallet of *Möttuls saga* – is brought, from which he produces a multicoloured cloak, woven by three elf-women over fifteen years. The cloak's quality is explained; if any lady or maiden has not kept faith 'misjafnt vel hefur haldið trú' (II, 31) with her lover, the cloak will reveal it, indicating how the woman sports with her lover, and thus prove who is *dyggust* (most worthy). This is quite enough adventure for Arthur, who is now ready to start eating, but the squire demands that the contest proceed immediately. Valven is sent to fetch the women to whom he gives an evasive account of the mantle's nature. The women assemble in the hall, admiring the splendid cloak; the king declares, equally evasively, that 'sú . . . er engin virðast lýtin á' (she who is without blemish) (294; II, 41) will win the cloak. The fit ends as the queen is about to try on the magic garment.

The final fit commences with the poet's lament that, although he has been successful with women in the past, now the only female interested in him is Elli, the personification of Old Age, who in Norse myth wrestled with and overcame the god Þórr; she is the woman who always gets her man. The successive failures of the women trying the cloak are narrated more briskly than in *Möttuls saga*; from the queen's attempt onwards, both the narrator and Kay make sarcastic comments about the poorness of the cloak's fit. On the queen, the back of the cloak is short, as if someone had stuck a 'fox' in there, probably an idiomatic term for a penis. The fool Girflet blurts out the truth, that most women are unfaithful to their husbands and that this is what is indicated of Estor's lady. The queen decides to make a joke, *leika af sér* (300; III, 22), of the trial, and decrees that every woman shall try the cloak. As in *Möttuls saga*, Kay's lady gestures towards the higher-ranking women who should precede her before she dons the garment (see Kalinke 1981, 219, for effects of suspense here); Valven's lady and Yvain's lady join the other disgraced women who huddle together in a circle, *húka í hring* (304; III, 37). Kardon's lady (presumably a reminiscence of the Karadín of *Möttuls saga*) is also unsuccessful, the cloak does not cover her *klettis bein* (304; III, 42), an obscure phrase probably meaning 'pudendum'. After the ladies of the most important knights have failed, the female guests are tested. The two-hundred-year-old queen of King Felix of the Old Men comes forward: the cloak expands down to the floor, leaving a hole over her 'goose'; age is no bar to lechery. Nor is stature: the queen of the dwarves, the queen of the Small Maidens, the wife of a certain Morit, and Perceval's lady also fail. The ladies stall, but there are a thousand and one hundred of them to get through, and the king grows hungry and impatient. Finally Kardon, the lady of Kaligras, is discovered; after a polite exchange with her lover, she puts on the cloak which fits perfectly; 'ei var hún stutt og ei var hún flá' (it was not short and it was not slack) (310; III, 69). The squire adds his praise; he has taken the cloak far and wide, but it has never fitted anyone before. In an extraordinary move, unparalleled in any other version of the mantle test, Arthur expels all the unfaithful women, including, one supposes, the queen, and rallies his downcast men 'því vér skulum sækja oss betri frúr' (for we shall find ourselves better women) (312; III, 77). The knights cheerfully agree that this will be a source of adventure and the feast proceeds. Kaligras and his wife are lauded as a loving couple, for no woman in England equals her in virtue and the cloak is deposited in a cloister in Cologne. The poet ends on a spiteful note; he wishes that the cloak were here to reveal the truth about women, for as Solomon observes, you should always keep your ears open to detect false women. The poem is coming to an end, but any woman who has heard it and who has laughed is clearly unfaithful; they should be consumed with fire from navel to knee until they confess!

The *Skikkjurímur* distance the adventure of the cloak from its original courtly context; in the Icelandic farmhouse where it was likely composed, chivalric mores are as fantastic as the freakish wedding guests. The poem strikingly combines escapism and realism; there is music in abundance, played on instruments both familiar – drum, harp, fiddle and pipe – and unusual: the tympanum, trumpet and organ (280; I, 41–2). The king's marvellous revolving chair allows him to oversee the dispensation of the finest drink; no mundane beer is consumed here, though the guests seem to anticipate cabbage soup with relish. The poem is markedly misogynistic; the punishment of burning genitals stems from church teaching about the likely fate of lecherous women in the next world. In contrast with *Möttuls saga*, there is no engagement with the problematic nature of male–female relations in a courtly context; king and nobles alike believe, optimistically, that their honour can be redeemed by getting a set of new and more virtuous women, 'worthier lovelies' (Kalinke 1981, 219). The poet's invocation of the proverbial wisdom of Solomon on the subject of women suggests that the new women will be as unfaithful as the previous ones. *Skikkjurímur* is notably interested in adventure and achievement: Arthur's demand for *ævintýri* before he feasts is a tradition which fosters knightly endeavour. His robust reponse to the women's failure recuperates the court's honour. Rather than leaving Arthur and his knights looking like ineffectual cuckolds, as in *Möttuls saga*, the test of the cloak is interpreted as a challenging provocation to new honour and adventure. Finally, in a neat narratorial touch, the poet claims that his poem is also a cleverly designed artefact. The *rímur* too function as a kind of chastity-test; they share the cloak's quality, or so the poet play-fully claims, of detecting the untrue woman: she who laughs at the poem. The man who is able, following Solomon's adjuration *eyru sín að hafa við* (to keep his ears open) (314; III, 83) will be disabused of his illusions about women, joining the poet in his clear-eyed, but unsuccessful dealings with the opposite sex.

Issues in recent scholarship

Jürg Glauser's useful overview (2005) of *riddarasögur* scholarship includes the translated *lais*, although they are not treated in detail. He notes that earlier studies of the translations tended to concentrate on the mechanics of adaptation and the evo-lution of a courtly Norse prose style; see, for example, Kalinke's (1979) article on the style of *Möttuls saga* and now Sif Rikhardsdóttir's discussion of the 'austere and objective narrative mode of the native prose' into which Marie's work is rendered in *Strengleikar* (2008, 150). Glauser (2005, 380–1) chronicles the debate about the pur-pose of the translations; Kalinke (1981, 20–45; edn 1987, xvii) arguing that a work such as *Möttuls saga*, which hardly reflects well on Arthur's court, is translated, as its own prologue insists, purely for entertainment value, while Simek (1982, 15) sug-gests, following Meissner (1902, 119), that the Norwegian court would have been educated in European courtly behaviour by hearing about the Arthurian court (see also Leach 1921, 153). Glauser characterizes this debate as a 'dichotomizing tendency . . . which is in the long run unfruitful . . . which no longer applies today' (see also Barnes 1989, 2000; Kalinke 1985). Damsgaard Olsen (1965, 92–117) has suggested that even a Scandinavian aristocratic audience was already familiar with chivalric behaviour, an argument with which Glauser broadly concurs. Sif Rikhardsdóttir, mainly writing from the standpoint of translation and post-colonial theory (see below), skirts round the either/or dichotomy of entertainment versus education, observing:

> The fact that the texts were adjusted to Nordic mentality by excluding or reducing elements that had no meaning within the receptive culture does not preclude their function as guidance in courtly mannerisms . . . Similarly the very notion that they were intended as 'entertainment' . . . indicates the extent to which the textual ideology of a leisured nobility free to pursue such frivolous matters has been assumed. (2008, 148, n. 14).

Driscoll's 1991 article inaugurated literary discussion of *Skikkjurímur*, while little has appeared on *Strengleikar*'s Arthurian *lais* beyond Power's notice of the similarities between Ingibjörg in *Helga þáttr Þórissonar* and *Januals ljóð*'s fairy mistress (Power, 1985). More recently, *Strengleikar* has attracted the attention of Sif Rikhardsdóttir, who contrasts the cases of Norway and England in comparing how vernacular literary culture processes Marie's *lais*. In Norway, French cultural superiority is implicit; the injunction of *Konungs skuggsjá* that French is a valuable language is evidence of the extent to which France is regarded as a source of desirable knowledge and custom.

New comparative work examining themes across European Arthurian texts is also bearing fruit. Chastity-test narratives, as Bart Besamusca has recently noted (2008), tend to fall into one of two categories: those in which internal commentators and the narrator draw didactic or social-moral conclusions from the test, and those where the moral message is occluded by humour. *Möttuls saga* appears to fall into the second category, for the narrator opines that women's misdeeds should be kept hidden. As Besamusca notes, Kæi's comments are not treated as humorous within the text, and there is inherent disapproval, not just of the women's infidelity, but of the kinds of sex Kæi suggests they have had; intercourse *a tergo*, for example. The interpretation of the cloak's signification is heuristic; depending largely on Kæi as reader of the cloak, the narrative makes manifest the considerable gap between the ideal and the real in Arthur's court. *Skikkjurímur*, however, by reverting to the traditional wisdom of Solomon about the deceitfulness of women, and by advocating the exposure and punishment of the unfaithful, belongs more clearly to the moral-didactic category.

In 'Queens and Bodies' (2009), I make use of the work of Peggy McCracken (1993) on the adulterous queen in French romance, reading the translated *lais* alongside the history of Hákon's reign, *Hákonar saga Hákonarsonar*, composed by the Icelander Sturla Þórðarson in 1264–5. The courtly description of the *lais* has a limited influence on Icelandic-Norwegian historiography, but anxiety about the roles and the bodies of royal women, about chastity and maternity, the queen's informal influence over the king, and the ways in which the royal female body displays the sovereignty of husband or father, are as relevant in the Norwegian context as in the French. The translated *lais* thus heightened awareness of the ways in which queenly bodies signified in the politics of the northern court.

The translated *lais* had a limited further circulation beyond the Norwegian court as demonstrated by the manuscript evidence from Iceland and the existence of the *Skikkjurímur*. However, the general neglect of the Scandinavian material in the wider Arthurian context, and the lack until recently of translation theories viable in a context where so little is known of the translator and his public, has meant that the texts have had little influence in wider European Arthurian studies. Now that scholarly editions and idiomatic translations are available it is to be hoped that these quirky, lively and individual versions of Arthurian tales will begin to be studied alongside their better-known sources and analogues.

Notes

[1] Richard O'Gorman points out, however, in a note to vv. 61–2 of his edition of *Chèvrefeuille*, that 'BN, n.a.f. 1104 states unambiguously that the message was written on the stick' (Marie de France, *Chèvrefeuille*, in *Early French Tristan Poems*, 2, ed. N. J. Lacy [Cambridge, 1998], p. 193).

[2] Unless otherwise noted, subsequent references to *Möttuls saga* are to the 1999 edition and translation by M. E. Kalinke.

[3] Subsequent references to *Skikkju rímur* are to the 1999 edition and translation by M. J. Driscoll.

Reference List

Texts and Translations

Strengleikar

Strengleikar eða Lioðabok. En Samling af romantiske Fortællinger efter bretoniske Folkesange (Lais), oversat fra fransk paa norsk ved Midten af det trettende Aarhundred efter Foranstaltning af Kong Haakon Haakonssøn, ed. R. Keyser and C. R. Unger (Christiania, 1850).

Elis saga, Strengleikar and Other Texts. Uppsala University Library, Delagardieska samlingen nos. 4–7 folio and AM 666 b quarto, introd. by M. Tveitane (Oslo, 1972).

Geitarlauf, in *Strengleikar*, Cook-Tveitane edn and trans., 1979, pp. 195–9.

Geitarlauf, ed. and trans. R. Cook, in *Norse Romance*, I, *The Tristan Legend*, ed. M. E. Kalinke (Cambridge, 1999), pp. 4–8.

Janual, in *Strengleikar*, Cook-Tveitane edn and trans., 1979, pp. 212–27.

Janual, ed. and trans. R. Cook, in *Norse Romance*, I: *The Tristan Legend*, ed. M. E. Kalinke (Cambridge, 1999), pp. 10–22.

Strengleikar: An Old Norse Translation of Twenty-one Old French Lais: Edited from the Manuscript Uppsala De la Gardie 4–7—AM 666b 4º, ed. and trans. R. Cook and M. Tveitane (Oslo, 1979).

Strengleikar, ed. Aðalheiður Guðmundsdóttir (Reykjavík, 2006).

The French Lais

Marie de France, *Le Lai de Lanval, accompagné du texte du* Ianuals lioð *et de sa traduction française avec une introduction et des notes par P. Aebischer*, ed. J. Rychner (Geneva and Paris, 1958).

Marie de France, *Les Lais de Marie de France*, ed. J. Rychner (Paris, 1966).

Le Lai du cort mantel, ed. Philip E. Bennett, in *Möttuls saga*, Kalinke edn, pp. 4–68.

Möttuls saga

Versions nordiques du fabliau français 'Le mantel mautaillié'. Textes et notes, ed. G. Cederschiöld and F.-A. Wulff (Lund, 1877).

Saga af Tristram ok Ísönd samt Möttuls saga, ed. Gísli Brynjúlfsson (Copenhagen, 1878).

'Möttuls saga', ed. Bjarni Vilhjálmsson, in *Riddarasögur*, I (Reykjavík, 1949), pp. 249–81.

'Möttuls saga', intro. by D. Slay, in *Romances: Perg 4:o nr. 6 in the Royal Library, Stockholm*, Early Icelandic Manuscripts in Facsimile, X (Copenhagen, 1972).

Die Saga vom Mantel und die Saga vom schönen Samson. Möttuls saga und Samsons saga fagra, ed. and transl. by R. Simek, Fabulae Medievales, 2 (Vienna, 1982).

Mǫttuls saga: with an Edition of Le Lai du cort mantel *by Philip E. Bennett*, ed. M. E. Kalinke, Editiones Arnamagnæanæ, B, 30 (Copenhagen, 1987).

Möttuls saga, ed. M. E. Kalinke, in *Norse Romance*, II: *Knights of the Round Table*, ed. M. E. Kalinke (Cambridge, 1999), pp. 3–31.

Skikkjurímur

Skikkjurímur, ed. Finnur Jónsson, in *Rímnasafn: Samling af de ældste islandske Rimer*, II, Samfund til udgivelse af gammel nordisk litteratur, 35 (Copenhagen, 1913–22), pp. 326–56.

Skikkjurímur, ed. M. J. Driscoll, in *Norse Romance*, II: *Knights of the Round Table*, ed. M. E. Kalinke (Cambridge, 1999), pp. 269–311.

Studies

Andrés Björnsson (1947). 'Um Skikkjurímur', *Skírnir*, 121, 171–81.

Barnes, G. (1975). 'The *riddarasögur* and medieval European literature', *Mediaeval Scandinavia*, 8, 140–58.

Barnes, G. (1989). 'Some current issues in *riddarasögur* research', *Arkiv för nordisk filologi*, 104, 73–88.

Barnes, G. (2000). 'Romance in Iceland', in M. Clunies Ross (ed.), *Old Icelandic Literature and Society*, Cambridge, pp. 266–86.

Besamusca, B. (2008). 'Characters and narrators as interpreters of fidelity tests in Arthurian fiction', paper given at the 22nd International Arthurian Congress, Rennes.

Björn K. Þórólfsson (1934). *Rímur fyrir 1600*. Safn Fræðafjelagsins, X, Copenhagen.

Bruckner, M. T. and Burgess, G. (2006). 'Arthur in the narrative lay', in G. Burgess and K. Pratt (eds), *The Arthur of the French*, Cardiff, pp. 186–214.

Damsgaard Olsen, Th. (1965). 'Den høviske litteratur', in H. Bekker-Nielsen, Th. Damsgaard Olsen and O. Widding (eds), *Norrøn Fortællekunst*, Copenhagen, pp. 2–117.

Driscoll, M. J. (1991). 'The cloak of fidelity: *Skikkjurímur*, a late medieval Icelandic version of *Le Mantel mautaillié*', *Arthurian Yearbook*, 1, pp. 107–33.

Driscoll, M. J. (1997). '"Words, words, words": textual variation in Skikkjurímur', *Skáldskaparmál*, 4, 227–37.

Einar Ól. Sveinsson (1964). 'Viktors saga ok Blávus: sources and characteristics', in Jónas Kristjánsson (ed.), *Viktors saga ok Blávus*, Riddarasögur, II, Reykjavík, pp. cix–ccix.

Finnur Sigmundsson (1966). *Rímnatal*, Reykjavík.

Glauser, J. (2005). 'Romance (translated *riddarasögur*)', in R. McTurk (ed.), *A Companion to Old Norse-Icelandic Literature*, Oxford, pp. 372–87.

Glauser, J. (ed.) (2006). *Skandinavische Literaturgeschichte*, Stuttgart, Weimar.

Hagland, J. R. (1985). 'Du problème de l'expansion de texte dans la Möttuls saga par rapport à l'original français', in R. Boyer (ed.), *Les Sagas de chevaliers (riddarasögur)*. *Actes de la Ve Conférence Internationale sur les Sagas (Toulon, juillet 1982)*, Paris, pp. 249–63.

Halvorsen, E. F. (1967). 'Möttuls saga', in *Kulturhistorisk leksikon for nordisk middelalder fra vikingetid til reformationstid*, 12, Copenhagen, cols 189–90.

Halvorsen, E. F. (1972). 'Strengleikar', in *Kulturhistorisk leksikon for nordisk middelalder fra vikingetid til reformationstid*, 17, Copenhagen, cols 301–3.

Holtsmark, A. (1959, 1960). Review of E. F. Halvorsen, *The Norse Version of the Chanson de Roland*, in *Maal og Minne*, 161–70 (in Norwegian); *Arv*, 16, 187–98 (in English).

Hunt, A. and Bromiley, G. (2006). 'The Tristan legend in Old French verse', in G. Burgess and K. Pratt (eds), *The Arthur of the French*, Cardiff, pp. 112–34.

Kalinke, M. E. (1979). 'Amplification in *Möttuls saga*: its function and form', *Acta Philologica Scandinavica*, 32, 239–55.

Kalinke, M. E. (1981). *King Arthur, North-by-Northwest: The* matière de Bretagne *in Old Norse-Icelandic Romances*, Bibliotheca Arnamagnæana, 37, Copenhagen.

Kalinke, M. E. (1985). 'Norse romance (*Riddarasögur*)', in C. J. Clover and J. Lindow (eds), *Old Norse-Icelandic Literature: A Critical Guide*, Islandica, XLV, Ithaca and London, pp. 316–63.

Kalinke, M. E. (1991). 'Chastity tests', in N. J. Lacy (ed.), *The New Arthurian Encyclopedia*, New York and London, pp. 81–3.

Kelly, K. C. (2000). *Performing Virginity and Testing Chastity in the Middle Ages*, London and New York.

Kjaer, A. and Holm-Olsen, L. (eds) (1986). *Det Arnamagnæanske håndskrift 81A fol.: Skálholtsbók yngsta*, Oslo.

Larrington, C. (2009). 'Queens and bodies: the translated Arthurian *lais* and Hákon IV's kinswomen', *JEGP*, 108, 506–27.

Leach, H. G. (1921). *Angevin Britain and Scandinavia*, Cambridge, MA.

Leach, H. G. (1966). 'The lais bretons in Norway', in M. Brahmer, S. Helsztynski and J. Krzyzanowski (eds), *Studies in Language and Literature in Honour of Margaret Schlauch*, Warsaw, pp. 203–12.

Lönnroth, L. (1978). *Den dubbla scenen. Muntlig diktning från Eddan till Abba*, Stockholm.

McCracken, P. (1998). *The Romance of Adultery: Queenship and Sexual Transgression in Old French Literature*, Philadelphia.

Meissner, R. (1902). *Die Strengleikar. Ein Beitrag zur Geschichte der altnordischen Prosalitteratur*, Halle a. S.

Power, R. (1985). '*Le Lai de Lanval* and *Helga þáttr Þórissonar*', *Opuscula*, VIII, Bibliotheca Arnamagnæana, 38, pp. 158–61.

Reichert, H. (1986). 'King Arthur's Round Table: sociological implications of its literary reception in Scandinavia', in J. Lindow, L. Lönnroth and G. W. Weber (eds), *Structure and Meaning in Old Norse Literature*, Odense, pp. 394–414.

Sif Rikhardsdóttir. (2008). 'The imperial implications of medieval translations: Old Norse and Middle English versions of Marie de France's *Lais*', *Studies in Philology*, 105, 2, 144–64.

Skårup, P. (1975). 'Les Strengleikar et les lais qu'ils traduisent', in *Les Relations littéraires Franco-Scandinaves au Moyen Age. Actes du colloque de Liège (avril 1972)*, Paris, pp. 97–115.

Tveitane, M. (1973). *Om språkform og forelegg i Strengleikar*, Bergen.

6

THE OLD NORSE-ICELANDIC TRANSMISSION OF CHRÉTIEN DE TROYES'S ROMANCES: *ÍVENS SAGA, EREX SAGA, PARCEVALS SAGA* WITH *VALVENS ÞÁTTR*

Claudia Bornholdt

> *Eigi hafða ek león þetta hingat til þess at þat væri berserkr.*
> I have not brought my lion here for it to act like a berserker.
> (Kalinke edn and trans. 1999, 80, 81)

The above comment by Sir Íven in *Ívens saga* helps illustrate a number of aspects characteristic of the three Scandinavian sagas that translate, or, to be more accurate, adapt Chrétien de Troyes's French romances *Yvain ou le Chevalier au Lion, Erec et Enide* and *Perceval ou le Conte du Graal* into the Old Norse language and Scandinavian culture. Just as Íven's lion does not act like a *berserkr*, the Arthurian knights in the Norse sagas most certainly do not act like uncultured men-beasts either, though their character and conduct differ quite a bit from those of the traditional heroes in French romance. The Old Norse Parceval, Íven and Erex are depicted in the sagas in a manner that brings them closer to a Scandinavian audience unfamiliar with the ideas and ethics prevailing in continental courtly literature. The Norse sagas bring an entertaining new subject matter to medieval Scandinavia and they unquestionably have the important didactic function of presenting models of behaviour. By comparing his lion and, implicitly, the lion's loyalty, strength and fighting ability, to a *berserkr*, Sir Íven's words conjure up a world familiar to the audience of the Norse sagas, a world in which it is not unheard of that the hero, be it the god Óðinn himself, a Norwegian king or a Norwegian or Icelandic farmer, is accompanied by his *berserkr(s)*. Thus, while having a beastly fighting companion is not necessarily unusual for a Scandinavian audience, the lion in *Ívens saga* does not behave like a typical *berserkr* but like a civilized, loyal companion to the courtly knight Íven. Unlike in Chrétien's romance, the religious symbolism of the lion is more or less lost in the saga. Instead the grateful lion is coupled with a figure drawn from the culture of its Norse audience, an approach found throughout the sagas of Parceval, Íven and Erex (on the motif of the grateful lion, see Kalinke 1994). The linking of the courtly lion with the barbaric *berserkr* illustrates that the Norse Arthurian sagas are not so much translations of French romances as adaptations that seek to integrate a new literature into the Norwegian and Icelandic culture and literary tradition and its code of ethics.

According to the epilogue of *Ívens saga,* the Norwegian *Hákon kóngr gamli* (King Hákon the Old) commissioned the translation of Chrétien de Troyes's *Yvain* from

French into Old Norse. Since the Norwegian King Hákon IV Hákonarson (r.1217–63) was referred to as 'the Old' only after the birth of his son, Hákon, in 1232, we have a time frame (1232–63) during which the translation of *Yvain* most likely was undertaken at the Norwegian court. Even though we lack comparable references in *Erex saga* and *Parcevals saga/Valvens þáttr* (Chrétien's *Perceval* is transmitted in two parts, as the saga of Parceval and the tale of Valven, that is, Gawain), it can be assumed that the translations of three of Chrétien de Troyes's Arthurian romances were composed in Norway some time during the reign of King Hákon Hákonarson. Whether this is indeed the case for *Erex saga*, however, continues to be a topic of discussion (see below).

The earliest more or less complete texts of the sagas are known today exclusively from Icelandic manuscripts, and *Erex saga* is transmitted in seventeenth-century paper manuscripts. Although both *Parcevals saga* and *Ívens saga* are preserved in fifteenth-century vellums, these are defective. Therefore, while it is generally assumed that Chrétien's romances were translated into Old Norse at the same time as *Tristrams saga* (see chapter 4), either by Brother Robert himself or by a group of translators working with him at the Norwegian court, we no longer have the original thirteenth-century translations. What we do have is the work of Icelandic copyists and redactors who adapted and modified the Norwegian translations. To what degree they altered the Norwegian texts remains a topic of intense debate. As far as we can deduce from the extant manuscripts, the thirteenth-century Norwegian translations were condensed but generally accurate retellings in prose of Chrétien's metrical romances (Kalinke 1981, 197; Hanna Þorleifsdóttir 2007, 167). Over the course of their transmission, however, the translations underwent various stages of editing and modification, leaving us today with Icelandic prose sagas that at times greatly deviate from their French sources, particularly *Erex saga*. Marianne Kalinke (1981, 183; 1985, 345–7) proposed five stages for the transmission of Chrétien's romances in Old Norse: (1) French romance; (2) Norwegian translation; (3) Norwegian/Icelandic copy; (4) Norwegian/Icelandic revision; and (5) Icelandic recreation. These stages, which might not be present in every case, make it very difficult, if not impossible, to judge which changes were made by the Norwegian translator and which were inserted later during the process of bringing the Norwegian translations to Iceland (Psaki 2002, 218–19, n. 4). Since the Norse adaptations of Chrétien's romances are extant exclusively in Icelandic manuscripts and since they contain 'substantial scribal intervention' (Kalinke 2002, 220; 1985: 332–6), it has been suggested – and indeed seems justified – that one should consider the extant sagas of Íven, Erex, Parceval and Valven not so much as Norwegian translations of Chrétien's romances but instead as examples of Icelandic literature (Kalinke 2002, 220; Jónas Kristjánsson 1988, 312). This is especially the case with *Erex saga* whose style much more closely resembles that of some of the indigenous Icelandic *riddarasögur*, 'chivalric sagas', than the Norse translations of the romances. Scholars do not concur whether Chrétien's *Erec et Enide* was translated at the same time and in the same place, namely Norway, as the other translations of French romance or whether the romance was translated in Iceland (Hallberg 1971, 135; Jakobsen 1989, *passim*; Kalinke 1996, 96, fn. 13). *Ívens saga* and *Parcevals saga/Valvens þáttr*, however, share so many syntactic-stylistic features as well as lexicon with the other translations of courtly French literature that they have traditionally been grouped with *Tristrams saga*, *Möttuls saga* and the *Strengleikar* in the so-called Tristram-group of the Norse *riddarasögur*, whereas *Erex saga* is considered to fall outside this group (Hallberg 1971, 134; Schach 1975, 132; Kalinke 1981, 131–77).

The sagas of Parceval, Íven and Erex transmit the content of Chrétien's romances in very condensed form. They drastically abbreviate and frequently eliminate passages, especially those containing extensive descriptions, psychological analysis, amorous casuistry, long monologues and authorial commentary (Kjær 1992, 115). They also add new prologues and epilogues. *Ívens saga* and *Parcevals saga/Valvens þáttr* remain faithful to the overall structure and content of their sources, whereas the redactor of the extant version of *Erex saga* has used some liberties in his rendition of Chrétien's romance. He modified details, rearranged episodes and added new material that he borrowed from contemporary Norse literature. As we shall see in greater detail below, many of the modifications in *Erex saga* seem to have been introduced in order to ground it more thoroughly in the socio-cultural background and literary tradition of medieval Iceland.

There can be little doubt that *Erex saga* in its preserved form belongs to the Icelandic literary milieu. It is quite a bit more complicated, however, to place *Ívens saga* and *Parcevals saga/Valvens þáttr* in a specific socio-cultural environment. It is just as difficult to discern authorial intention and the possible didactic purpose for all three works. For decades the critical debate concerning the translated *riddarasögur* – and thus also of the three sagas based on Chrétien de Troyes's romances – was split between two positions that either consider the translations as entertainment and 'primarily escapist fiction' or as didactic models for the Norwegian and Icelandic audiences, positions that are most vehemently presented in the work of Marianne Kalinke and Geraldine Barnes respectively (Psaki 2002, 218, n. 2; for a review of the debate, see Barnes 1989; Weber 1986). In more recent scholarship this polarized debate has been advanced inasmuch as the translated *riddarasögur* are considered more in terms of the indigenous Norwegian and especially Icelandic literary traditions and no longer solely from the perspective of the continental tradition of courtly romance (Psaki 2002, 217). This is a step in the right direction since, as mentioned above, *Parcevals saga* with *Valvens þáttr*, *Ívens saga* and *Erex saga* are more than merely translations of the French romances. They are adaptations targeting a Scandinavian audience living in Norway in the thirteenth century and in Iceland in the fourteenth century and beyond (Kramarz-Bein 1999, 66). Ultimately it is impossible to determine with certainty whether we ought to read the three sagas in the context of the royal milieu of the Norwegian court in the mid-thirteenth century (Barnes 2007, 380; 1977, 1982, 1984; Kramarz-Bein 1999, 2007; Kretschmer 1982) or as sagas that underwent a gradual transformation by Icelandic scribes and represent the rural and possibly clerical culture of later medieval Iceland (Kalinke 1996: 100; 1981, 1985; Jakobsen 1988, 1989; Jónas Kristjánsson 1988: 312; Weber 1986). Both approaches are valid inasmuch as the sagas were composed in thirteenth-century Norway and thus the text of the original translation remains the underlying layer for the later Icelandic redactions. To what extent the Norwegian translations were altered by later Icelandic redactors differs from saga to saga.

Without intending to make a judgement call about the actual chronology of the three sagas, they are discussed below in the order of *Parcevals saga*, *Ívens saga* and *Erex saga*, since this order may be said to represent the stages of transmission and visible Icelandic alteration. *Parcevals saga* with *Valvens þáttr* is the most didactic of the three sagas. It is arguably best understood in the context of the courtly milieu of thirteenth-century Norway as it reveals the didactic intentions of the Norwegian translator, whose unique style is well preserved in this saga. *Ívens saga*, as preserved today, represents an intermediary position. It contains features that are representative of the so-called Norwegian Tristram-group of the *riddarasögur*, especially in respect to style and lexicon, but at the same time it also contains material that seems to have entered the saga in later Icelandic redactions. *Erex saga* stands apart from the other two translations/adaptations, not only because of its late transmission but also because of stylistic differences and alterations to the plot. This saga is best understood as an Icelandic saga, whether or not it originally was translated from the French in Norway, presents a gradual 'Icelandicization' of the attitudes, taste and language of the work' (Jónas Kristjánsson 1988, 312), or, as has been suggested as well, was actually first composed in later medieval Iceland (Jakobsen, 1989).

Parcevals saga and *Valvens Þáttr*

The Norwegian translator of Chrétien's *Perceval* separated the stories of Perceval and Gawain. The first part, *Parcevals saga*, focuses on the adventures of the protagonist Parceval as narrated by Chrétien up to v. 6513, while the second part, *Valvens þáttr* (The Tale of Gawain), is devoted to the adventures of Gawain, ending at Chrétien's v. 9098, more than one hundred verses before the French romance breaks off. The extant manuscripts of *Parcevals saga* and *Valvens þáttr* present a significantly reduced version of Chrétien's romance (by about 40 per cent) but include a new prologue and epilogue in *Parcevals saga* and a brief transitional sentence at the opening of *Valvens þáttr*.

It has been suggested that the same Robert who names himself *bróðir* and *abóti* in *Tristrams saga* and *Elis saga* (deriving from the *chanson de geste Elie de St Gille*) respectively is also responsible for the translation of Chrétien's *Perceval* (Schach 1975; Hallberg 1971; Kramarz-Bein 1999, 63–4; 2007, 136–7). While this is difficult to prove with certainty, there can be little doubt that the translation was completed either by Brother Robert himself or by translators working with or shortly after him at the Norwegian court. The language, syntax and style of *Parcevals saga* and *Valvens þáttr* clearly indicate that the translator was a Norwegian who worked in the same environment as the translator(s) of *Tristrams saga*, *Möttuls saga* and *Ívens saga* (Psaki 2002, 202).

The manuscripts preserving *Parcevals saga* and *Valvens þáttr* are exclusively of Icelandic provenance and they are divided into two branches that are based either directly on the lost original Norwegian translation or on a no longer extant inter-mediate copy that was produced before 1350. The first branch is represented by a vellum fragment of one leaf that dates to about 1350 (Royal Library, Copenhagen, Ny kgl. Saml. 1794b, 4to). The second branch, which dates to *c*.1400–25, transmits the complete text of *Parcevals saga* and *Valvens þáttr* (Royal Library, Stockholm Perg. 4:o nr 6). It contains a lacuna between fols 45v and 46r that can be partially filled with text supplied by the fragment 1794b, 4to.

Parcevals saga and *Valvens þáttr* are characterized by the so-called *høvisk stil* 'courtly style' (Halvorsen 1962, 315–18). The Norwegian translator, whom we must consider responsible for the stylistic features, used rhymed proverbs, puns, word-plays, strings of alliterating words and synonymous and alliterating collocations (Kalinke 1999, 106; 2002, 221). The most distinct stylistic feature of *Parcevals saga* and *Valvens þáttr* are rhymed couplets, especially at the end of chapters (chapters 4–8, 11–16) where they deliver a sort of commentary on the events either by one of the protagonists or by the narrator (see chapter 2). An example of the former is the closing sentence in chapter 5, in which the young and inexperienced Parceval reacts to his teacher Gormanz's praise of his good spirit and potential for becoming a good knight: 'skal ek aldri vera *flýjandi* meðan ek em upp *standandi*' (Wolf edn 1999, 126) (I shall never take to flight while I can still stand upright) (Maclean trans. 1999, 127).[1] Another example, this time with additional alliteration, is Blankiflúr's utterance concluding her lamentation at Parceval's bed (end of chapter 7): 'Sendi **guð** yðr **gott** til *handa*, hvat sem hann vill **gera** af várum *vanda*' (132) (May God bestow on you his largesse, whatever he does in our distress) (133). An example of authorial commen-tary in rhymed couplets can be found at the end of chapter 8, which concludes with the loving embraces of Blankiflúr and Parceval the night after Parceval has defeated Blankiflúr's opponent Gingvarus and sent him to King Arthur: 'Ást er öllum hlutum *kærari*, hverjum þeim er tryggr er *elskari*' (136) (Love is dearer than any thing other to everyone who is a true lover) (137).

The rhymed couplets mostly occur at chapter endings, but are not limited to that position, as the following authorial rhymed and alliterating comment on Parceval's efforts during his training with Gormanz attests:

Góð náttúra er gott *nemandi* þeim er at góðu eru *kunnandi*. Gott kemr aldin af góðum *viði*: svá er ok góðr maðr með góðum *siði*. (126)

(Good character brings a good return for those who good things can discern. Good fruit comes from a good tree: so a good man has good habits naturally.) (127)

A comparison with Chrétien's verses reveals that the Norse translator based the rhymed couplets on them without, however, translating literally:

> Et quant nature li aprent
> Et li cuers del tot i entent,
> Ne li puet estre rien grevaine
> La ou nature et cuers se paine. (Roach edn 1959, vv. 1481–4)

(And since nature was his teacher and his heart was set upon it, nothing for which nature and his heart strove could be difficult.) (Kibler trans. 1991, 399–400)

The rhymed couplets in *Parcevals saga*, which seem so out of place in a prose saga, may have been inserted as a 'concession to the poetry of the original' (Clover 1974, 67). In combination with the other stylistic devices, such as alliteration and semantic repetition, which are used 'to signal important dialogue and action', they clearly function to elevate the style and to emphasize the content of selected passages (Kalinke 1981, 155–8). Given their location in the saga, their content and the fact that the rhymed couplets frequently take the form of proverbs and maxims that deliver commentary on events, we can conclude that their function is to highlight the saga's intended didactic purpose (Álfrún Gunnlaugsdóttir 1982, 228; Kramarz-Bein 1999, 66; Psaki 2002, 216; Kalinke 2002, 222).

Parcevals saga is often considered the most didactic of the Norse adaptations of Chrétien's romances as it focuses to a much larger degree than *Ívens saga* and *Erex saga* on the hero's education and his training to become a courtly knight (Kramarz-Bein 1999, 68–71). The saga is considered 'besonders höfisch', since it makes the courtly training and education of the hero itself into a theme (Kramarz-Bein 2007, 135). It is thought to be a handbook of chivalry because of the saga's strong 'emphasis on tutelage in practical and ethical fundamentals of chivalry' (Barnes 2007, 380; 1984, *passim*) and at the same time an *Entwicklungsroman* (Weber 1986, 437–51) and a *þroskasaga*, or *Bildungsroman* (Álfrún Gunnlaugsdóttir 1984), because it focuses more on instruction in morality than chivalry (see Kalinke 1996, 98). *Parcevals saga* has also been proposed as a *riddara skuggsjá,* a 'Knight's Mirror' that is analogous to the thirteenth-century Norwegian *Konungs skuggsjá,* 'King's Mirror' (Barnes 1984; Kalinke 2002, 222).

Considering that *Parcevals saga*, like Chrétien's *Perceval*, is the only saga and the only Arthurian romance that is concerned with the growing up and instruction of a young, initially very naive hero, the saga's focus on Parceval's education is perhaps not as significant as is often stated, since the education of the hero lies at the very core of the subject matter of *Perceval*. Nonetheless, the frequent and deliberate use of proverbs and maxims and the careful placement of didactic commentary in rhymed couplets that are oftentimes accompanied by alliteration suggest that the Norwegian translator and the later Icelandic redactors intended to place special emphasis on the idea of the hero's education and socialization. The emphasis on the acquisition of appropriate courtly behaviour situates the story of the young Parceval quite neatly within the context of King Hákon Hákonarson's thirteenth-century Norwegian court and its interest in the continental court culture. This interest is expressed by the sheer number of continental works translated at the royal court in the thirteenth century as well as in the composition of *Konungs skuggsjá* (Barnes 2007, 397). Assuming that the extant *Parcevals saga* indeed preserves a text that closely resembles the original Norwegian translation, it is also possible to go one step further and postulate that *Parcevals saga* was composed with a didactic intention and the political and ideological goal of strengthening the Norwegian monarchy (Kramarz-Bein 2007, 138). This interpretation is not without problems, however, once we consider that King Arthur seems just as helpless and a victim of circumstances in *Parcevals saga* as he is in Chrétien's romance, for example, in the account of the red knight's behaviour at Arthur's court (Kalinke 1981, 38). Moreover, King Arthur and the depiction of royal power in general do not seem to be a priority for the Scandinavian translator and the later copyists of *Parcevals saga*. It is the hero's behaviour that is of importance and this behaviour clearly serves as an example for the praiseworthy growth and socialization of a human being (Kalinke 2002, 222).

Chrétien opens his romance with a prologue in which he praises his patron Philip of Flanders and then proceeds immediately to the first adventure of the young Perceval: his meeting with the knights in the forest. Chrétien does not explain who Perceval is, why he is roaming alone in the woods nor why he is so naive and uneducated. The translator-adaptor of *Parcevals saga* makes an effort to fill in some of this background information. The heading for the first chapter introduces the overall content of the saga: 'Hér byrjar upp sögu ins prúða Parcevals riddara, er enn var einn af Artús köppum' (108) (Here begins the story of the proud knight Parceval, who was another of Arthur's champions) (109). The ensuing new introduction provides an explanation for Parceval's growing up in the wilderness: he is the son of a married farmer, who holds the rank of a knight and who has settled with his family in the wilderness because he had captured and abducted the daughter of a king. The knight and his family hide in the woods from society and to avoid retribution for the deed. Growing up in the woods, the young Parceval was instructed by his father in archery, swordplay and javelin throwing, and now, after his father's death, the twelve-year-old boy spends his time riding in the woods on his pony, killing animals and birds. At this point the plot picks up Chrétien's story: Parceval meets five knights in shining armour, believes them to be God and learns from them about King Arthur.

This new beginning to the story has been situated in the realm of folktale tradition, not least because of the specific choice of words, as Parceval's father and mother are introduced as *karl* (man, commoner) and *kerling* (woman, wife). It has been suggested that the new introduction was not part of the original Norwegian translation (Álfrún Gunnlaugsdóttir 1984, 234), but instead that it is a later Icelandic addition that was modeled after Icelandic tales of abducted brides in which the couple are forced to live in exile, such as, for example, in *Víglundar saga* or *Orkneyinga saga* (Kalinke 2002, 223). This explanation is quite plausible and, yet again, it is nearly impossible to locate these changes with certainty in Iceland. The motif of the abducted bride and the couple that lives in exile to avoid social retribution could just as well have been borrowed from one of the bridal-quest stories in *Þiðreks saga*, a saga that was certainly known and presumably also composed in Norway in the mid-thirteenth century.

While we cannot know where the new introduction was added to *Parcevals saga*, it is obvious that the new content sought to supply background information that explains the young hero's situation. The new introduction and the first chapter heading ('Here begins the story of the proud knight Parceval') provide a framework for the story. This frame is closed by a new epilogue that summarizes and at the same time concludes Parceval's adventures:

> Hann reið nú brott ok létti eigi fyrr en hann kom til Fögruborgar, ok varð Blankiflúr unnasta hans honum harðla fegin ok allir aðrir þeir sem þar váru fyrir. Fekk Parceval þá Blankiflúr ok gerðiz ágætr höfðingi yfir öllu ríki hennar, svá ágætr ok sigrsæll, at aldri átti hann svá vápnaskipti við riddara, at eigi sigraðiz hann, ok mætti hann öllum inum snörpustum riddurum er váru um hans daga. Ok lýkr hér nú sögu Parcevals riddara. (182)

> Now he rode away and did not stop until he came to Fagraborg, and Blankiflúr his beloved was overjoyed to see him again, and so were all the others who were there. So Parceval married Blankiflúr and became a splendid ruler over all her kingdom, so famous and victorious that never did he have an encounter with any knight in which he did not gain the victory. And he fought all the fiercest knights who were alive in his day. And now here ends the story of Parceval the Knight. (183)

This epilogue supplies a satisfactory and harmonious ending to the story of Parceval, an ending that is lacking in Chrétien's unfinished romance. It explicitly stresses the hero's worldly achievements as husband, king and model knight. As happens in Chrétien's account, Parceval's spiritual journey had already come to a conclusion at the end of his stay with the hermit on Easter Sunday. There 'nám [hann] á þessum tveimr dögum eina góða bæn ok lifði síðan sem góðr kristinn maðr' (182) (he learned by heart a good prayer, and lived ever after as a good Christian man) (183). In the French romance the account of Perceval's adventures ends abruptly after the hero has received communion. The plot then turns to Gawain's adventures and never returns to Perceval. The Norse saga remedies this unresolved ending of Parceval's story by inserting an epilogue that lists all of Parceval's accomplishments in respect to God, his wife and his role as a king and knight (Psaki 2002, 211). It thus combines the two realms that are central to the subject matter, the spiritual and the secular, and confirms that the hero has achieved an understanding of and success in both. *Parcevals saga* harmonizes both realms inasmuch as Parceval first makes peace with God and then settles into his secular life as husband, king and exemplary knight.

One contentious aspect of *Parcevals saga* is its depiction and therefore understanding of the Grail. The Norse translator seems to have attempted to explain an idea that was utterly foreign or at least incomprehensible to him and his audience. Chrétien spreads out his information about the appearance, nature and function of the Grail over several verses (3220–9; 3234–9; 3245–53; 3290–3; 3000–3). The Norse saga merely translates – or rather recounts – Chrétien's very first mention of the Grail in verses 3220–3. There Chrétien explains that *un graal* is carried in the hands of a fair, charming and well-dressed maiden. In *Parcevals saga* we learn that a beautiful maiden walked in and 'carried in her hands, just as though it were a gospel-book [*textus*], something which they call in the French language a grail [*braull*], but we may call it "processional provision" [*gangandi greiða*]' (149). While Maclean translates the Latin term *textus* with 'gospel-book', 'Evangelistary' has also been suggested (Foote 1969: 58). The term *braull* presumably is a possible misreading of OF *graal*. It seems appropriate to translate the otherwise unattested Old Norse *gangandi greiði* as 'processional provision', as Maclean does, thereby giving the expression a sacred or even liturgical connotation that is missing from other suggested translations, such as 'walking purveyor of hospitality' (Barnes 1993, 497), 'herumgehende Bewirtung' (Kramarz-Bein 1999, 67) or 'hospitality bestowed while walking' (Kratz, 1977b: 376). The depiction of Chrétien's Grail in the saga is somewhat similar to that in Wolfram von Eschenbach's *Parzival* in that the Grail is characterized by its ability to sustain those in its presence (Kramarz-Bein 2007, 142), but otherwise the actual form, qualities and symbolism of the Grail remain obscure in the saga. Clearly the translator tried to explain to his audience what is to be understood by *braull* (or *graal*), but his explication 'serves in fact to obfuscate further the nature and function of the *graal*' (Kalinke 1981, 77).

While the attempt to explain the Grail to the Scandinavian audience was not very successful, *Parcevals saga* otherwise renders the content of the French romance quite adequately, albeit in greatly condensed form. Most interpretations of *Parcevals saga* and *Valvens þáttr* are grounded in the differences that exist between the Norse saga and the French romance, that is, the omissions, deletions, alterations, condensation and occasional amplification undertaken by the Norse translator and/or later Icelandic redactors. Many of these interpretations are plausible, though we always have to keep in mind the special circumstances of the saga's transmission. It is impossible to detect with certainty what exactly the original Norwegian translation looked like and whether its idiosyncrasies and changes were inserted in Norway by the Norwegian translator or later in Iceland by the Icelandic copyist(s). Any interpretation that exclusively reads the extant saga in the context of the Norwegian court in the thirteenth century operates on dangerous ground, since the preserved text of the saga might in fact more closely represent the context of later Icelandic society and the literary environment of the indigenous Icelandic sagas. The most significant changes that were made to Chrétien's romance – the addition of a new prologue and epilogue, the division of the romance into two parts (the saga of Parceval and the tale of Gawain), and the omission, condensation and amplification of details and some scenes – could have occurred in either Norway or Iceland.

Recent interpretations of the saga have sought to reach a balance between the two extreme positions of interpreting the saga solely in either a Norwegian or an Icelandic context (Kalinke 2002; Psaki 2002). Psaki suggests that *Parcevals saga* 'agrees in substance with *Perceval* in describing the hero's progress from total ignorance of – but fascination with – knightly concerns, through his mastery of these but failure in the spiritual realm, to his eventual subordination of the knightly to the spiritual and his consequent success in both' (Psaki 2002, 202). In a similar vein, Kalinke proposes that the original Norwegian translation from which the extant Icelandic redaction derives focused on the moral, social and human maturation of the eponymous protagonist of *Parcevals saga*, which is also the core of Chrétien's romance. As is indicated by the many proverbs and maxims interspersed in the text, oftentimes in prominent places and in the notable form of rhymed couplets, the saga certainly has a didactic purpose. In line with Barnes's idea of the knight's mirror, Kalinke suggests that the saga might best be understood as a *speculum virtutum* that depicts 'the gradual socialization and education, in physical skills, social values, and virtuous habits, of the young hero' (Kalinke 2002, 222). While Chrétien's romance relates the maturation of an uneducated simpleton into a model of chivalry, the Old Norse-Icelandic *Parcevals saga* depicts the maturation of an individual whose development is complete once he has become a good Christian, taken a wife and understood and executed his responsibilities as ruler (Kalinke 2002, 223; Psaki 2002, *passim*). These values and virtues are central to *Parcevals saga* and they would have appealed just as much to a Norwegian audience in the thirteenth century as to an Icelandic audience in later centuries.

Ívens saga

Ívens saga, the Old Norse translation of Chrétien's *Yvain*, reduces the romance by about 60 per cent (Hanna Þorleifsdóttir 2007, 167) and consequently presents a much more straightforward plot whose figures represent idealized courtly heroes and are therefore less problematic than Chrétien's. As is the case with *Parcevals saga*, the stylistic particularities of *Ívens saga* most likely can be attributed to the thirteenth-century Norwegian translator who composed the saga in the amplificatory rhythmical prose of the court style with frequent use of alliteration and synonymous and antithetical collocations (Kalinke 1999, 35; 1979). The original Norwegian translation, which is no longer extant, probably adhered quite closely to Chrétien's text while many of the changes in content, the result of condensation and amplification, occurred during the later transmission of the saga in Iceland (Kalinke 1981, 68). In some instances it is even possible to detect the exact changes that were made by the Icelandic copyists (Kalinke 1981, 183–92). A note attached to a late seventeenth-century paper copy written by Magnús Ólafsson (AM 588a 4to) attests to the process of change: he explains that the original from which the manuscript had been copied was more expansive and longer, *miklu vitlòftigra og ordfyllra* (Kalinke 1981, 16).

Ívens saga is preserved in three primary manuscripts: the vellums Stockholm Perg. 4:o nr 6 (*c*.1400–25) and AM 489 4to (*c*.1450) and the paper manuscript Stockholm Papp. fol. nr 46, written in 1690. The last is based on the no longer extant Icelandic **Ormsbók* (*c*.1350–1400). The Stockholm 6 codex contains thirteen romances, including *Parcevals saga* with *Valvens þáttr*, and serves as the basis for the critical editions. It has two lacunae of approximately one leaf each (after fol. 26 and fol. 35) which can be partially filled, however, on the basis of the other two primary manuscripts (Kalinke 1999, 35).

Ívens saga opens with an introduction that focuses on the virtues of King Arthur. Instead of translating Chrétien's didactic comment that King Arthur should be taken as a model of chivalric behavior – *la cui proesce nos enseigne / que nos soiens preu et cortois* (Roques edn 1967, vv. 2–3) (whose valour teaches us to be brave and courteous) (Kibler trans. 1991, 295) – the saga author presents a comparison between King Arthur and Charlemagne:

> Hinn ágæti kóngr Artúrus réð fyrir Englandi, sem mörgum mönnum er kunnigt. Hann var um síðir kóngr yfir Rómaborg. Hann er þeira kónga frægastr er verit hafa þann veg frá hafinu ok vinsælastr annarr en Karlamagnús. Hann hafði þá röskustu riddara er í váru kristninni. (Kalinke edn 1999, 38)

> The excellent King Arthur ruled England, as is known to many. After a time he became king of Rome. He was the most illustrious of the kings who had lived on this side of the ocean and the most popular other than Charlemagne. He had the bravest knights who lived in Christendom. (Kalinke trans. 1999, 39)[2]

As has been observed for other Norse translations of French sources, the depiction of King Arthur in *Ívens saga* tones down instances of criticism of the fabled king. In *Yvain* Chrétien offers criticism of the king already at the very beginning of the romance when Arthur leaves the company of his knights and goes to take a nap. The knights are very surprised at this and are greatly disturbed by his behaviour which they discuss at length (vv. 42–52). The saga merely tells us: 'Þetta undruðuz allir menn, þvíat aldri fyrr hafði hann þetta gert' (38) (everyone was amazed at this because this had never happened before) (39). Later, when Yvain's host explains that he cannot receive any assistance from King Arthur and his knights to defend his kingdom and daughter against the giant Harpins de la Montaingne because Queen Guinevere had been abducted, Chrétien has the father pass explicit judgement on the king's behaviour. He blames Kay for not looking after the queen. He calls King Arthur a fool and the queen imprudent – 'Cil fu fos et cele musarde' (v. 3920) – for entrusting herself to Kay. The saga tones this down by not mentioning King Arthur and merely calling the queen foolish for entrusting herself to Kæi: 'víst var hún heimsk er hún gaf sik í geymslu þvílíks riddara' (78) (Surely she was foolish when she entrusted herself to such a knight) (79).

The saga furthermore abbreviates the scene in which a settlement is reached between the two daughters of the Lord de la Noire Espine. Whereas Chrétien's King Arthur argues at length with the older sister about the outcome of the inheritance quarrel, the saga reduces the long scene that follows the combat between Íven and Valven to a single sentence giving Arthur's judgement: 'En meyjarnar skyldu skipta til helmings allt þat er þær erfðu eptir föður sinn' (94) (And the maidens were to divide equally everything they had inherited from their father) (95). Arthur's role as just king is reduced (Kjær 1992, 124), but this very reduction contributes to the overall impression that Arthur appears to be in control of the situation (Jordan 2007, 158–9). As indicated by the opening comparison of King Arthur and Charlemagne, *Ívens saga* arguably presents King Arthur as the ideal of the ideal ruler (Kretschmer 1982, 150). It certainly makes an effort to remove explicit criticism of King Arthur's behaviour and actions.

Ívens saga is greatly condensed but, as is the case for *Parcevals saga*, the Norwegian translator and the later Icelandic redactors do not alter the plot by rearranging or adding scenes and sequences, as will be seen occurs in *Erex saga*. There is one longer scene not found in *Ívens saga* – Chrétien's verses 4697–5101, which give the background to the episode of the two daughters of the Lord de la Noire Espine – but this omission is occasioned by a lacuna after fol. 35 in the manuscript Stockholm 6 (Kalinke edn 1999, 35). Otherwise the saga stays very close to Chrétien's romance; at times passages from Chrétien are translated almost literally (Hanna Þorleifsdóttir 2007, 169). The most noticeable changes to the content that affect the overall impression one gains of the saga result from condensation. The saga shortens and omits many monologues, excursuses, authorial commentary, direct speech uttered by secondary characters and overly descriptive passages and scenes dominated by psychological analysis (Jordan 2007, 148). At times, the condensation is so extreme that the plot becomes somewhat confusing. This is most obvious in connection with the inheritance struggle of the two sisters. Due to the lacuna in the manuscript, we lack the background that explains why Íven engages Valven in single combat to fight on behalf of one of the sisters. In chapter 13 we suddenly learn that Íven is accompanied by a maiden (84), but we know neither who she is nor where she came from. The maiden is mentioned again in chapter 14 and this time we learn that Íven had promised to fight for her, but we lack pertinent information (90). Moreover, the saga reverses the roles of the two sisters. In Chrétien's romance Yvain fights on behalf of the younger sister and Gawain on behalf of the older sister who tries to cheat her sister out of her inheritance. In the saga, the younger sister, whom Valven defends, is the wicked one, whereas Íven represents the older sister. Finally, probably as a result of the drastic condensation, the name of

Íven's lady love, Laudine, is omitted from the saga, as is the name of Arthur's queen, Guinevere (Kjær 1992, 126).

Overall *Ívens saga* places more emphasis on action and reduces reflective passages, such as the narrator's excursus on love, and the passage devoted to personified Love in *Yvain* (vv. 1360–1409) is omitted in its entirety. As a result of these changes, the role of the narrator is greatly reduced. The saga entirely avoids using the narrator's voice in the first person and omits the narrator's direct address of characters. An example of such an omission is the description of Íven and Valven's single combat. Whereas Chrétien has the narrator discuss Yvain and Gawain's friendship as well as the ambivalent relationship between the emotions of love and hate (vv. 5995–6063), the saga author merely presents the circumstances of the battle without delving into the intricacies of the conflict and the pending battle of two close friends: 'Hér varð undarligr hlutr, þvíat hér börðuz þeir tveir menn með heipt er hvárr vildi sitt líf gefa fyrir annars líf. En nú váru þeir dauðligir óvinir ok hvárr vildi öðrum fyrirkoma' (90) (This was now a strange thing, because here two men were fighting with deadly hatred each of whom would give his life for the other. But now they were deadly enemies and each wanted to destroy the other) (91; see Jordan 2007, 153). By eliminating such stylistic features as authorial commentary, excursuses, monologues and extensive reflections by the characters and on the characters' actions, the style of *Ívens saga* with its focus on action and fast-paced dialogue closely resembles that characteristic of medieval Icelandic literature, and consequently it has been argued that the story of Íven was transformed into an adventure story that is modelled after the indigenous sagas (Jordan 2007, 148).

Just as commentary by the author is avoided to blend out judgement on the characters and their actions, the weaknesses, inner conflicts and inner progression of the individual characters are toned down while their actions are emphasized. Gawain's role, for instance, is reduced in the saga to that of Íven's friend and exemplary Arthurian knight. All that sheds a doubtful light on Gawain's actions and motivation in Chrétien's romance is eliminated. For example, Chrétien's Gawain implores Yvain in a long speech after the wedding celebrations to depart with King Arthur and his knights in order to seek adventure, uphold his reputation and not fall prey to the embraces of his wife and a life dominated by pleasure and ease (vv. 2486–509). The Norse saga removes the implicit allusion to the *recreantise* of Erec and Enide in Gawain's words and it also eliminates all hints of the misogyny embedded in Gawain's speech. In the saga, Gawain's words are merely summarized and related in indirect discourse: 'þá talaði herra Valven við herra Íven, at hann skyldi fylgja brott kónginum ok þar eigi lengi vera í þeim kastala ok fordjarfa svá sinn riddaraskap ok atgervi' (64–6) (Sir Valven spoke with Sir Íven and said that he should accompany the king and not stay in the castle any longer and thus ruin his knightly reputation and accomplishments) (67). While Sir Valven does convince Íven to take leave of his wife, he is not blamed for this. It is not the fact that Íven left his wife to seek adventure and thereby maintain his reputation that is responsible for the crisis in Íven's life, but rather Íven's neglecting to return to her at the agreed-upon time. Accordingly, the saga does not blame Valven for Íven's missing the deadline either. Valven is not mentioned at all in the scene that depicts how Íven 'hugsaði til at um var liðit þann tíma, er hans frú hafði honum sett' (66) (remembered that the date had passed that his lady had set for him) (67). The French romance on the other hand explicitly blames Gawain by stating that he had caused Íven 'to delay so long that the entire year passed and a good bit of the next, until it reached mid-August' (Kibler trans. 1991, 329; see Jordan 2007, 155–6).

Ívens saga contains several passages that reveal the influence of the indigenous literary tradition. There is, for one, the aforementioned moment when Íven compares his lion to a *berserkr*: 'Eigi hafða ek león þetta hingat til þess at þat væri berserkr' (80) (I have not brought my lion here for it to act like a berserker) (81). Chrétien's Yvain refers to the lion as a *chanpïon* 'champion' (v. 4448). The saga also stresses the motifs of friendship and kinship. Compared to Chrétien's Yvain, who frequently acts out of compassion for the less fortunate, the Norse Íven acts out of a strong sense of duty to his family and friends (Jordan 2007, 160–1; Kretschmer 1982, 172) and the need to maintain his honour, a motif that is a motivating force for the heroes in the Arthurian sagas (Kalinke 1977, 142–4; Kalinke, 1973, 1975; Kretschmer 1982, 174–6). In *Ívens saga* this becomes most obvious at the moment when Íven laments his behaviour after realizing that he has overstayed his leave. He does this in a beautifully composed, rhythmical passage characterized by antithetic alliterative pairs (see chapter 2; Kalinke 1981, 164–5):

> Til hvers skal ek lifa? Vesall maðr var ek, svá ógeyminn. Hvat skal ek útan drepa mik sjálfr? Ek hefi týnt huggan minni ok fagnaði, ok um snúit af sjálfs míns glæp virðing minni, ok vent tign minni í týning, yndi mitt í angrsemi, líf mit í leiðindi, hjarta mitt í hugsótt, unnustu mína í óvin, frelsi mitt í friðleysi; eða hví dvel ek at drepa mik? (74)

> (For what reason should I live? I was a wretch of a man, so heedless. What am I to do but kill myself? I have lost my consolation and joy, and through my own fault brought down my honor and turned my reputation into loss, my delight into suffering, my life into loathing, my heart into anxiety, my beloved into my enemy, my freedom into outlawry; why do I delay in killing myself?) (75).

This monologue transmits vv. 3525–56 of *Yvain*. Chrétien emphasizes that Yvain's greatest offence is the loss of joy caused by his behaviour: 'Que fet quant ne se tue / cil las qui joie s'est tolue?' (vv. 3525–6) (Why does the wretch who's destroyed his own happiness not kill himself?) (Kibler trans. 1991, 339) and 'Et je doi la mort redoter / Qui ai ma joie a duel changiee?' (vv. 3546–7) (And so should I, whose joy has changed to grief, fear death?) (339). In addition to the motif of lost joy, the saga names the loss of comfort, reputation, worthiness, freedom, as well as loss of the beloved and his distress (Jordan 2007, 163). In *Ívens saga* the protagonist's loss of reputation, honour and freedom are additions *vis-à-vis* the French source. The central role that is allotted to the hero's reputation, his honour and personal freedom is deeply rooted in medieval Icelandic literature and culture.

In many respects *Ívens saga* occupies a position between *Parcevals saga* and *Erex saga*. It is composed in the same courtly style as *Parcevals saga* and its plot too is greatly reduced. Moreover, at the end of *Ívens saga* the protagonist, like Parceval, has completed his journey and, having been reinstated, has found joy and happiness. *Ívens saga* shares with *Erex saga* the focus on the characters and their actions, however, as will be seen below. Furthermore, in *Ívens saga* dialogue dominates the narrative (Hanna Þorleifsdóttir, 2007) as well as the sequence of adventures the hero faces and successfully completes.

Erex saga

The most fascinating of the three Norse adaptations of Chrétien's romances is *Erex saga*; it is unique in 'the most marked deviation not only from its source in respect to content and structure but also in respect to style from the other translations known or thought to have been produced at the Norwegian court of King Hákon Hákonarson' (Kalinke edn 1999, 219). The Icelandic redactor significantly modified Chrétien's romance and transformed it into a fast-paced adventure story that was better suited to the experiences and expectations of his Icelandic audience (see Farrier 1990). The saga also contains a noticeable 'sermonizing tone' in its many 'didactic comments with religious overtones' (Blaisdell and Kalinke trans. 1977, xii) that suggests clerical influence on the composition (Kalinke edn 1999, 219; Barnes 2007, 391–2).

Except for two small vellum fragments from *c.*1500 (Lbs. 1230 8vo III) that contain twenty lines from the beginning of the saga, *Erex saga* is otherwise preserved only in seventeenth-century Icelandic paper manuscripts which derive from fourteenth-century vellums: AM 181b fol. (*c.* 1650) from Stockholm Perg. 4:o nr 6 (which also contains *Ívens saga* and *Parcevals saga*), and Stockholm Papp. fol. nr 46 (*c.*1690), from the now lost fourteenth-century Icelandic **Ormsbók* (see Kalinke edn 1999, 220; Kalinke 1981, 72–4, 251). In the two seventeenth-century paper manuscripts the saga's hero is consistently referred to as 'Erex', whereas in the older vellum fragment Lbs. 1230 III he is named 'errek' (Erek). This discrepancy suggests that an earlier version of the saga did indeed transmit the name as it is found in Chrétien's romance, that is, 'Erec', and that 'Erex' is a later corruption that was most likely introduced by the Icelandic redactor (Kalinke edn 1999, 260, n.1).

As is the case with the other Norse translations/adaptations of Chrétien's romances, *Erex saga* is exclusively transmitted in Icelandic manuscripts, making it difficult to determine with certainty when the saga was originally composed and what its exact form and content would have been in a thirteenth-century translation, if the translation actually had occurred in Norway. The extant version of *Erex saga* presents the basic plot of Chrétien's romance in greatly reduced form. Descriptions, such as of equipment, clothes and horses are deleted as are thoughts, the expression of inner conflict by the protagonists as well as commentary by the narrator. The saga also rear-ranges some of Chrétien's episodes and adds two new adventures and a brief epilogue. All these changes leave us with a saga that is one of a kind, in which the motivation for episodes as well as the characterization of some of the protagonists have been changed. In addition to modifications in content, the saga also greatly differs in style from the other Norse Arthurian sagas. Unlike *Parcevals saga* and *Ívens saga*, there are very few instances in *Erex saga* of the alliterative and rhythmical language char-acteristic of the so-called court style; instead *Erex saga* reflects the laconic style of the classical Icelandic sagas.

Erex saga opens *in medias res*, omitting Chrétien's address to the audience and his explanation for having set out to compose the romance. The saga begins at King Arthur's castle in Kardigan where Erex, a handsome man of great accomplishments, resides as one of the twelve knights of the Round Table. There is good entertainment in the castle and at the height of the merriment King Arthur announces the hunt for the hart. The successful hunter will receive a kiss from the most beautiful maiden at court. As happens in *Erec et Enide*, Valven (Gawain) warns the king that this reward might lead to discord at the court, since 'fyrri munum vér berjaz en þola þat at annars unnasta sé fríðari kölluð en annars' (Kalinke edn 1999, 222) (we would rather fight than let someone else's beloved be declared more beautiful than one's own' (Kalinke trans. 1999, 223).[3] While Arthur acknowledges in *Erec et Enide* that he is aware of the controversy that may result from singling out one of the court's ladies as the most beautiful, he nonetheless insists on his plan by stating that 'the word of a king must not be contravened' (Carroll trans. 1991, 38). This scene sheds some dubious light on Chrétien's King Arthur who seems to be willing to endanger the peace at his court for the purely entertaining hunt and the reward it entails. Arthur's reply to Gawain in the saga reflects a shift of emphasis. The king is presented as a powerful and sover-eign ruler whose will is to be obeyed by his retainers: 'Kóngr reiddiz orðum hans ok mælti: "Hvárt sem þér líkar vel eða illa, Valven, þá skal fara sem áðr; þvíat engi þjónustumaðr á at neita því, sem hans meistari býðr honum"' (222) (The king became angry at his words and spoke: 'Whether you like it or not, Gawain, we shall do as I have said, for no vassal must refuse to carry out what his lord commands' (223). As has been observed for *Parcevals saga* and *Ívens saga*, the depiction of King Arthur in *Erex saga* also shows didactic tendencies in that he is presented as a sovereign king who serves as a model of royal behaviour (see Kalinke 1981, 40, 44). For example, at Erex's wedding feast, Arthur reflects on his power and might and rejoices, but the narrator comments on his humility, that Arthur 'miklar sik eigi af þegnavaldi' (234) (does not pride himself on account of his power over his vassals) (235).

During the hunt Erex accompanies the queen and one of her maidens and they encounter a knight and a dwarf. Without provocation the latter lashes out at both the maiden and Erex with his whip. Unable to avenge his humiliation and defend his honour on the spot, Erex takes leave from the queen and pursues the dwarf and his knight to a castle. There he meets his future bride, Evida (Enide), whose father offers him lodging. He engages the knight in combat, defeats him and thus avenges the blow he had earlier received from the knight's evil dwarf. Eventually he returns to King Arthur's court with Evida who then receives the honour of the kiss as the most beautiful maiden present.

While the saga follows the basic plot of Chrétien's romance, it also introduces a number of significant and substantial changes in the relationship of Erex and Evida. In *Erec et Enide* we learn that Erec arrives at the dwelling of an elderly vavasour who asks his beautiful daughter to take care of Erec's horse. The first meeting of Erec and Enide unfolds in a courtly and modest manner: Enide stands back, is embarrassed and blushes when she first sees Erec, while Erec is astonished at her great beauty. After taking care of Erec's horse, Enide takes him by the hand and, as instructed by her father, leads him upstairs where she sits next to him during dinner. Afterwards Erec inquires about the vavasour's and his daughter's situation. He learns about the sparrow-hawk contest and that anyone wishing to compete has to claim the sparrow-hawk for his lady. He borrows his host's armour and then asks that Enide be permitted to accompany him so that he can compete for the sparrow-hawk. After hearing about Erec's name and reputation, the host quite literally hands over his daughter to Erec, giving him the missing 'item' needed to compete against the knight. In Chrétien there is no word about love between Erec and Enide until after Erec has successfully defeated his opponent and the young couple are on their way to King Arthur's court.

In *Erex saga* the situation is quite different. The two protagonists, Erex and Evida, experience love at first sight, for as soon as Erex dismounts and Evida comes to tend to his horse he notices her great beauty: 'ok þegar feldi hann allan sinn elskuhug til hennar. En er hún sá Erex, þá feldi hún allan sinn elskuhuga til hans' (226) (and at once he fell very much in love with her. And when she saw Erex, she fell very much in love with him' (227). Evida's father notices their affection and he himself leads away Erex's horse while the maiden waits on the guest and engages him in pleasant conversation. When his host returns, Erex asks to be given Evida in marriage. Pleased by Erex's ancestry and social standing, the father agrees to the match, provided that his daughter approves – 'ef þat er hennar vili' (226). Evida consents and the two are betrothed. Only now do they enjoy their dinner and Erex learns about the sparrow-hawk contest and the knight Malpirant (Yder in Chrétien). This change in the saga emphasizes the love between the young couple and at the same time deletes any impression that Evida is merely an 'object of bargaining' that Erex requires to avenge himself on Malpirant (Kalinke 1975, 17). Instead the saga presents Erex and Evida as a couple that is deeply in love. Evida is not unquestioningly handed over by her father; she is explicitly asked to give her consent to the betrothal and thus she becomes an empowered partner to Erex. Throughout *Erex saga* Evida maintains a position that accords with that of women in the *Íslendingasögur*, 'Sagas of Icelanders' (see Kalinke 1981, 181–3).

After the wedding we are told that Erex settles 'um kyrt ok ann svá mikit sinni unnustu at hann fyrirlætr alla gleði ok skemtan ungra manna. Vel er hann virðr af öllum góðum mönnum, en þó fær hann nokkut ámæli fyrir sitt hóglífi' (236) (into a life of ease, and he loves his beloved so much that he forsakes all the pleasures and amusements of young men. He is esteemed by all good men, and yet he receives some blame for his life of ease' (237). The narrator comments: 'Ok angrar þat hans frú mjök er hún heyrir honum hallmælt (236) (And it distresses his wife greatly that she hears him reproached) (237). Evida expresses her worries in a low voice as she lies next to Erex: 'Harmr er mér þat, herra minn, er þú fær ámæli fyrir þá ást er þú hefir á mér, ok þínu hóglífi' (236) (It distresses me, my lord, that you are reproached on account of the love you have for me and for your life of ease) (237). Compared to Chrétien's romance, the saga greatly softens the public criticism of Erex's behaviour and Evida lays much less blame on herself as the cause of Erex's life of ease. Chrétien repeatedly stresses that Erec is criticized by his retainers, who have lost all respect for him and confidence in his ability to serve as their lord. Erec is ridiculed and loses his authority. This notion is absent in the saga adaptation where the narrator states that Erex is still esteemed by all his men, even though he is reproached for his life of ease, a criticism that is much less severe than the one Erec receives from his retainers in the French romance.

The subsequent adventure sequence drastically reduces the passages in which Erex and Evida reflect on their behaviour and actions and we hear very little about the conflict between the spouses. While Erec's repeated command that Enide should not speak is certainly the dramatic and psychological centre of the adventure sequence and an important key to the interpretation of Chrétien's romance, the saga author downplays the psychological component and the spousal conflict and instead focuses on the action and adventures. Here the author intervenes most significantly as he conflates, reorganizes and even adds adventures (see Kalinke 1981, 192–3; Kalinke 1970, 343–55; Kalinke 1971, 54–65), as the following diagram shows. The shaded sections in *Erec et Enide* and *Erex saga* are not found in the French romance and saga respectively.

The saga conflates Erec's first two encounters with three and five robbers respectively into just one encounter with eight robbers. Afterwards Erex meets and defeats a single knight, Chrétien's Guivret the Short, who in the saga becomes the large and strong knight Guimar, Erex's cousin. Next the saga places Erex's encounter with the two giants who have captured a knight; in *Erec et Enide* this occurs after Erec has met up with Kay. Erex frees the knight and sends him and his wife to King Arthur's court. There now follow two new adventures: an encounter with a winged dragon and a combat with seven armed men. Both of these interpolated adventures, which were probably inspired by and borrowed from *Þiðreks saga*, tell of captured knights whom Erex releases from their captors and sends to King Arthur's court, thus continuing the type of adventure like the previous one with the two giants (see Blaisdell 1964). Following these three rescue missions is the episode in which Erex swoons, Evida is captured and Earl Placidus (Count Oringles in Chrétien) attempts to force her into

Erec et Enide	*Erex saga*
Three robbers (killed by Erec) Five robbers (killed by Erec)	Eight robbers (killed by Erec)
Count Galoain (attempt to elope with Enide; the count withdraws after the fight)	Earl Milon (attempt to elope with Evida; the count withdraws after the fight)
Guivret the Short (joust ends in friendship)	Guimar (large and strong knight); Erex's cousin; joust ends in friendship)
	Two giants (killed by Erex; the rescued knight is sent to Arthur)
	Winged dragon (carries the knight Plato, duke of Vigdæiborg and the son of Sir Valven's sister, in its jaw; Erex kills the dragon and sends the rescued knight to Arthur)
	Seven armed men who have four captured knights tied to their horses (Erex kills the seven evil knights and sends the four freed knights to Arthur)
	Earl Placidus (Erex's apparent death, attempted wedding with Evida; Erex kills Placidus)
Kay (on Gawain's horse)	Kæi (on Gawain's horse)
Gawain invites Erec to join Arthur's court; Erec spends one night at Arthur's court	
Two giants (damsel in distress; abducted knight, Cador of Cabruel, whom Erec frees and sends to Arthur)	
Count Oringles (apparent death of Erec; Enide forced into marriage; Erec kills Oringles)	
Guivret the Short (battle with Erec who is defeated)	Reconciliation of Erex and Evida; Erex loses consciousness but is found and taken in by King Guimar (Erex's cousin); no battle and no defeat of Erex
Erec recovers at Guivret's castle	Erex recovers at Guimar's castle
Joy of the Court adventure	Joy of the Court adventure

marriage with him. After Erex has rescued Evida and killed the presumptive groom, he encounters Kay in the forest. Erex defeats Kay, who is riding Valven's horse, spares his life but takes the horse away from him. Unlike in the French romance, Erex does not meet Gawain nor does he spend a night at Arthur's court. After his battle with Kay, Erex and Evida are finally reconciled, but then Erex loses consciousness a second time. His cousin Guimar finds him, helps him and takes him to his castle to recover from his wounds. It is noteworthy that Erex does not engage in combat with Guimar. In the saga, Erex undergoes a strenuous sequence of battles that pitch him against eight robbers, the large and strong knight Guimar, two giants, a winged dragon, seven armed men, Earl Placidus and finally Sir Kay. Erex defeats all of his attackers and rescues a total of six knights, all of whom he sends to Arthur's court.

The reconciliation of Erex and Evida takes place after Erex has successfully proved his valour in every battle. After his last such battle, his combat with Kay, Erex addresses Evida:

> Í mörgum þrautum höfum við um hríð verit, ok hefir guð ór öllum vel leyst. En nú hefi ek reynt af þér sanna ást, dygð ok trúfesti. Er nú ok meiri ván, at skjótr verði skilnaðr okkarr, þvíat fast angra mik stór sár ok langt matleysi. (252)

> (For some time we have been engaged in many a struggle, and God has seen us through it all. And I have now experienced from you true love, virtue, and fidelity. But now it is to be expected that we shall soon be parted, because I am suffering greatly on account of my grievous wounds and continuing lack of food.) (Kalinke trans. 1999, 253)

These words stress the fact that Erex and Evida have completed the adventures together, as a couple. The conflict between the spouses that plays such a central role in Chrétien's romance is reduced in the saga. There is agreement with Chrétien inasmuch as after their departure from his father's court Erex orders Evida to 'ríða fyrir sér ok óttaz ekki herfurður eða hverr váði sem at hendi ferr, ok tala ekki við sik' (238) (ride ahead of him and not to be afraid of any ghosts or any other danger they might encounter, and not to talk to him) (239). Upon seeing the eight robbers, Evida 'minniz á þögn er henni var skipuð, en má þó ekki annat fyrir ástar sakir við Erex en snúa nú aptr ok segir honum, þvíat hún var langt fram undan í veginn riðin' (238) (remembers that she has been ordered to keep silence, but she cannot do anything else on account of her love for Erex than turn back now and tell him, because she had ridden far ahead on the path) (239). Erex's reaction to her disobedience is not reported in direct discourse, however. All we learn is that she gets ingratitude (óþökk) from him for this. She is also reproached by Erex – 'fær hún óþökk' – when she tells him about the pursuit of Earl Milon (243). These are the only incidents in the saga in which the command to keep silent is mentioned. The inner conflict in Enide that takes up much space in Chrétien is lacking in the saga, as is the actual motivation for and enforcement of the order of silence on Erec's part.

In *Erex saga* Evida is presented as a strong and self-determined person. She assists Erex at all turns in his adventures and her character and loyalty are never questioned, not by the narrator/author, not by herself and not by Erex. When Evida believes Erex to be dead, she reproaches herself: 'Vesöl em ek orðin af dauða bónda míns ok þess annars, at með minni tungu kom ek honum á þessa ferð, er ek þagða eigi yfir rangligu ámæli vándra manna' (250) (I have become wretched on account of the death of my husband and also because I brought him on this journey because of my tongue, when I did not keep silent concerning the wrongful reproaches of evil men) (251). Although Evida regrets that she warned Erex of his diminished reputation, the saga author removes all suspicion that her behaviour was inappropriate. Moreover, she considers the courtiers 'evil men' and their criticism of Erex to be 'wrongful'. Until the moment when she believes Erex to be dead, Evida herself never regrets her decision to look after her husband's reputation, which reflects, in fact, the expected role of women in the indigenous Icelandic sagas.

Even though Evida's role is reduced by the omission of her monologues and expression of inner conflicts, it is, however, at the same time greatly increased. Evida is given self-determination in making decisions concerning her marriage to Erex and she clearly is an equal partner in their relationship. Unlike Erec and Enide in Chrétien's romance, Erex and Evida fall in love at first sight and Evida is betrothed to Erex only after she has given her consent to the match. This motif of spousal consent to the marriage is again taken up in *Erex saga* in the Earl Placidus episode. In the French romance, Oringles summons his chaplain and Enide is given to the count by force and he marries her even though she vigorously rejects him (Roques edn 1966, vv. 4729–35; Carroll trans. 1991, 95). Conversely, in the saga the court priest refuses to marry Evida to Earl Placidus, explaining 'Þat eru guðs lög eigi, nema hún gefi leyfi til' (250) (That is contrary to God's law, unless she consents) (251). Even though Evida objects to the marriage, the earl prepares a feast and continues trying, in vain, to obtain her consent. Unlike in the romance, in the saga the marriage never takes place and Evida is depicted much less as a victim and much more as an active participant in the events.

In the concluding 'Joy of the Court' episode the role played by the female characters is once more altered. In Chrétien's romance Erec rides into the garden alone, leaving Enide and his other companions behind (Roques edn, vv. 5814–29; Carroll trans. 1991, 109). He defeats the knight Maboagrains and releases him from the promise he had made to his beloved. Having loved the maiden ever since childhood and having been loved by her in return, he had rashly agreed to grant her a boon without knowing its nature, and as a consequence had to remain in the garden until a knight came along and defeated him in combat. The situation is entirely different in the saga. Erex and Evida jointly ride through the gate into the garden and together they find the maiden in the tent. Malbanaring, as Maboagrains is called in the saga, appears and insults Erex, blaming him for wanting to steal his possession, the maiden, and challenging him to single combat. After the fight, Malbanaring tells his story, explaining that he had taken the maiden from her father 'þó með hennar vilja' (256) (though with her consent)

(257) after he had granted her a boon. She asked him to stay with her in the garden and never part from her unless a knight came along and defeated him. She believed this would never happen. As the daughter of an earl she thought it a disgrace, *ósæmð*, if people were to find out that she was married only to a knight, and she was afraid that her father would conquer her with a large retinue (257). This explanation by the maiden Elena for her deed places her in a much better light than in Chrétien's romance. Elena asks Malbanaring, to whom she is married without her father's consent, to stay in the garden in order to hide from her father's anger and retaliation. Her actions are not selfish and seemingly pointless, as is the request for the boon in Chrétien's *Erec et Enide*, but rather a necessity to ensure the survival of the couple's love.

Just as the saga does not blame Evida and her femininity for tempting Erex away from his social duties and into the marital bed, so Elena also does not lure her lover into the garden exclusively to enjoy his love and attention. In fact, *Erex saga* lacks the implicit and explicit hints of misogyny that are present in Chrétien. Instead, Erex and Evida seek to repair Erex's diminished honour as a couple and they succeed together, both observing the roles allotted to them by society. We can attribute these changes to the saga author's 'own perception of reality, which derives from his own cultural background, ethical as well as literary' (Kalinke 1981, 181). *Erex saga* presents a couple that acts in the manner of the great couples in the Icelandic family sagas. Their adventures are placed in the social context of Icelandic marriage and kinship relationships. The woman explicitly consents to marriage and Erex proves his ability to protect his wife and, by extension, his family and retinue from outside aggression. This is underscored by the proliferation of the abduction motif in *Erex saga*. Chrétien uses this motif twice: in the second attack during the adventure sequence, where one of the five attacking knights wants to win Enide in single combat with Erec, and in the Count Galoain episode. The saga multiplies this motif: it occurs during the first adventure, the attack by the eight knights; the Earl Milon episode; in Guimar's encounter with Erex (he challenges Erex's right to Evida); in the interpolated adventure of the seven armed men; in Earl Placidus's attempt to marry Evida against her will; and in the final Joy of the Court episode (see Kalinke 1981, 100–1).

Underscoring the importance of the couple's joint achievements and Erex's responsibility towards his family, *Erex saga* closes with a short epilogue that relates the future of Erex and Evida, an ending that is in full agreement with the conventions of Icelandic sagas (Kalinke 1981, 128). We learn that the couple had two sons who were named after Erex's and Evida's fathers and who both became kings and distinguished men and 'líkir föður sínum at hreysti ok riddaraskap' (258) (like their father in valor and chivalrous deeds) (259). Honour is the motivating principle of the saga (Kalinke 1975, 14; 1973), and accordingly the epilogue reports that Erex and Evida ruled their kingdom 'með sæmð ok heiðri ok fullum friði' (258) (with honor and glory and in complete peace) (259). The saga's final sentence reiterates that this saga is not only a tale about honour but also the story of a loving and exemplary couple, for 'lýkr hér

þessari sögu af þeim ágæta Erex kóngi ok hans frú, hinni vænu Evida' (258) (here
ends the saga of that excellent King Erex and his wife, the beautiful Evida) (259).

Notes

[1] Subsequent references to *Parcevals saga* are to Wolf's edition and Maclean's translation (1999).
[2] Subsequent references to *Ívens saga* are to Kalinke's edition and translation (1999).
[3] Subsequent references to *Erex saga* are to Kalinke's edition and translation (1999).

Reference List

Texts and Translations

Erex saga

Erex saga Artuskappa, ed. F. W. Blaisdell, Editiones Arnamagnæanæ, B, 19 (Copenhagen, 1965).

Erex saga, ed. and trans. M. E. Kalinke, in *Norse Romance*, II: *Knights of the Round Table*, ed. M. E. Kalinke (Cambridge, 1999), pp. 222–58.

Erex saga and Ívens saga: The Old Norse Version of Chrétien de Troyes's Erec *and* Yvain, trans. F. W. Blaisdell and M. E. Kalinke (Lincoln, NE, 1977).

The Saga of Erex, trans. M. E. Kalinke, in *Norse Romance*, II: *Knights of the Round Table*, ed. M. E. Kalinke (Cambridge, 1999), pp. 223–59.

Ívens saga

Ívens saga, ed. by M. E. Kalinke, in *Norse Romance*, II: *Knights of the Round Table*, ed. M. E. Kalinke (Cambridge, 1999), pp. 38–98.

Iven's Saga, trans. M. E. Kalinke, in *Norse Romance*, II: *Knights of the Round Table*, ed. M. E. Kalinke (Cambridge, 1999), pp. 39–99.

Ívens saga, in *The Sagas of Ywain and Tristan and Other Tales. AM 489 4to* (Copenhagen, 1980), facs 46v–56v.

Ívents saga, ed. Bjarni Vilhjálmsson, in *Riddarasögur*, II (Reykjavík, 1949), pp. 1–78.

Ívents saga, in *Romances: Perg. 4:o nr 6 in The Royal Library, Stockholm*, Early Icelandic Manuscripts in Facsimile, X (Copenhagen, 1972), facs 24–39.

Ívents saga, ed. F. W. Blaisdell, Editiones Arnamagnæanæ, B, 18 (Copenhagen, 1979).

*Parcevals saga (*with *Valvens þáttr)*

Parcevals saga, ed. Bjarni Vilhjálmsson, in *Riddarasögur*, IV (Reykjavík, 1954), pp. 195–285.

Parcevals saga. Valvens þáttr, in *Romances. Perg. 4:o nr 6 in The Royal Library, Stockholm*, Early Icelandic Manuscripts in Facsimile, X (Copenhagen, 1972), facs 39–61.

Parcevals saga, ed. K. Wolf, in *Norse Romance*, II: *Knights of the Round Table*, ed. M. E. Kalinke (Cambridge, 1999), pp. 108–82.

The Story of Parceval, trans. H. Maclean, in *Norse Romance*, II: *Knights of the Round Table*, ed. M. E. Kalinke (Cambridge, 1999), pp. 109–83.

The Tale of Gawain, trans. H. Maclean, in *Norse Romance*, II: *Knights of the Round Table*, ed. M. E. Kalinke (Cambridge, 1999), pp. 185–205.

Valvens þáttr, ed. Bjarni Vilhjálmsson, in *Riddarasögur*, IV (Reykjavík, 1954), pp. 287–314.

Valvens þáttr, ed. K. Wolf, in *Norse Romance*, II: *Knights of the Round Table*, ed. M. E. Kalinke (Cambridge, 1999), pp. 184–204.

Chrétien de Troyes's Romances

Le Chevalier au lion (Yvain), ed. M. Roques, in *Les Romans de Chrétien de Troyes*, IV (Paris, 1967).
Chrétien de Troyes. *Le Roman de Perceval ou Le Conte du Graal*, ed. W. Roach, 2nd rev. edn (Geneva and Paris, 1959).
Erec and Enide, trans. C. W. Carroll, in *Chrétien de Troyes: Arthurian Romances*, ed. W. W. Kibler (London, 1991), pp. 37–122.
Erec et Enide, ed. M. Roques, in *Les Romans de Chrétien de Troyes*, I (Paris, 1966).
The Knight with the Lion (Yvain), trans. W. W. Kibler, in *Chrétien de Troyes: Arthurian Romances* (London, 1991), pp. 295–380.
The Story of the Grail (Perceval), trans. W. W. Kibler, in *Chrétien de Troyes: Arthurian Romances* (London, 1991), pp. 381–494.

Studies

Álfrún Gunnlaugsdóttir (1982). 'Quelques aspects de *Parcevals saga*', in R. Boyer (ed.), *Les Sagas des chevaliers. Actes de la Ve Conférence internationale sur les Sagas (Toulon, juillet 1982)*, pp. 217–33.
Álfrún Gunnlaugsdóttir (1984). 'Um Parcevals sögu', *Gripla*, 6, 218–40.
Barnes, G. (1977). 'The *riddarasögur*: A medieval exercise in translation', *Saga Book of the Viking Society for Northern Research*, 19, 403–41.
Barnes, G. (1982). 'Scribes, editors, and the riddarasögur', *Arkiv för nordisk filologi*, 97, 36–51.
Barnes, G. (1984). 'Parcevals saga: riddara skuggsjá?', *Arkiv för nordisk filologi*, 99, 49–62.
Barnes, G. (1989). 'Some current issues in riddarasögur research', *Arkiv för nordisk filologi*, 104, 73–88.
Barnes, G. (1993). '*Parcevals saga*', in P. Pulsiano and K. Wolf (eds), *Medieval Scandinavia: An Encyclopedia*, New York and London, pp. 496–7.
Barnes, G. (2007). 'The "Discourse of counsel" and the "Translated" *riddarasögur*', in J. Quinn, K. Heslop and T. Wills (eds), *Learning and Understanding in the Old Norse World: Essays in Honour of Margaret Clunies Ross*, Turnhout, pp. 375–97.
Blaisdell, F. W. (1964). 'The composition of the interpolated chapter in Erex saga', *Scandinavian Studies*, 36, 118–26.
Clover, C. (1974). 'Scene in saga-composition', *Arkiv för nordisk filologi*, 89, 57–83.
Farrier, S. E. (1990). 'Erex saga and the reshaping of Chrétien's Erec et Enide', *Arthurian Interpretations*, 4, 1–11.
Foote, P. G. (1969). 'Gangandi greiði', in Bjarni Guðnason, Halldór Halldórsson and Jónas Kristjánsson (eds), *Einarsbók. Afmæliskveðja til Einars Ól. Sveinssonar. 12. desember 1969,* Reykjavík, pp. 45–58.
Hallberg, P. (1971). 'Norröna riddarsagor. Några språkdrag', *Arkiv för nordisk filologi*, 86, 114–38.
Halvorsen, E. F. (1962). 'Høvisk litteratur', in *Kulturhistorisk leksikon for nordisk middelalder fra vikingetid til reformationstid*, 7, Copenhagen, cols 308–13.
Halvorsen, E. F. (1973). 'Norwegian court literature in the Middle Ages', *Orkney Miscellany*, 5, 17–26.
Hanna Steinunn Þorleifsdóttir (2007). 'Dialogue in the Icelandic copies of Ívens saga', in V. Johanterwage and S. Würth (eds), *Übersetzen im skandinavischen Mittelalter*, Studia Medievalia Septentrionalia, 14, Vienna, 2007, pp. 167–76.
Jakobsen, A. (1988). 'Et misforstått tekststed i *Erex saga*', *Maal og Minne*, 185–7.
Jakobsen, A. (1989). 'Var oversetteren av Erex saga islending?', in B. Eithun, E. F. Halvorsen, M. Rindal and E. Simensen (eds), *Festskrift til Finn Hødnebø 29. desember 1989*, Oslo, pp. 130–41.
Jónas Kristjánsson (1988). *Eddas and Sagas: Iceland's Medieval Literature*, trans. Peter Foote, Reykjavík.

Jordan, N. (2007). 'Eine alte und doch immer neue Geschichte. Die *Ívents saga Artúskappa* und der *Iwein* Hartmanns von Aue als Bearbeitungen von Chrétiens *Yvain*', in V. Johanterwage and S. Würth (eds), *Übersetzen im skandinavischen Mittelalter*, Studia Medievalia Septentrionalia, 14, Vienna, 2007, pp. 123–39.

Kalinke, M. E. (1970). 'The structure of the *Erex saga*', *Scandinavian Studies*, 42, 343–55.

Kalinke, M. E. (1971). 'A structural comparison of Chrétien de Troyes' *Erec et Enide* and the Norse *Erex saga*', *Mediaeval Scandinavia*, 4, 54–65.

Kalinke, M. E. (1973). 'Honor: the motivating principle of the *Erex saga*', *Scandinavian Studies*, 45, 135–43.

Kalinke, M. E. (1975). 'Characterization in *Erex saga* and *Ívens saga*', *Modern Language Studies*, 5, 11–19.

Kalinke, M. E. (1979). 'Alliteration in *Ívens saga*', *Modern Language Review*, 74, 871–83.

Kalinke, M. E. (1981). *King Arthur, North-by-Northwest: The* matière de Bretagne *in Old Norse-Icelandic Romances*, Bibliotheca Arnamagnæana, 37, Copenhagen.

Kalinke, M. E. (1985). 'Norse romance (*riddarasögur*)', in C. J. Clover and J. Lindow (eds), *Old Norse-Icelandic Literature: A Critical Guide*, Ithaca, NY, pp. 316–63.

Kalinke, M. E. (1994). 'The cowherd and the saint: the grateful lion in Icelandic folklore and legend', *Scandinavian Studies*, 66, 1–22.

Kalinke, M. E. (1996). 'Scandinavia', in N. J. Lacy (ed.), *Medieval Arthurian Literature: A Guide to Recent Research*, New York and London, pp. 83–119.

Kalinke, M. E. (2002). 'The saga of Parceval the knight', in A. Groos and N. J. Lacy (eds), *Perceval/Parzival: A Case Book*, New York and London, pp. 223–40.

Kjær, J. (1992). 'Franco-Scandinavian literary transmission in the Middle Ages: Two Old Norse translations of Chrétien de Troyes – Ívens saga and Erex saga', in K. Busby (ed.), *The Arthurian Yearbook*, New York, pp. 113–34.

Kramarz-Bein, S. (1999). 'Höfische Unterhaltung und ideologisches Ziel. Das Beispiel der altnorwegischen *Parcevals saga*', in S. T. Andersen (ed.), *Die Aktualität der Saga. Festschrift für Hans Schottmann*, Ergänzungsbände zum Reallexikon der Germanischen Altertumskunde, 21, Berlin and New York, pp. 63–84.

Kramarz-Bein, S. (2007). 'Die altnorwegische *Parcevals saga* im Spannungsfeld ihrer Quelle und der mittelhochdeutschen und mittelenglischen Parzival-Überlieferug', in B. Besamusca and F. Brandsma (eds), *Arthurian Literature*, XXIV: *The European Dimensions of Arthurian Literature*, Cambridge, pp. 135–56.

Kratz, H. (1977a). 'The *Parcevals saga* and *Li contes del Graal*', *Scandinavian Studies*, 49, 13–47.

Kratz, H. (1977b). 'Textus, Braull and gangandi greiði', *Saga Book of the Viking Society*, 19, 371–82.

Kretschmer, B. (1982). *Höfische und altwestnordische Erzähltradition in den Riddarasögur. Studien zur Rezeption der altfranzösischen Artusepik am Beispiel der* Erex saga, Ívens saga *und* Parcevals saga, Hattingen.

Psaki, F. R. (2002). 'Women's counsel in the riddarasögur: the case of *Parcevals saga*', in S. M. Anderson and K. Swenson (eds), *Cold Counsel: Women in Old Norse Literature and Mythology*, New York and London, pp. 201–24.

Schach, P. (1975). 'Some observations on the translations of Brother Robert', in *Les Relations littéraires franco-scandinaves au Moyen Age. Actes du Colloque de Liège*, Paris, pp. 117–35.

Weber, G. W. (1986). 'The decadence of feudal myth: towards a theory of *riddarasaga* and romance', in J. Lindow, L. Lönnroth and G. W. Weber (eds), *Structure and Meaning in Old Norse Literature*, Odense, pp. 415–54.

7

THE OLD SWEDISH *HÆRRA IVAN LEONS RIDDARE*

William Layher

The Arthurian romance *Hærra Ivan Leons riddare* 'Sir Ivan, the Knight with the Lion' is one of a trio of Old Swedish works translated during the years 1303–12 at the Norwegian court of Hákon V Magnússon (r.1299–1319) and his wife, Queen Eufemia. Although the Norwegian royal line had a distinguished tradition of literary patronage – Hákon's grandfather Hákon IV Hákonarson (r.1217–63) had a number of Arthurian romances and other courtly texts translated into Old Norse during his reign – the three Old Swedish texts were translated not at the king's behest but rather under the direction of Queen Eufemia (d.1312). Known collectively as the *Eufemiavisor* or 'Eufemia-poems' (a term coined by scholars but not attested in the medieval record), these romances are *Hærra Ivan* (1303), a unique and otherwise unattested bridal-quest epic called *Hertig Fredrik af Normandie* (1308?) and *Flores och Blanzeflor* (1312).

    Hærra Ivan marks a new development in the reception of Arthurian narrative in early fourteenth-century Norway – new not just for reasons of content, but also for reasons associated with its unique literary form. In contrast to the prose *Ívens saga* that preceded it, *Hærra Ivan* was translated into rhyming *Knittelvers* in Old Swedish. Indeed, *Hærra Ivan* is defined by a series of firsts: first work of secular literature in Old Swedish; first use of end rhyme in narrative in the North; first text translated for the edification of a foreign audience; first work of literature in medieval Scandinavia whose patron was known to be a woman. The relevance of *Hærra Ivan*, then, is not limited to its retelling of the tale of the knight with the lion, although the romance certainly offers interesting insights into the Arthurian reception on the Scandinavian mainland. Rather, its literary value rests chiefly with the fact that, save for the serendipitous circumstances under which it was translated, the text might never have materialized at all.

Manuscript transmission

The manuscript transmission of the *Eufemiavisor* does not reach back to Eufemia's time. The Old Swedish romances survive only in copies from the fifteenth or early sixteenth centuries, with the exception of a single vellum leaf of *Flores och Blanzeflor* that was written around 1350. *Hærra Ivan* is transmitted in six manuscripts, all of them miscellanies and all in Stockholm. ABCEF are in the Royal Library; manuscript D is at the National Archives (Riksarkivet).

A. Cod. Holm. D4, folio, paper and vellum (*c.*1430), 2r–57r. On the table of contents for this manuscript (the vellum leaf 1rv), the romance is entitled *Aff herra iwan oc herra gaffwian* 'Concerning Sir Ivan and Sir Gawain'.

B. Cod. Holm. D4a, known as 'Codex Verelianus' or 'Fru Märetas bok', folio, paper (1448), 207–349. The text is prefaced by a rubric on fol. 207: *Här byggyndäs en book aff konung artus och hans ärligom mannom och aff herra wadion rödh* 'Here begins a book about King Arthur and his valiant men and about Sir Wadein the Red'.

C. Cod. Holm. D3, known as 'Fru Elins bok', folio, paper (1488), 3–168. The romance lacks a title.

D. Skokloster-samlingen E8822 [was Cod. Skokloster 156], folio, paper (second. half of the fifteenth century), 34v–72v. The text appears under the rubric *Her æwter star en sagæ aff H iwan fager ath høræ* 'Now comes a tale about S(ir) Ivan, pleasant to hear'. This manuscript contains only the first 3354 verses.

E. Cod. Holm K4, folio, paper (1450–1500), 78r–162v. This version of *Hærra Ivan* is in Old Danish. The text, a fragment lacking a title or other rubric, breaks off after verse 5272.

F. Cod. Holm. K47, quarto, paper (*c.*1500, no later than 1504), 1r–111v. Another version of the romance in Old Danish, this *Hærra Ivan* bears the title *Om Kong Artus oc Keyser Karol Magnus* 'Concerning King Arthur and Emperor Charlemagne' that was written in a younger hand in the margin.

None of the extant versions of *Hærra Ivan* was copied from another. While the redactions in the manuscripts A, B, C, D, E appear to derive from a single common source, version F – the youngest of the surviving copies – was translated into Old Danish from a unique branch of the Old Swedish transmission, a source that often preserved a more original wording (Noreen edn 1931, xii–xiii). It is unsurprising that *Hærra Ivan* and other texts from the Old Swedish literary corpus were translated into Old Danish in the late fifteenth century, for the 'distance' that separated these two languages (linguistically, culturally, geographically) was easily overcome. What is notable in the transmission of *Hærra Ivan* is that both of the Old Danish versions (E and F) were produced independently of one another, indicating a livelier reception in the southern regions of this literary/cultural area than is commonly realized.

Despite the fact that the translations were undertaken at the Norwegian court, the *Eufemiavisor* remained exclusively within the East Norse tradition. There is no evidence of an Icelandic or Norwegian reception of the romances. While we cannot trace the path of the manuscript transmission from original translation to the oldest copy D4 (*c.*1430), we do know that manuscripts of *Hærra Ivan* and *Hertig Fredrik* were held at a royal castle along the west coast of Sweden in 1340. This information is gleaned from a written inventory prepared in that year for King Magnus Eriksson of Sweden (r.1319–64) and Norway (r.1319–43), Eufemia's grandson, which lists many of the costly items in Bohus castle, near present-day Göteborg. Included in this document – alongside mention of leather shoes, furniture, barrels of fish and spices, polar bear skins and tournament helmets – is an extensive list of books that were either in the king's possession or loaned (or perhaps gifted) to others, among them two of the *Eufemiavisor*, namely *unum Yvan* 'an Ivan' and *i. librum de hærtogh Fræthrik* 'the book about Duke Fredrik' (Lange and Unger edn 1847, 3.1, 179). Although the title of *Hærra Ivan* is reproduced in the inventory in a casual, abbreviated manner, as *unum Yvan*, it is notable that the other text, *Hertig Fredrik*, is identified in more detail. The disparity in titles may well indicate that *Hærra Ivan* was sufficiently well known as a work of literature for a more elaborate description to be unnecessary, whereas *Hertig Fredrik* was still considered obscure in 1340, so that for the purposes of the inventory (and its subsequent readers) a fuller identification was necessary.

Editions

The first edition of *Hærra Ivan* (Liffman and Stephens, 1845–9) offered a diplomatic text, based on the oldest manuscript, Cod. Holm. D4 from the first decades of the fourteenth century, a (more or less) systematic account of manuscript variants and a detailed overview – one that is still consulted today – of each of the six manuscripts of *Hærra Ivan*. In addition, admirers of the 'New Philology' will appreciate Liffman and Stephens's prescience in including a folio-sized foldout leaf in this edition, on which was printed, in parallel columns, the same passage from the romance in all six manuscripts and, for the sake of comparison, from two Icelandic manuscripts of *Ívens saga*. Unfortunately the text of the 1849 edition was riddled with minor errors, and the apparatus was unwieldy.[1]

These deficits were addressed almost a hundred years later in the critical edition by Erik Noreen (1931), which was based on the oldest manuscript, Cod. Holm. D4. Noreen's edition is authoritative and reliable, but it reflects the editorial practice of its day: the text is highly reconstructed and occasionally Noreen departs from his lead manuscript in order to incorporate variants he considered more original. His judgements were far from haphazard, however, and the interested scholar may consult Noreen's archive of notes and deliberations, which offer a behind-the-scenes look at his editorial process and a justification for his emendations (Noreen 1929). Despite its minor inconsistencies the Noreen edition is the standard work on *Hærra Ivan*, and the foundation for any critical engagement with the text.

The first English translation of the entire text brought *Hærra Ivan* before an international audience (Williams and Palmgren trans. 1999).[2] The English translation was published in facing-page format, opposite an edition of the Old Swedish text that is based on Noreen's edition, yet not identical to it. Williams did not set out to replace Noreen's edition, but rather to improve upon it by rectifying some of Noreen's emendations and bringing the Old Swedish text into closer conformity with its lead manuscript, D4 (Williams and Palmgren edn 1999, 7–9). With this edition the reader can easily reconstruct the exact wording of the oldest version of *Hærra Ivan*. For broader inquiries into the textual history of *Hærra Ivan*, however, the Noreen edition, with its robust apparatus, will continue to be essential.

Author

The translator of *Hærra Ivan Leons riddare* is anonymous.[3] Since the translation of the *Eufemiavisor* is so deeply indebted to the precise alignment of specific cultural, literary and political factors at the Oslo court in the early fourteenth century there is good reason to conclude that only a small handful of candidates would have possessed all of the necessary prerequisites to complete the task. One such candidate was Peter Algotsson, a well-educated aristocrat from a powerful dynasty in Västergötland, who in 1288 was forced into a lengthy political exile at the Norwegian court. Son of a lawman and brother of a bishop, Peter was made a canon of Skara cathedral in 1278. His career soon turned to politics, however, and in 1279 he became the chancellor of the Swedish King Magnus Ladulås. Peter may well have been involved in diplomatic errands for the Swedish monarchy as early as 1273, as there is a letter from Duke Johann of Braunschweig attesting that a certain Petrus Camerarius was despatched there from the Swedish court in order to negotiate a marriage contract – presumably because Peter had a university education (later documents name him 'magister Petrus') and some facility with the German language.[4] His fortunes turned in 1288, when he left his royal position and fled to Norway. Peter soon was taken up into Norwegian political circles. In the early 1290s Peter was sent to the courts of England and Scotland to negotiate marriages for the Norwegian king – nothing came of these overtures, and soon the king's interest swung to possible alliances in the Baltic region – but the errands confirm that Peter was held in high regard, and, further, that he had deep and first-hand knowledge of the chivalric ways of various courts in northern Europe. Indeed, there is a letter sent in 1293 from King Edward I of England to Peter (published in the collection of Norwegian diplomata), thanking him in very warm terms for the falcons and hawks he had sent as a gift (Lange and Unger edn 1847, 19, 422–3). In sum, Peter Algotsson – or someone very much like him – had the skills necessary to undertake the task of producing the first rhyming works in Old Swedish: an intimate knowledge of foreign languages and their customs, a long-standing record of diplomatic service to the monarchy, and a position that kept him at the Oslo court as an intimate of the royal house. With regard to Peter's literary abilities, it is worth noting that Peter's older brother, Brynolf Algotsson, bishop of Skara, is known as the first poet in medieval Sweden to compose rhyming verse in Latin. A flair for literary composition may have run in the family.

Regardless of the translator's actual identity, *Hærra Ivan* and *Flores och Blanzeflor* attest his facility with Old French, while *Hertig Fredrik af Normandie* ('Duke Fredrik of Normandy') shows that he knew German as well. The source of *Hertig Fredrik* was a bridal-quest romance written in Middle Low German or a dialect incorporating many northern German linguistic features (see Layher 2000, 2002, 2003). Scholars have long doubted that *Hærra Ivan* was based solely on Chrétien's *Yvain*. Since the 1870s scholarship has maintained that *Hærra Ivan* (and to a lesser extent *Flores och Blanzeflor*) demonstrates that the translator also had a working knowledge of Old Norse, since some of the unique aspects of the Old Swedish romances – minor details or turns of phrase which were not derived from the Old French sources – are also attested in the thirteenth-century Norse translations of the same works (*Ívens saga* and *Flóres saga ok Blankiflúr*), which were almost certainly still in circulation at the Norwegian court. The implication is that the Old Swedish poet borrowed occasionally from *Ívens saga*, lifting phrases and motifs from it when his French text left something to be desired (Klockhoff 1881; Kölbing 1872, xii–xxxviii; Nordfelt 1920). While the parallels between *Hærra Ivan* and *Ívens saga* are indeed intriguing, a new look at their interconnections is urgently needed, especially since one of the most detailed treatments of this topic, found in Kölbing's introduction to his edition of *Ívens saga* (1872), was based on an incomplete understanding of the manuscript filiations and the textual variation in the redactions.

Few if any of the claims of literary borrowing prove that the Old Swedish translator could have acquired his innovative details *only* from *Ívens saga*, and indeed there is ironclad evidence that the translator of *Hærra Ivan* had access to additional channels of Arthurian reception unknown to us. In verse 73 of *Hærra Ivan* the sharp-tongued Sir Kay at Arthur's court is described as *hærra Kæyæ quaþsprak* 'Sir Kay the slanderer' (Williams and Palmgren edn. 1999, v. 73). The epithet *quaþsprak* is a loan from Middle Low German or Middle Dutch (MLG *quât* evil, malice; *sprake* 'speech' [Schiller and Lübben 1875–81, III, 398; IV, 341]). It is unclear how this word ended up in the Old Swedish *Hærra Ivan*, since both *Yvain* and *Ívens saga* describe Sir Kay's speech in this passage – his propensity to malicious, slanderous commentary – but do not give him a descriptive surname. But the fact that this same word appears in a similar context in Hartmann von Aue's translation of Chrétien's *Erec et Enide* from the late twelfth century – *von sînem valsche er was genant / Keiîn der quâtspreche* 'on account of his untruthfulness he was called Kei the *quâtspreche*' (Cormeau and Gärtner edn 1985, vv. 4663–4)[5] – is evidence of Ripuarian or Low German/Dutch influence reflected in the Middle High German *Erec* and Old Swedish *Hærra Ivan*. By what means this term reached the Swedish translator shortly after 1300 we do not know.

The case of *quaþsprak* is just one example in which a distinctive word, phrase or scene in *Hærra Ivan* cannot be traced back to *Ívens saga*. Another example – one frequently cited as the *locus classicus* proving that *Hærra Ivan* borrowed from *Ívens saga* (Hunt 1975, 171) – is the prologue of the Old Swedish romance, where the poet sets the scene by introducing Arthur and Charlemagne as 'þe værþoghasta konunga tva / þær man æ hørþe sagt i fra' (the two most worthy kings / about whom stories have ever been told) (Williams and Palmgren edn 1999, vv. 5–6). The pairing of Charlemagne and Arthur is not attested in Chrétien, but it does occur in the prologue to *Ívens saga*.

> Hinn ágæti kóngr Artúrus réð fyrir Englandi, sem mörgum mönnum er kunnigt. Hann var um síðir kóngr yfir Rómaborg. Hann er þeira kónga frægastr er verit hafa þann veg frá hafinu ok vinsælastr annarr en Karlamagnús.
>
> (The excellent King Arthur ruled England, as is known to many. After a time he became king of Rome. He was the most illustrious of the kings who had lived on this side of the ocean and the most popular other than Charlemagne.) (Kalinke edn and trans. 1999, 38–9)

Does this prove that the Swedish translator borrowed the detail from *Ívens saga*? It does not, if we consider that the twinned references in the saga do not stress an equivalency between Arthur and Charlemagne – as is the case in *Hærra Ivan* – and that the saga merely refers to Charlemagne as a means of underscoring Arthur's popularity: he is the most popular king other than Charlemagne. And further, the reference to Arthur being king of Rome reflects an understanding that had a widespread distribution prior to the translation of *Hærra Ivan*, and presumably derives from Geoffrey of Monmouth's account in the *Historia regum Britanniae* of Arthur's military campaigns against the Romans. The *Historia regum Britanniae* was translated in Iceland at the beginning of the thirteenth century and became known as *Breta sögur* (Kalinke 2009, 185; Würth 1998, 81–2). The Arthurian section of the *Historia* is thus the oldest Arthurian narrative in the North. One of the two redactions of *Breta sögur* is the so-called *Hauksbók* (AM 544 4to), a compendious codex produced between 1301 and 1314 and named after its compiler Haukr Erlendsson, a native Icelander who moved to Norway in 1301, where he served as lawman until his death in 1334. Thus, Geoffrey's Arthurian narrative presumably was available in Norway, either in the original Latin or, what may be more likely, in the Icelandic manuscript that Haukr used as the basis for his redaction of *Breta sögur*.

Patronage and date

Ultimately the translation of *Hærra Ivan* was undertaken because of the efforts of one key person: its patron, Queen Eufemia of Norway, who married the Norwegian Duke Hákon Magnússon in 1299. Eufemia, a northern German noblewoman, was raised at the court of Duke Witzlaw II of Rügen, a powerful and influential figure in the Baltic region and long-standing ally of the Danish king. She probably was Witzlaw's youngest daughter, but due to incomplete and sometimes contradictory data in the chronicle records it cannot be proved that this was the case; Witzlaw II may have been Eufemia's father, her foster-father or perhaps her grandfather. To be sure, the oldest document mentioning her, a Hanseatic report from 1299 announcing the upcoming engagement of Eufemia to Hákon, claims that she was the *filiam principis Rujanorum* 'daughter of the prince of Rügen' (*Hanserecesse* 1870–97, 1, 42), and in 1302 Witzlaw II himself referred to Eufemia as *domine regine norwegie filie mee predelicte* in his will and testament – he used the same wording to refer to his other daughters Margareta and Helene (Fabricius edn 1841–58, 3, 128f.). The testimony of both of these charters, contemporary with the events they mention, strongly suggests that Witzlaw II was indeed her father. The issue is relevant to Eufemia's engagement as a literary patron if we consider that Witzlaw's son, Witzlaw III of Rügen, was famed as a Minnesänger in his own right. Witzlaw III claims to have learned to compose courtly stanzas as a child under the direction of a poet known as 'der Ungelærde' (the unlearned) at the Rügen court in Stralsund, who also may have served as an inspiration for Eufemia, the younger sister of Witzlaw III. On Eufemia's role as literary patron see Mitchell (1997), Layher (1999), Würth (2000).

Hákon's marriage to Eufemia was a political masterstroke for the Norwegian monarchy. It successfully altered the balance of power in the region by forging a closer alliance between Norway and territories that held long-standing ties to Denmark. In the same way, the translation of *Hærra Ivan* can also be seen as a diplomatic overture towards the East, one that marks a deliberate shift in Norwegian politics in the years around 1299. Prior to this Norway had traditionally considered its sphere of influence to include England, Scotland, the Scottish islands, Iceland and the Faroes, but with the marriage to Eufemia and the production of the Old Swedish romances came a reorientation of political and cultural sensibilities: the gaze was now directed to the South-east, that is, toward Sweden.

The tale of *Yvain* was already well known in Norway by the time the Old Swedish *Hærra Ivan* appeared. The Old Norse *Ívens saga* was translated during the reign of Hákon Hákonarson (r.1217–63) and its Old French source may well have remained at the Norwegian court. The apparent redundancy presses the question of why another rendition, one translated into an unfamiliar foreign idiom, might have seemed desirable in the early fourteenth century. *Hærra Ivan* was indeed an old and familiar tale, but it was cloaked in a new guise and designed for cultural export. Its ostensible function, as we understand it today, was to bind its intended recipient, a Swedish nobleman, more closely to the Norwegian monarchy in the years just after 1300. Thus we see the transformation of an Arthurian tale into a political overture.

According to the colophon at the end of *Hærra Ivan* the romance was translated in 1303. The relevant passage provides details about the translation:

> Þa þusand vinter, þry hundraþ ar
> fran Guþs føþilse liþin var
> ok þær til þry, i þæn sama tima

varþ þæsse bokin giorþ til rima.
Eufemia drotning, þæt maghin I tro,
læt þæssa bokena vænda svo
af valske tungo ok a vart mal
– Guþ naþe þe æþla frugho sial –
þær drotning ivir Norghe var
mæþ Guþs miskun þrættan ar. (Williams and Palmgren edn 1999, vv. 6431–40)

(When one thousand winters, three hundred years
had passed since God's birth
and another three, that is when
this book was turned into verse.
Queen Eufemia, you may believe me,
had this book translated
from French into our language
– God have mercy on the noble lady's soul –
who was queen of Norway
for thirteen years by the grace of God.) (Williams and Palmgren trans. 1999, vv. 6431–40)[6]

The date 1303 indicates that *Hærra Ivan* was the first of the three *Eufemiavisor* to be translated, but this chronology is subject to some debate. While there is no disagreement that *Flores och Blanzeflor* was the third in the series – the colophon is unambiguous in all manuscripts that the work was completed 'shortly before she [Eufemia] died' (Olson edn 1921, v. 2185) – it cannot be proved that *Hærra Ivan* was the first. The unresolved issue concerns the date of translation of *Hertig Fredrik af Normandie*, which according to the manuscripts may have occurred in 1300 or 1301 or as late as 1308. The question of primacy is relevant inasmuch as it determines with which text the 'breakthrough' in Old Swedish literature was accomplished – with the translation of a familiar and canonical Arthurian romance held in high renown, *Hærra Ivan*, or with the exuberant, slightly untidy and obscure *Hertig Fredrik*. Attempts to answer the question by clarifying the relative chronology of *Hærra Ivan* and *Hertig Fredrik* through an evaluation of their stylistic quirks (comparing the rhythm of their *Knittelvers* lines, for example, or their degree of literary borrowing) have not produced reliable results (see Sawicki 1939; Jansson 1945). Nevertheless, given the lingering uncertainty over the date of translation for *Hertig Fredrik* the scholarly consensus should prevail that *Hærra Ivan* was the first of the *Eufemiavisor* to be translated.

There is no evidence that Eufemia spoke Swedish or any other Nordic language. Neither was Swedish the language of Eufemia's husband nor her court. It is obvious, then, that the *Eufemiavisor* were intended for a specific, foreign recipient. That person was in all likelihood the distinguished and highly accomplished Swedish nobleman Erik Magnusson, Duke of Södermanland and brother of King Birger Magnusson of Sweden. In 1302 Erik was betrothed to Eufemia and Hákon's only child, their infant daughter Ingebjörg. In 1303, the following year – if the chronology of the *Eufemiavisor* is credible – *Hærra Ivan* was translated. The Old Swedish romances appear to have been intended as literary gifts for Erik Magnusson, translated into his native tongue in order to strengthen and uphold his fidelity to the Norwegian court until such time as the lengthy (and occasionally politically turbulent) engagement could be brought to its fruition in marriage in 1312. Indeed, the trio of romances and their dates of translation have been conveniently 'mapped' on to the chronology of the engagement of Erik and Ingebjörg, with each of the romances appearing to respond to a specific moment in this relationship. If the heady days of the engagement's early years are celebrated by the gift of *Hærra Ivan*, then the nadir of the engagement, when political tensions between King Hákon Magnússon and Erik threatened to cancel the betrothal, could well be marked by the appearance of *Hertig Fredrik* in 1308, which enthralls the listener with a tale about a crafty knight whose love for a sequestered princess enables him to persevere against her antagonistic and overly protective father. By the same token *Flores och Blanzeflor*, the last romance translated in 1312, celebrates the story of two ideal lovers who against all odds and despite all sorts of delays finally marry. This attractive yet rather simplistic view of literary patronage as a compassionate queen's attempt at social outreach to a potential son-in-law (or perhaps better: as an attempt at foreign policy?) and as an admonition to fulfil marital duties is deep-rooted in the scholarship on the *Eufemiavisor*, and perhaps in need of revision. But if we return to the appearance of *Hærra Ivan* in 1303 and the question of its primacy among the *Eufemiavisor*, the notion of translation as 'gift' provides additional support in favour of *Hærra Ivan* being the first of the Old Swedish romances to be completed. At the same time this view allows us to discount romantic notions about Eufemia's literary patronage being motivated by the content of the romances and their ostensible 'message' to Erik Magnusson.[7] If we regard the *Eufemiavisor* as unique and therefore highly valuable repositories of cultural capital in Old Swedish, then it follows that *Hærra Ivan*, a romance of international renown, would be the first text to appear in that tongue because the value of *Yvain* had already been demonstrated at the Norwegian court through the Old Norse translation. It stands to reason that the most appropriate vehicle for the literary innovations introduced in the *Eufemiavisor* would be a text whose worth was already established. As an end-rhymed, Old Swedish romance *Hærra Ivan* becomes a literary work suffused with exponential cultural, and therefore also political, value.

Source

Hærra Ivan is a translation of Chrétien's *Yvain*, but we do not know which branch of the *Yvain* transmission was the basis. Although the translator's skill with Old French is indisputable, several of the discontinuities that exist between *Hærra Ivan* and *Yvain* suggest that at times he misread his source manuscript or, equally possible, retained a variant that was transmitted in that particular source. One example is v. 2267, which describes how Sir Ivan is discovered sleeping by a lady on horseback accompanied by *iomfrughor þre* 'three damsels' instead of the usual two. This detail is found only in manuscripts A, F, G of *Yvain* (Foerster edn 1965, v. 2889). A similar situation obtains in lines 4666–9 of *Hærra Ivan*, describing the two monstrous 'sons of the Devil' against whom Sir Ivan must fight. In *Yvain* these men are said to be the offspring of a mixed union between a demon and a human mother. The Old Swedish text claims that one of them was born of woman while the other was born of a sheep (*aff et far*) – a rendering of the Old French text that seems nonsensical, even comic, but manuscript S from the thirteenth century is corrupt and reads *mouton* 'sheep' instead of *netun* 'demon': 'Que de fame et de muton furent' (Foerster edn 1965, v. 5273), and this suggests that the manuscript from which *Hærra Ivan* was translated had the corrupt reading. Until a comparative analysis of the entire manuscript transmission of both texts has been undertaken, no firm conclusions can be drawn about the French source used by the Swedish translator.

The translator of *Hærra Ivan* worked judiciously, making few substantial changes to the overarching scope of the romance. It has been claimed that of all the vernacular translations of *Yvain* the Old Swedish *Hærra Ivan* comes closest in length to the French romance, totalling 6446 verses to the 6818 verses in Chrétien (Hunt 1975, 70). While the numbers are indisputable they do not paint a complete picture of the translator's fidelity to his source. The translator omitted or condensed a considerable amount of Chrétien's rhetoric (see Coffer 1976; Hunt 1975), but at the same time his occasionally prolix tendencies and his predilection for padding his verses with courtly formulas and other formulaic phrases have added to the total length. The sum of the difference between *Yvain* and *Hærra Ivan* is thus more than the disparity of 372 verses.

There are few outright innovations, but J. Sullivan has identified some intriguing shifts of emphasis in the representation of youth and older age in the 'Pesme Aventure' (Dire Adventure) episode of *Hærra Ivan* (Sullivan 2009, 110–13) and of this episode in the *Yvain* tradition as a whole (Sullivan 2007). Another striking change occurs in the characterization of the lion in *Hærra Ivan*. In the Old Swedish romance the animal appears to be female. Although the Swedish word for 'lion' is neuter in the dragon/ lion episode – *et leon* (v. 2695) and *leonit* (v. 2698) – whenever the pronoun occurs it is feminine, such as *hon* as subject (v. 2726) and *hænne* and *hana* as object (vv. 2737, 2743). The shift in gender is especially notable because of the added emphasis it lends to the lion's expressions of grief during the so-called suicide scene, which in *Hærra Ivan* (as in *Ívens saga* also) is marked not by the beast's attempted suicide but by its service to the unconscious hero: the lion takes Sir Ivan's sharp sword in its mouth – 'hon tok sværþit mæþ sinne tan' (v. 2837) – and removes it to a safe distance so that the hero will not injure himself further (vv. 2839–46). The lion's grief in this scene over the apparent death of its lord is expressed most intensely: the lion 'lop ater ok fram þæræ, / sum hon monde galin væræ / mæþ iæmerlik lat ok skriaþe sva / at þæt var ømkæ at høræ pa' (ran back and forth, / as if it were crazy, / with distressing cries and such howling / that it was sad to hear) (vv. 2841–4). The re-gendering of the lion through the use of the feminine pronoun *hon*, even though the Swedish noun *leon* is neuter, causes this highly emotional passage to ring with echoes of a previous scene, namely the lament of Wadein's widow who, like the lion, mourns the loss of her male hero. The Swedish poet describes the enraged courtiers searching for the invisible Sir Ivan 'sum þæt leon þær grymæst ær, / þær se þe diur ok ække fær' (like the fiercest lion / which sees the animals but cannot catch them) (vv. 919–20), a characterization unique to the Old Swedish text which, through its use of the lion simile, anticipates the later scene in the woods, when the lion (like Wadein's widow) is desperate to avenge the wounds Ivan has suffered but can see no adversary to attack. The analogy is underscored by the use of the same word to describe the inarticulate laments of both grieving parties (the widow and the lion) – their mourning is *ømkelik* 'pitiable' (vv. 945, 2832). The lion simile recurs to characterize the ferocity of Ivan's combat with Count Aliers and his army, in that the poet describes Sir Ivan riding on the battlefield 'ræt sum en leon þær varþer vreþ' (just like a lion turned angry) (v. 2516). The oddity is that the lion here is *en leon*, that is, masculine, a shift in the grammatical gender of the noun from neuter to masculine that facilitates an understanding of that animal as a symbol for the valiant and virile Sir Ivan. And finally, although the word 'lion' occurs in all three genders in Old Swedish, it is telling that the only attested use of the feminine pronoun for this animal is found in *Hærra Ivan*. This raises the possibility that the shift was deliberate and that in this romance Sir Ivan's companion was meant to be understood as female.

Some peculiarities in the Old Swedish lexicon of the oldest manuscript of *Hærra Ivan* may offer some clues about the nature of the source of the translation. *Hærra Ivan* was copied into Cod. Holm D4 by two hands, with hand 1 responsible for the first part of the text and hand 2 for its remainder. But hand 2 also left his mark on the earlier parts of *Hærra Ivan*, in that this scribe retroactively corrected a few words of the text that had been entered by hand 1. For example, on six occasions on fol. 2r and 2v the word *mælte* 'he/she said' was crossed out and the synonyms *sagdhe* or *taladhe* inserted in its place. The most logical explanation for these changes is that it is an attempt to exercise 'quality control' over the text. The systematic deletion of the term *mælte* (which was far more common in Old Danish and Old Norwegian than in Old Swedish) appears to be motivated by concerns about readership. It is tempting to see the improvements introduced by hand 2 as an attempt to compensate for the linguistic deficits of the copyist's exemplar, which may well have been produced in a milieu close to Oslo, thus making the romance appear more 'Swedish' and therefore better positioned to appeal to a Swedish audience.

Literary context

Hærra Ivan does not represent the full extent of the Swedish reception of Arthurian material in the early fourteenth century. Further points of contact are documented elsewhere, such as in *Hertig Fredrik af Normandie* – where an ostensibly Arthurian narrative arc is grafted rather clumsily onto a bridal-quest epic structure (Layher 2003, 70–4) – and in *Fornsvenska Legendariet* 'Old Swedish Legendary' (Stephens edn 1847–58), a devotional and hagiographic compilation translated into Old Swedish between 1276 and 1307. The Old Swedish Legendary contains an intriguing digression about the death of Arthur and the torment of his soul that cannot be linked to any known source.

The legendary was probably compiled, translated and written at one of the prominent Swedish monasteries such as Skänninge or Skara. Its text is based on hagiographic, historiographic and devotional texts in Latin and Middle Low German. The legendary survives in eight complete or fragmentary manuscripts from the fourteenth to sixteenth centuries, but the three short Arthurian episodes discussed here are found only in a fragment dating from the earlier stages of the transmission, perhaps from as early as the beginning of the fourteenth century.[8] The dating of this fragment, Cod. Holm. A124, is subject to debate. The orthography is archaic, suggesting a dating to just after 1300 (Collijn 1913, 276–7) but linguistically the fragment seems to belong to the middle of the fourteenth century (Jansson 1934, 56). While only the second of these episodes is unique, all three give insight into specific modalities of the Swedish reception of Arthur through Latin chronicles.

The Arthurian passages have been edited and translated into English (Cross, 1961). The first episode is based on details found in Geoffrey of Monmouth's *Historia regum Britanniae*. It summarizes the main points of Arthur's biography: his conquests, his battle against the Roman emperor Leo, his wounding in battle and his retreat to another land for healing, whence he never returned. The account also describes the emblem on Arthur's shield as an image of the Virgin Mary, and acknowledges the belief of many that Arthur is still alive. The third section in Cod. Holm. A124, consisting of only three sentences, concerns Merlin. This passage gives a somewhat garbled account of Merlin's family history – 'his mother was the daughter of the King of Temecia, a nun who was never known by man though she was not a maid' – and ends with a brief reference to Merlin's written prophecies. This material is found in the *Chronicon Pontificum*. The middle section, concerning Walwanius (Gawein), is unique. According to this account there was a priest who said a daily Mass for Arthur's soul. On Midsummer's Eve, Walwanius appeared in a dream to this priest and invited him to a feast at Arthur's court. Travelling there in a dream the monk saw that the banquet was magnificent, but that strife and discord soon arose and all the men took to arms and killed one another. The next day they were raised up again. Walwanius's final message to the priest, which is couched in the *contemptus mundi* rhetoric of the

Church, explained that such were the daily torments suffered by men like Arthur, who seek worldly honour instead of the blessings of heaven. Intriguing in this exemplum is the fact that Gawain plays the familiar role as an emissary of Arthur's court. Of further interest is the similarity between the daily clashes fought by the Arthurian knights at court and the fierce battles of the *einherjar* in Valhalla, the deceased warriors who gather at Odin's mead-benches. Cross ultimately discounts these parallels (Cross 1961, 86–8), noting that a cleric well versed in homiletic literature would not need to draw upon examples from Norse mythology in order to construct an exemplum of this type.

Readership and cultural context

The different rubrics and titles given to *Hærra Ivan* in the manuscripts provide insight into how late medieval audiences regarded the romance. The rubric in the oldest manuscript, Cod. Holm. D4, *Aff herra iwan oc herra gaffwian* 'Concerning Sir Ivan and Sir Gawain', bears a striking resemblance to the title of the Middle English tale *Ywain and Gawain* from the fourteenth century, this despite the fact that Gawain's role in the Old Swedish romance is no larger than it is in Chrétien, and that no literary connection exists between the Nordic version and its fourteenth-century English counterpart. The reference to Gawain in the rubric of manuscript D4 may have been inspired by the prominent status that he held in the courtly discourses of medieval Sweden as a marker of chivalric prowess, as demonstrated by another mention of Gawain in the Old Swedish chronicle known as *Erikskrönikan* from around 1330: 'if Gawain or Perceval had been here, they would have been dressed no less sumptuously . . .' (Pipping 1963, 79). For the scribe of D4, the name Gawain may well have served as a signal and guarantor of the literary quality of the romance.

   According to a rubric at the front of the codex E8822 in the Swedish National Archives, this is a devotional manuscript copied by 'Frater Johannis de Nedrosia' for the edification of his fellow monks and other readers at the convent of Friars Minor in Bergen. This manuscript was written in a hybrid dialect known as *birgittinernorsk* (Birgittine Norwegian) that blended Norwegian with Swedish linguistic forms. It was regularly used in documents circulating among the Birgittine houses of Scandinavia, beginning in the early fifteenth century. It is unclear whether Johann of Nidaros translated his Old Swedish source into *birgittinernorsk* so as to appeal better to his readership, or whether he was simply copying a source that had already been adapted into that idiom; the witness of manuscript E8822 confirms, at least, that a manuscript of *Hærra Ivan* was circulating in this clerical milieu. For *Hærra Ivan* to appear in a devotional codex of this type is incongruous, but the fact that the romance, the last item copied into the miscellany, is described as *fager at høræ* (pleasant to hear) should not be construed as a commentary on the aesthetics of the text or on its literary appeal in fifteenth-century Norway, nor does it imply that the text was thought to possess any edifying qualities. Rather, the phrase is boilerplate scribal jargon, used to highlight texts or prayers that warrant the reader's special attention, and the phrase appears in other rubrics in this same manuscript, such as in reference to Christ's Passion on fols 5r–9v, which is *fager ath høre oc lesa* (pleasant to hear and read), the disquisition on the struggle between the body and the soul on fols 16v–21v, a *fager tingh ath høra* (pleasant matter to hear), or as a means of calling attention to the *fager tingh* on fols 24v–29v about Adam and the creation of the world. In this context the rubric for *Hærra Ivan* means simply that the romance is 'worthwhile hearing'.

The rubric for *Hærra Ivan* in manuscript D4a announces the romance by referring to King Arthur, his brave knights and, oddly enough, to the knight whom Sir Ivan kills at the fountain: 'Här byggyndäs en book aff konung artus och hans ärligom mannom och aff herra wadion rödh' (This is the beginning of a book about King Arthur and his renowned men and about Sir Wadein the Red). The name of the character called Sir Wadein the Red[9] is unique to the Old Swedish version of the tale, but the connection between this knight and a particular colour has deep roots in the *Yvain* tradition, reaching back to Chrétien's Esclados le Ros. In neither Nordic translation of *Yvain* does the name of the *Esclados* figure resemble that given by Chrétien. In the manuscript Stockholm Perg. 4:o nr 6 of *Ívens saga* the guardian of the fountain is named *Sodal raudi* 'Sodal the Red', another onomastic innovation that nevertheless preserves the crimson identity of this antagonist. He is named *Nadir* in the manuscript AM 489 4to, but the text immediately following the name is illegible. AM 489 must have included the surname 'the Red', since the manuscript Add. 4857 in the British Library, a seventeenth-century copy of AM 489 made when it was still in better shape, has the genitive form *Nadis hinnz rauda* 'Nadir the Red' (Blaisdell edn 1979, 56, n. 13). Nordfelt advanced the theory (1920, 115) that the Old Swedish *Wadein* and the Icelandic form *Nadir* derive from Chrétien's *Noradin* (Foerster edn 1965, v. 596), a reference to Nur ad-Din, the Sultan of Syria who distinguished himself by besieging Antioch during the Second Crusade (d.1174). Chrétien alludes to this figure by having Sir Kay name him as the valiant champion with whom everyone wants to fight when drunk with wine. The implication of Nordfelt's argument, which relies on a lengthy chain of assumptions about corrupted French manuscripts and the Norse translator's hapless misreadings of his sources, suggests that the Old Swedish translator based his name *Wadein* on the form of the name given in the edition of *Ívens saga*, that is, Kölbing's (1872). This hypothesis fails on the basis of the manuscript evidence, for we cannot know for certain how this character was named in the lost thirteenth-century archetype of *Ívens saga* that might have served as a reference for the Swedish translator; indeed, the two main manuscripts, representing different branches of transmission, disagree on precisely this issue (he is *Sodal* in Stockholm 6 but *Nadir* in AM 489). In addition, the Old Swedish text seems to have no use for Chrétien's *Noradin*, who in the Stockholm 6 redaction of *Ívens saga* is called *herra Nodan*. In the Swedish translation Chrétien's exotic and obscure *Noradin* is replaced by canonical figures in medieval tradition, namely Perceval and Theoderic: Sir Kay claims that Sir Ivan is so reckless that he would be willing to fight *hærra Percefal ok Diderik van Bærna* 'Sir Percefal and Dietrich von Bern' (v. 555). The name *Wadein* is thus no more 'estranged' from its presumed source than are the names this character bears in the Old French manuscripts of *Yvain*: *esclados*, *escladoc*, *elcadoc*, *achadot*, *acarduel* and *acardeu* (Foerster edn 1887, v. 1970) – all of which demonstrate that onomastic corruption was the rule rather than the exception. Indeed, it is not beyond the pale to wonder whether *Wadein* was coined by the Old Swedish translator of *Hærra Ivan*, and that in view of this figure's role in the romance it might have been designed as an aptronym constructed on the basis of the Old Swedish verb *väþia* (also *vädya*), meaning 'to challenge', 'to stand up against'.

The Swedish translator, like his Norse counterpart before him, preserved the distinctive characteristics of the Esclados figure, the colour red, even though the name of the knight who guards the fountain was subject to variation. *Hærra Ivan* is, of course, only 'about' Wadein the Red to the extent that he dies in v. 800 of his injuries after having uttered his last words to his courtiers:

> Iak ma mik sare for Iþer klagha:
> en riddare mik hær æptir iaghæ,
> han haver mik sva sara skænt
> þæt mit lif ær nu braþlika ænt. (vv. 795–9)

> (I must complain bitterly to you:
> a knight is pursuing me here;
> he has injured me so badly
> that my life will soon be over now.) (vv. 795–9)

These words highlight a difference between Wadein the Red and Chrétien's Esclados, that is, the fact that Wadein speaks twice in the Old Swedish romance during his fateful encounter with Sir Ivan: the first time to express his amazement that Sir Ivan remained in the saddle despite being struck by his lance (vv. 719–22), and again – his last words – to his courtiers inside the castle. This stands in contrast to the enigmatic and sinister silence that marks the scene in *Yvain*. The latter innovation may say less about the characterization of Wadein the Red in *Hærra Ivan* than it does about the Swedish translator's attempt to make things perfectly clear at all times by inserting direct speech and overt editorial commentary into passages that in *Yvain* were couched in indirect speech or implicit in the context of the scene itself. Further evidence of the translator's attempt to clarify his account can be seen in the glosses he adds to Chrétien's text that explain foreign terminology to his Nordic audience. For example, the narrator mentions that Sir Ivan walked into a garden and saw a maiden reading aloud from a *romanz*, which is defined in the next verse as 'a type of book so called in France' (vv. 4775–6), and subsequently a reference to Cupid (v. 4791) is followed by the identification 'who is called the god of love' (v. 4793).

In the Old Danish manuscript K47 the title given to *Hærra Ivan* is *Om Kong Artus oc Keyser Karol Magnus*, which derives not from the content of the romance but from its prologue. Since the prologue to *Hærra Ivan* both agrees with but also diverges from *Yvain* and *Ívens saga*, it deserves closer scrutiny. The prologue promises *skæmtan* 'entertainment' to those who desire to hear the tale:

> I nampn faþers ok sons ok þæs hælgha anda
> vil iak taka mik til handa
> forna saghu fram at føra
> þem til skæmptan þær a viliæ høra
> af þe værþoghasta konunga tva
> þær man æ hørþe sagt i fra:
> Karlamaghnus ok konung Artus;
> til dyghþ ok æro varo þe fus.
> Artus var konung af Ængland.
> Han van Rom mæþ sværþ ok brand
> ok var þær kesar mæþ mykle æra.
> Han frælste Ængland af harþe kæra
> ok skat þær romara fyrra giorþo,
> sva at ængin han siþan kræfia þorþe.
> Annar var Karlamaghnus af Franz.
> Þæt vil iak Iþer sighia til sanz,
> mot heþna mæn for kristna at striþæ
> varo ænge fræmbre i þera tiþæ.
> Baþe þe hærra iak sæghir i fra
> þe have þera framfærþ skipat sva,
> ivir alla væruldina gar þera lof
> hvar hærra ok førstæ søkiæ hof.
> Konunga synir þe søkto þera hem,
> hærtoghar, iærlar, grevar þiænte þem;
> riddara synir þe giorþo ok sva
> ok alle þe þær viþer kunno na.
> Um þænne værþugh konung Artus dagha
> varo kæmpæ starke þera lif þorþo vagha
> for riddarskap ok fruor æræ.
> Þæt ær illæ þe æru nu færræ
> for fruor lof viliæ pris at vinnæ;
> man kan þem nu næplik finnæ. (vv. 1–32)

> (In the name of the Father, the Son, and the Holy Spirit
> I will take upon myself
> to tell an old tale
> as entertainment for those who want to listen
> about the two most worthy kings
> about whom stories have ever been told:
> Charlemagne and King Arthur;
> they were eager for virtue and honor.
> Arthur was the king of England.
> He conquered Rome with sword and fire
> and was emperor there with great glory.

He freed England from hardship
and from tribute which the Romans formerly imposed,
so that nobody has dared demand it since.
Charlemagne was the other one.
In truth I want to tell you:
where Christians battled against the heathens,
none was more outstanding in those days.
The two rulers I am telling about
have governed their actions in such a manner
that their praise has spread over the entire earth,
wherever lords and princes hold court.
The sons of kings sought them out;
dukes, earls, and counts served them;
sons of knights did so as well,
and all those who were able to do so.
In the days of the worthy King Arthur
there were strong champions who dared risk their life
for chivalry and the honor of ladies.
It is a pity there are fewer now
who want to gain honor in order to win praise from the ladies;
now they are scarcely to be found.) (vv. 1–32)

The prologue to *Hærra Ivan* strikes a markedly different tone than does the prologue to *Yvain*. The translator echoes the grandeur and spectacle found in his Old French source by referring to the lasting fame of Arthur, king of England, and to the glory of those who served him, but the *laudatio temporis acti* in the Old Swedish text laments not the decline in morals or the worth of love, as is the case in Chrétien: 'But today very few serve love: nearly everyone has abandoned it; and love is greatly abased ... Now love is reduced to empty pleasantries, since those who know nothing about it claim that they love, but they lie' (Kibler trans. 1991, 295). Instead, the prologue to *Hærra Ivan* mourns the decline in chivalry and the unwillingness of knights to fight and strive for glory. This subtle shift in emphasis is characteristic for *Hærra Ivan* as a whole. On many occasions the translator seems more concerned with deeds than with sentiment, with plot instead of introspection.

Repeatedly the translator's otherwise remarkable fidelity to his Old French source falters as the discourse turns to love. One example of this can be found in an early scene in *Hærra Ivan*, when the invisible Sir Ivan and the grieving widow react to Wadein's bloody wounds in the castle bedchamber. Chrétien's account elaborates upon the reciprocity of injury – upon the 'wound of love' that Yvain has suffered, caused by the beauty of the widow (Foerster edn 1965, vv. 1364–74) – and Yvain delivers a lengthy monologue expressing his love for the sorrowing woman (vv. 1428–1505). There is precious little of this in *Hærra Ivan*. While the poet does acknowledge that Sir Ivan has fallen in love – he mentions Sir Ivan wishing to win the lady for himself and hoping to change her mind from 'no' to 'yes' – the deep emotional register and elaborate rhetoric of Chrétien's scene is reduced to twenty-three verses and becomes remarkably flat (vv. 1082–1104). After gazing at the beautiful widow, Sir Ivan does little else; the Old Swedish text ends the encounter with a brief summary: 'Han sat sva længe ok þænkte þær a / til fruan monde þæþan ga' (He sat thus for a long time, thinking about this / until the lady left) (vv. 1105–6).

It would be inaccurate to characterize the Old Swedish translator as uninterested in emotions, however, for the characters express their feelings openly to one another. Especially during the scenes in which Luneta performs shuttle diplomacy between the sequestered widow and the eager Sir Ivan, the three of them speak much as they do in *Yvain*, and considerable effort is expended to match the tone and rhetoric of Chrétien's account. It is only on occasions when the discourse in *Yvain* fails to advance the plot that the Old Swedish translator abbreviates his account or, in other situations, such as during the first face-to-face encounter between Sir Ivan and the widow, that the translator distils the rapid-fire *bons mots* of Chrétien's scene into a sequence of pedestrian statements. Verbal jousting and flirtatious wordplay characterize this scene in *Yvain*, where the following takes place:

> '. . . but sit down now and tell me what has overpowered you.'
> 'My lady,' he said, 'the power comes from my heart, which commits itself to you; my heart has
>   given me this desire.'
> 'And what controls your heart, good sir?'
> 'My eyes, my lady.'
> 'And what controls your eyes?'
> 'The great beauty I see in you.'
> 'And what wrong has beauty done?'
> 'My lady, such that it makes me love.'
> 'Love, then whom?'
> 'You, my dear lady.'
> 'Me?'
> 'Indeed yes.'
> 'In what way?' (Kibler trans. 1991, 320)

The same scene in *Hærra Ivan* is drab and bereft of sparkle:

> "Nu sitin nær mik, min hiærte kære,
> ok sighin þæt mik mæþ rættan skil,
> huru þæt ær Iþer sva komit til
> þæt I mæþ hiærta ok sinne
> ælskin mik for alla qvinna."
> "Þæt vil iak giærna sighia Iþer,
> iak kænnis þær opinbarlika viþer,
> Iþer fæghrind haver mit hiærta spænt,
> þæt mit lif ær braþlika ænt
> utan iak naþer af Iþer ma fa;
> min kæra frugha, I þænkin þær a." (vv. 1512–22)

> ("Now sit down beside me, my dearest,
> and tell me clearly,
> how it has come about

> that with heart and mind
> you love me above all women."
> "This I will gladly tell you;
> I confess it openly:
> your beauty has fettered my heart
> so that my life will soon be ended,
> unless I can find favor with you;
> my dear lady, consider this.") (vv. 1512–22)

The translator made an effort to render the conventional trope about the lover's eyes controlling his heart – *Iþer fæghrind haver mit hiærta spænt* (v. 1519) – but the sentiment is stilted. While some have criticized the narrator as lacking the 'stylistic sophistication' to translate the *sens* of Chrétien's romance accurately (Coffer 1976, 305), the above scene indicates that a further impediment was likely the difficulty of rendering enjambment and other poetic techniques in *Knittelvers*, a verse form still in its infancy in Old Swedish that had never before been used for a narrative project of this scope and complexity (Layher 2008).

We are also justified in speculating about the degree to which Norse audiences – specifically those at the Norwegian court – were familiar with the setting and diction of Arthurian romance in the years before 1312. The contrast between *Hærra Ivan* and *Hertig Fredrik* on this issue is illuminating, in that the latter text assumes a greater familiarity with Arthurian names and themes. Their different approaches to the topic of King Arthur's Round Table are illustrative (Reichert 1981 and 1986). In *Hærra Ivan*, for example, the symbolism of the Round Table is almost entirely absent. It is mentioned only once, in v. 2117, as a piece of furniture at Arthur's court – 'Þe sattos viþer þæt sivala borþ' (they [the assembled knights] sat down at the round table) – whereby the use of the definite pronoun *þæt* instead *et* in this verse – it is 'the' round table rather than 'a' round table – suggests that the Swedish audience was meant to recognize the special significance of the table and its round shape. This innovation is surprising, considering that the Round Table does not exist in Chrétien's *Yvain*. In *Hertig Fredrik*, in contrast, the Round Table is mentioned frequently in the same breath as the company of Arthurian knights. It is the *sihwalfua bordh* 'round table' at which the knights gather: *Aff thet sihwalfua bordh thet kompanj* 'the company of the Round Table'; *thet sihwalfua bordh / thet førra hafdhe margt stolt eet ordh* 'the Round Table that used to host such proud and noble words' (Noreen edn 1927, vv. 19, 1823). Intriguing too is the solitary passage in *Hertig Fredrik* where the Old French locution *table ronde* is matched by the Old Swedish neologism *tavelrunda* – but here, too, as before, the table is mentioned in the context of the group of Arthurian knights who congregate there: 'the tolff kompana komo ther med æræ / aff the tavelrunda skara' (the twelve compatriots arrived [at the tournament] with great honour, those of the Round Table) (vv. 1666–7).

Hærra Ivan, its singularity notwithstanding, is hardly a peripheral or inconsequential text. In matters of content it is firmly embedded in the Nordic literary tradition yet also attuned to new modalities of literary contact across mainland Scandinavia. Its translation ushered in a new era of courtly representation through literary activity. And with its innovative use of rhyming verse *Hærra Ivan* accomplished the final breakthrough that had been lacking thus far in the Norse reception of Arthur: the articulation of an Arthurian romance using a similar auditory device, the rhyming couplet, as its French source.

Notes

[1] Both Old Danish redactions of *Hærra Ivan* (E and F) appeared in a diplomatic edition towards the end of the nineteenth century (Brandt 1869–77, vols 1–2). To date this is the sole edition of the Old Danish text.

[2] The 1999 translation was not the first English version of the romance. An abridged translation appeared in English in 1902, in a slim and rather obscure volume printed in London that featured a collection of heroic and adventuresome tales meant for children (Schück 1902, 58–119). This translation of *Hærra Ivan*, which appears to be based on an abridged Swedish prose version by Henrik Schück, the famed Swedish medievalist, in the late nineteenth century, was done by William Frederick Harvey, a barrister at law and lecturer in English at the University of Lund. This is undoubtedly a translation of the Old Swedish *Hærra Ivan* (and not of Chrétien's *Yvain*), since the knight whom Sir Ivan confronts at the fountain is named 'Red Vadoin' (Schück 1902, 65).

[3] One issue debated at considerable length in nineteenth- and early twentieth-century studies of the *Eufemiavisor* concerns the coherence of the text corpus: whether the three *Eufemiavisor* had been translated by the same person or by several different translators (see Klockhoff 1881; Olson 1916; Nordfelt 1921; Noreen 1930). Sawicki (1939) offers a detailed overview of this debate and a cogent summary of the evidence in favour of a single translator, while Jansson (1945) reinforces the view that the *Eufemiavisor* form a discrete corpus translated by the same person.

[4] The idea that Peter Algotsson may have been the translator of the *Eufemiavisor* was debated in the years after 1945 (Beckman 1947, 1948; Ståhle 1949), but note also the caveat by S. Mitchell (1997, 236 and 240, n. 28), that an Icelandic annal records the death of 'Bishop Peter of Skara in Götaland' in 1299. I have argued elsewhere that this death notice is not for Peter Algotsson – who was never bishop in Skara – but rather for the old bishop Peter of Västerås, who died in Nidaros in 1299 (Layher 1999, 231–2). The date of death for Peter Algotsson is not known.

[5] This passage in *Hærra Ivan* has been widely discussed (see Sawicki 1939, 65; Jansson 1945, 175; Gutenbrunner 1954), but note the rebuttal to Gutenbrunner's implausible reconstruction (Blaisdell 1963).

[6] Subsequent references to *Hærra Ivan* are to the edition and translation by Williams and Palmgren.

[7] Würth suggests: 'Thematisch eignete sich der Iwein-Stoff hervorragend als Geschenk für einen frischverlobten Edelmann, da der Text unter anderem die implizite Ermahnung enthält, nicht zugunsten der ritterlichen Ehre die ehelichen Pflichten zu vernachlässigen' (The Iwein material was thematically outstandingly suitable as a present for a newly betrothed nobleman, since the text contains among others the implicit admonition not to neglect one's marital duties in favour of knightly honour) (2000, 279).

[8] On the sources of the Legendary, see Jansson 1934 and 1959. The edition published by Stephens (1847–58) lacks the fragment discussed here.

[9] The name is subject to some variation in *Hærra Ivan*: it appears as *wadoin* (A), *Wadein* (B), *wadyan* (D), *vadion* (E, F).

Reference List

Texts and Translations

Diplomatarium Norvegicum, ed. C. C. A. Lange and C. R. Unger (Christiania, 1847).

Erec, ed. C. Cormeau and K. Gärtner (Tübingen, 1985).

Erikskrönikan enligt Cod. Holm. D2 jämte avvikande läsarter ur andra handskrifter, ed. R. Pipping (Uppsala, 1963).

Ett forn-svenskt legendarium, ed. G. Stephens (Stockholm, 1847–58).

Flores och Blanzeflor. Kritisk upplaga, ed. E. Olson (Lund, 1921).

Fornsvenska Legendariet. Handskrifter och språk, ed. V. Jansson (Stockholm, 1934).

Hanserecesse. Die Recesse und andere Akten der Hansetage von 1256–1430 (Leipzig, 1870–97).

Hærra Ivan, ed. and trans. H. Williams and K. Palmgren, in *Norse Romance*, III: *Hærra Ivan*, ed. M. E. Kalinke (Cambridge, 1999).

Hærra Ivan, in *Mediaeval Stories*, trans. H. Schück (London, 1902), pp. 58–119.

Herr Ivan: kritisk upplaga, ed. E. Noreen (Uppsala, 1931).

Hertig Fredrik av Normandie. Kritisk upplaga på grund av Codex Verelianus, ed. E. Noreen (Uppsala, 1927).

Ívens saga, ed. F. W. Blaisdell, Editiones Arnamagnæanæ, B, 18 (Copenhagen, 1979).

Ívens saga, ed. and trans. M. E. Kalinke, in *Norse Romance*, II: *Knights of the Round Table*, ed. M. E. Kalinke (Cambridge, 1999), pp. 33–102.

Ívents saga, ed. E. Kölbing, in *Riddarasögur* (Strassburg, 1872), pp. 73–136.

The Knight with the Lion (Yvain), trans. W. W. Kibler, in *Chrétien de Troyes: Arthurian Romances* (London, 1991), pp. 295–380.

Der Löwenritter (Yvain), ed. W. Foerster, Christian von Troyes sämtliche erhaltene Werke, II (Halle, 1887; rpt Amsterdam, 1965).

Romantisk Digtning fra Middelalderen, ed. C. J. Brandt (Copenhagen, 1869–77).

Urkunden zur Geschichte des Fürstenthums Rügen, unter den eingeborenen Fürsten, ed. C. G. Fabricius (Stralsund, 1841–58).

Studies

Beckman, B. (1947). 'Om tiden och sättet för Hertig Fredriks försvenskning', *Arkiv för nordisk filologi*, 62, 263–7.

Beckman, B. (1948). 'En diplomatisk aktion av konung Valdemar', *Historisk Tidskrift*, 321–34.

Blaisdell, F. W. (1963). 'Names in the "Erex saga"', *Journal of English and Germanic Philology*, 62, 143–54.

Busby, K. (1993). *Les Manuscrits de Chrétien de Troyes*, Amsterdam and Atlanta, GA.

Coffer, K. B. (1976). 'Herr Ivan: a stylistic study', *Scandinavian Studies*, 48, 299–315.

Collijn, I. (1913). 'Nyfunna fragment af fornsvenska handskrifter bland räkenskapsomslagen i Kammerarkivet', *Samlaren*, 34, 275–93.

Cross, J. E. (1961). 'King Arthur in the Old Swedish legendary', *Medium Ævum*, 30, 80–8.

Gutenbrunner, S. (1954). 'Über die Quellen der Erexsaga', *Archiv für das Studium der neueren Sprachen*, 190, 1–20.

Halvorsen, E. F. (1957). 'Breta sǫgur', in *Kulturhistorisk leksikon for nordisk middelalder fra vikingetid til reformationstid*, II, Copenhagen, cols 220–3.

Hunt, T. (1975). 'Herr Ivan Lejonriddaren', *Mediæval Scandinavia*, 8, 168–86.

Jansson, V. (1934). *Fornsvenska Legendariet. Handskrifter och språk*, Stockholm.

Jansson, V. (1945). *Eufemiavisorna. En filologisk undersökning*, Uppsala.

Jansson, V. (1959). 'Fornsvenska legendariet', in *Kulturhistorisk leksikon for nordisk middelalder fra vikingetid til reformationstid*, IV, Copenhagen, cols 518–22.

Kalinke, M. E. (2009). 'The Arthurian legend in *Breta sögur*: historiography on the cusp of romance', in Margrét Eggertsdóttir et al. (eds), *Greppaminni: Essays in Honour of Vésteinn Ólason*, Reykjavík, pp. 184–98.

Klockhoff, O. (1881). *Studier öfver Eufemiavisorna*, Uppsala.

Layher, W. (1999). 'Queen Eufemia's legacy: Middle Low German literary culture, royal patronage, and the first Old Swedish epic (1301)', unpublished Ph.D. thesis, Harvard University, Cambridge, MA.

Layher, W. (2000). 'Origins of the Old Swedish epic "Hertig Fredrik af Normandie": a Middle Dutch link?', *TijdSchrift voor Skandinavistiek*, 21, 223–49.

Layher, W. (2002). '"Herzog Friedrich von der Normandie" ("Hertig Fredrik af Normandie")', in B. Wachinger et al. (eds), *Die deutsche Literatur des Mittelalters: Verfasserlexikon*, 11, Berlin and New York, cols 653–6.

Layher, W. (2003). 'Ein verlorenes Brautwerbungsepos? Wo ist *Herzog Friedrich von der Normandie in der deutschen Literatur einzuordnen?', in W. Harms, C. S. Jaeger and H. Wenzel (eds), *Ordnung und Unordnung in der Literatur des Mittelalters*, Stuttgart, pp. 61–80.

Layher, W. (2008). 'The big splash: endrhyme and innovation in medieval Scandinavian poetics', *Scandinavian Studies*, 80, 407–36.

Mitchell, S. A. (1997). 'Courts, consorts and the transformation of medieval Scandinavian literature', *NOWELE*, 31/32, 229–42.

Nordfelt, A. (1920). 'En svensk riddardikt och dess original', *Studier i modern språkvetenskap*, 7, 87–125.

Nordfelt, A. (1921). 'Det historiska beviset för Eufemiavisornas ålder', *Studier i modern språkvetenskap*, 8, 71–82.

Noreen, E. (1929). *Studier rörande Eufemiavisorna*, III: *Textkritiska studier över Herr Ivan*, Uppsala.

Noreen, E. (1930). 'Undersökningar rörande det inbördes förhållandet mellan de s.k. Eufemiavisorna', *Samlaren*, 11, 35–68.

Olson, E. (1916). 'Textkritiska studier över den fornsvenska Flores och Blanzeflor', *Arkiv för nordisk filologi*, 28, 129–75, 225–66.

Reichert. H. (1981). 'Wie beliebt war König Artus' Tafelrunde bei den Skandinaviern?', in H. Uecker (ed.), *Akten der fünften Arbeitstagung der Skandinavisten des deutschen Sprachgebiets, 16.–22. August 1981 in Kungälv*, St. Augustin, pp. 169–83.

Reichert. H. (1986). 'King Arthur's Round Table: sociological implications of its literary reception in Scandinavia', in J. Lindow, L. Lönnroth and G. W. Weber (eds), *Structure and Meaning in Old Norse Literature*, Odense, pp. 394–414.

Sawicki, S. (1939). *Die Eufemiavisor. Stilstudien zur nordischen Reimliteratur des Mittelalters*, Lund.

Schiller, K. and Lübben, A. (1875–81). *Mittelniederdeutsches Wörterbuch*, 6 vols., Bremen.

Ståhle, C. I. (1949). 'Till frågan om tillkomsten av "Hertig Fredrik"', *Arkiv för nordisk filologi*, 64, 237–45.

Sullivan, J. (2007). 'Youth and older age in the dire adventure of Chrétien's *Yvain*, the Old Swedish *Hærra Ivan*, Hartmann's *Iwein* and the Middle English *Ywain and Gawain*', *Arthurian Literature*, 24, 104–20.

Sullivan, J. (2009). 'Rewriting the exercise of power in the Landuc segment of the Old Swedish *Hærra Ivan* and Chrétien's Yvain', *Neophilologus*, 93, 19–33.

Verwijs, E. and Verdam, J. (1885–1911). *Middelnederlandsch woordenboek*, 's-Gravenhage.

Würth, S. (1998). *Der 'Antikenroman' in der isländischen Literatur des Mittelalters. Eine Untersuchung zur Übersetzung und Rezeption lateinischer Literatur im Norden*, Basel and Frankfurt a. M.

Würth, S. (2000). 'Eufemia. Deutsche Auftraggeberin schwedischer Literatur am norwegischen Hof', in F. Paul (ed.), *Arbeiten zur Skandinavistik. 13. Arbeitstagung der deutschsprachigen Skandinavistik in Oslo*, Frankfurt a. M., pp. 269–81.

8

ARTHURIAN ECHOES IN INDIGENOUS ICELANDIC SAGAS

Marianne E. Kalinke

The *Saga af Tristram ok Ísodd* excepted, the translations of Arthurian literature into Old Norse and Old Icelandic did not lead to the creation of an indigenous Icelandic Arthurian literature, as occurred, for example, in the German-language area. The translated Arthurian *riddarasögur* left echoes, however, in both the Sagas of Icelanders and the indigenous romances by incorporating certain motifs and episodes from the corpus. To judge by some Arthurian motifs not found in the translations, acquaintance with the *matière de Bretagne* in the North also seems to have been transmitted through oral tradition. The favourite donor of Arthurian motifs was the Tristan legend, which not only had an impact on the *riddarasögur*, the indigenous romances that developed in the wake of the translated literature but also on the *Íslendingasögur* 'Sagas of Icelanders'. Indeed, the most interesting use of the Arthurian material occurs in the Sagas of Icelanders, where acculturation to native literary traditions resulted in striking adaptations of the foreign motifs.

The *Saga af Tristram ok Ísodd* is paradigmatic for the type of transformation that occurred when the literary conventions of a courtly culture encountered those obtaining in the Sagas of Icelanders. Tristanian motifs, introduced through the Norse translation *Tristrams saga ok Ísöndar* and most likely also through oral versions of the legend, were adapted under the impact of indigenous literary and cultural norms. In his version of the Tristan legend the anonymous Icelandic author of the *Saga af Tristram ok Ísodd*, thought to have been composed in the fourteenth century, produced a veritable pastiche of Tristanian and Arthurian motifs, but left a work rather far removed in spirit and ethos from the traditional Tristan legend. Scholars have puzzled over this very strange Tristan romance, considering it a 'boorish account of Tristram's noble passion' (Leach 1921, 186), or 'a completely confused retelling of Brother Robert's *Tristrams saga*' (Mitchell 1959, 471), or a 'parody of the genre' of Arthurian romance (Kalinke, 1981a: 199), or a transformation of 'tragedy into burlesque' (Schach 1987, 98), or a witness 'to the comparatively early knowledge in Iceland of the so-called "vulgar" Tristram-tradition' (Thomas 1983, 88). More recently, Geraldine Barnes has suggested an alternative approach to this intractable text, that it should be read not as 'a deliberatively debased version of *Tristrams saga* but the subject matter of an autonomous work, composed in a narrative form whose style and ethos differ from the "courtly" mode of Thomas and Brother Robert' (1999, 385). She argues that the saga might be a 'sympathetic parody of *Tristrams saga*' in that the *Saga af Tristram ok Ísodd* 'replicates certain key characteristics and situations of the latter but incorporates them into a new narrative mode', that is, the narrative mode of the indigenous Icelandic romances (387).

Whereas some of the oddities in the Icelandic version 'can be viewed as the marks of a generic consistency' (Barnes 1999, 384) as known from Icelandic romance, it is more likely that the transformation of the legend in the *Saga af Tristram ok Ísodd* occurred under the impact of the Sagas of Icelanders, not the imported romances and the indigenous romances composed in their wake. The cultural assimilation is most evident in the portrayal and behaviour of the protagonists in the love triangle. While the Icelandic *Saga af Tristram ok Ísodd* transmits the distinctive structure, themes and motifs of the legend, modifications in the portrayal of the protagonists and their relation to each other resulted in a romance quite different from the traditional Tristan legend. In effect, the Icelandic author retold the narrative in such a manner as to make the object of desire Tristram rather than Ísodd and the recipient of Tristram's allegiance his uncle rather than Ísodd. The Icelandic *Tristrams saga* may be said to reflect not so much the differences between courtly continental and indigenous Icelandic romance but rather differences in the expression of male and female sexuality in courtly romance and in the *Íslendingasögur*.

The *Saga af Tristram ok Ísodd* does not end with the tragic death of the lovers, for unlike the continental Tristan as known through the Norwegian translation, his Icelandic counterpart does consummate the marriage with *Ísodd svarta*, 'Ísodd the Dark', as Isolt with the White Hands is called in the saga. Consequently, the Icelandic saga does not conclude with Tristram's death, but rather continues by informing us of the fate of Tristram's son and in turn of that of his grandchildren. This ending, which is totally at odds with the traditional Tristan legend, expresses the Icelanders' interest in genealogy and the penchant of the indigenous sagas to conclude their narratives by looking into the future and remarking on the descendants of a saga's protagonists (Barnes 1999, 389).

There is every indication that the specific character of the Icelandic *Saga af Tristram ok Ísodd* and its drastic divergence from the continental legend is the result of acculturation to an Icelandic sexual and homosocial sensibility at odds with that in the foreign import, romance (Lurkhur 2008, 9, 137). Whereas 'romances typically adhere to a gender scheme in which men, as autonomous agents and knights, are sharply distinguished from women, who are passive subjects' (Lurkhur 2008, 6), this is not the case in the *Saga af Tristram ok Ísodd,* where the distinction is blurred. The traditional gender roles of romance are inverted, commencing with the story of Tristram's parents, here named Kalegras and Blenziblý. When Kalegras kills Blenziblý's lover in a tournament, she reacts by falling in love with him, for she has never seen anyone his equal. She sends for Kalegras and has her messenger tell him that she desires his love. When Kalegras enters her chamber, she takes the initiative by kissing him.

Without any hesitation the two get into bed, where they remain passionately entwined – for three years – while ignoring all attempts by others to communicate with them. Whether intentional or not, the author has here injected a most exaggerated form of the *recreantise* motif in Chrétien's *Erec et Enide*, known in Iceland in translation as *Erex saga* (Kalinke, 1981a, 201–3).

Blenziblý's sexual aggressiveness anticipates the role Ísodd plays when Tristram woos her for his uncle. Abetted by her mother, Ísodd repeatedly woos Tristram for herself: 'þá vildi hún þó heldr eiga Tristram en nokkurn annan, þann er hún hafði fréttir af' (Jorgensen edn 1999, 270) (she wanted to marry Tristram more than any other man she had ever heard of' (Hill trans. 1999, 271).[1] Tristram is not interested, however, and when his uncle offers to grant him the woman and the kingdom, because it would be 'giptusamligra fyrir aldrs sakir' (276) (a more auspicious match on account of their age) (277), Tristram rejects the offer. To be sure, Tristam and Ísodd engage in the adulterous relationship, but the narrator's explanation is that 'mátti hann þó fyrir engan mun við sköpunum vinna' (288) (he was by no means able to withstand the fates) (289).

Lurkhur argues that 'the main thrust of the narrative tension is directed towards the relationship between Tristram and his uncle rather than to Tristram and the queen' (2008, 207) and that 'the value placed on family loyalty in *Tristram ok Ísodd* prevails to such an extent that the relationship between Tristram and his uncle Mórodd outweighs the relationship between Tristram and Ísodd' (300). This explains Tristram's repeated rejection of Ísodd on his bridal-quest mission and subsequently also Mórodd's magnanimous offer to Tristram of the bride. This too can be interpreted in light of medieval Icelandic culture. King Mórodd offers Ísodd to Tristram because he considers this 'a more auspicious match on account of their age', and he adds 'en ek ann þér allvel konunnar ok ríkisins' (276) (and I freely grant you the woman and the kingdom) (277). Tristram rejects the offer, but in his response refers only to the kingdom, when he says: 'ek vil ekki kóngr vera, meðan yðr er við kostr' (276) (I do not want to be king while you are able to be) (277). Mórodd's offer of Ísodd to Tristram on the one hand and Tristram's refusal on the other may be a reflection of the importance Icelandic culture placed on the equality of marital partners. Mórodd's offer rests on similarity of age, while Tristram's refusal alludes to the importance of the social station of the marital partners. In medieval Iceland the issue of the couple's *jafnræði*, their being equally matched, was of prime importance, and the term comprised both social prestige and wealth (Jochens 1995, 21, 24). At the end of the saga the narrator seems to confirm that *jafnræði* is indeed a concern, for he says that the reason why Tristram did not accept Ísodd the Fair from King Mórodd was 'at hann unni honum hins bezta ráðs' (288) (he wanted him to have the best match' (289). The phrase *hit bezta ráð* 'the best match' implies that Tristram wants his uncle to have a 'match' *ráð* that is not only 'equal' *jafn*, but that is also absolutely the best. The narrator's comment suggests that in Tristram's opinion Ísodd was Mórodd's equal, but not his own. Tristram himself ends his adulterous liaison with Ísodd because he places service to his uncle above his love for Ísodd. A certain heathen king attacks England and Tristram leads his uncle's forces against him. The main part of Tristram's army is slain and the situation seems hopeless. The narrator then reports that Tristram 'heitir til sigrs á sjálfan guð, þvíat hann skal af láta fiflingum við Ísodd dróttning (282) (promised to God Himself that in return for victory he would leave off his dalliance with Queen Ísodd) (283).

In the *Saga af Tristram ok Ísodd* there occurs an inversion of romance conventions and the Tristan legend itself. The crux of the story is not so much Tristram's relationship to Ísodd but rather his relationship to his uncle. The narrative focus is to such an extent on Tristram that Ísodd is effectively marginalized. 'With its emphasis on homosocial relationships at the expense of heterosocial love' the Icelandic *Tristrams saga* bears the cultural imprint of the Sagas of Icelanders (Lurkhur 2008, 9). The Icelandic version of the Tristan legend, which was known in Iceland through Brother Robert's *Tristrams saga ok Ísöndar* – recall that the Norwegian translation is transmitted solely in Icelandic manuscripts – is ideologically on an entirely different plane than the traditional legend.[2] As Barnes has noted (1999, 387–8), 'the moral turmoil and anguish, and the tragic consequences of fatal attraction which dominate Thomas's story are of little consequence to the Icelandic romance.' A very different ethos pervades the Icelandic saga, much of it the result of accommodation to the diverging cultural norms expressed in the indigenous Icelandic literature. That acculturation occurred when romance encountered the *Íslendingasögur*, that is, Sagas of Icelanders, is also evident in the transformation of Tristanian motifs in *Grettis saga*, the life of Grettir, Iceland's most famous outlaw, and *Kormáks saga*, the life of Kormákr, one of Iceland's medieval poets.

The 'ambiguous-oath' episode in *Tristrams saga ok Ísöndar* inspired the inclusion of a similar episode, the so-called *Spesar þáttr* 'Tale of Spes' in *Grettis saga*, thought to have been composed in the early fourteenth century. In *Tristrams saga ok Ísöndar* Ísönd offers to undergo trial by red-hot iron to prove her innocence and thus lay to rest what she states are slanderous charges of adultery. Before the appointed day of the trial, Ísönd sends word to Tristram that he is to meet her in disguise at a ford in the river and that he is to carry her from the ship across the water. He appears with his face stained yellow and in shabby clothes, and she summons him and asks him to carry her from the boat. He does so and she tells him to fall on top of her when they reach land. She hikes up her dress and he falls on her. Her men want to beat him to death but she defends him, saying that he is a weary pilgrim, weak from his long journey. When she takes the oath, she states:

> Aldri var sá karlmaðr fæddr af kvennmanni, at nær mér nökkviðri kæmi nema þú, kóngr, ok sá hinn píndi pílagrímr, er bar mik af bátnum ok fell á mik, öllum yðr ásjáöndum. Svá hjálpi mér guð í þessari freistni, ok svá skíri hann mik af þessu járni. (Jorgensen edn 1999, 150)

> (There was never a man born of woman who got next to my naked flesh except you, king, and that poor pilgrim who carried me from the boat and who, in sight of all of you, fell on top of me. May God help me in this trial and clear my name with this iron.) (Jorgensen trans. 1999, 151)

Ísönd carries the glowing iron without being burned, and the narrator comments: 'Ok gaf guð henni með sinni fagri miskunn fagra skírn, sætt ok samþykki við kónginn, herra sinn ok eiginbónda, með fullri ást, sæmd ok mikilli tign' (150) (And God in his gentle mercy granted her purification, reconciliation, and harmony with the king, her lord and husband, with an abundance of love, honor, and high esteem) (151).

Grettis saga was produced by an author well versed in the earlier literature of his country. While he himself refers to several sagas, it is evident that he is also indebted to a number of works not mentioned by name. These are primarily Sagas of Icelanders, but one of his more interesting loans, though not acknowledged, comes from the Tristan legend, namely the ambiguous-oath episode. Toward the end of *Grettis saga*, the action moves to Constantinople. The eponymous protagonist Grettir had been killed by a certain Þorbjörn Þórðarson, who was banned from Iceland for the deed. He goes first to Norway and then to Constantinople. He is pursued by Þorsteinn drómundr, 'the Galleon', Grettir's brother, who finally catches up with Þorbjörn in Constantinople and kills him with the very weapon with which he had killed Grettir. As punishment for the killing Þorsteinn is to be incarcerated for life unless someone ransoms him. To pass the time Þorsteinn sings in the dungeon. His voice is so remarkable that a wealthy noblewoman named Spes, who hears him singing, ransoms him. She is married to a certain Sigurðr, a wealthy man but one of lower birth; the narrator notes that she had married him for money (Scudder trans. 1997, 274). We are told that the couple had little love for each other and that Spes felt that she had married beneath her; in other words, that the expected *jafnræði* did not exist. Spes and Þorsteinn fall in love and she bestows much money on him. Her husband becomes suspicious, accuses her of squandering their money and of having an affair. On three different occasions her husband and his friends attempt to catch Spes and her lover in *flagrante delicto*, but each time the lovers outwit their pursuers. Finally Spes declares that she no longer wants to be embarrassed by her husband's accusations and that she will ask the bishop to decide how she might clear herself of the false charges. She is to swear an oath declaring her innocence.

While the adulterous affair between Spes and Þorsteinn resembles that of Ísönd and Tristram, it differs inasmuch as the suspicious husband never actually catches the lovers together. Furthermore, *Grettis saga* contains an additional element not found in *Tristrams saga*, namely the husband's accusation that the wife had given away money. Nonetheless, the ambiguous-oath episode itself is clearly modelled after the same in the Tristan legend. On the appointed day Spes appears in her finest clothes, accompanied by many elegant women. It is a rainy day, the roads are wet, and she has to cross a muddy ditch to get to the church. At the ditch a large crowd has gathered, including a tall beggar who offers to carry Spes across the mud. She hesitates but then gets on his back. He struggles along on crutches and just before reaching the opposite bank he stumbles and falls forward. Spes is flung up on the bank, while he sinks into the mud. He attempts to take hold of her dress, but instead grabs her knee and naked thigh with his muddy hand. She jumps up and curses him roundly, but the surrounding crowd plead for mercy. Spes gives him some gold coins and then says: 'Haf þat nú, karl; aldri mun þat gott, at þú hafir eigi fullt fyrir þat, er ek hafi hrakit þik' (Guðni Jónsson edn 1936, 283) (Take this, old man. It would be wrong if you were not paid in full for my ill treatment of you) (Scudder trans. 1997, 182). This sets the stage for the oath.

When Spes comes to church she says to her husband:

> . . . vil ek sverja, at engum manni hefi ek gull gefit ok af engum manni hefi ek saurgazk líkamliga, útan af bónda mínum ok þeim vándum stafkarli, er tók sinni saurugri hendi á lær mér, er ek var borin yfir díkit í dag. (284)

> (I swear that I have not given any man gold and been defiled by him apart from my husband and that wicked beggar who put his muddy hand on my thigh when he carried me over the ditch today.) (188)

This is the oath she then swears and people said that she left nothing out. Spes then asks for a divorce, saying she did not want to put up with her husband's slanders. The narrator reports:

> fluttu þetta frændr hennar. Varð þá svá með atgangi þeira ok býtingum, at þau váru skilin, ok Sigurðr fékk lítit af gózinu; var hann gǫrr ór landi brott. Fór þar, sem víða eru dœmi til, at inir lægri verða at lúta; gat hann ok engu fram komit, þó at hann hefði rétt at mæla. (284)

> (Her kinsmen presented the request, and through their agency and gifts of money, the divorce was granted. Sigurd received little of their wealth and was banished from the country. In this case, as in others, the weaker were forced to yield. He did not manage to have his way even though he was in the right.) (188)

The narrator's wry comment on might over right reflects conditions not infrequent in the Sagas of Icelanders, as does the intimation that Spes got her way through bribery. The narrator reports that Spes took over all of Sigurðr's wealth and that she was considered a paragon among women. Yet, the narrator continues:

> Þá er menn hugðu at eiðstaf hennar, þótti mǫnnum, sem grunr hefði í verit, ok ætluðu, at vitrir menn myndi hafa diktat fyrir henni þessi atkvæði. Gátu menn þá upp grafit, at sá stafkarl, sem hana hefði borit, var Þorsteinn drómundr, en þó fekk Sigurðr enga rétting þessa máls. (284–5)

> (On closer scrutiny her oath seemed suspect, and it was assumed the terms had been laid down for her by clever men. It was discovered that the beggar who had carried her over the ditch was Thorstein Dromund, but Sigurd did not manage to win redress in the matter.) (188)

The scene in which Spes is carried across the muddy ditch by her disguised lover who falls and takes hold of her thigh is clearly modelled after the similar scene in the Tristan legend. And this staged mishap, like the one in the Tristan legend, enables Spes to swear an oath that is true, the meaning of which is different, however, from what the audience, including Sigurðr, believe. In its incorporation into *Grettis saga*, the ambiguous-oath episode has undergone significant acculturation. Although Þorbjörn is wealthy, Spes considers herself to have married beneath her; the word used is *vargefin* (274), which suggests the same as lack of *jafnræði*, although the latter term does not occur. The episode concludes on a typically Icelandic note, with the divorce. Since the oath has shown Spes to be innocent, she is able to use her husband's 'false accusations' as a reason for divorce. This too is to be understood in an Icelandic context where a woman could sue for divorce (Jochens 1995, 55–6).

Since the nineteenth century scholars have noted the indebtedness of the *Spesar þáttr* to the Tristan legend, but have disagreed as to whether the source is the courtly version of the legend, as represented by Brother Robert's translation of Thomas's *Tristan*, or the *version commune* of Béroul. The most recent study of the *Spesar þáttr* posits the Icelandic *Saga af Tristram ok Ísodd* as the source and interprets the Spes tale in an intertextual and alluding relationship to this romance (Kramarz-Bein 2000, 175–6, 178–9).[3] Which version of the Tristan legend was the actual source that inspired the author of *Grettis saga* does not really matter in our context. There is no doubt that he knew some form of the legend, incorporated the ambiguous-oath episode into the outlaw saga, but adapted it to his own ends and Icelandic cultural conditions.

The *Íslendingasögur*, or Sagas of Icelanders, are also known as Family Sagas, since many of these sagas deal with the lives of prominent Icelanders and their extended families through several generations. A subgroup, known as *skáldasögur*, is devoted to the lives of famous Icelandic poets, or skalds. At the heart of four of these sagas is a tale of tragic love, and it has been suggested that the basic plot of one of the skald sagas, namely *Kormáks saga*, was inspired by some version of the Tristan legend.[4] Whether this is the case for the entire work is debatable, but one of its episodes is undoubtedly indebted to the Tristan legend, to its so-called Harp-and-Rote episode. Chapters 49–50 of *Tristrams saga ok Ísöndar* recount the visit of an Irish harper to the court of King Mark, the Irishman's abduction of Ísönd, and Tristram's rescue of the queen and her return to her husband.

According to the saga, Tristram was absent from court one day when an Irish vassal, carrying a harp, arrives by ship at King Mark's court. The saga relates that the Irishman had loved Ísönd for a long time – she recognizes him when he arrives – and that was the reason for his visit. He identifies himself as a minstrel, and after the king and his courtiers have eaten, Mark asks the visitor to entertain the court by playing an Irish tune in return for which he could have whatever he wanted. After the Irishman has performed he asks for Ísönd as his reward. Mark remonstrates and says that he cannot have her. In response the visitor says that if the king denies him what he has promised, then he may no longer rule as king,

> því sá höfðingi, sem opinberliga lýgr ok gengr á eiða sína ok orð, á aldri at hafa vald né ríki yfir dugandismönnum. En ef þú neitar þessu, er ek hefi mælt, þá legg ek undir dóm einarðra manna . . . ef þú synjar mér þat, er þú héz mér, þá átt þú engan rétt í þessu kóngsríki, ok þat skal ek með mínum vápnum sanna í móti þér. (128)

> (for that nobleman who openly lies or who breaks his oath or his word, shall not have power or dominion over valiant men. Should you deny what I demand, then I will commend the case to the judgment of honest men . . . If you deny me what you have promised me, then you have no right to this kingdom, and I will prove this with my weapons) (129).

Since no one is willing to engage in combat with the Irishman, Mark surrenders his wife to him. Upon returning to the court and learning the news, Tristram takes his fiddle and pursues the couple. When he reaches their tent, the Irishman is trying to console Ísönd, who is weeping and wailing. He asks Tristram to cheer up Ísönd with his fiddle, in exchange for which he will give him a coat and a good robe. Tristram entertains Ísönd for the entire evening as the tide rises and the gangway floats away. Tristram offers to take Ísönd to the ship on his horse, but rides off instead into the woods, saying: 'Þú sóttir Ísönd með þinni hörpu, en nú hefir þú týnt henni sakir einnar gígju' (130) (You won Ísönd with your harp, and now you have lost her because of a fiddle) (131).[5] When he returns Ísönd to the king, he remarks that 'lítit sómir konu at unna þeim manni, er hana gefr upp fyrir einn hörpuslátt' (132) (there is little honor for a woman to love a man who would surrender her for a performance on a harp) (133). King Mark does not respond.

A somewhat transformed but nevertheless still quite recognizable version of the Harp-and-Rote episode occurs in *Kormáks saga*, the biography of the prolific Icelandic love poet Kormákr Ögmundarson (*c*.930–70), presumably composed in the early thirteenth century. According to the saga, Kormákr loves a beautiful woman named Steingerðr to whom he is betrothed, but who instead is given in marriage to a man named Þorvaldr tinteinn. One time she accompanies her husband on a voyage to Denmark, but on the way Vikings accost the ship, plunder it and abduct Steingerðr. Kormákr comes upon Þorvaldr on an island, learns what has happened, and asks the hapless husband why he had not pursued the Vikings. Þorvaldr admits that he did not have the manpower, in response to which Kormákr asks: 'Segir þú ómátt þinn á' (Einar Ól. Sveinsson edn 1939, 296) (Are you admitting that you're not up to it?) (McTurk trans. 2002, 63). Kormákr and his brother Þorgils row up to the Viking ship which lies anchored offshore. Steingerðr has in the meantime been offered in marriage to one of the men on board ship. Kormákr kills him and then swims back to land with his brother, the latter with Steingerðr in tow. Kormákr returns Steingerðr to Þorvaldr, who now unexpectedly tells his wife to go with Kormákr, saying that 'hann drengiliga hafa eptir sótt' (298) (he had pursued her like a man) (64). Kormákr says that this is also his wish, but just as unexpectedly Steingerðr objects, saying that 'ekki skyldu kaupa um knífa' (298) (she was not going to exchange one knife for another) (64).[6] The incident concludes with Kormákr telling Steingerðr to go with her husband. Finlay (2001) argues that the proposed parallels with *Tristrams saga* are 'overstated', that *Kormáks saga* does not contain the motif of the rash promise, and that the episode could have been inspired 'by either some version of Tristan, or the story of Lancelot' (264). Icelanders did know some version of the Lancelot tale (see below), yet the points of convergence of the abduction motif in *Kormáks saga* and the Tristan legend are pronounced. The abduction episode in *Kormáks saga* suggests acquaintance with the Arthurian tradition, most likely the Tristan legend, be that in oral or written form (see Bjarni Einarsson 1976, 109–10).

The abduction episode undergoes an odd transformation: not only is Steingerðr's husband willing to give her to his rival – unlike King Mark in *Tristrams saga ok Ísöndar*, but like the king in the Icelandic *Saga af Tristram ok Ísodd* – but Steingerðr refuses the opportunity to return to Kormákr, the man to whom she had been betrothed before she was married off to Þorvaldr. Throughout her marriage she finds herself in situations where Kormákr kisses her, both secretly and in full view of Þorvaldr, but where she and Kormákr also spend a night together, yet 'hvíldi sínum megin bríkar hvárt þeira' (272) (slept on separate sides of a screen) (49). This too appears to be an echo of a Tristanian motif, namely the sword-between-the-lovers motif, although this also occurs in the story of Sigurðr and Brynhildr, as told in Eddic poetry and *Völsunga saga* (Finlay 2001, 260–1).

The manner in which Tristanian motifs are realized in *Kormáks saga* and *Grettis saga* reveals that we are on generic ground that diverges strikingly from that of romance. As is the case with Ísodd's husband in the *Saga af Tristram ok Ísodd*, Þorvaldr's offer of his wife to his rival seems to be predicated on the Icelandic notion that in a marriage there should be *jafnræði*, an 'equal match'. Steingerðr's seeming independence of men, however, as suggested by her refusal to return to her lover, reflects the independence of Icelandic women, which is also the case in the behaviour of Spes in *Grettis saga*, who, to be sure was not Icelandic. In romance a woman's decision to divorce her husband and join her lover, as happens in *Grettis saga*, would have been unthinkable; hence the continuing dilemma of the lovers in *Tristrams saga ok Ísöndar* after Ísönd's innocence appears to have been attested in the ambiguous-oath episode. Similarly, a husband's declaration that the lover is the more suitable partner and therefore the offer of his wife to the lover, as happens in the *Saga af Tristram ok Ísodd* and in *Kormáks saga*, is equally unacceptable in the realm of romance. While the authors of the indigenous *Grettis saga* and *Kormáks saga* knew the Tristan legend and borrowed from it, the motifs underwent a drastic transformation in the cultural transfer.

The authors of the indigenous Icelandic sagas knew and borrowed material not only from *Tristrams saga ok Ísöndar*, but also from the *Strengleikar* collection, which contains two of Marie de France's Arthurian lais, *Geitarlauf* (*Chèvrefeuille*) and *Januals ljóð* (*Lanval*). Unlike the other Arthurian translations produced at the court of King Hákon Hákonarson, which are transmitted in Icelandic manuscripts, the *lais* in the *Strengleikar* collection are extant, with but one exception, solely in a late thirteenth-century Norwegian manuscript, De la Gardie 4–7 (see chapter 2). Nonetheless, at least three lais, *Bisclavret*, *Guigemar* and *Lanval* were known in Iceland. *Guiamars ljóð* (the translation of *Guigemar*) was copied in 1737 in Iceland and entitled *Gvímars saga* in the manuscript, Lbs. 840 4to. This copy derives from a sister text of that found in the Norwegian manuscript (Kalinke 1979). An Icelandic redaction of *Bisclaretz ljóð*, entitled *Tiódels saga*, is preserved in twenty-four manuscripts. Except for the striking divergence that in this version the werewolf becomes a white bear, *Tiódels saga* ultimately derives from the Norwegian translation of *Bisclavret* (Kalinke, 1981b).

One *lai* attributed to Marie de France, *Eliduc*, which is one of the twelve *lais* in the manuscript Harley 978 (British Library), is not transmitted in the *Strengleikar* collection, even though the other eleven *lais* are found in the Norwegian manuscript De la Gardie 4–7, their translations hewing close to the texts in the Harley manuscript. Nonetheless, *Eliduc* was known in Iceland and may in fact at some point have been translated independently of the other lais. Evidence for acquaintance with this lai in Iceland is furnished by *Völsunga saga* 'Saga of the Völsungs', the prose version of the heroic eddic poems devoted to the Völsungs and the Niflungs. *Völsunga saga* contains an analogue to the weasel episode in *Eliduc*, where a maiden is restored to life through imitating how a weasel brings its mate back to life. In the saga, Sigmundr, who had severely injured his son Sinfjötli when as a werewolf he bit him, restores him by imitating the behaviour of two weasels, one of which had bitten the other in the throat. As occurred with the Tristan loans in *Grettis saga* and *Kormáks saga*, a motif from courtly literature was incorporated into an indigenous Icelandic saga but also transformed, for the leaf that cures Sinfjötli is brought to Sigmundr by a raven, the god Odin's bird (see Clover 1986).

The Arthurian lai *Januals ljóð* appears to have been known to the anonymous author of *Helga þáttr Þórissonar*, 'The Tale of Helgi Þórisson', a *þáttr* (short tale) found in *Flateyjarbók* (GKS 1005 fol.), an Icelandic vellum manuscript produced in the years 1387–90. The manuscript is the largest of the medieval Icelandic manuscripts (it consists of 225 large folios) and contains the biographies of the Norwegian kings, *Konungasögur*, 'Kings' Sagas', into which are woven some Sagas of Icelanders, including sagas of skalds, such as *Hallfreðar saga*, 'Saga of Hallfreðr', as well as *þættir*, a number of them exemplary tales. *Helga þáttr Þórissonar*, which is classified among the mythical-heroic narratives, relates a story of the encounter between the Christian and pagan realms, between the Christian King Óláfr Tryggvason and the pagan King Guðmundr (Guðni Jónsson edn 1954, 345–53). The plot of the short tale, like *Januals ljóð*, commences when the protagonist finds himself in the woods and comes upon twelve women on horses; their leader Ingibjörg is the daughter of the mythical King Guðmundr of Glæsisvellir, an otherworldly realm. Despite certain differences between the account in the *þáttr*, in which Helgi joins in a sumptuous feast and for three days enjoys the favours of Ingibjörg, who bestows wealth upon him when he leaves, there are so many correspondences between vv. 39–156 of the French *lai* (Rychner edn, 1958) and the Icelandic *þáttr* that the former via its Norse translation *Januals ljóð* most likely was the source of the Icelandic adaptation and incorporation into a very different type of narrative (Power 1985). Unfortunately, one leaf is missing in the manuscript De la Gardie 4–7 and this contains the beginning of *Januals ljóð*. The Norse version begins only with the translation of vv. 157–8, but it is safe to assume that the missing leaf contained a fairly accurate rendering of the *lai*.

Unlike the Arthurian loans that were transformed when they were incorporated into the Sagas of Icelanders and *fornaldarsögur* 'Mythical-Heroic Sagas', the Tristanian motifs in the indigenous Icelandic romances more or less retained their original character and function, although they underwent a certain amount of adaptation to the particular context of a romance. Paul Schach (1968) published a broad survey of the influence of *Tristrams saga ok Ísöndar* on Old Icelandic Literature, and the following discussion is indebted to him. *Rémundar saga keisarasonar*, 'The Saga of Rémundr, the Emperor's Son', which presumably dates from the first half of the fourteenth century, bears the impact of the Tristan legend more than any other indigenous Icelandic romance. The story commences with the protagonist's dream that he has come to a strange country where he is married to a beautiful princess with whom he exchanges rings. When he awakens, the ring is still on his finger. The plot revolves around Rémundr's search for the woman of his dreams. The saga is believed to be an analogue of *Artus de la Petite Bretagne*, a fourteenth-century French prose romance, which is not, however, about King Arthur but rather a knight named after him, who falls in love with a princess he sees in a dream and whom he seeks (Schlauch 1934, 65).

Rémundar saga borrows the hall-of-statues motif from *Tristrams saga ok Ísöndar* as well as the motif of the quest for healing. In *Tristrams saga* (chapter 80) the eponymous protagonist constructs a hall and fashions a group of life-size statues for it. This sculptural group consists of Ísönd, Bringvet, the evil dwarf, the giant, a lion, Ísönd's dog and King Markis's counsellor. Ísönd, who is at the centre of this group, is so lifelike and animated that the statue appears to be alive. Tristram was wont to visit this place:

> Ok jafnan sem hann kom inn til líkneskju Ísöndar, þá kyssti hann hana, svá opt sem hann kom, ok lagði hana í fang sér ok hendr um háls, sem hún væri lifandi, ok ræddi til hennar mörgum ástligum orðum um ástarþokka þeira ok harma. (Jorgensen edn 1999, 188)

> (As soon as he got to the statue of Ísönd he kissed it, and as often as he came he took it in his arms, embracing it as if it were alive, and speaking many loving words to it about their love and their sorrow.) (Jorgensen trans. 1999, 189)

When Kardín, the brother of Ísodd the Dark, sees the statues he believes them to be real. In fact, upon seeing the ferocious-looking giant he panics and faints (Kalinke, 2009).

The motif of the lifelike statues appears in *Rémundar saga*. After having seen the maiden in his dream, Rémundr has a statue of the maiden fashioned and placed at the entry to a church, where Rémundr's father sees and greets her, taking her to be a real person. His son informs him, however, that this is no woman created by God but rather a likeness of the woman he had seen in his dream. And Rémundr embraces the statue and joyfully kisses it. The narrator comments: 'Og hér meguð þér sjá, hvað heit ástin er' (Bjarni Vilhjálmsson edn 1954, 179) (And here you can see how hot love is).

Subsequently Rémundr takes the statue with him wherever he goes, and the narrator comments that he thus alleviates his distress. Rémundr now goes into the woods every day and has the statue brought along. And every day he sits in a clearing, where he

> hana faðmandi og blíðlega kyssandi og hjá sér stundum niður leggjandi og á hana horfandi og eftir lítinn tíma upp takandi. Þótti honum létt sínum harmi og trega, sem hann þvingar á marga vega. (179)

> (embraces it and gently kisses it, and sometimes he lays it down beside him and gazes at it, and after a while he picks it up again. It seemed to him that his grief and sorrow had lightened which weigh him down in so many ways.)

The above translation does not replicate the striking stylistic feature of the passage, that is, the use of the present participle – *faðmandi*, *kyssandi*, *leggjandi*, *horfandi*, *takandi* – to convey state of being and duration. This Latinate feature is one of the characteristics of the so-called Tristram group of translations (see chapter 2), and it subsequently also became a stylistic feature of some of the indigenous romances. *Rémundar saga* thus reveals its indebtedness to *Tristrams saga* not only in the motif of a lifelike statue of the beloved but also in the ornate Latinate style.

The plot is set in motion when Rémundr and an entourage of twelve men have one day again paused in the woods where Rémundr caresses the statue of his beloved. A knight in full armour suddenly appears as if out of nowhere and charges Rémundr with lewdness. The stranger, named Eskupart, accuses Rémundr of consorting with a statue that is an image of his own beloved and challenges him to combat. Despite the stranger's enormous size Rémundr manages to kill him but not before a piece of the stranger's sword lodges in his head. The same thing, it should be noted, occurs to Tristram in the Icelandic *Tristrams saga ok Ísoddar* and it is thought that its anonymous author borrowed the motif from *Rémundar saga* (Schach 1968, 90). Before he dies, the knight places the spell on Rémundr that the sword fragment can only be removed by the maiden whom Rémundr is longing for. Thus begins Rémundr's quest for healing. This is somewhat different, however, from that on which Tristram embarks in the Norse *Tristrams saga ok Ísöndar*. Unlike Tristram, who travels by boat in search of healing, Rémundr travels by cart and becomes known as *hinn kranki kerrumaðr*, 'the sick man of the cart'.

The reference to Lancelot, *Le Chevalier de la charrete*, is obvious, although Lancelot is not wounded when he travels around by cart. A lost Norse translation of Chrétien de Troyes's *Lancelot* has been posited (Halvorsen 1959, 25), but this is unlikely, given that *Lancelot* is the only Arthurian romance by Chrétien that was not translated into other languages in the Middle Ages (Skårup 1980, 76–7).[7] There is no reason why a fourteenth-century Icelandic author could not have become acquainted with the story of Lancelot other than through a translation of *Le Chevalier de la charrete*. There is ample evidence that Icelandic authors knew foreign literary motifs and tales other than those found in the translations undertaken in the thirteenth century and extant today. What *Rémundar saga keisarasonar* reveals is that the anonymous four-teenth-century Icelandic authors had access to a remarkable treasure trove of Arthurian motifs both via the Old Norse-Icelandic translations and through oral tradition.

Acquaintance with the story of Lancelot in Iceland is also suggested by a strange transmutation in the Icelandic *Saga af Tristram ok Ísodd* of an episode in the Norwegian translation, *Tristrams saga ok Ísöndar*, in which Tristram leaps into Ísönd's bed over the flour that had been strewn to entrap him. He had been bled that day and the exertion of the leap caused his veins to reopen and to leave blood in the bed. In the *Saga af Tristram ok Ísodd* the scenario is quite different. The trap is the same, but no one had been bled that day. Tristram does not sleep in the same quarters as Ísodd and the king, but in a separate building. By means of a rope he hauls himself up to the window of Ísodd's chamber, and from there he jumps into Ísodd's bed. But he hits the edge of the bed with his hand in such a manner that it bleeds. The queen then stabs her own hand with a pair of scissors, and when the king asks her the next day about the blood, she claims to have scratched herself with the scissors when she got out of bed during the night (Jorgensen edn 1999, 280). The blood-in-the-bed motif is also found in *Le Chevalier de la charrete*, where Lancelot gains access to the queen's bedroom through a window, but in bending the bars he injures his hand (Kibler edn 1981, vv. 4636–47) and blood from his hand is subsequently found in the queen's bed. She explains this as the result of a nose bleed (vv. 4782–3). Whether the inspiration for the specific character of Tristram's nocturnal visit came from acquaint-ance with some version of the Lancelot story cannot be determined, but the Icelandic *Saga af Tristram ok Ísodd* and *Le Chevalier de la charrete* share entry through a window and the wound incurred thereby.

That Icelanders knew versions of the Tristan legend other than the courtly version translated in *Tristrams saga ok Ísöndar* is suggested by *Göngu-Hrólfs saga* 'The Saga of Hrólfr the Walker', an indigenous Icelandic romance, the eponymous protago-nist of which acquired his cognomen from the fact that he was so large that no horse could carry him for an extended period. Hrólfr becomes the emissary of a certain Earl Þorgnýr of Jutland, a very old man and widower, who had loved his wife very much. In good weather he would sit on her burial mound and hold meetings there or watch games being played. One day, a swallow drops a long, golden hair, as long as a man is tall, wrapped in a silk scarf on to his knee. The earl vows to win in marriage the woman to whom the hair belongs. Hrólfr becomes the proxy wooer in this bridal quest. The motif of questing for the woman to whom hair dropped by a swallow belongs derives from the Tristan tradition, but not the courtly version. It is found in Eilhart von Oberge's *Tristrant*, where two swallows are seen fighting over a woman's beautiful hair. King Mark vows to marry only the woman from whose head the hair comes and Tristrant undertakes the bridal quest.[8] Unlike what happens in the Tristan legend, the proxy wooer Hrólfr ends up marrying the woman whom he was seeking for his lord, who unfortunately dies a violent death at the hands of a *berserkr* (Kalinke 1990, 147–54).

The motif of fashioning an image that may be said to generate the plot in the Icelandic *Rémundar saga* also occurs in *Þiðreks saga*, which was composed at the court of King Hákon Hákonarson (r.1217–63) in Norway. *Þiðreks saga* is a large compilatory work based chiefly on lost Low German sources. The author/translator/compiler of the saga knew *Tristrams saga ok Ísöndar*, which should not come as a surprise, since both works originated at Hákon's court in Bergen, an important Hanseatic city. Several *þættir*, that is, short stories, incorporated into *Þiðreks saga* make use of the hall-of-statues motif (Schach 1968, 93–9). In 'Velents þáttr', an analogue to the story of Wayland the Smith in the eddic poem *Völundar kviða*, Velent secretly fashions a statue that is so lifelike that his king, Niðungr, believes it to be real and greets it (Guðni Jónsson edn 1954, 95–6). This is similar to what happens in *Rémundar saga* (see Kramarz-Bein 2002, 214–18). In a second tale, in 'Herburts þáttr ok Hildr' Þiðrekr hears about the beauty of Hildr, daughter of a certain King Artus, and sends his nephew Herburt as his proxy wooer to her father. He remains at court for some time, becomes Hildr's steward and falls in love with her. When Hildr asks Herburt about his uncle, whose proxy wooer he is supposed to be, Herburt draws a picture of Þiðrekr on a stone wall and depicts him as a rather dreadful-looking man (see Kramarz-Bein 2002, 219–24). As a result, Hildr asks why Herburt does not woo her for himself, which he then does, and the couple elope (321–3). Finally, in 'Írons þáttr' (341–4) the motif of creating a likeness is coupled with that of the hunt for the beloved. Íron neglects his wife Ísolde for the hunt and this frequently results in his absence for as long as twelve nights. On one of these occasions, when it has snowed, she leaves town, goes to a linden tree, takes off all her clothes, and stretches out in the snow. When her husband once again wants to leave for the hunt, she takes him to the linden tree and suggests that he might be better off hunting animals closer to home. He recognizes his wife in the likeness and henceforth ceases his hunting expeditions (see Kramarz-Bein 2002, 224–31). Unlike *Rémundar saga*, however, the three tales do not transmit the complete motif complex from the Tristan legend, that is, the fashioning of a lifelike image which the protagonist addresses and caresses as though it were a woman of flesh and blood.

That there exists a relationship between the Tristan legend and *Þiðreks saga* is also evident in the names that appear in the latter (Schach 1964, 284–6). Repeatedly women are named *Ísold* and *Ísolde*, the form of the name suggesting German derivation, and even a Tistram appears. Þiðrekr's sister is named Ísolde. She marries Count Herþegn and they have three sons, one of whom they name Tistram. Earl Íron and his wife Ísolde have a daughter who is named Ísolde like her mother. King Hernið, who is killed by a dragon, is married to an Ísold. Þiðrekr informs the widow of her husband's death and then he marries her himself. The fact that Earl Íron's wife is named Ísolde supports the interpretation of her likeness in the snow as an echo of the Tristan legend, but none of the other characters so named, or Tistram, is in any way connected to the Tristan legend. Like the authors of some Icelandic romances, the author of *Þiðreks saga* used names that would have resonated with his audience.

A variation of the image drawn on a wall in 'Herburts þáttr ok Hildr' in *Þiðreks saga* occurs in the Icelandic *Jarlmanns saga ok Hermanns* 'Saga of Jarlmann and Hermann', most likely composed in the late fourteenth or early fifteenth century. It is a bridal-quest romance in which the desired bride Ríkilát is famed as a physician and the proxy wooer Jarlmann pretends to be ill to gain access to her (Bjarni Vilhjálmsson edn 1954, 181). Jarlmann draws an image of his lord and foster-brother Hermann on a wall that is so impressive that Ríkilát says she cannot imagine that any woman would not choose him (184–5). The motif of the likeness most probably does not derive directly from the Tristan legend, but rather from *Rémundar saga*, to judge by certain verbal similarities (Schach 1968, 91–2). Nonetheless, there are enough echoes of the Tristan legend in *Jarlmanns saga ok Hermanns* to show that the author indubitably composed the saga with Tristram's story in mind (Kalinke 1990, 170–4). One might even say that the saga contains an implicit criticism of Tristram's behaviour. Like Ísodd's mother in the Icelandic *Saga af Tristram ok Ísodd*, Ríkilát's father offers his daughter to the proxy wooer Jarlmann, but he responds that he does not want to be called a *drottins-svikari* 'traitor to one's lord' (197).

It is noteworthy that the motif of the *drottinssvikari* occurs in one of the oldest Arthurian narratives in the North, in *Januals ljóð*, the translation of *Lanval* (see chapter 5). There King Arthur's queen attempts to seduce the eponymous protagonist, but he rejects her, saying that he has long served the king and neither wants to betray his faith – 'mentir ma fei' – nor wrong his lord – 'mesferai a mun seignur' (Rychner 1969, 80, vv. 272, 274). In the Norse translation the rejection appears to be more pointed. He tells the queen that neither for her sake nor her affection 'vil ec vera svicare, ne suivirðing herra mins' (will I be a deceiver or a disgrace to my lord) (Cook edn and trans. 1999, 12). By translating *svicare* with 'deceiver' and *suivirðing* with 'disgrace' (13), Cook is able to transmit the alliteration of the original text, but the full impact of the Norse *svikari*, which means 'traitor', is lessened. Although *Jarlmanns saga ok Hermanns* is undoubtedly indebted to the Tristan legend, it is remarkable that like Janual, but unlike Tristan, Jarlmann refuses to become a *drottinssvikari*.

In *Rémundar saga* and *Tristrams saga ok Ísöndar* the eponymous protagonists fashion a statue of the beloved that they treat as though the image were of flesh and blood. In one Icelandic romance, *Þjalar-Jóns saga*, 'Saga of File Jón', also known as *Jóns saga Svipdagssonar ok Eireks forvitna*, 'Saga of Jón Svipdagsson and Eirekr the Curious', the bridal quest is generated by an image of a maiden. Prince Eirekr discovers a chest containing the image of a maiden so beautiful and lifelike that it could have been taken for human had it been warm and able to speak (Tan-Haverhorst edn 1939, 7). This statue had been made by a mysterious stranger named Gestr 'Guest', a name appearing frequently in the Icelandic sagas and suggesting the person so named is in disguise. Eirekr discovers the statue when he attempts to ascertain Gestr's identity, and he vows to embark on a quest to find and marry her (see Kalinke 1990, 179–82).

Tristanian echoes are evident in another narrative that is extant today solely in *rímur* form, that is, in *Haralds rímur Hringsbana* 'Rímur of Haraldur Hringur's Slayer'. This metrical narrative, thought to have been composed during the first half of the fifteenth century, is probably based on an earlier *Haralds saga Hringsbana*, which has not been preserved.[9] *Haralds rímur* contains a proxy wooing, by a son, Haraldur, for his father, King Hringur of Denmark; a substituted bride, of a farmer's daughter named Signý like the princess, for the desired bride; and a voyage for healing. The tale departs from the canonical Tristan legend inasmuch as the king actually marries the substituted bride and only learns later that his son had betrayed him and taken the princess for himself. He attempts to kill his own son but is killed by him instead. Haraldur is subsequently wounded in combat with a stranger who, before being killed by Haraldur, curses him that the wound can only be healed by his sister. As is the case with some of the narratives discussed above, the author of *Haralds rímur* used the Tristanian motifs in a novel way. One of the more interesting mutations of the substituted-bride motif is the appearance of a stranger named Svipall, who in reality is the god Odin, and who proposes the substitution of the farmer's daughter for the princess. As happens in the Icelandic *Saga af Tristram ok Ísodd* and *Jarlmanns saga ok Hermanns*, the father's proxy wooer is considered a more appropriate match for Signý, daughter of the king of England. The royal steward remarks that things would turn out badly, if the proxy wooer does not get the bride himself (Ólafur Halldórsson edn 1973, 34, II.18).

Authors of the indigenous Icelandic romances revealed their general acquaintance with the *matière de Bretagne* through allusions and name-dropping. The late medieval Icelandic romance *Sigurðar saga þögla* 'Saga of Sigurðr the Taciturn' is set 'á dögum Arturii konungs hins fræga, er réð fyrir Bretlandi, sem síðan hefir England kallað verið' (Bjarni Vilhjálmsson edn 1954, 99) (in the days of the famous King Arthur, who ruled over the land of the Britons, which has since been called England). *Samsons saga fagra* 'Saga of Samson the Fair' is set in the days of King Arthur of England, Samson's father (Bjarni Vilhjálmsson edn,1954: 347), but this is not the legendary king. Yet, *Samsons saga* has repeatedly been linked in manuscripts and by scholars with the Arthurian translations thought to have been undertaken in Norway (Kalinke, 1981a: 223–4), and Henry Goddard Leach listed the saga in his hypothetical chart of foreign romances in Scandinavia (1921, 382). Apart from some of the personal and place names occurring in the saga and the fact that the plot contains the chastity-testing mantle known from *Möttuls saga*, there is no evidence positing a lost Arthurian romance as source (Kalinke 1981a, 224). Only the motif of the magic mantle derives indubitably from an existing Arthurian narrative, namely *Möttuls saga*, to which the saga refers at its end, but under the alternate title, *Skikkju saga* 'Mantle Saga'.

Samsons saga fagra provides additional information concerning the origin and properties of the magic mantle. This is procured from the Land of Little Maidens by a certain Kvintelin as punishment for his having abducted Samson's beloved, Princess

Valentina. The mantle had been woven by four elf-women over a period of eighteen years (380). In addition to being able to expose unfaithful women, as it does in *Möttuls saga*, this mantle can also expose thieves and reveal which maidens are lazy (390, 396).[10] On Samson's wedding day to Valentina the mantle is tested and it turns out that very few come off well, whereas the bride passes the test with flying colours. The mantle test is a blind motif in *Samsons saga*, however, since it neither serves any particular purpose nor advances the plot. Nonetheless, at the conclusion of the saga, the anonymous author situates the events in *Samsons saga* as having occurred prior to those in *Möttuls saga*. The narrator informs us that the mantle eventually came into the hands of a Viking who carried it off to Africa, where it remained until a powerful and jealous woman named Elida sent it to England, to King Arthur, and there a story about the mantle, entitled *Skikkju saga*, originated (401). The woman who according to *Samsons saga* sent the mantle to King Arthur is quite different from the exceedingly *fríð ok dýrlig* 'beautiful and illustrious' maiden who sent the magic garment to the court of Arthur in *Möttuls saga* (Kalinke edn 1999, 13). This Old Norse translation of *Le Lai du cort mantel* concludes by informing us that Karadin and his beloved, who was the only person at Arthur's court whom the mantle fitted, placed the magic garment in a monastery for safe keeping (29).

It has been suggested that the Arthurian motifs in *Samsons saga fagra* derive from a Lancelot romance, since several motifs, notably a cart, play a significant role in the saga: the evil Kvintalin has a dwarf named Grelent fashion for him a magic cart on wheels; Princess Valentina comes upon it and falls asleep in it. This cart is to be the means of her abduction. The cart motif has led to the thesis that *Samsons saga* derives from an oral version related to Ulrich von Zatzikhoven's *Lanzelet* (Simek 1985, 210–12), the source of which, according to the romance, was a French, presumably Anglo-Norman, book Ulrich had received from Hugh de Morville, one of the hostages at the court of Emperor Henry VI after Richard Lionheart returned to England in 1194 (Ranawake 2000, 46). In not quite 500 verses, this late twelfth-century German romance tells about a magic mantle, but unlike the garment in *Möttuls saga* and its French source, this is not a chastity-testing mantle but rather one that reveals the failure of men and women to adhere to the conventions of the courtly game of love, in the spirit of Andreas Capellanus's *De amore*. Consequently the reference to *Skikkju saga*, that is, *Möttuls saga*, at the end of *Samsons saga* most likely is accurate: the author of *Samsons saga* knew *Möttuls saga* and borrowed its chastity-testing mantle for his own composition.

A most popular motif in Arthurian romance, to judge by its many appearances in late medieval Icelandic romances is that of the grateful lion in *Ívens saga*. No fewer than six narratives contain the figure of the grateful lion which derives either directly from the thirteeenth-century Norwegian translation of Chrétien de Troyes's *Yvain* or from an Icelandic intermediary. In *Ívens saga* we read that the eponymous protagonist rides into a forest one day and hears howling and roaring. He comes upon a fire-spewing serpent and a lion engaged in a frightful struggle. Íven considers which of the two animals he should assist and decides to aid the lion since the animal seems to be appealing to him for help. Íven slays the serpent and then prepares to defend himself against the lion. The animal crawls towards him, however, 'sem hann vildi biðja sér friðar með tárum, ok gaf sik svá í vald herra Íven' (Kalinke edn 1999, 72) (as though it wanted to ask for peace with its tears, and thus it surrendered to Sir Íven) (Kalinke trans. 1999, 73–5). The knight and lion henceforth become inseparable companions, and Íven receives the epithet *leóns riddari* 'Knight with the Lion' (78).

Analogues of the grateful-lion episode appear in *Ectors saga* (chapter 10), the fragmentary *Grega saga*, *Kára saga Kárasonar* (chapter 18), *Konráðs saga keisarasonar* (chapter 8), *Vilhjálms saga sjóðs* (chapter 13), and *Sigurðar saga þögla* (chapters 15–16). In all of these sagas the serpent, *ormr*, from *Ívens saga* is transformed into a flying dragon, *flugdreki*, spewing fire and poison and carrying a lion in its claws. In *Sigurðar saga þögla*, 'Saga of Sigurðr the Taciturn', which, as noted earlier, is set in the days of King Arthur, the eponymous protagonist decides to save the lion, when he recalls that he has the image of a lion on his shield. He kills the dragon and then heals the wounded lion, which, it turns out, exhibits both *frœkleika* 'valour' and *viturleika* 'wisdom' and is as gentle as a cat (Bjarni Vilhjálmsson edn 1954, 148). *Sigurðar saga þögla* contains the most expansive account of the protagonist and his lion (see Kalinke, 1981a: 231–6), even including information about the lion that derives from learned sources, such as the *Physiologus*.

The fragmentary *Grega saga* contains a dragon–lion episode that combines motifs from both *Ívens saga* and *Þiðreks saga*. The grateful lion becomes Grega's companion and the author of the saga includes an adaptation of the Fjallsharfir (Harpins de la Montaingne) episode from *Ívens saga* (Kalinke edn 1999, 79), in which the lion attacks and kills in quick succession not one giant, as in *Ívens saga*, but three (Loth edn 1960, 204–5). Íven's lion becomes further anthropomorphized in *Konráðs saga keisarasonar*, 'Saga of Konráðr the Emperor's Son'. After Konráðr has rescued the lion, the protagonist addresses the animal and says that he has heard that the lion is most wise and understands human speech, and therefore he offers to become his liege lord, while the lion is to accompany and serve him faithfully. And the narrator comments that in response the lion shed tears like a human being, rolled over on its back, and is reconciled. Konráðr puts the lion on a leash and subsequently addresses the animal repeatedly as if it were a human being (Bjarni Vilhjálmsson edn 1954, 312).

The author of *Sigurðar saga þögla* knew not only *Ívens saga* but also *Þiðreks saga*, from which he borrowed the detail of the lion on Sigurðr's shield. As noted earlier, the author of *Þiðreks saga* knew *Tristrams saga ok Ísöndar* from which he borrowed names and the Hall-of-Statues motif. At the conclusion of the saga Þiðrekr marries Ísold, the widow of King Hernið, who had been killed by a dragon. The narrator reports that Hernið has learned that a dragon lies in a certain forest and he decides to find it and either gain fame or find death, *vinna frægð eða fá bana* (Guðni Jónsson edn

1954, 561). The narrator comments that he decides to attack the dragon more out of impetuosity and for the sake of fame than wisdom. The dragon picks him up with its claws and flies with him to its lair, where it casts Hernið to its young, which devour him. Subsequently Þiðrekr comes upon the dragon as it is engaged in a fierce struggle with a lion. He recalls that his shield bears the image of a lion and decides to help this animal. Þiðrekr's sword is useless, however, and he prays to God to help him. He uproots a tree, intending to kill the dragon with it, but the animal picks up the lion with its claws and at the same time wraps its tail around Þiðrekr, and flies to its lair. There the dragon and its young devour the lion. Having had its fill, the dragon straightens out its tail and Þiðrekr is released. He finds a sword, which turns out to have belonged to Hernið, and kills the dragon and its young (563–4).

The author of *Þiðreks saga* knew not only *Tristrams saga* but also other translations that were produced at the court of Hákon Hákonarson in Bergen, among them *Ívens saga*. Kramarz-Bein noted the frequency of anthropomorphized animals in *Þiðreks saga* and posited influence from *Ívens saga* and its lion, which may have inspired a similar portrayal of Þiðrekr's horse Falka (2002, 259–63). The impact of *Ívens saga* on *Þiðreks saga* goes beyond the portrayal of animals, however, for the dragon–lion episode presumably is based on the same in *Ívens saga*. As is the case with the three stories that incorporate the Hall-of-Statues motif from *Tristrams saga*, the dragon–lion episode is transformed in *Þiðreks saga*, for the eponymous protagonist is not able to save the lion. Moreover, the creeping dragon from *Ívens saga* becomes a flying dragon in *Þiðreks saga* and this flying dragon becomes the model for the same in the late medieval Icelandic romances. An episode with a flying dragon is even incorporated into *Erex saga* (Kalinke 1981a, 194–7, 244–6; see also chapter 6), which derives ultimately from Chrétien de Troyes's *Erec et Enide*. The interpolated episode that is not found in the French romance most likely was borrowed from *Þiðreks saga*.

A survey of Tristanian and Arthurian motifs in the indigenous Icelandic romances reveals not only direct borrowing from such translations as *Tristrams saga ok Ísöndar* and *Ívens saga* but also loans from within the corpus of indigenous Icelandic romance. *Þiðreks saga* is a unique case, since the work is thought to be a compilation based on German heroic poems about Dietrich von Bern (Theoderic). The saga was produced in the Bergen area, where King Hákon Hákonarson, who commissioned the translation of several Arthurian narratives, held court. There is no certainty whether *Þiðreks saga* derives from an already existing Low German compilation or whether the compilation occurred in the process of translation. There seems to be no doubt, however, that the work as we know it bears traces in the form of allusions, motifs, structure and style of the translations undertaken at Hákon's court (Kramarz-Bein 2002). While the author of *Þiðreks saga* adopted and adapted the dragon–lion episode from *Ívens saga* in the thirteenth century, the authors of fourteenth- and fifteenth-century Icelandic romances borrowed the grateful-lion episode from *Ívens saga* but shaped their own versions under the influence of the dragon–lion tale in *Þiðreks saga*.

Notes

[1] Subsequent references to the *Saga af Tristram ok Ísodd* are to the Jorgensen and Hill edition and translation (1999).

[2] See also Bagerius 2009, 116–17.

[3] The article by Kramarz-Bein contains a thorough review of scholarship on the *Spesar þáttr* and its relationship to the Tristan legend.

[4] One of the most ardent proponents of this thesis was Bjarni Einarsson in his monograph *Skáldasögur* (Reykjavík, 1961). In 'Skald sagas in their literary context. 2: possible European contexts' Alison Finlay (2001) discusses at length Bjarni Einarsson's theses with special attention to *Kormáks saga* (see pp. 245–65).

[5] That the Icelandic redaction of the saga appears to have lost some text is suggested by Gottfried von Strassburg's *Tristan*. There too the Irishman, named Gandin, offers Tristan 'the finest clothes that we have in this pavilion', if Tristan can console Isolt. When Tristan rides off with her, he says, like Tristram, that what Gandin had taken away with his harp, he now takes away with his. But he then adds: 'You bestow magnificent clothes, friend. I have the best that I saw in your tent!' (Gottfried von Strassburg, *Tristan*, trans. A. T. Hatto (London, 1967), pp. 216, 218). Tristan's reference to having received clothes, as promised, is missing in the saga, but presumably was found in the Norwegian translation. The episode is related in vv. 13,110–425 (Gottfried von Straßburg, *Tristan*, vol. I, ed. K. Marold, Berlin and New York, 1977).

[6] The expression *kaupa um knífa* 'exchange one knife for another' is a euphemism referring to the male sexual organ.

[7] Simek considers it 'surprising if, of all well known romances in Old French ... Lancelot was the only one not to be translated into Old Norse' (1985, 205). He fails to consider, however, that this Arthurian romance by Chrétien de Troyes was not translated at all into any language in the Middle Ages.

[8] See *Eilhart von Oberg. Tristrant*, ed. D. Buschinger (Göppingen, 1976), vv. 1381–1434.

[9] Echoes of this no longer extant medieval narrative are found in a younger *Haralds saga Hringsbana*, most likely composed in the seventeenth century (Ólafur Halldórsson edn 1973, 17) and thought by Margaret Schlauch 'to have been constructed as a deliberate reply to the French romance' (1934, 151). H. G. Leach provides a summary of this seventeenth-century *Haralds saga Hringsbana*, which has not been published (see Leach and Schoepperle 1915, 269–72).

[10] That the mantle can also reveal whether maidens are lazy is a striking element, since it also occurs in the late eighteenth-century novel *Der kurze Mantel* by Benedikte Naubert, the sources for which are thought to have been the sixteenth-century prose version *Le Manteau mal taillié* and the ballad 'The boy and the mantle'. The ability of the mantle to identify lazy maidens presumably derives from the ancient folktale about Frau Hulda or Frau Holle, who punishes lazy and impertinent women (see introduction to *Möttuls saga* (1987), xxx–xxxi).

Reference List

Texts and Translations

Chrétien de Troyes. *Lancelot or, The Knight of the Cart (Le Chevalier de la Charrete)*, ed. and trans. William W. Kibler (New York and London, 1981).
Ectors saga, ed. A. Loth, in *Late Medieval Icelandic Romances*, I, Editiones Arnamagnæanæ, B, 20 (Copenhagen, 1962), pp. 79–186.
Flateyjarbók, ed. Guðbrandur Vigfusson and C. R. Unger (Christiania, 1860–8).
Göngu-Hrolfs saga, trans. Hermann Pálsson and P. Edwards (Edinburgh, 1980).

Göngu-Hrólfs saga, ed. Guðni Jónsson, in *Fornaldar sögur Norðurlanda*, III (Reykjavík, 1954), pp. 161–280.

Grega saga, ed. A. Loth, in 'Fragment af en ellers ukendt "Grega saga"', *Opuscula*, I, Bibliotheca Arnamagnæana, 20 (Copenhagen, 1960), pp. 201–6.

Grettis saga Ásmundarsonar, ed. Guðni Jónsson, Íslenzk fornrit, 7 (Reykjavík, 1936).

Gvímars saga, ed. M. E. Kalinke, in *Opuscula*, VII, Bibliotheca Arnamagnæana, 34 (Copenhagen, 1979), pp. 106–39.

Haralds rímur Hringsbana, ed. Ólafur Halldórsson, Íslenzkar Miðaldarímur, 1 (Reykjavík, 1973).

Helga þáttr Þórissonar, ed. Guðni Jónsson, in *Fornaldar sögur Norðurlanda*, IV (Reykjavík, 1954), pp. 345–53.

Janual, ed. and trans. R. Cook, in *Norse Romance*, I, *The Tristan Legend*, ed. M. E. Kalinke (Cambridge, 1999), pp. 10–22.

Jarlmanns saga ok Hermanns, ed. Bjarni Vilhjálmsson, in *Riddarasögur*, VI (Reykjavík, 1954), pp. 171–235.

Konráðs saga keisarasonar, ed. Bjarni Vilhjálmsson, in *Riddarasögur*, III (Reykjavík, 1954), pp. 269–344.

Kormak's Saga, trans. Rory McTurk, in *Sagas of Warrior-Poets* (London, 2002), pp. 3–67.

Kormáks saga, ed. Einar Ól. Sveinsson, in *Vatnsdæla saga, Hallfreðar saga, Kormáks saga*, Íslenzk fornrit, VIII (Reykjavík, 1939), pp. 201–302.

Mágus saga jarls hin meiri, ed. Bjarni Vilhjálmsson, in *Riddarasögur*, II (Reykjavík, 1954), pp. 135–429.

Lanval, ed. J. Rychner, in *Les Lais de Marie de France* (Paris, 1969), pp. 72–92.

Marie de France. *Le Lai de Lanval, accompagné du texte du* Ianuals lioð *et de sa traduction française avec une introduction et des notes par P. Aebischer*, ed. J. Rychner (Geneva and Paris, 1958).

Mǫttuls saga: With an Edition of Le Lai du Cort Mantel *by Philip E. Bennett*, ed. M. E. Kalinke, Editiones Arnamagnæanæ, B, 30 (Copenhagen, 1987).

Möttuls saga, ed. M. E. Kalinke, in *Norse Romance*, II: *The Knights of the Round Table*, ed. M. E. Kalinke (Cambridge, 1999), pp. 1–31.

The Saga of Grettir the Strong, trans. B. Scudder, in *The Complete Sagas of Icelanders*, II, ed. Viðar Hreinsson (Reykjavík, 1997), pp. 49–191.

Saga af Tristram ok Ísodd, ed. P. Jorgensen, in *Norse Romance*, I: *The Tristan Legend*, ed. M. E. Kalinke (Cambridge, 1999), pp. 244–90.

The Saga of Tristram and Ísodd, trans. J. Hill, in *Norse Romance*, I: *The Tristan Legend*, ed. M. E. Kalinke (Cambridge, 1999), pp. 245–91.

Sagan af Kára Kárasyni, ed. Einar Þórðarson (Reykjavík, 1886).

Samsons saga fagra, ed. Bjarni Vilhjálmsson, in *Riddarasögur*, III (Reykjavík, 1954), pp. 345–401.

Sigurðar saga þögla, ed. Bjarni Vilhjálmsson, in *Riddarasögur*, III (Reykjavík, 1954), pp. 95–267.

Vilhjálms saga sjóðs, ed. A. Loth, in *Late Medieval Icelandic Romances*, IV, Editiones Arnamagnæanæ, B, 23 (Copenhagen, 1964), pp. 1–136.

Þiðreks saga af Bern, ed. Guðni Jónsson (Reykjavík, 1954).

Þjalar Jóns saga, ed. L. F. Tan-Haverhorst, in *Þjalar Jóns saga. Dámusta saga* (Diss. Leiden, 1939), pp. 1–47.

Studies

Bagerius, H. (2009). *Mandom och mödom. Sexualitet, homosocialitet och aristokratisk identitet på den senmedeltida Island*, Göteborg.

Barnes, G. (1999). 'Tristan in late medieval Norse literature: saga and ballad', in *Tristan und Isolt im Spätmittelalter, Chloe. Beihefte zum Daphnis*, 29, pp. 373–96.

Bjarni Einarsson (1961). *Skáldasögur. Um uppruna og eðli ástaskáldasagnanna fornu*, Reykjavík.

Bjarni Einarsson. (1976). *To skjaldesagaer. En analyse af Kormáks saga og Hallfreðar saga*, Bergen, Oslo and Tromsø.

Clover, C. J. (1986). '*Vǫlsunga saga* and the missing lai of Marie de France', in R. Simek, Jónas Kristjánsson and H. Bekker-Nielsen (eds), *Sagnaskemmtun: Studies in Honour of Hermann Pálsson*, Vienna, Cologne and Graz, pp. 79–84.

Finlay, A. (2001). 'Skald sagas in their literary context, 2: Possible European contexts', in R. Poole (ed.), *Skaldsagas: Text, Vocation, and Desire in the Icelandic Sagas of Poets*, Ergänzungsbände zum Reallexikon der Germanischen Altertumskunde, 27, Berlin and New York, pp. 232–71.

Halvorsen, E. F. (1959). *The Norse Version of the Chanson de Roland*, Bibliotheca Arnamagnæana, 19, Copenhagen.

Jochens, J. (1995). *Women in Old Norse Society*, Ithaca, NY.

Kalinke, M. E. (1981a). *King Arthur, North-by-Northwest: The* matière de Bretagne *in Old Norse-Icelandic Romances*, Bibliotheca Arnamagnæana, 37, Copenhagen.

Kalinke, M. (1981b). 'A werewolf in bear's clothing', *Maal og Minne*, 137–44.

Kalinke, M. E. (1990). *Bridal-Quest Romance in Medieval Iceland*, Islandica, 46, Ithaca and London.

Kalinke, M. (2008). 'Female desire and the quest in the Icelandic legend of Tristram and Ísodd', in N. J. Lacy (ed.), *The Grail, the Quest and the World of Arthur*, Cambridge, pp. 76–91.

Kalinke, M. E. (2009). '*Tristrams saga ok Ísöndar*, chapter 80: ekphrasis as recapitulation and interpretation', in *Analecta Septentrionalia*. Ergänzungsbände zum Reallexikon der Germanischen Altertumskunde, 65, Berlin, pp. 221–37.

Kramarz-Bein, S. (2000). 'Der *Spesar Þáttr* der *Grettis saga*. Tristan-Spuren in der Isländersaga', in H. Beck and E. Ebel (eds), *Studien zur Isländersaga. Festschrift für Rolf Heller*, Ergänzungsbände zum Reallexikon der Germanischen Altertumskunde, 24, Berlin and New York, pp. 152–81.

Kramarz-Bein, S. (2002). *Die Þiðreks saga im Kontext der altnorwegischen Literatur*, Beiträge zur nordischen Philologie, 33, Tübingen and Basel.

Kolbrún Haraldsdóttir (1993). 'Flateyjarbók', in P. Pulsiano and K. Wolf (eds), *Medieval Scandinavia: An Encyclopedia*, New York and London, pp. 197–8.

Leach, H. G. (1921). *Angevin Britain and Scandinavia*, Harvard Studies in Comparative Literature, VI, Cambridge and London.

Leach, H. G. and Schoepperle, G. (1915). 'Haraldssaga Hringsbana and the Tristan and Svanhild romances,' *Scandinavian Studies*, 2, 264–76.

Lurkhur, K. A. (2008). 'Redefining gender through the arena of the male body: the reception of Thomas's *Tristran* in the Old French *Le Chevalier de la Charette* and the Old Icelandic *Saga af Tristram ok Ísodd*', unpublished Ph.D. thesis, University of Illinois, Urbana.

Mitchell, P. M. (1959). 'Scandinavian literature', in R. S. Loomis (ed.), *Arthurian Literature in the Midddle Ages*, Oxford, pp. 462–71.

Power, R. (1985). '*Le Lai de Lanval* and *Helga þáttr Þórissonar*', *Opuscula*, 8, Bibliotheca Arnamagnæana, 38, Copenhagen, pp. 158–61.

Ranawake, S. (2000). 'The emergence of German Arthurian romance: Hartmann von Aue and Ulrich von Zatzikhoven', in W. H. Jackson and S. A. Ranawake (eds), *The Arthur of the Germans: The Arthurian Legend in Medieval German and Dutch Literature*, Cardiff, pp. 38–53.

Schach, P. (1960). 'The *Saga af Tristram ok Ísodd*: summary or satire?', *Modern Language Quarterly*, 21, 336–52.

Schach, P. (1962). 'Tristan in Iceland', *Prairie Schooner*, 36, 151–64.

Schach, P. (1964). 'Tristan and Isolde in Scandinavian ballad and folktale', *Scandinavian Studies*, 36, 281–97.

Schach, P. (1968). 'Some observations on the influence of *Tristrams saga ok Ísöndar* on Old Icelandic literature', in E. C. Polomé (ed.), *Old Norse Literature and Mythology: A Symposium*, Austin, TX and London, pp. 81–129.

Schach, P. (1987). '*Tristrams saga ok Ýsoddar* as burlesque', *Scandinavian Studies*, 59, 86–100.

Schlauch, M. (1934). *Romance in Iceland*. Princeton.

Schultz, J. A. (1996). 'Ulrich von Zatzikhoven', in N. J. Lacy (ed.), *The New Arthurian Encyclopedia*, New York and London, pp. 481–2.

Simek, R. (1985). 'Lancelot in Iceland', in R. Boyer (ed.), *Les Sagas de Chevaliers (Riddarasögur). Actes de la Ve Conférence Internationale sur les Sagas (Toulon, Juillet 1982)*, Paris, pp. 205–16.

Skårup, P. (1980). 'Forudsætter Rémundar saga en norrøn Lancelots saga kerrumanns', *Gripla*, IV, pp. 76–80.

Thomas, M. F. (1983). 'The briar and the vine: Tristan goes north', *Arthurian Literature*, III, Cambridge, pp. 53–90.

9

ARTHURIAN BALLADS, *RÍMUR*, CHAPBOOKS AND FOLKTALES

M. J. Driscoll

The *matière de Bretagne*, especially the legend of Tristan, remained popular – and productive – in late medieval and early modern Scandinavia, not least in Iceland. One clear indication of this is the continued transmission of the Old Norse translations and adaptations from French – the so-called *riddarasögur* – well into the modern era. *Erex saga*, for example, the Old Norse translation of Chrétien's *Erec et Enide*, is found in eleven manuscripts, only one of which, a fragment comprising two parts of a single leaf, is from before the Reformation; the others are all post-medieval, the youngest from the beginning of the twentieth century (Kalinke and Mitchell 1985, 39).

Another indication of the enduring popularity of this material is the use of names and motifs borrowed from Arthurian romance in the late and post-medieval Icelandic romances or *lýgisögur* (surveyed in Kalinke 1981, 221–41; also see chapter 8). One example is *Sigurðar saga þögla*, said to take place 'á dögum Arturi hins fræga, er réð fyrir Bretlandi, en síðan hefur England kallat verit' (in the days of the famous King Arthur, who ruled over Britain, which has since been called England),[1] and another is *Samsons saga fagra*, which begins 'Artus hét kongr er réð fyrir Englandi' (Arthur was the name of a king who ruled over England). Grateful lions, deriving ultimately from *Ívens saga*, were especially popular and appear in many of the late- and post-medieval *lygisögur* (Driscoll 1992, lxxiv–lxxvii), including the very late folktale-like narrative *Vígkæns saga kúahirðis*, which is preserved only in a single nineteenth-century manuscript but also appeared in a popular printed edition from 1886 (Einar Ól. Sveinsson 1929, lvii–lviii; Kalinke 1981, 233–9).

Motifs deriving from the Tristan legend are found in *Rémundar saga keisarasonar*, *Haralds saga Hringsbana* – which Margaret Schlauch thought 'seem[ed] to have been constructed as a deliberate reply to the French romance' (Schlauch 1934, 151) – *Jarlmanns saga ok Hermanns* and several other romances, but also in 'Spesar þáttr', the final section of *Grettis saga* (Schach 1969, 111–21). Similarly, several episodes in *Kormáks saga* appear to have been influenced by the Tristan legend to such an extent that Bjarni Einarsson could refer to Kormákr as 'Tristan Íslands' (Bjarni Einarsson 1961, 163).

Arthurian matter also formed the basis for new works in other genres, such as the ballad, examples of which are found in Icelandic, Danish, Faroese and Norwegian, all probably dating from the fifteenth and sixteenth centuries. In the sixteenth and seventeenth centuries Arthurian material found its way from Germany to Scandinavia, principally Denmark, in the form of chapbooks, or *Volksbücher*, the Danish translations of which in turn generated Icelandic versions, both in prose and verse. Finally, a group of Icelandic folktales contains echoes, however faint, of the story of Tristan and Isolde.

Tristrams kvæði

The traditional ballad was never as popular in Iceland as it was in mainland Scandinavia and the British Isles; the lack of alliteration – a requirement in Icelandic poetry to the present day – presumably made ballad metres sound odd to Icelandic ears, while the dominance of the *rímur*, or metrical romances, as the preferred form for narrative verse in late medieval and early modern Iceland meant that the ballad had no real place in the literary landscape. There are, however, some fine examples of the genre among the one hundred or so Icelandic ballads – known as *fornkvæði* (literally old poems) or *sagnadansar* (literally saga-dances) – which have come down to us, perhaps none finer than *Tristrams kvæði* (ÍF 23[2]; ed. Jón Helgason 1962–81), whose simple refrain, 'Þeim var ekki skapað nema (að) skilja' (They were fated only to be parted), seems to capture so beautifully the pathos of the Tristan story.

Texts of *Tristrams kvæði* are preserved in seven manuscripts from the seventeenth and eighteenth centuries, as well as several younger copies made of these. Its original date of composition is generally reckoned to have been some time in the fifteenth century, perhaps as early as 1400. Scholars identify four separate versions of the ballad.[3] These vary somewhat in length, version A comprising thirty-three stanzas,[4] version C thirty and versions B and D both twenty-two; otherwise there are no significant divergences between them, though version B has a different refrain, the somewhat less appropriate 'Og er sá sæll sem sofna náir hjá henni' (and fortunate is he who gets to fall asleep next to her).[5]

The metre of *Tristrams kvæði* is rather unusual – so much so that it is sometimes referred to as 'Tristramsháttur' (Tristram's metre) (Vésteinn Ólason 1979, 37) – having four stressed syllables in the first and third lines but only two, rather than the normal three, in the second and fourth.

Unlike many of the Icelandic ballads, *Tristrams kvæði* has no parallels among the ballads of other traditions – the Danish and Faroese Tristan ballads, discussed below, are unrelated – and, although some scholars have posited a Norwegian original (e.g., Liestøl 1931, 86), there appears to be no reason to see it as anything other than an original Icelandic composition.

The ballad relates the story of Tristram's death, the result of a wound incurred (at London Bridge according to version C) while fighting against the 'heathen dog':

> Tristram framdi bardagann
> við heiðinn hund;
> margur fékk á þeirra fundi
> blóðuga und.
>   Þeim var ekki skapað nema skilja. (ÍF 23 C, 2)

> (Tristram fought a battle
> against the heathen dog;
> many a man received at their meeting
> a bloody wound.
>   They were fated only to be parted.)

Tristram refuses to be treated by any physician, asking instead that Ísodd *bjarta* (the bright) be sent for. His men set off, instructed to hoist blue sails if she is with them on the return voyage, but black otherwise. Initially the king is reluctant to let her go, saying that Tristram is doomed to die, but the second time she asks he relents. The king expresses his doubt that she will return safely, but Ísodd says that it is up to God to decide whether she returns and that she will not forget her duties while away. They set off and the blue sails are hoisted. Ísodd *svarta* (the black), who is standing outside, twice (or thrice in version A) declares that the sails are black, causing Tristram to die of grief:

> Tristram snerist í sinni sæng,
> so sárt hann stakk;
> heyra mætti mílur fimm
> hans hjartað sprakk.
>   Þeim var ekki skapað nema skilja. (ÍF 23 C, 18)

> (Tristram turned in his bed,
> so great was his pain;
> for five miles around could be heard
> his heart break.
>   They were fated only to be parted.)

Ísodd *bjarta* comes ashore and hears singing and bells tolling. She makes her way to the church, where priests are standing round with candles. She bends down over the body and dies. Ísodd *svarta* declares that they may not enjoy each other even in death and has them buried on either side of the church. A tree grows from each grave, their branches meeting above the church:

> Uxu upp þeirra af leiðunum
> lundar tveir;
> fyrir ofan miðju kirkju
> mættust þeir.
>   Þeim var ekki skapað nema skilja. (ÍF 23 C, 30)

> (Up from their graves
> grew two trees
> above the middle of the church
> they met.
>   They were fated only to be parted.)

There are several points of contact between *Tristrams kvæði* and the *Saga af Tristram ok Ísodd* – i.e., the younger, Icelandic version of the story, dated to around 1400, as opposed to Brother Robert's Old Norse *Tristrams saga ok Ísöndar* – the most striking of which is the name and cognomen of Tristram's wife. In *Tristrams saga* the hero's beloved, the queen, is called Ísönd, while the woman he marries is named Ísodd; in the younger saga, and in the ballad, both women are named Ísodd, the queen with the epithet *fagra* (the fair; beautiful) in the saga and *bjarta* (the bright) in the ballad, while Tristram's wife is known in both as Ísodd *svarta* (the black). On the basis of this, Eugen Kölbing argued that the ballad must derive from the younger saga (Kölbing 1878, xvii) while Wolfgang Golther suggested that both sagas must have been known to the composer of the ballad (Golther 1907, 188). This was also the opinion of Paul Schach, who argued that the author of the ballad took his inspiration from the older saga and the names of the two women from the younger (Schach 1957–61, 123). In a later article, however, he seems to favour the idea that the author of the saga knew the ballad, while still feeling that 'the whole spirit of the poem . . . point[s] unmistakably to the final chapters of *Tristrams saga* as the major source' (Schach 1964, 286). Vésteinn Ólason has noted several verbal parallels between the ballad and the younger *Saga af Tristram ok Ísodd* which are most likely to have come about if the author of the latter had been familiar with the former (Vésteinn Ólason 1982, 213–16). This, if true, would indicate that *Tristrams kvæði* must have been composed before *c*.1400, making it the oldest of the extant Icelandic ballads. It should, however, be remembered that in most continental versions of the story the two women are namesakes – this is, indeed, the point – so the fact that they also share the same name in the two younger Icelandic manifestations of the story need not necessarily prove that there is any direct connection between them. Icelandic literary history is not, after all, an entirely self-contained system.

As a ballad *Tristrams kvæði* works well, whatever its origin. It is well constructed, making particularly effective use of repetition at key points in the narrative. Unlike most ballads, however, it does seem to presuppose familiarity with the underlying story: how else could one understand why 'þeim var ekki skapað nema að skilja'?

The Danish Tristan ballads

There are two Danish ballads which derive from the Tristan legend. The first of these, *Tistram og Isold* (DgF 470; ed. Olrik 1905–19), is preserved in nine manuscripts, all but one from the first half of the seventeenth century. There is some textual variation between them, but not so great as to preclude their deriving from a single original, probably dating from the sixteenth century. This appears to belong among the young-est of the Danish ballads, and, like many others, to have originated and circulated in an aristocratic milieu.

The narrative tells how Sir Thisterum sends word to the Lady Isall – to use the forms of the names found in the texts – asking that she meet him in their trysting place 'i rosens lund' (in the wildrose wood). That evening, accompanied only by her maid, she rides out to the appointed place. Somewhat curiously, given the obviousness of the situation, the narrator takes pains to assure us that nothing untoward happened there:

> De satte dem både til jorden neder
> alt i hverandres arm;
> i-hvad de snakkede og hvad de talte,
> det var foruden harm.
>
> Den rider og den frue
> de havde hverandre så kære;
> det vil jeg for sanden sige,
> dem fulgte både tugt og ære. (DgF 470, 9–10)
>
> (They sat themselves both down on the ground
> all in each other's arms;
> whatever they said and whatever they spoke
> it was without harm.
>
> This knight and this lady
> they held each other so dear;
> this I will say in truth,
> decency and honour accompanied them.)

After a time the maid says that they have lingered too long. The two lovers part, praying to God that they will be able to meet again soon. Returning, Isall is confronted by her husband, who angrily asks what she has been doing in the wildrose wood, and why her cheek is pale; such behaviour is unbecoming to the queen of the land, he says. Her maid hastily intervenes, saying that they had assisted a fair lady who had that night given birth to a son. This seems to placate the king – though this is not stated – and the maid's presence of mind is richly rewarded by her lady in the ballad's final stanza.

Although reminiscent of a number of trysting scenes in *Tristrams saga*, the situation depicted here does not correspond directly to any of them. The quick-witted serving maid, referred to as 'jomfru' (maiden) or 'tjenestemø' (serving girl), is clearly reminiscent of Bringvet, and in the excuse that they had helped a woman in childbirth there may be an echo of Ysolt's well-known abilities as healer. The suspicious husband, identified in some texts as King Magnus, brief though his appearance is, certainly corresponds well to the figure of King Markis. None of this necessitates any direct connection with the saga, however, and the form 'Isall', which seems more easily derivable from the French 'Ysolt' than the Old Norse-Icelandic 'Ísönd', could suggest that the ballad's immediate source might rather lie in some other, non-Scandinavian, form of the Tristan legend.

The other Danish Tristan ballad, *Tistram og Jomfru Isolt* (DgF 471; ed. Olrik 1905–19), differs in many respects from that just dealt with, both in terms of its transmission history and its relation to other Tristan-related material. The ballad is preserved in fourteen manuscripts altogether, dating from the sixteenth to the eighteenth centuries. Scholars have identified five main versions, designated A–E in *Danmarks gamle Folkeviser*.[6] Although it is difficult to say anything with any certainty about the ballad's original date of composition, the mere fact that it exists in such a relatively large number of versions suggests that it must have been in circulation for some time before first being written down, presumably in the latter half of the sixteenth century, the date of the earliest manuscripts. The five versions vary in length and complexity, but common to all of them is the notion of interdiction: the young Tistram is advised by his mother not to go to the emperor's hall as it will bring him sorrow and shame; he sets out nevertheless, initially winning himself esteem and glory. The maid Isolt notices him and expresses her desire to meet/kiss/wed him, a suggestion angrily rebuffed by the Lady Grimholt, the empress and, ostensibly, Isolt's mother, who sets out to prevent the two coming together. In the shorter versions, A, B and C, the two lovers are able to win each other, and Lady Isolt, according to version B, 'sover i Herre Tistrams arm' (sleeps in Sir Tistram's arms). An attempt by the Lady Grimholt in versions B and C to poison the two lovers fails, as Tistram forces her to drink the poison instead. In the longer versions, D and E, the reason for the interdiction is made clear: Tistram and Isolt are brother and sister of whom it is prophesied that 'de skulde hverandre trolove' (they would pledge their troth to each other). To avert this, the two are separated and Isolt is sent to the emperor and empress of Rome and reared there as their own child. In these versions, the empress is successful in poisoning them, and Isolt lies, not sleeping, but 'død i Herre Tistrams arm' (dead in Sir Tistram's arms).

The principal manuscripts all date from roughly the same period, the latter part of the sixteenth century and beginning of the seventeenth. Version B, which includes Grimholt's attempt to poison the couple, is the earliest to have been written down, being found in 'Jens Billes Håndskrift', written in the period 1555–9.[7] The editors of *Danmarks gamle Folkeviser* believed the simplest version to be the most original, and that the changes and additions in the other versions were attempts to explain how the basic situation could have come about, as is reflected in their ordering of the versions. At the same time, however, the longer versions seem better to reflect, and may therefore better preserve, the original story: this is argued by Gísli Brynjúlfsson (1878, 333), and appears to be the underlying assumption in Paul Schach's article on the ballads, though he only goes as far as to say, in a footnote, that he believes 'that those versions of the ballad which have preserved the tragic fate theme basic to the Tristan story within a coherent narrative whole are closer in spirit and form to the original poem than those which are characterized by lack of coherence and motivation and the replacement of the death of the lovers by the fairy-tale happy ending' (Schach 1964, 288, fn. 24). Either way, the ballad as we have it has little to do with the medieval *Tristrams saga* apart from the names of the protagonists, although there are some points of similarity with the Faroese *Tístrams táttur* and the Icelandic folktales, discussed below.

The Faroese ballads

In contrast to Iceland, the Faroe Islands have a rich ballad tradition; indeed, the ballad was the pre-eminent form of artistic expression in the Faroes for many centuries. Arthurian material is found in the short but powerfully dramatic *Tístrams táttur* and in the long ballad-cycle *Ívint Herintsson*.

Tístrams táttur (CCF 110; ed. Djurhuus 1968) is extant in a single redaction recorded by V. U. Hammershaimb in 1848. His informant was Anne Hansdatter, a seventy-seven-year-old woman living at Sjúrðargarður, Fámjin, on the island of Suðuroy.[8] The ballad comprises thirty-seven four-line stanzas, in which the events are treated in rapid succession, the narrator in several places breaking in to avow the veracity of the story with phrases such as 'tað var mær av sonnum sagt' (truly it has been told to me). There is a five-line refrain, 'Burt skal eg ørind ríða' etc. (I must ride away), which is also found in several other Faroese ballads.[9]

Tístrams táttur is certainly the most dramatic – and arguably the most 'northern' – of the Scandinavian Tristan treatments. Like the Icelandic *Tristrams kvæði*, it concentrates on the tragic fate of the two lovers, stating at the very outset:

> Tað var áður í fyrdinni,
> saman untust tvey,
> Tístram og hún Ísin frú,
> av harmi sprungu tey. (CCF 110, 1)

> (It was long ago in the past,
> two [people] loved each other,
> Tístram and the Lady Ísin,
> they died of grief.)

Tístram and Ísin are inseparable; it is said of them that 'tað mátti ei annað úti vera, tá ið annað tað var inni' (the one could not be outside if the other was inside). Tístram's parents, in order to prevent the union – for which no reason is given, other than the mother's wickedness – send him to France where he is to seek the hand of the daughter of the king; if he refuses, the letter he bears with him from his father to the king dictates that he should be put to death. Before departing, Tístram meets Ísin in the garden; he pledges his fidelity to her and promises to return. Upon his arrival in France Tístram makes his way to the king's hall and presents him with the letter. The king informs his daughter of the coming of a suitor, which news she takes joyfully. Tístram, however, steadfastly refuses to comply, saying:

> Frættir tað ikki Ísin frúgv,
> eystur í síni lond,
> at eg lovist tíni dóttur,
> giftist tær í hond. (CCF 110, 22)

> (The Lady Ísin shall not hear,
> in her land in the east,
> that I was betrothed to
> and married your daughter.)

He is then taken and hanged. His men return and are met on the shore by Ísin, who upon hearing of Tístram's fate, immediately sails back to France. In a scene clearly reminiscent of Guðrún's vengeance on Atli, as described in *Atlakviða* and *Völsunga saga*, she makes her way to the king's hall and sets fire to it, killing all who are inside, women and children alike. As the flames engulf him, the king asks what he has done to warrant this attack and is told it is because he has taken Tístram's life. Ísin then makes her way to the gallows on which Tístram hangs, cuts him down and lays him on the grass, whereupon she, like Ísodd in *Tristrams kvæði*, dies of a broken heart.

Although there are several striking parallels between the Icelandic and Faroese ballads of Tristan, there does not appear to be any direct connection between them (Schach 1964, 286–7).

The ballad cycle *Ívint Herintsson* (CCF 108; ed. Djurhuus 1968) is extant in three redactions. The longest of these (A) comprises five separate *tættir*, or sub-ballads:

Jákimann kongur (80 stanzas)
Kvikilsprang (60 stanzas)
Ívints táttur (80 stanzas)
Galians táttur I (100 stanzas)
Galians táttur II (60 stanzas)

The two shorter redactions (B and C) consist of three parts, leaving out *Ívints táttur* and conflating the last two into a single sub-ballad, called *Galians táttur* in B (119 stanzas) and *Galiants kvæði* in C (122 stanzas). These versions were all recorded in the late eighteenth and early nineteenth century, having been transmitted orally for several hundred years before that.

In the first part, common to all three versions, Jákimann, the troll-like king of Húnaland (Land of the Huns), vows that he will win the hand of the sister of King Hartan (called Artan in B and C), 'um enn hun ikki vil' (whether she's willing or not). He travels to Hartan's hall and presents his suit to the king, who, after some deliberation, says his sister should decide for herself. When she sees Jákimann she is horrified by his appearance and refuses to have anything to do with him. Herint hears of this (in C he is sent for by the sister) and travels to Hartan's hall, where he also asks for the princess's hand. He then challenges Jákimann three times to single combat; Jákimann, thinking Herint will be easy prey, finally agrees and the two fight for three full days. Fearing that neither can ever defeat the other, the king's sister has the church bells rung, allowing Herint to win, after which the two are married.

The next part, also common to all versions, opens with the birth of their three sons, Ívint, Viðferð (called Fótur in C) and Kvikilsprang (Kvikil spraki in B, Kvikilsprá or Kvikilbragd in C). Kvikilsprang journeys to Girtland (presumably Greece) to woo the princess Rósinreyð (Rósin moy in B, Rósumund in C). His suit is rejected by the king, and he fights with the king's men, killing many. He is eventually overcome and cast into a dungeon, where he spends nine nights. Rósinreyð goes to her father and asks him to allow her to have the knight. The king will not hear of this and so she sends word to Kvikilsprang's brother Ívint. He arrives and frees Kvikilsprang, and the two kill all but twelve of the king's men. The king asks Kvikilsprang for quarter but he cleaves him in twain. He and Rósinreyð are then married and Kvikilsprang becomes king of Girtland.

The third sub-ballad, *Ívints táttur*, which is found only in the A version and may be a later addition (Liestøl 1915, 169), relates how the third brother, Brandur *hin viðførli* ('the far-traveller', a name borrowed from *Þiðreks saga*), orders his horse to be saddled and makes his way *á heiðin skógv* (into a heathen wood). He fights first with one giant, whom he kills, and then another, the son of the first, whom he also kills, but then he himself falls into a poisoned spring and dies. Hearing of this, his brother Ívint sets out to avenge him, encouraged by his father Herint. He goes to see King Hartan, explaining to him what has happened, and the king accompanies him on his journey for three days. Once alone in the forest, Ívent rides through the night, killing a flying dragon and various other monsters on the way. He finally lies down to sleep. When he awakens he finds his horse lying dead, all its bones broken. He sees a giant horse nearby and saddles it. The scene now shifts to the giants, who see a knight approaching. Regin, the giant's son, goes out against him. Ívint slays him, cutting him in two, and Regin's mother, *tann grimma gívur* (the ugly hag), bewails her loss. Ívent makes his way into the giant's hall, where he kills the mother. He then returns to his uncle Hartan and tells him all that has happened. Hartan invites him to go with him back to his hall.

Galians táttur I begins by informing us that it was Hartan's custom not to sit down to eat until he had been brought some piece of news. One day a man comes, telling of a wondrous hind which has been seen outside the hall. Ívint sets off in pursuit of it, accompanied by *kongasynir og sveinar* (princes and valets). They are unable to catch it and become lost in the forest. When asked by one of his men where they are to spend the night, Ívint says that he knows of a rich widow who lives nearby with whom they can stay; 'hon hevur ikki hjá manni sovið í fimtan vetra skeiði' (she hasn't slept with a man in fifteen years). Ívint sleeps with the widow, but when he tells her the following morning that she needn't expect him to return to her she mixes up a potion which inflicts him with an incurable disease. Returning to the king's hall, Ívent lies languishing in the king's hawk-loft. Nine months later the widow gives birth to a son, who grows up with his mother ignorant of the identity of his father. One day, when he is fifteen, he is teased by the other boys, who mention his father's illness. He goes to his mother, who explains that she had been raped by his father after which she had given him the potion. He threatens to kill her if she has been the cause of his father's death. She says he must be mad – *ein galin mann* – for wanting to kill his mother. He then says that, if this be so, Galian shall henceforth be the name by which he will be called. She gives him another potion which he is to administer to his father. He then sets off to Hartan's hall, accompanied part of the way by his mother, who tells him to call on her if he ever needs her help. Once there the knight Reyður rides out against him, but is defeated. Entering the hall he asks to be taken to Ívint. He is able to cure him and there is great rejoicing in Hartan's hall.

Galians táttur II informs us of another of Hartan's curious customs, viz., that every year at yuletide he sends one of his men off *í Botnar norður*, the legendary abode of the giants in the north, in search of adventure. Galian is keen to go but the king says he is too young. He sets out anyway, killing fifteen trolls the first day, fifteen more the second and on the third rescuing a fair maiden. He then fights a dragon which succeeds in swallowing both him and his horse, though this proves to be too big a mouthful and he is able to cut himself free. He is badly affected by the dragon's poison, however, and remembering what his mother had said, calls on her to help him; she arrives with another potion for him to drink and a fresh horse. He returns to Hartan's hall, where he is challenged by Ívint, who does not recognize him. The two clash until Galian gains the upper hand, at which point he says that only a mad man would kill his own father; instead, he forces him to marry his mother, while he at the same time marries the fair maid he had rescued from the giant.

The connection with the Arthurian tradition is clear enough, not least in that King Hartan/Artan – presumably a corruption of Artús – will not sit down to eat without having heard some piece of news, a peculiarity of his mentioned in *Parcevals saga*, *Möttuls saga* and *Skikkjurímur*. Ívint is obviously to be identified with Ivain/Íven, whose saga contains both a fight with a dragon and the motif of the nubile widow, while the pursuit of the marvellous hind is known from *Erex saga*. Some of the motifs appear to derive from other, non-Arthurian, sources. The poisoning motif, for example, may be a loan from *Mírmanns saga*, while the central wooing episode in the story of Kvikilsprang probably derives from *Hrólfs saga Gautrekssonar*, where Hrólfr's foster-brother Ásmundr sets off to woo Ingibjörg, daughter of the king of Ireland (Liestøl 1915; Kölbing 1875, 396–401).

The Norwegian ballads *Iven Erningsson* and *Kvikkjesprakk*

Iven Erningsson, a Norwegian ballad comprising eighty-seven four-line stanzas in the version published in *Norsk folkediktning* (ed. Bø and Solheim 1967),[10] recounts much of the matter contained in *Ívints táttur* and the two *Galians tættir*. The poem begins with Iven and his men in the forest at nightfall looking for a place to spend the night. Iven says he knows of a widow, Gjertrud, who lives nearby. They are well received and Iven sleeps that night with the widow. When he declines the following morning to marry her she puts a curse on him whereby he shall 'liggje i femten åri sjuk'e i sterke sott!' (lie in a terrible illness for fifteen years). No doctor is able to heal him. Gjertrud bears a son by Iven, Junkar, who, when he turns fifteen, asks his mother who his father is. She tells him, and also of the curse, which she says she has no intention of lifting. Junkar says if she doesn't cure him it will cost her her life, after which she declares that the boy who wants to kill his mother must be mad (*gallen*). He says he will henceforward be known as Galite. He gets a potion from her and sets off to find his father. He finds him in the hall of the Danish king and administers the potion. After three draughts Iven is fully recovered. There is then a fragmentary description of a journey by Galite to Trollebotn where he kills all the trolls there, after which he is challenged by Iven, whom he defeats, revealing at the same time his identity. He then tells Iven that if he doesn't agree to wed his mother it will cost him his life. The ballad ends with the wedding of Iven and Gjertrud, after which Galite proclaims: 'I gjår var jeg eit hittebån, i dag en riddarson' (yesterday I was an orphan, today the son of a knight).

Closely related to this is *Kvikkjesprakk*, a Norwegian ballad comprising sixty-eight four-line stanzas (ed. Bø and Solheim 1967).[11] The eponymous hero, brother of Iven Erningsson (there are said to be three brothers, but only two are named), sets out with his page for Girklond (Greece, but in other versions to Jutland), intending to woo the fair Rosamund, daughter of King Ljodvor. The king rejects his suit, after which he is attacked by 150 of the king's men, whom he defeats and then, at the suggestion of the king's page, by a fierce lion, which he kills. The page then offers him ale, which he drinks until he falls asleep, after which he is put in irons and cast into the dungeon. Kvikkjesprakk's own page then rides home and relates what has happened, after which Iven travels to Girklond, kills the king and releases his brother from the dungeon. The two then proceed to kill everyone, *både katt og hund* (both cat and dog), sparing only the lovely Rosamund. Iven returns home, leaving Kvikkjesprakk to rule over Girklond.

These two Norwegian ballads do not in their present form contain any Arthurian material (apart from the name of the protagonist in the former), but are clearly related to the Faroese *Ívint Herintsson* cycle (Liestøl 1915; Kölbing 1875).

The Icelandic folktale of Tristram og Ísól *bjarta*

The story of Tristan and Isolde also forms the basis for an Icelandic folktale, five versions of which are printed in *Íslenzkar þjóðsögur og œvintýri* (ed. Árni Böðvarsson and Bjarni Vilhjálmsson 1954–61). Each has a different title, as the protagonists are variously named Tristam, Tistram, Tristran or, in one version, Fertram, and Ísól, Ísodda or, again in one version, Helga. The versions vary greatly in length and narrative coherence, and none presents the entire story. Rather, each focuses on certain key scenes and motifs, which, in the context of the individual tales, are frequently blind; indeed the shortest versions, A and, especially, E, are scarcely coherent as they stand. Although these tales have, in their present form, only a tenuous connection to the medieval *Tristrams saga*, the presence of these Tristanian motifs shows that they must nevertheless derive ultimately from it.

By conflating the different versions, and ignoring the variants which are at odds with the story as we otherwise know it, the basic plot is as follows: the king and queen of a certain country are childless, causing them distress. The king has to go away (on a military expedition or to collect taxes); before departing he tells the queen that if she is not pregnant by the time he returns he will kill her. That evening, as the queen is bewailing her fate she is approached by a strange woman who offers to help her. The woman takes her in a boat to a camp, which turns out to be the king's, and gives her brightly coloured clothes to wear. The king is told that there is a beautiful woman in the camp and asks that she be brought to him. She spends the night with the king, unrecognized. The following morning the woman takes her back and tells her that she is pregnant. The king returns and in due course she gives birth to a child, a girl, who on account of her great beauty is called Ísól *bjarta* (the bright). The queen dies shortly thereafter, having given Ísól a pair of scissors and a magic belt.

The king, in mourning for his wife, neglects his duties and is urged by his counsellors to take a new wife. He agrees and a party sets out in search of a suitable bride. The journey goes well at first but they are blown off course, eventually making land in an unknown country. Going ashore, they encounter a beautiful woman combing her hair with a golden comb; with her is her daughter and a thrall. The woman tells them that she is the widow of a powerful king who has been slain by pirates, from whom she and her daughter have fled, accompanied by their slave. They tell her the nature of their mission and she agrees to accompany them and marry the king. The king, for his part, is happy with their choice and the two are wed. He is, however, kept in ignorance of the existence of the new queen's daughter, Ísól (or Ísóta) *svarta* (or *blakka*) (the black).

Ísól bjarta lives in a castle by the shore built for her by her father. She devotes much of her time to the care of the sick. One day on the beach she encounters a chest which has been washed ashore; in it she finds a beautiful baby boy with a note explaining that he should be baptized and named Tistran. The boy grows up there and the two become very fond of each other, promising eventually to marry.

The queen and her daughter one day entice Ísól out into the forest, where they push her and her two servants, called Eyja and Meyja or variants thereof, into a deep pit. The two servants die from hunger, but Ísól is protected by her belt, and is able to escape by digging steps into the wall of the pit with her scissors, which she however drops into the pit as she emerges. She is taken in by an old couple who live in the forest, cooking and sewing for them in return. She makes herself a cape of bark and leaves and, calling herself Næfrakolla, gets work in the palace kitchens. Meanwhile, Ísól svarta has taken her stepsister's place. (In some versions Tistram is given a drink of forgetfulness by the queen so that he will forget Ísól bjarta and marry Ísól svarta, while in others the latter has simply assumed the former's identity.)

Tistram and Ísól/Ísóta are to be married. Tistram has asked Ísól to prepare the wedding garments, but being unable to sew she asks Næfrakolla to do it for her. This she does, preparing a plain garment for Ísól but a beautiful garment with golden seams for Tistram. On the wedding day Ísól asks Næfrakolla to take her place, as she herself is pregnant by her thrall and must give birth. Næfrakolla agrees, but is made to promise that she will not under any circumstances speak to Tistram. She does, however, reciting a series of cryptic verses relating to experiences she and Tistram had had. Later, as they are about to go to bed, Tistram asks Ísól svarta, who has given birth and disposed of the baby (eating it in one version), about the things she had said earlier. She is unable to answer and the ruse is exposed. The queen and her daughter reveal themselves to be witches and are killed. Tistram and Ísól bjarta are reunited and marry.

As is clear from this summary, a fair number of themes and motifs have survived, albeit occasionally in transferred or garbled form, from the 'classical' story of Tristan and Ysolt – principally the Old Norse translation *Tristrams saga ok Ísöndar*, though there are also points of contact with the younger *Saga af Tristram ok Ísodd* and *Tristrams kvæði*. Foremost among these are the pair of 'fair' and 'dark' women with similar or identical names and the discovery of the helpless hero on the shore by the woman he will eventually love (here presumably influenced by another common motif, that of the discovery of a child born to lead his people, e.g., Moses and Scyld Sceafing). At the same time, it is also clear that the tale makes use of elements from other folkloric traditions. Finally it may be noted that while the classical story of the two lovers ends tragically in virtually all its manifestations, the Icelandic folktale ends, as folktales will, with the two being united in marriage and living happily ever after (Schach 1964, 289–96).

Wigalois

The Middle High German verse epic *Wigalois*, subtitled *Der Ritter mit dem Rade* (ed. Kapteyn 1926), composed by Wirnt von Grafenberg in the early thirteenth century (*c*.1210–15?), tells the story of Gawain's son, known as Guinglain in Renaut de Beaujeu's *Le Bel Inconnu* or Gliglois in the eponymous thirteenth-century French romance. Although not as well known as Gottfried von Strassburg's *Tristan* or Wolfram von Eschenbach's *Parzival*, Wirnt's *Wigalois* was popular throughout the Middle Ages – there are some thirty-seven manuscripts of it extant – and, recast in prose, in the early modern period, first appearing in print in Augsburg in 1493 and reprinted at least eight times over the next two centuries.

Like many German chapbooks, *Wigalois* found its way to Denmark. The earliest known imprint is from 1656 and bears the title *En smuck lystig Historie, om den berømmelige Ridder og Heldt Her Viegoleis med Guldhiulet, hvorledes hand veldelig offvervant den stercke Kempe oc Hedning Roas af Glois, med fleere hans ridderlige Gierninger. Som tilforn ey haffver været paa Danske, men nu offversat aff det Tydske*

Sprock udi dette Aar (A fine merry story of the famous knight and hero Sir Viegoleis with the golden wheel, how he forcefully vanquished the powerful heathen warrior Roas of Glois, along with others of his chivalric deeds, previously unavailable in Danish but now in this year translated from the German language). There were at least thirteen further imprints, the latest from Christiania (present-day Oslo) in 1855 (Paulli 1921, 209–18).

According to the work's modern editor, Jørgen Olrik, the Danish translator was 'ingen Sprogkunstner af Rang' (no first-rate wordsmith), whose 'Kundskaber i det tyske Sprog synes ogsaa at have været middelmaadige' (knowledge of the German language seems also to have been mediocre). Among other things he has consistently avoided translating the word *Tafelrunde* (the round table), presumably not knowing how to render it in Danish. A number of minor changes appear to have been made for religious reasons, where obvious references to Catholic practices have been omitted or altered; these need not have been the work of the Danish translator, however, who may have used a German text different from those now known (Olrik 1921, xxxii–xxxiii).

The Danish chapbook was translated into Icelandic in the seventeenth century as *Gabons saga og Vigoleis*. A translation of the saga is attributed to Magnús Jónsson í Vigur (1637–1702), known as Magnús *digri* (the stout), an important figure at the time who copied or had copied a great many manuscripts (Jón Helgason 1955). Although it is not entirely certain, it seems likely that it is Magnús's translation which is preserved in Stockholm Papp. 4:o nr 22, a composite manuscript from the second half of the seventeenth century. The text of the saga was copied, according to the colophon, in March 1683, so the translation must have been undertaken sometime before that date, but after 1656, the year in which the Danish text was first published; this period, in particular the latter half of it, saw a great deal of literary activity on Magnús's part, so this could well be his text.

Two further translations, apparently independent both of the one by Magnús Jónsson and of each other, were made in the course of the eighteenth century, one preserved in the manuscript BL Add. 11157, copied in 1761 by the poet and scribe Jakob Sigurðsson (*c.*1727–79), and the other in the manuscript Lbs 2232 8vo, a large composite manuscript from the late eighteenth and early nineteenth century. This latter text is defective, breaking off near the end. Both these translations follow the original Danish text more closely than does that of Magnús í Vigur, who appears to have taken more liberties (Seelow 1989, 106–13).

As noted by Seelow there are no *rímur* based on the saga, unusual enough in itself. There is a set of *Rímur af Vególus og köppum hans*, composed by Gunnar Ólafsson (*c.*1727–95). They appear to be unrelated to the saga, however, but the similarity of the names of the protagonists is certainly striking.

The Danish chapbook *Tistrand og Indiana*

One of the more interesting, not to say curious, manifestations of the Tristan story in Scandinavia is a Danish chapbook, apparently first published in Christiania in 1775, with the title *En Tragœdisk Historie om den œdle og tappre Tistrand, Hertugens Søn af Borgundien, og den skiønne Indiana, den store Mogul Kejserens Daatter af Indien* (A tragic story of the noble and valiant Tistrand, son of the Duke of Burgundy, and the fair Indiana, daughter of the great Mogul, emperor of India). Over the next century the text was repeatedly reprinted – at least nineteen times – in both Denmark and Norway, generally with the title *En meget smuk Historie om den œdle og tappre Tistran, en burgundisk Hertugsøn, og den skjønne og dydige Indiane, Keiserens, den store Moguls Datter af Indien* (A very beautiful story of the noble and valiant Tistran, son of the Duke of Burgundy, and the fair and virtuous Indiane, daughter of the emperor, the great Mogul of India). There was also a Swedish translation, printed three times in Jönköping between 1855 and 1860, and at least six separate translations into Icelandic, making this by any standard a very popular work indeed.[12]

Although the 1775 Christiania edition is the earliest known printing of the story in its entirety, nearly half of it had already appeared in serial form in the weekly newspaper *Nordske Intelligenz-Sedler*, also published in Christiania, starting in November 1771 and breaking off nearly a year later, with a seven-month hiatus between January and August 1772. In this serialized version, entitled 'En tragœdisk Historie om den tappre Tistrand og den skiønne Indiana' (A tragic story of the valiant Tistrand and fair Indiana), no information was given on the work's origin, but the title page of the 1775 edition, and those of several of the subsequent reprints, announce it to have been 'Nu nyligen af Tydsk paa Dansk oversat' (now recently translated from German to Danish). No corresponding German text has survived, however, nor is there any further evidence for the existence of one, but most scholars, until recently at least, have nevertheless accepted that there must have been a German original.

Wolfgang Golther pointed out a number of similarities between the Danish text – which he considered '[ein] dichterisch ganz wertlose[s] Erzeugnis' (a product entirely devoid of literary merit), albeit one worthy of note from a cultural-historical perspective – and the German prose romance *Tristrant und Isalde*, first printed at Augsburg in 1484 (ed. Brandstetter 1966), but noted also that there were a great many differences, some of which resulted in 'eine unbeabsichtigt komische Wirkung' (an unintentionally comic effect) (Golther 1907, 252–3).

The plot is as follows: Tormona, wife of King Alfonsus of Spain, dies in childbirth, along with the new-born prince, leaving the king with no heir. He sends for his two nephews, Tistrand and Røderich,[13] with the idea that one of the two can be chosen to succeed him. One day, shortly after Tistrand's arrival, Kunchin, son of the emperor of China, arrives in Spain with an army of 200,000 men, demanding, through an emissary, that the Spanish king surrender to him outright or meet him in single combat. He is betrothed to the beautiful Indiana, daughter of the grand Mogul of India, and intends to present her with the kingdom of Spain, and the king's head, as a *morganaticum*. Tistrand offers to fight Kunchin in the king's place. He succeeds in defeating him, but is badly wounded by Kunchin's poisoned sword. The only one who can cure him, he is told, is Indiana, renowned for her healing powers, who has unfortunately vowed to avenge Kunchin. He journeys to India, but keeps his identity secret, claiming to be French and to have received his wound in the war with the English. Indiana is suspicious but treats him anyway, after which he returns to Spain.

Røderich is envious of Tistrand and conspires against him. Tistrand suggests that the king should marry in order to produce an heir, suggesting Indiana, of whom both he and his uncle have dreamt, as the perfect match. Tistrand journeys once again to India, where he kills a dragon, winning him the favour of the Mogul, who supports the proposal of a union between Alfonsus and Indiana. The Mogul offers Tistrand the hand of his youngest daughter as a reward for having slain the dragon, but Tistrand declines, as he already has his eye on Innanda, daughter of Dagobert, king of France. On the journey back to Spain Tistrand and Indiana unwittingly drink a magic potion which had been given to Indiana's servant, Galmeje, intended for the bridal couple. Although consumed with love for each other, they agree, at the suggestion of Indiana, to limit themselves to simple expressions of affection: Tristand may kiss her hand, while she strokes him on the cheek. They must do this, she explains, because her body has been given to Alfonsus and she will not defile the marriage bed for as long as he lives.

Alfonsus and Indiana are married with great pomp and circumstance, and Indiana quickly becomes beloved by the people, not least for her healing abilities. Tistrand, as the king's chief adviser, sleeps in the king's own chamber, which, the narrator tells us, must have been hard for the young man, seeing the woman he loved in another man's arms. Suspecting that something is not entirely right, Tistrand's increasingly malevolent cousin Røderich keeps a sharp eye on the couple. He makes his suspicions known to the king, persuading him to hide in a shrub near the place in the garden where he knows the two often meet. Indiana notices the king is there and when Tistrand arrives tips him off, so that nothing untoward happens, and the king remains convinced of their innocence. Tistrand occasionally visits Indiana's bed in order to catch a glimpse of her white arm as she sleeps. Røderich has sand sprinkled on the floor around Indiana's bed, hoping in this way to catch him out. Realizing this, Tistrand leaps over the sand, but develops a nose-bleed as a result of the effort. When the blood is discovered Røderich accuses them of adultery. This time the king is convinced and has the two lovers condemned to death; they manage to escape into the forest, however, where they live in chastity together, sleeping with a naked sword between them, Indiana insisting that she is still Alfonsus's wife, whatever may have happened.

Three years pass until one day the king comes upon their hut in the forest while he is out hunting. They are asleep together in the bed, but the king notices the naked sword between them and decides that they have been innocent all along. The two are rehabilitated and return to court. In their absence, Røderich has consolidated his position in the kingdom and has, among other things, increased the tax burden on the people, mostly to his own benefit. Once returned, Indiana persuades the king to lower taxes again, making her even more popular. Røderich begins to plot the deaths of both the king and queen, but he is finally found out and arrested. Tistrand returns to Burgundy and travels from there to France, where he marries Innanda and succeeds Dagobert as king of France. Both couples have children. Tistrand is unable to forget Indiana, however, and often secretly gazes upon an image of her. Innanda discovers this and, realizing that her husband loves another woman, cools towards him.

Indiana has a castle near the French–Spanish border, and Tistrand journeys there with his brother-in-law, Duke Carl, to meet her. But she says that they must not meet again and Tistrand returns to France. He helps his brother-in-law abduct an English princess, but is wounded in the process by a poisoned arrow. As his wounds worsen he realizes that only Indiana can save him. Ships are sent off to Spain to fetch her and are instructed to fly red flags if she is on board, but black if she is not. As the ships are seen approaching on the horizon Tistrand asks what colour the flags are and is told by Innanda that they are black. He dies of grief, just as Indiana and King Alfonsus step ashore. Queen Indiana berates Innanda for having allowed Tistrand to die, kisses Tistrand's lips for the first time and then dies herself of grief.

After their deaths the truth of the potion is revealed by Galmeje, and the king has the two buried together in a silver coffin with a crystal lid. Out of each of their breasts a lily grows, the two plants intertwining, which has subsequently become the symbol of France. They are buried together in St Diogenes's cloister where many people go to see them, greatly contributing to the cloister's coffers. Their bodies remain uncorrupted and after many years Pope Cleo has them canonized. Tistrand and Indiana's children marry each other, thus uniting the crowns of France and Spain.

While the general outline of the story presented here is, as Golther said, recognizably the same as the classical story of Tristan and Isolde, there are indeed a great many differences between them. Most obviously, the scene of the action has shifted from Cornwall, Ireland and Brittany to Spain, France and India, and while the names of the chief protagonists are not entirely unlike those of their medieval counterparts many of the other characters have quite different names, Morholt, for example, brother of the queen of Ireland, becoming Kunchin, son of the emperor of China. The malevolent Røderich, while obviously modelled on the character Andret (Antret, Auctrat), has a much greater role to play here. The most fundamental difference between the two, however, is that although Tistrand and Indiana are fated for ever to love only each other, they choose not to enter into an illicit sexual liaison. Moreover, each has children with their respective spouses, who after their parents' deaths are married, achieving in the second generation what was impossible in the first. The medieval story of adulterous love has been transformed into an eighteenth-century novel of sensibility, preaching faithfulness to one's spouse and devotion to one's sovereign as the ultimate good.

Another way in which *Tistrand og Indiana* reveals itself to be a product of its time is in the significant role played in the story by politics, and in particular the politics of trade. One of King Alfonsus's reasons for agreeing to send Tistrand to woo Indiana on his behalf is that it would allow him to re-establish trade relations with the Great Mogul, who, on account of Kunchin's death, has prohibited the Spanish from trading in India. For his part, the Mogul is also keen to resume ordinary trade relations with Spain, and for this reason urges his daughter to accept Alfonsus's proposal, prompting her to say: 'Intet Fruentimmer paa Jorden er mere ulykkelig end Konger og Fyrsters Døttre, de andre kand efter Kiærlighed gifte sig, men vi maa være som et Offer for det ganske Land til dets Handel og Velfærds Bedste' (No women on earth are more unfortunate than the daughters of kings and princes; the others can marry for love but we must be as an offering for the good of the commerce and welfare of the entire country) (*Tistrand og Indiana* 1775, 39–40). Much later in the story, it is mentioned that both Spain and France have established permanent trading stations in India and have large naval fleets to service them.

Most scholars, as was mentioned, have accepted the statement on the title page of the first several editions that *Tistrand og Indiana* is a translation from German, despite the lack of any further evidence for a German text. Golther claimed there could be no question of the existence of this German original, as could be seen from the 'vielen deutschen Wendungen und Redensarten' (many German phrases and expressions) in the text. Moreover, he argued, conditions in eighteenth-century Denmark were not as conducive to the production of such a work as they were in Enlightenment Germany. On the lack of any evidence for a printed edition of the text, Golther suggested that the German original need never have been printed, and that the Danish text could just as easily have been translated from a manuscript as from a printed book (Golther 1907, 252–3).

Danish scholars too have largely accepted the idea of a German original, but have been more interested in determining whether the translator was a Dane or a Norwegian. Rasmus Nyerup, having recently acquired a copy of the 1792 edition at the Copenhagen *Børs*, discusses the work at length in an article on 'Almuens Morskabslesning' in the journal *Iris og Hebe*; citing a number of Norwegianisms in the text, Nyerup concludes that 'Oversætteren maa have været en Normand' (the translator must have been a Norwegian) (Nyerup 1796, 207–9). Richard Paulli, who calls the work 'et Vildskud paa Tristan-Romanernes Stamme, en Beardejdelse af det gamle Stof i orientalsk Rokokostil' (a stray shoot on the Tristan legend's trunk, an adaptation of the old matter in oriental rococo style) also believes that 'muligvis er det dog ikke Danmark, men Norge, hvem Æren tilkommer for at have oversat denne Kuriositet, eftersom det ældste kendte Tryk er udkommet i Kristiania' (it is possible that it is not Denmark but Norway to whom the honour of translating this curiosity belongs, since the earliest known imprint of it came out in Christiania) (Paulli 1936, 193–4).

Tue Gad does not agree with Golther's assessment of the language of the text of the 1775 edition, calling it 'godt dansk, uden germanismer' (good Danish, without Germanisms). While he does not preclude that there may have been a German original, now lost, he says, 'det kan også tænkes, at det er en person m/k i Danmark eller Norge der har omarbejdet den tyske prosaroman, og at den danske bog af reklame-grunde lanceres som en oversættelse fra tysk, i lighed med så mange andre folkebøger' (it can also be that it was a person, male or female, in Denmark or Norway who has recast the German prose romance, and that for marketing purposes the Danish book was launched as a translation from German, like so many other chapbooks) (Gad 1987, 23).

Seemingly unaware of Gad's article, Marianne Kalinke argues in an article published in 1991 that *Tistrand og Indiana* 'is an original Dano-Norwegian version of the Tristan legend and not a translation' (Kalinke 1991a, 60). Kalinke goes further, however, claiming that the novel was also intended as 'an eighteenth-century king's mirror' – the article's subtitle – the impetus for which was the so-called 'Struensee affair', where Caroline Mathilde, English wife of the mentally unstable, and probably schizophrenic, King Christian VII, conducted, quite openly, an adulterous relation-ship with the king's German physician, Johann Friedrich Struensee. Taking advantage of his situation, Struensee acquired such power that he was for some sixteen months the effective ruler of Denmark, resulting in 1772 in his execution and her banish-ment to Germany, where she died three years later, aged twenty-four. This, argues Kalinke, is precisely how rulers and their courtiers ought not to behave; rather than succumbing to the temptations of the flesh, as Struensee and Caroline Mathilde had done, they should follow the example of Tistrand and Indiana, whose love remained chaste. There are, to be sure, a number of parallels between the story of the lovers' triangle as presented in the novel and the events in the Danish court in the period 1770–2, which Kalinke explores in detail, but these are of such a general nature, and the timing so close – the novel was appearing in serialized form in Christiania even as the events ostensibly inspiring it were unfolding in Christiansborg – that her attempts to see *Tistrand og Indiana* as a *roman à clef* seem somewhat forced, not least as they presuppose an audience sympathetic to Struensee, which is rather unlikely to have been the case at the time.

Three years after Kalinke's article appeared the Danish scholar Jonna Kjær published a short *Festschrift* article on *Tistrand og Indiana*. Like Kalinke – whose *roman à clef* theory she rejects entirely – she sees the text as a Norwegian produc-tion, whose language is 'ganske gennemgående præget af norvagismer' (characterized throughout by Norwegianisms) (Kjær 1994, 83). She suggests, however, that it may well be a translation after all, though not from German but from Icelandic. There is an Icelandic *Saga af Tistran og Indíönu*, about which more will be said presently, but it, or rather they, quite clearly derive from the Dano-Norwegian chapbook. Kjær seems herself to have come round to this idea, as in an article written two years later she refers to the four Icelandic manuscripts of the saga known to her as containing translations of the Danish novel (Kjær 1996a, 153).

Jonna Kjær has written a third article on *Tistrand og Indiana*, also published in 1996. In it she attempts to identify the reasons for the novel's great popularity, contrasted with *Historie om Herr Tristan og den smukke Isalde*, a translation of the German prose romance *Tristrant und Isalde*, from Marbach's *Volksbücher* (Leipzig, 1839), published in 1857 by H. P. Møller – and never reissued. Kjær shows how the story has been greatly simplified in the Danish translation, with many of the elements present in Marbach's text being left out, including those potentially of interest to nineteenth-century readers, such as reflections on love and duty. These very same elements, she says, have free rein in the Danish novel, which she sees as 'un roman de femmes en ce sens qu'il a été particulièrement apprécié par un public féminin' (a woman's novel, in the sense that it was particularly appreciated by women), but also possibly written by a woman. The female protagonists are in sharp contrast, with Isalde presented as *la femme dangereuse* (the dangerous woman), while Indiane is virtuous – the word even appearing in the novel's title – her morals without fault, *un modèle idéalisé* (an idealized model) for female readers.

> Dans l'ensemble, la comparaison entre les deux romans fait de Tristan og Isalde un texte sec et démodé, tandis que Tistran og Indiane est un mélange fascinant d'évasion et d'actualité. La lecture de ce dernier a sans aucun doute pu faire rêver sur la vie de beau monde des riches et des puissants, mais elle a pu donner aussi des leçons pratiques de morale. Il est significatif que ce roman n'insiste pas sur l'amour comme maladie et lié à la mort, car il enseigne au contraire l'amour «calme», discipliné et altruiste qui rend possible une bonne vie aux niveaux individuel et collectif. (Kjær 1996b, 298)

> (On the whole, the comparison between the two novels shows *Tristan og Isalde* to be an arid and outdated text, while *Tistran og Indiane* is a fascinating mixture of escapism and topicality. The reading of the latter was without doubt able to make the reader dream of the beautiful lives of the rich and powerful, but it could also provide practical moral lessons. It is significant that this novel does not insist on depicting love as a disease and linked to death, for it teaches on the contrary 'calm', disciplined and altruistic love, which makes it possible to lead a good life both on the individual and the collective level.)

Tistrand og Indiana in Iceland

The story of Tistrand and Indiana made its way, seemingly not long after its first publication in Norway, to Iceland, where it was translated into Icelandic not once but several times. The earliest of the translations, and that closest to the Danish text, is found in the manuscript JS 410 8vo, part of a large collection of sagas in various hands from the eighteenth and nineteenth centuries. The text, which is entitled 'Saga af Tistran, einum burgundiskum Hertogasyni, og Indiönu, Dóttur Moguls ens mikla Keisarans af Indialandi' (The saga of Tistran, son of a Burgundian duke, and Indiana,

daughter of the great Mogul, the emperor of India), is written in an unidentified hand
of the late eighteenth or early nineteenth century. The Icelandic text, like the Danish
original, is divided into eleven numbered chapters, the short introductions to which
are also retained. Although the translation follows the Danish closely, even slavishly,
some concessions to saga style are made. The opening sentence, for example, following the summary, begins: *Það er upphaf þessarar sögu* . . . (This story begins . . .).

An entirely separate translation is preserved in the manuscript Lbs 3433 8vo, an
unbound collection of texts of various kinds in the hand of the clergyman Jens V.
Hjaltalín (1842–1930). The text is undated, but several other items in the manuscript
are dated to the mid-1860s. There is no title, but 'Tistrans saga' has been added later
in pencil. Like the previous translation, the text is divided into eleven chapters and
follows the Danish quite closely, but the summaries – a convention of print extremely
rare in Icelandic manuscripts – are not included.

A third translation, written in good saga-style, albeit of the post-classical variety,
with few obvious traces of Danish influence, is found in three manuscripts, two from
the very end of the nineteenth century and one from the beginning of the twentieth.
In two of these the saga is given the title 'Saga af Tístran Róbertssyni og Indiönu
Mógulsdóttir' (The saga of Tístran Róbertsson and Indiana Mógulsdóttir).[14] The text,
like that of the previous translations, is divided into eleven chapters, but several small
but significant changes have been made, particularly in the first chapter. There is, for
example, no stillborn prince; instead it is simply said of King Alfons and his wife that
þeim var ekki barna auðið (they were without issue). In a more substantial change,
the information that Kunchin, called Kunkvín in the Icelandic, is betrothed to Indiana
and intends to present her with King Alfons's head as a morning gift, given by the
emissary when he first comes to the Spanish court in the original Danish and the other
translations, is here not introduced until after Kunkvín has been killed by Tístran, at
the beginning of chapter 2.

Tistrand og Indiana was also the basis for three sets of *rímur*, that most Icelandic
of literary genres. The first, and certainly the best-known, of these are by Sigurður
Breiðfjörð (1798–1846), the pre-eminent *rímur*-poet of the nineteenth century.
Sigurður composed his *Rímur af Tistrani og Indiönu* in the autumn of 1828 while
staying with his uncle, the clergyman Jóhann Bjarnason at Helgafell on Snæfellsnes.
Jóhann, who is described as a man excessively fond of wine, women and other worldly
pleasures (Páll Eggert Ólason 1948–52, III, 20–1), asked his nephew to compose a set
of *rímur* for the entertainment of his household, and Sigurður, finding a copy of the
Danish chapbook on his uncle's bookshelf, decided to use it as the basis for his *rímur*.
Most *rímur* are based on existing prose sagas, so composing a set of *rímur* on the
basis of a foreign novel was rather unusual, though there certainly are other examples – including Sigurður's own *Núma rímur*, composed while he was in Greenland
in 1831–3.[15] Sigurður's original manuscript has not survived but there are two early
copies, one an autograph, made before the *rímur* were printed in Copenhagen in 1831.

The printed text differs somewhat from that of these early manuscripts, incorporating a number of improvements presumably made by Sigurður himself (Sveinbjörn Beinteinsson 1961, xii).

Sigurður was rather free with his source – *rímur* tend, by and large, to follow their sources quite closely, though Sigurður's treatment of his source is similarly free in his *Núma rímur*, on which he himself comments in the preface to it – skipping over some sections and amplifying others as he saw fit. Not surprisingly, he tended to dwell on the types of scenes generally favoured by *rímur*-poets: descriptions of journeys by sea (in the third, fifth, sixth, eleventh and thirteenth fits), erotic passion (in *ríma* five) and, not least, battles (in fits two, four, six, seven, nine and eleven). By the standards of the *rímur*, Sigurður was an innovative poet, introducing two new metres in his *Tístrans rímur* (there are fourteen individual fits, each in a different metre); he also uses an unusually large number of original kennings, many of them exceedingly complex (Sveinbjörn Beinteinsson, 1961; Kjær, 1996a).

Sigurður Breiðfjörð's *Rímur af Tístrani og Indíönu* are probably best known because of the extremely negative, not to say vicious, review of them written by the poet and naturalist Jónas Hallgrímsson (1807–45) in the third number of the journal *Fjölnir* (1837). Jónas takes issue with both the substance and style of *Tístrans rímur*, but his attack is really directed not so much at them in particular as at the entire genre: *rímur*, he argues, even the best of them, are simply bad poetry. Not only are they 'flestallar þjóðinni til mínkunar' (most of them to the discredit of the nation), but they 'eíða og spilla tilfinníngunni á því sem fagurt er og skáldlegt og sómir sjer vel í góðum kveðskap' (destroy and corrupt the feeling for what is beautiful and poetic and befitting good poetry) (Jónas Hallgrímsson 1837, 18). Jónas, who apparently does not recognize the story as a version of the Tristan legend, refers to Sigurður's source for the *rímur* as *einhvur ligasaga*, using the disparaging term *lygasaga* (lit. 'story of lies') frequently used to describe the post-classical Icelandic romances.[16] This he has not bothered to read, he says

> því hún er auðsjáanlega so eínskjisverð og heímskulega ljót og illa samin, að hennar vegna stendur á litlu, hvurnig með hana er farið. Það er auðvitað, að einu gjildir, hvurt hún væri sönn eður ekkji, ef hún væri falleg á annað borð – ef það væri nokkuð þíðing í henni og nokkur skáldskapur (því þegar á að snúa sögu í ljóð, verður að vera skáldskapur í henni sjálfri, eígi hann að birtast í ljóðunum) – ef hún lísti eínhvurju eptirtektarverðu úr mannlegu lífi eíns og það er eða gjæti verið, og síndi lesandanum sálir þeírra manna, sem hún talar um, og ljeti það vera þesskonar sálir, sem til nokkurs væri að þekkja. Enn hjer er ekkji því að heílsa. Af Tistranssögu er ekkjert að læra. Hún er ekkji til neíns, nema til að kvelja lesandann, og láta hann finna til, hvursu það er viðbjóðslegt, að hlíða á bull og vitleísu. (Jónas Hallgrímsson 1837, 19–20)

> (because it is clearly so abject and ridiculously ugly and badly written that it matters little how it was handled [by the poet]. Obviously it would make no difference whether the story was true or not were it otherwise beautiful – were there in it any meaning or any poetry (for if a story is to be put into verse there must be poetry in it if that poetry is to appear in the verses) – if it described anything worthy of attention in human life as it is or as it could be and revealed to the reader the souls of the people with which it dealt and made them the type of souls that are worth knowing.

But such is not the case here. Nothing can be learnt from the story of Tistran. It is pointless, only
distressing the reader and making him see how revolting it is to listen to tosh and twaddle.)

With his review, Jónas is commonly credited with having 'dealt the whole genre
such a staggering blow that it never really recovered from it' (Stefán Einarsson 1957,
224), and while it is true that the *rímur* did eventually lose the place in the hearts of
common folk in Iceland they had once had, Jónas was an example, rather than a cause,
of a change in taste, one largely confined at this time to the expatriate literary elite
in Copenhagen. Among ordinary people in Iceland *rímur* continued to be composed,
recited, copied and enjoyed throughout the nineteenth century and even into the twentieth (Páll Valsson 1999, 154–67).

Criticism of Sigurður Breiðfjörð's *Rímur af Tístrani og Indíönu* came also from
within his own camp, however, from Níels Jónsson (1782–1857), nicknamed *skáldi*
(the poet), a prominent poet in his own right, who composed another set of *rímur*
based on the Danish chapbook in direct response to Sigurður's. These *rímur* have
never been printed, but are preserved in half a dozen manuscripts, including the autograph Lbs 982 8vo, where their full title is given as 'Lítil Tilraun að snúa í Rijmur
saugunni af þeim Tistrani Hrobjartar Hertogasyni af Borgund og Indiaunu Drottníngu
Móguls Dóttur af Indialandi eptir daunskri útleggjíngu frá ári 1844' (A small attempt
to turn into rímur the saga of Tistran, son of Robert, Duke of Burgundy, and Queen
Indiana, daughter of the Mogul of India, following the Danish translation, from the
year 1844).[17] In a long preface Níels criticizes Sigurður for not doing justice to the –
in his estimation very fine – story, for which reason he has felt obliged to produce his
own *rímur* based on it.[18] He says:

> Hvort ein saga er í sjálfri sér sönn eða diktur, miðar hún til að gefa hugmyndir um persónur og
> athafnir þeirra, þess vegna líka um sálarefnin, sem þær orsaka, og þennan eiginlegleika hefir saga
> þessi til að bera á þolanlega hárri tröppu og það svo, að hún rétt með farin og vel að gáð gjörir það
> efunarmál, hvort hún geti að öllu leyti diktur verið. En Breiðfjörð hefir gjört hana því gagnstæða og
> að öfuglíki, og höfundinn að erki beinasna. Allir hennar tilburðir koma úr lofti, tildraga og orsaka
> lausir eins og ofanrigningur á skjá . . .

> (Regardless of whether a story is true, as such, or invented, its aim is to convey impressions of indi-
> vidual characters and their actions, and therefore also the emotions brought about by these actions,
> and this story is able to do this to a reasonably high standard, to such a degree that, if correctly
> treated and fully understood, makes it doubtful that it could be completely fictitious. But Breiðfjörð
> has done just the opposite and made of it a travesty and of the author a complete ass. Its events
> come all out of nowhere, without rhyme or reason, like rain out of the blue . . .)

Although Níels's criticism is in some ways reminiscent of that of Jónas, there is no
indication in the preface that he knew of the review in *Fjölnir*. In any case, as this last
sentence makes clear, his chief complaint is that Sigurður has made deliberate changes
to the plot – something, as was mentioned, *rímur*-poets generally did not do – changes
which render many of the actions meaningless; it is not a criticism of Sigurður as a
poet, and still less of the genre as a whole.

It is unlikely that Sigurður ever saw these *rímur*, or Níels's long preface, as they were written only shortly before his death. Níels had previously composed verses disparaging *Tístrans rímur*, however, which, although never printed, circulated widely in manuscript. Sigurður was aware of these, and responded to them, with palpable annoyance, in the eleventh *mansöngur* to his *Rímur af Gísla Súrssyni*, composed in 1838.[19] He certainly knew of, and was deeply offended by, the attack in *Fjölnir*, to which he responded several times in verse and in the essay 'Andsvar til Fjölnirs', of which there are many copies in manuscript.

There is yet another set of *rímur* based on the Danish chapbook, '[Rímur af] Tistran sem var eirn Burgundiskur Hertoga Son og Indiane Dóttur Keysarans af India' (Rímur of Tistran, who was the son of a Burgundian duke, and Indiane, daughter of the emperor of India), composed by Filippus Salómonsson (1799–1835) – his only known venture into *rímur*-writing – who lived on the farm of Grænanes in Norðfjörður in eastern Iceland. These were composed in 1833, apparently in ignorance of Sigurður's *rímur* (Sveinbjörn Beinteinsson 1961, xvi), and are only preserved in a single manuscript, Lbs 2040 8vo, written in 1857. Like the other two, they appear to be based directly on the Danish text, rather than on one of the Icelandic translations.

A fourth version of the prose saga is found in three manuscripts, all written by the same man, Magnús Jónsson (1835–1922), from the farm of Tjaldanes in western Iceland.[20] The earliest of these is from 1875 and the latest from 1899. The text, which is called simply 'Sagan af Tistran ok Indíönu', is a prose retelling of Sigurður Breiðfjörð's *rímur*. Magnús was unusual among scribes in prefacing his manuscripts with information about his texts. In the preface to Lbs 1493 4to, written in 1899, he says:

> Saga af Tistran ok Indíönu er nú ecki svo óvíða til í afskriftum, þessi saga er alls ólík hinni gömlu Tistrans sögu, eða öllu heldr önnr saga, ok mun sjálfsagt vera samsett eptir rímunum.

> (The saga of Tistran and Indíana is nowadays found in quite a few manuscripts. This saga is completely different from the old Tistrans saga, or really any other saga, and is probably based on the *rímur*.)

Jonna Kjær mentions this text in her first article, referred to above, even using it to support her suggestion that the Danish chapbook may be a translation from Icelandic. She finds the text interesting, she says, because it is 'påfallende fri og anderledes, først og fremmest på grund af tilføjelse af nogle meget flotte og stærke skildringer af erotisk længsel' (strikingly free and different, primarily owing to the addition of some very fine and powerful descriptions of erotic desire) (Kjær 1994, 83). These descriptions, here recast in prose, go back to Sigurður Breiðfjörð's *rímur*. Interestingly, Jónas Hallgrímsson singled out Sigurður's treatment of the love between Tístran and Indiana, 'það sem skáldskapurinn hefði gjetað verið mestur í' (the thing that could have been the most poetic), as one of the worst aspects of the *rímur* – 'so ljótt og við-bjóðslegt' (so ugly and disgusting) (Jónas Hallgrímsson 1837, 20–1) – further proof, if any were needed, that tastes differ.

Notes

[1] The texts throughout are given in normalized orthography; the translations are my own.

[2] Ballads are normally referred to by their numbers in the standard editions; for Icelandic ballads this is Grundtvig and Jón Sigurðsson's *Íslenzk fornkvæði* (ÍF), for Danish *Danmarks gamle Folkeviser* (DgF) and for Faroese *Corpus carminum Færoensium* (CCF).

[3] A single stanza preserved in the manuscript AM 153 8vo corresponds exactly to none of the others, and may represent a fifth version.

[4] The final stanza, which is in the *ríma*-metre *ferskeytt* and therefore presumably not originally part of the poem, is omitted in some editions, e.g., ed. Grundtvig and Jón Sigurðsson 1854–85.

[5] Marianne Kalinke, perhaps ascribing an unwarranted degree of artistic sensibility to a simple ballad, suggests that this 'presumably alludes to the eventual union of Tristram and Ísodd in death' (Kalinke 1991b).

[6] Gísli Brynjúlfsson, 1878 includes a sixth text, version F, which in *DgF* is classed as a variant of E.

[7] See Rossel et al. 1976, 380–2; this text was also given as version A in Gísli Brynjúlfsson 1878.

[8] Hammershaimb's transcript is now part of AM Acc. 4c (II [4]); for a description of the manuscript see Chesnutt and Larsen 1996, 62–86.

[9] CCF 55A, 65A, 84, 101A; a similar refrain is found in CCF 156B.

[10] Another version, entitled 'Ivar Erlingen og Riddarsonen' and comprising sixty-two verses, is printed in Landstad (ed.) 1968; Liestøl (1915, 156–65) prints a transcription, fifty-seven verses, made by Hans Ross.

[11] Another version, entitled 'Kvikkisprak Hermoðson' and comprising sixty-one verses, is printed in Landstad (ed.) 1968.

[12] On the publication history, see Gad 1987, 31; the Swedish translations are listed in Hjalmar Linnström 1867–84, I, 637.

[13] The forms of the names used here are those of the 1775 Christiania edition; in most subsequent editions 'Tistrand' loses his final 'd' and 'Alfonsus' his final 'us', while 'Røderich' becomes 'Røderik' and 'Indiana' 'Indiane'.

[14] Lbs 2114 4to and Lbs 3941 8vo; the third, Lbs 4650 4to, has only the rubric 'Hjer hefur söguna af Týstran og Indíönu' (Here begins the saga of Tístran and Indíana).

[15] *Núma rímur*, generally regarded as among Sigurður Breiðfjörð's absolute best, are based on J. K. Höst's Danish translation of Jean-Pierre Claris de Florian's novel *Numa Pompilius, second roi de Rome*, first published in Paris in 1786 (see Sveinbjörn Sigurjónsson 1937). Another well-known example are *Pontus rímur*, by Magnús Jónsson (*c.*1530–91), the earliest evidence for the existence of a German *Volksbuch* in Iceland (see Seelow 1989, 250–2).

[16] For a discussion of this term, see Driscoll 1997, 3–4.

[17] The date, 1844, is presumably that of the composition of the *rímur*, rather than the publication of the Danish chapbook (none of the extant printings are from 1844).

[18] The *rímur* themselves have never been printed but the preface appears in Finnur Sigmundsson 1946, 130–43.

[19] These were printed in Copenhagen in 1857 and reprinted at Bessastaðir in 1908.

[20] There is a fourth manuscript written by Magnús in 1913, but as it is in private ownership I have not had the opportunity to see it. On Magnús and his manuscript production, see Driscoll 1997 and 2009.

Reference List

Texts and Translations

En Tragædisk Historie om den ædle og tappre Tistrand, Hertugens Søn af Borgundien, og den skiønne Indiana, den store Mogul Kejserens Daatter af Indien (Christiania, 1775).

'Ivar Erlingen og Riddarsonen', ed. M. B. Landstad, in *Norske folkeviser* (Oslo, 1968), pp. 157–68.

'Iven Erningsson', ed. O. Bø and S. Solheim, in *Folkeviser*, Norsk folkediktning, VI (Oslo, 1967), I, 99–111.

'Ívint Herintsson', ed. N. Djurhuus, in *Føroya kvæði, Corpus carminum Færoensium* (Copenhagen, 1968), V, 199–242.

'Kvikkisprak Hermoðson', ed. M. B. Landstad, in *Norske folkeviser* (Oslo, 1968), pp. 146–56.

'Kvikkjesprakk', ed. O. Bø and S. Solheim, in *Folkeviser*, Norsk folkediktning, VI (Oslo, 1967), I, 69–78.

Rímur af Tístrani og Indíönu, orktar af Sigurði Breiðfjörð (Copenhagen, 1831).

'Rímur af Tistrani og Indíönu', ed. Sveinbjörn Beinteinsson, in *Tístransrímur*, Rímnasafn, III (Reykjavík, 1961).

'Sir Tistrum and Maid Isallt', trans. S. A. J. Bradley, in *The Tristan Legend: Texts from Northern and Eastern Europe in Modern English Translation*, ed. J. Hill (Leeds, 1977), pp. 148–55.

'The Icelandic ballad of Tristan (Tristrams kvæði)', trans. J. Hill, in *The Tristan Legend: Texts from Northern and Eastern Europe in Modern English Translation*, ed. J. Hill (Leeds, 1977), pp. 29–38.

'Thisterom and Isall', trans. S. A. J. Bradley, in *The Tristan Legend: Texts from Northern and Eastern Europe in Modern English Translation*, ed. J. Hill (Leeds, 1977), pp. 146–7.

'Tistram og Isold', ed. A. Olrik, in *Danmarks gamle Folkeviser*, VIII (Copenhagen, 1905–19), pp. 29–36.

'Tistram og Jomfru Isolt', ed. A. Olrik, in *Danmarks gamle Folkeviser*, VIII (Copenhagen, 1905–19), pp. 37–46.

'Tístrams táttur', ed. V. U. Hammershaimb, in *Færøsk Anthologi*, STUAGNL, XV (Copenhagen, 1891), I, 216–22.

'Tístrams táttur', ed. N. Djurhuus, in *Føroya kvæði, Corpus carminum Færoensium* (Copenhagen, 1968), V, 283–5.

'Tístrams táttur', trans. B. Lockwood, in *The Tristan Legend: Texts from Northern and Eastern Europe in Modern English Translation*, ed. J. Hill (Leeds, 1977), pp. 156–8.

'Tristram og Ísól bjarta', ed. Árni Böðvarsson and Bjarni Vilhjálmsson, in *Íslenzkar þjóðsögur og ævintýri, safnað hefur Jón Árnason* (Reykjavík,1954–61), II, 308–17; IV, 486–95.

'Tristrams kvæði', ed. S. Grundtvig and Jón Sigurðsson, in *Íslenzk fornkvæði* (Copenhagen, 1854–85), 186–207.

'Tristrams kvæði', ed. Jón Helgason, in *Íslenzk fornkvæði. Islandske folkeviser*, I–VIII, Editiones Arnamagnæanæ, Series B, vols. X–XVII (Copenhagen, 1962–81), I, 137–43; III, 198–201; IV, 121, 221–26; V, 22–5.

'Tristrams kvæði', ed. and trans. R. Cook, in *Norse Romance*, I: *The Tristan Legend*, ed. M. E. Kalinke (Cambridge, 1999), pp. 227–39.

Tristrant und Isalde. Prosaroman nach dem ältesten Druck aus Augsburg vom Jahre 1484, ed. A. Brandstetter (Tübingen, 1966).

Vigoleis, ed. J. Olrik, in *Danske Folkebøger fra 16. og 17. Aarhundrede*, V (Copenhagen, 1921), pp. 1–116.

Wigalois: Der Ritter mit dem Rade, ed. J. M. N. Kapteyn (Bonn, 1926).

Studies

Bjarni Einarsson (1961). *Skáldasögur. Um uppruna og eðli ástaskáldasagnanna fornu*, Reykjavík.

Chesnutt, M. and Larsen, K. (1996). 'History, manuscripts, indexes', in *Føroya kvæði, Corpus carminum Færoensium*, VII, Copenhagen.

Driscoll, M. J. (1992). 'Introduction', in *Sigurðar saga þögla: The Shorter Redaction*, Reykjavík, pp. xiii–clxvi.

Driscoll, M. J. (1997). *The Unwashed Children of Eve: The Production, Dissemination and Reception of Popular Literature in Post-Reformation Iceland*, London.

Driscoll, M. J. (2009). '"Um gildi gamalla bóka". Magnús Jónsson í Tjaldanesi und das Ende der isländischen Handschriftenkultur', in *Text, Reihe, Transmission: Unfestigkeit als Phänomen skandinavischer Erzählprosa 1500–1800*, Beiträge zur Nordischen Philologie, XLII, Tübingen and Basel.

Einar Ól. Sveinsson (1929). *Verzeichnis isländischer Märchenvarianten, mit einer einleitenden Untersuchung*, FF Communications, LXXXIII, Helsinki.

Finnur Sigmundsson (1946). *Níels skáldi*, Menn og minjar: íslenskur fróðleikur og skemmtun, V, Reykjavík.

Gad, T. (1987). 'En tragoedisk Historie. . .', *Magasin fra Det kongelige Bibliotek og Universitetsbiblioteket I*, 2. árgang nr. 3 (1987), 17–31.

Gísli Brynjúlfsson (1878). 'Danske, islandske og færøiske Kvad om Tistram og Isodd', in *Saga af Tristram ok Ísönd samt Möttuls saga*, Copenhagen, pp. 327–70.

Golther, W. (1907). *Tristan und Isolde in den Dichtungen des Mittelalters und der Neuen Zeit*, Leipzig.

Jón Helgason (1955). 'Um Magnús Jónsson í Vigur og bækur hans', in *Kvæðabók úr Vigur, AM 148, 8vo*, Íslenzk rit síðari alda. flokkur 2. bd. 1, Copenhagen, pp. 7–14.

Jónas Hallgrímsson (1837). 'Um Rímur af Tistrani og Indíönu, "orktar af Sigurdi Breidfjörd"', *Fjölnir*, III, 18–29.

Kalinke, M. E. (1981). *King Arthur, North-by-Northwest: The matière de Bretagne in Old Norse-Icelandic Romances*, Bibliotheca Arnamagnæana, 37, Copenhagen.

Kalinke, M. E. (1991a). 'En tragœdisk Historie om den ædle og tappre Tistrand: an eighteenth-century king's mirror', *Danske studier*, 57–75.

Kalinke, M. E. (1991b), 'Tristrams kvæði', in N. J. Lacy (ed.), *The New Arthurian Encyclopedia*, New York, p. 474.

Kalinke, M. E. and Mitchell, P. M. (1985). *Bibliography of Old Norse-Icelandic Romances*, Islandica, XLIV, Ithaca, NY.

Kjær, J. (1994). '*Tristan og Indiana* eller "Lykkens tumlebold" – fortællinger om Tristan og Isolde i Norden', in *Michelanea. Humanisme, litteratur og kommunikation. Festskrift til Michel Olsen i anledning af hans 60-årsdag den 23. april 1994*, Aalborg, pp. 81–7.

Kjær, J. (1996a). 'Les *Rímur af Tístran og Indíönu* (1831) de Sigurður Breiðfjörð – une version islandaise du mythe de Tristan et Iseut', in *Tristan und Isolde. Unvergängliches Thema der Weltkultur, XXX. Jahrestagung des Arbeitskreises 'Deutsche Literatur des Mittelalters', 27. September–1. Oktober 1995*, Wodan, LVII, Greifswald, pp. 141–54.

Kjær, J. (1996b). 'Tristan og Isalde et Tistran og Indiane: deux romans populaires danois du XIXe siècle. Etude de réception', in *Tristan-Tristant. Mélanges en l'honneur de Danielle Buschinger à l'occasion de son 60ème anniversaire*, Wodan, LXVI, Greifswald, pp. 279–98.

Kölbing, E. (1875). 'Beiträge zur Kenntnis der färöischen Poesie', *Germania*, XX, 385–402.

Kölbing, E. (1878). 'Zur Überlieferung der Tristan-Sage', in *Tristrams saga ok Ísondar, mit einer literarhistorischen Einleitung, deutscher Uebersetzung und Anmerkungen*, Heilbronn.

Linnström, H. (1867–84). *Svenskt Boklexikon, Åren 1830–1865*, Uppsala.

Liestøl, K. (1915). 'Iven Erningsson', in *Norske trollvisor og norrøne sogor*, Kristiania, pp. 155–88.

Liestøl, K. (1931). 'Islendske folkevisor', in *Nordisk kultur*, IX, A, Copenhagen, pp. 84–9.

Nyerup, R. (1796). 'Almuens Morskabslæsning. Historien om Tistrand', *Iris og Hebe* (October–December 1796), 193–210.

Olrik, J. (1921). 'Indledning. Vigoleis', in *Danske Folkebøger fra 16. og 17. Aarhundrede*, V, Copenhagen, pp. iii–xxxiv.

Páll Eggert Ólason (1948–52). *Íslenzkar æviskrár frá landnámstímum til ársloka 1940*, Reykjavík.

Páll Valsson (1999). *Jónas Hallgrímsson: Ævisaga*, Reykjavík.

Paulli, R. (1921). 'Bibliografi: Vigoleis', in *Danske Folkebøger fra 16. og 17. Aarhundrede*, V, Copenhagen, pp. 211–17.

Paulli, R. (1936). 'Bidrag til de danske Folkebøgers Historie', in *Danske Folkebøger fra 16. og 17. Aarhundrede*, XIII, Copenhagen, pp. 169–291.

Rossel, S. H. et al. (1976). 'Nøgle, navne, kilder', *Danmarks gamle Folkeviser*, XII, Copenhagen.

Schach, P. (1957–61). 'Some observations on Tristrams saga', *Saga-Book of the Viking Society*, XV, 102–29.

Schach, P. (1964). 'Tristan and Isolde in Scandinavian ballad and folklore', *Scandinavian Studies*, XXXVI, 281–97.

Schach, P. (1969). 'Some observations on the influence of *Tristrams saga ok Ísöndar* on Old Icelandic literature', in E. C. Polomé (ed.), *Old Norse Literature and Mythology: A Symposium*, Austin, TX, pp. 81–129.

Schlauch, M. (1934). *Romance in Iceland*, New York.

Seelow, H. (1989). *Die isländischen Übersetzungen der deutschen Volksbücher. Handschriftenstudien zur Rezeption und Überlieferung ausländischer unterhaltender Literatur in Island in der Zeit zwischen Reformation und Aufklärung*, Reykjavík.

Stefán Einarsson (1957). *A History of Icelandic Literature*, Baltimore, MD.

Sveinbjörn Beinteinsson (1961). 'Um Tístransrímur', in *Tístransrímur*, Rímnasafn, III, Reykjavík, pp. ix–xix.

Sveinbjörn Sigurjónsson (1937). 'Inngangur', in *Númarímur eftir Sigurð Breiðfjörð*, Reykjavík, pp. xi–lxiv.

Vésteinn Ólason (1979). 'Inngangur', in *Sagnadansar*, Reykjavík, pp. 7–88.

Vésteinn Ólason (1982). *The Traditional Ballads of Iceland: Historical Studies*, Reykjavík.

10

ARTHURIAN LITERATURE IN EAST SLAVIC

Susana Torres Prieto

The title of the present chapter requires at least a few clarifications for the non-specialist in medieval Slavic studies. First of all, the term Slavic is, above all, a linguistic identifier. For many decades now, it has been a conventional way of classifying the vast territories stretching from Bohemia to Muscovy and from Gdansk to Dubrovnik. Following the linguistic criteria of the development of Slavic into three large linguistic branches, all those territories were divided into areas of Western – or Central – Slavic, South Slavic and East Slavic. This terminology, however, did not account for religious and cultural differences or the process of formation of modern states.

In the late 1960s the great Byzantinist Dimitri Obolensky coined a term that took into account precisely the cultural and religious history of these territories: the 'Byzantine Commonwealth' (Obolensky 1971). It focused, therefore, on the role of Byzantium's political, artistic and religious influence in the formation of the new states and, in doing so, it cut across linguistic differentiations (it excluded Poland, for example, but included Bohemia and Moravia). Focusing rather on the process of textual transmission, Ricardo Picchio established a new difference between two areas that presented, according to him, distinct attitudes towards literacy, literature and textual transmission. Picchio divided the Slavic world into *Slavia Orthodoxa* and *Slavia Romana*, a denomination that subsumed all the many accountable differences in literary production. According to Picchio (Picchio 1972), those territories that, after the schism of 1054, had entered within the sphere of cultural influence of the Roman Church had had a literary and artistic development closer to that of their Western neighbours, whereas those territories that had remained under the religious authority of Byzantine Orthodoxy had gone through a completely different process of literary development, due to social as well as doctrinal characteristics.

Arthurian literature had a much wider diffusion and impact on vernacular literature in *Slavia Romana* than it ever did in *Slavia Orthodoxa*. While translations and adaptations exist in Bohemia from the fourteenth century, in *Slavia Orthodoxa*, which included the territories of East Slavic language and part of those of South Slavic (Serbia, Bulgaria and Macedonia), the development of non-religious literature, and indeed of Arthurian romance, was, if not necessarily more sparse, certainly less attested in written form. This should not be surprising if we take into account the fact that literature was strictly restricted to the Orthodox monastic milieu, where the compilation in written form of any non-religious text was made only sporadically.

Between these two cultural regions, however, there are 'contact areas' whose turbulent history prevents us from assigning them clearly to either of these groups. One of these permeable areas is the Balkans (Serbia, Croatia and Dalmatia) and another would be present-day Belarus and the Ukraine, that is, those territories that, at some point or another, were part of the Grand Duchy of Lithuania. In the present chapter, we shall present the evidence currently available to us of the knowledge and transmission of Arthurian romance in *Slavia Orthodoxa*, since its presence in *Slavia Romana* has already been presented elsewhere in the series Arthurian Literature in the Middle Ages (Thomas 2000).[1]

We have indirect evidence from a relatively early time, for example, of the existence of courtly poetry at the courts of the Nemanja dynasty in Serbia, as well as of the intense translating activity of courtly literature in Dalmatia.[2] There is also evidence of the existence of courtly poetry in the East Slavic principalities, which have traditionally been named Kievan Rus' – but whose limits soon surpassed those of current-day Ukraine – which emerged as political entities as the Varangian traders established commercial settlements by the river routes as far as Byzantium. This courtly poetry, the *byliny*[3] (singular *bylina*) survived only orally until the nineteenth century, when they started to be collected,[4] and subsequently enjoyed a dual existence, oral and written, which contributed to their oral survival by means of a process that Zumthor has called *archéocivilisation*.[5] This process conferred on the *byliny* certain characteristics, such as their limited degree of improvisation[6] and the focalization of the action at a certain court, in the case of the *byliny* the Kievan court, which becomes the physical and spiritual headquarters of a group of heroes in a permanent campaign situation either of 'reconquest' against a foreign invader, or against a mythical creature.

The *byliny* are poems averaging between 200 and 400 verses in length that were most likely originally sung, not recited, to judge by their verse pattern.[7] Although the name *byliny* traditionally groups together all those poems of loosely understood heroic content that share a common verse type, the differences in content and point of view of the three traditional cycles (the mythological, the Kiev and the Novgorod cycles) are not to be underestimated.[8] The accepted division of the whole corpus into three cycles attempts to account for the differences in content and ideology among them. In terms of relevance and proportion, which match both structural and ideological parameters, the Kiev cycle constitutes the paradigm of the *byliny*.

The Kiev cycle contains some elements that we could call Arthurian, the most relevant of which is, naturally, the court.[9] The court is the starting and the returning point of the *bogatyr*'s, that is, the hero's, quest. It is also the social entity from which he acquires prestige and recognition. Unlike Camelot, however, the court at Kiev is not presided over by a worthy king. Prince Vladimir, a fictional character rather than a historical one, is unfailingly morally inferior to any of the Kievan heroes, whose moral righteousness and military prowess shine the brighter by comparison to their prince. Given the compulsive lack of romance in Slavic epics, it is no surprise that there is no queen Guinevere at the Prince's Court.

Parallel to the function of the hero's journey, his quest, around which all episodes and actions are structured, the court is the central element of what I have called the semiotic universe of the *byliny* (Torres Prieto 2005, 195–217). This semiotic universe in the *byliny* is conformed to four elements whose characterization is unvarying and which, according to Jauss's concept, fulfilled the 'horizon of expectations' of the audience (Jauss 1982, 94–7) in terms of defining *byliny* as a genre; they were the hero, the antagonist, the prince and the court. It is precisely in the use, function and disposition of these four elements of the *byliny* semiotic universe where, I would argue, parallels to the Arthurian romance are more significant and noteworthy.

The *bylinic* hero, the *bogatyr*, is always on the move. There is no such thing as a static *bylina* and very often the narration of the hero's adventures develops as he is travelling, like the Arthurian knight, *au venture*. There are no tournaments in the *byliny* and the hero either sets out to find his antagonist, for example, a dragon, or finds him or her, as he is on his way, usually to the court. The motives for starting his trip, or his quest, are usually two: the defence of the Motherland (*sic*) and the search for a bride. He is always successful in the first quest, and almost always fails in the second one. In fact, the search for a bride, either by abduction or liberation, within the Kiev cycle, is left to minor heroes.

God's intervention is present in more than one instance, either directly or by proxy. There are cases where the assistance is not decisive in the confrontation with the antagonist itself, but very important in the resolution of the episode. The grand triad of Kievan heroes, Il'ia Muromets, Dobrynia Nikitich and Alesha Popovich, all receive the help of God, one way or another, either in the fact that they are aided in the middle of the combat or in the procurement of advice or the means to overcome the antagonist. This feature is essential to the definition of the hero as a fully Christian hero.[10]

The strength of the *bogatyr* relied on three elements: the strength of the *bogatyr* himself, the special qualities of his horse and the wonderful attributes of his weapons (Putilov 1988, 68). The horse not only carries the hero across the plains, sometimes galloping impossible distances or at an amazing speed, but also acts as an adviser, warning the hero of immediate danger or as a rescuer. The hero and horse constitute a unit and the long descriptions of the hero saddling his horse before departing are some of the most detailed scenes of the *byliny*.

There seem to be three main types of antagonists in the *byliny*: supernatural beings, foreign enemies and women. In the worst of scenarios, the hero will have to face a woman who is also foreign and uses supernatural powers, that is, a sorceress. The creatures the hero has to fight often have anthropomorphic characteristics or behaviours. The curious mix of animal and human characteristics is certainly not exclusive of the East Slavic or Russian traditions. The process of bestialization of the antagonist, giving way to all kinds of strange creatures in medieval literature, particularly in travel books, but also in romances like *Perceforest*, is all the more significant in the *byliny*, where the real, foreign enemies, called generically Tartars, are described as half-human and half-animal.

The heroes have to confront all these different creatures who, even when representing a real and historical threat, are nevertheless described with fantastic attributes. Some would say that this proves a clear influence of the fairy tale on the *byliny*, others that this represents a previous step in the development of the *byliny* into the historical song, in which the enemies are clearly human. Both are possible, but it is also feasible that this is one of the characteristics of the *byliny*, in line with what A. E. Alexander called the 'suspension of disbelief' (1973, 58–60). The equation of a national threat with a semi-human, bestialized creature is, nevertheless, quite strong.

Women as antagonists of the hero are generally presented using magic. The hero, in these instances, does not set out in search of a wife, but rather he comes across these women, who add to their magic practices their promiscuity as they offer themselves to the hero. Construing the treatment of women in the *byliny* simply as an expression of misogyny is a failure to see that some female characters are also the best helpers of the hero: the mother, the sister and sometimes a good Russian wife. What is more important in the negative portrayal of female characters is their foreignness and their magical practices that antagonize the hero rather than the fact that they are women. The portrayal of women probably suggests a male monastic milieu in which the social role of women was linked to motherhood or *caritas*. More significantly, women help the hero in many instances when other women, or men, have placed the hero in danger.

The prince in the *byliny* is a certain Prince Vladimir who cannot be traced back to any historical figure, though it is very probably a composite abstraction of two of the most prominent rulers of Kievan Rus': Prince Vladimir I Sviatoslavich, the Saint (who ruled between 980 and 1015) and Vladimir Vsevolodich Monomakh (1053–1125). The poems of the Kievan cycle have as one of their recurring scenarios the prince's court in Kiev, and very often the conversations between Prince Vladimir and the Kievan heroes take place in the dining-hall, in the course of a banquet. This is perhaps one of the other main characteristics of the royal figure: like King Arthur, he is often surrounded by the Kievan heroes, dining at his table, when action breaks out. It is also the Kievan court to which the heroes return after battles, after capturing an enemy or liberating prisoners.

The relation between the heroes and the prince is that of loyalty and respect of the former for the latter. However arguable or dishonourable the behaviour of the prince may be, the heroes pay him unconditional respect and he is the central figure around whom they all gather and whom they always obey. He is thankful to his *bogatyrs*, for bringing back collected taxes, for example. Nonetheless, the prince can also be depicted quite negatively, and it is sometimes precisely his faulty behaviour that triggers the beginning of a new adventure for the always righteous hero who will diligently complete his task without resentment.

The Kievan court, the place at which the heroes arrive and from where they depart, has a clear function only in the *byliny* of the Kievan cycle.[11] Only *bogatyrs* are linked to Kiev. Other heroes who might arrive in Kiev, not being *bogatyrs*, are foreigners and their intention when they arrive in Kiev is to ridicule the court and its members. The court is certainly a symbol and functions as the goal of the hero in the poems. It thus plays a similar role to that of Camelot in the Arthurian cycle, as a representation of something else, as a metaphor of the unity of the different heroes, as brothers in arms, under the authority of Prince Vladimir.

However, if the existence of courts in reality was a means to enhance the authority of the ruler and to 'reinforce his personal ties with individuals' (Shepard 2003, 14), the court of Kiev is usually where the hero is scorned, questioned, incarcerated. Of course this is directly linked to the figure of the prince, whose portrayal is not very favourable. So, instead of being an agreeable place suitable for 'the rest of a warrior', like Camelot, or the court of Charlemagne as depicted in the *chansons de geste*, it turns into a hostile but necessary destination. In this sense, the epic Kiev presented in the *byliny* is far from a poetic realisation of the dreams of an ideal government, the place for the recreation of a Golden Age, as it has been traditionally understood. The court of Kiev, while depicted as the necessary place to which a *bogatyr* goes, is not described in favourable tones, nor is Prince Vladimir. Unlike the court of King Arthur, the Kievan court is a place of conspiracy and of dissolute conduct. This hostile and shameful environment, against whose conspiracies the hero has to fight and which denies him the glory he deserves, enhances by contrast the virtues of the *bogatyr*, who nevertheless fulfils his duty against all odds.[12]

The *byliny* represent a highly hybrid genre, particularly in respect to the generic classifications made ad hoc as it were for narratives that have been preserved in other literary traditions. If analysed from the point of view of their content, the *byliny* lack the intimate approach to courtly love necessary in romance, since it is the defence of the land that constitutes the main task of the hero if he wants to be successful. If the analysis is structural, the quest of the hero and shameful behaviour of the ruler seem to remove both from the realm of the *chansons de geste*. Are they, then, *chansons de geste* in the form of romance? Or uncourtly romances devoid of love? Or adventure tales closer to Odyssean accounts? Or a little bit of everything? It should not be forgotten that the *byliny* most likely originated at a time when the Rus' principalities were immersed in internal strife as well as fighting external enemies, either the Mongol Yoke or the Teutonic Knights. The permanent state of campaign is clearly reflected in the hero's ethos and in the choice of themes of the *byliny*.

Another socio-cultural fact to bear in mind is the lack in East Slavonic society of what Sarah Kay has called the 'clerical department' of aristocratic households (Kay 2000, 85–6). Indeed, in *Slavia Orthodoxa*, literary activity was mainly restricted to the monasteries, except for a very few sporadic examples. It was within the monastic, and not the courtly environment, as was the case in *Slavia Romana*, that the translations and adaptations of epic works were made or epic songs were most likely created. In both cases, the absence of courtly love would first and foremost reflect the ideology of the translator or copyist, through whom any romantic elements were filtered and who would impose on the epics and romances created or adapted in the monasteries a Christian moralistic approach.

Notwithstanding that acquaintance with Arthurian material in Early Rus' principalities cannot be documented, either through one of the above-mentioned routes of cultural influence, or through the much discussed Norse route (Mel'nikova, 1996), certain references to Arthurian literature in the *byliny* do seem to be present, and they seem to provide us with the information lacking in the preserved versions to grasp the full meaning of some of the poems. These parallels are to be found particularly in the story of Tristan. For example, Dobrynia forces his wife to recognize him when he returns to Kiev from Constantinople, by placing his wedding ring in her wineglass, a motif transmitted in the Tristan legend.[13] And the action of Marinka scraping off Dobrynia's footprints after his escape from her castle, a fact that has puzzled scholars for decades and to which many possible interpretations have been given, might be better understood in light of the trap set for Tristan by the dwarf Frocin with the flour on the floor. However, the very late written record of the *byliny*, and the absence of evidence of their transmission for centuries, renders any comparative approach speculative, subject to the easy temptation of finding parallels in motifs that could be literary universals or secondary additions introduced during centuries of oral transmission. Is the literary existence of a court presided over by a ruler at whose service a phalanx of heroes perform great deeds conclusive evidence that Arthurian literature was known in Rus' and that, furthermore, a local narrative tradition, the *byliny*, was modelled upon it? Maybe. Despite a healthy dose of scepticism in light of the materials *currently available* to us, the fact is that even if the Arthurian tradition was transmitted at second or third hand, even if oral adaptations were never written down, even if the attested literature is but a distant echo of Camelot, the Early Rus' found the means to create a parallel courtly universe in which they could also recreate their own 'myth of common identity' (Franklin 1998, 188).[14]

Of all the heroes linked to the ruler of Camelot, Tristan was, without a doubt, the most popular in Slavic, and not only in East Slavic oral tradition, as we have seen. In addition to the Czech 'Tristan' produced in Bohemia, his adventures also became known in Belarus in the sixteenth century. The latter two translations, however, were not made from the same originals and they did not arrive in the Slavonic realm by the same route.[15] Like *Tandariáš a Floribella*, the long fourteenth-century Czech adaptation *Tristram a Izalda* (around 9,000 verses), was based on German sources – on Eilhart von Oberge's twelfth-century version, Gottfried von Strassburg's courtly romance *Tristan* and Heinrich von Freiberg's continuation[16] – but the sixteenth-century Belarusian translation *Tryščan* was made from an Italian adaptation of the French prose version, Luce del Gat's *L'Estoire de Monseigneur Tristan* (c.1235), popularly known as the Prose Tristan.

The Czech *Tristram a Izalda* dates to the early fifteenth century and is preserved in two fifteenth-century manuscripts (1449 and 1483).[17] Compared to its German models, the Czech *Tristram*, as noted by Thomas, 'alternates between medial-style realism and low-style burlesque' (Thomas 2000, 253). This departure from the 'courtly ethos of the German romance' responds, according to Thomas, to a change of audience, from the Bohemian court to the 'increasingly influential Czech-speaking members of the gentry and the merchant class' (Thomas 2000, 252).[18]

In Belarus, the story of Tristan, *Trysčan*, is extant in a single manuscript whose dating is far from precise, although indirect evidence allows us to postulate the last quarter of the sixteenth century as the date of the redaction, which, needless to say, however, is not the date when it can be assumed that Tristan's adventures were first translated or known in Belarus. The same codex that contained this Belarusian *Tryščan*, owned by the Unikhovski family, also contained a Slavic translation of *Buovo d'Antona* (*Istorija o knjažati Kgvidone*), the Italian translation of the Anglo-Norman romance of *Bevis of Hampton*,[19] and a translation of Miklós Oláh's *Athila*, via a Polish translation of the Latin original in Cyprian Bazylik's *Historia spraw Atyle kroal węgierskiego* in Krakow in 1574. This date is, in fact, the *terminus post quem* of the manuscript. The *terminus ante quem* would be the date of the first annotation made in the codex by a member of the Unikhovski family, in 1594.[20]

This single manuscript of *Tryščan* (MS 94) is currently at the Raczynski Public Library in Poznan. It was discovered and described for the first time by O. M. Bodianskii in 1846 (Bodianskii, 1846). The Belarusian 'Tristan' occupies the first 127 pages of the 344 pages of the codex (pagination was added by a later hand). Written in cursive script, in a single column, the incipit reads: 'Here begins the tale of the knights from the Serbian books, in particular the famous knights Tristan, Antsolot [Lancelot] and Bovo, and many other valorous knights.'[21] The *incipit* already provides a clue to its provenance, and it also is the source of an ongoing controversy, namely, is this 'Tristan' *really* Belarusian.

In the first edition of the manuscript by A. N. Veselovskii, the language is identified as sixteenth-century Belarusian (1888, 127). E. Sgambati further points out that the Belarusian used, while being a literary language, is rather a combination of the local vernacular and both East Slavic and Polish. It is, after all, a form of codification of the vernacular with some literary features rather than a Belarusian recension of Church Slavonic (Sgambati 1983, 13 and notes 1 and 2 on that page). The text is pervaded, in any case, by Italianisms and Serbisms, which clearly betrays its Dalmatian–South Slavic origin. The fact that the name of the translator, or even the name of the person for whom the translation was made, or the one who could have commissioned the translation, remains unknown does not contribute to clarifying the place where the translation took place.[22]

The Belarusian *Tryščan*, at least its first part, presumably was directly linked to the Italian *Tristano Veneto*, probably through a no longer extant Serbian text, although the absence in *Tryščan* of errors and omissions in the *Tristano Veneto* (as attested by the manuscript codex 3325 of the National Library of Vienna) points rather to the existence of a prototype for these two related texts that has been lost (Sgambati 1983, 24–46).[23] The Belarusian *Tryščan* has a second part, however, that has not been attested as such in any other text of the Tristan tradition,[24] although Sgambati has tentatively traced echoes of the Tuscan Tristan tradition in it (Sgambati 1983, 47–68). Some of the episodes, though not in the same sequence, could indeed derive from the *Tavola Rotonda* and the *Tristano Riccardino*, but others are, simply, a new creation, as will be seen. That the second part of *Tryščan* has a different textual origin than the first is well attested by factual incongruences between it and what is narrated in the first part, such as Tryščan's statement, upon returning Ižota to King Marko, that it was the *second* time that he had recuperated his wife with his sword, although in *Tryščan* he does not engage Palamidež (Palamedes) in combat because he escapes on his horse.

The second part (chapters 32–43), therefore, recounts the escape of Tryščan and Ižota to Domolot,[25] to the court of King Artiuš and Queen Ženibra; Tryščan's first encounter with Antsolot (Lancelot); Geush's (Kay's) challenge to Tryščan and his defeat. Then it narrates Antsolot's pursuit of the lovers and his second encounter with Tryščan. The three decide to return to Domolot, and this is followed by Tryščan's fight with Gavaon (Gawain) and other knights at King Artiuš's court. At this point, King Samsiž (Lasansis of Enchanted Arms?) of Black Island arrives at the court of Domolot. After defeating all knights, including Antsolot, he also defeats King Artiuš and they are all taken as prisoners to the Black Island. Queen Ženibra, following Antsolot's request, begs Tryščan to rescue King Artiuš and his knights. They embark in Tryščan's vessel (Tryščan, Ižota, Ženibra and Govornar [Governal]) and arrive first at an island where a queen demands that all the newcomers be castrated before they may pay homage to her, or else be incarcerated. Tryščan refuses to be castrated and he is taken to the dungeons, from where he escapes when Ižota manages to throw his sword to him. He subsequently liberates all the other incarcerated knights, kills the queen and her brother and, after refusing the offer to become the lord of those lands, departs with Ižota, Ženibra and Govornar in search of King Samsiž. On their voyage, they dock at yet another harbour where a treacherous crusader lives who makes a fortune by killing every guest and taking his possessions. Tryščan kills the treacherous crusader and he is, once again, invited to stay in that land as lord of the realm. He again refuses, but realizing that, at this pace, he is never going to arrive at the Black Island where King Samsiž dwells, he decides to disguise himself and Govornar as merchants (with 'Latin vestments') and have both Ižota and Ženibra dress as nuns. Pretending to be a merchant, under the name of Sir Latin, and after having refused a few offers to sell the ladies, whom he passes off as his sisters, and even his chessboard, he is challenged by King Samsiž to fight for the ladies and his kingdom. Claiming he does not know how to fight, his real self is revealed in the middle of the battle, and King Samsiž begs for clemency. Thereupon, King Artiuš and all his knights are freed and they can all return to Domolot. Tryščan and Ižota continue their trip to King Marko's court and, on their way, Tryščan successively fights a French knight of King Peremot (Faramon), Smerdodug the infidel, Palamidež, Antsolot (a fight whose fatal outcome is eventually prevented by Ižota), Divdan (Dinadan), Iaščor (Hector des Mares), Librun (Le Brun?), Galets (Galahad) – these last two along with Antsolot – until they finally arrive at King Marko's court, where Tryščan delivers Ižota to his uncle. Tryščan eventually departs and arrives at a tournament in the land where Ižota of the White Hands lives. There, Tryščan fights Klimberko and Erdin (Kaherdin), whom he kills. While trying to recuperate from his many wounds, he receives 'a letter from the air' in which Ižota protests her love ('My lord, just as a fish cannot live without water, I cannot live without you'). Tryščan sends a letter to King Marko asking him to permit Ižota to come and heal him. Ižota arrives at the place where Tryščan is and begins healing him, and at this point the narrative abruptly stops. The last lines of the manuscript read: 'I do not know whether he recovered from those wounds or died. This is all that is written about him.'

Aside from this second part, the differences between *Tryščan* and the traditional legend of Tristan and Yseut are many, even in its first part where the text corresponds to the Veneto version. For a start, Tryščan and Ižota fall in love before taking the potion, which renders meaningless and thus invalidates one of the main aspects of the myth of the doomed lovers, who are attracted to each other because they are mistakenly put under a spell that was not intended for them.[26] In the more Christianized versions of the romance, the potion was certainly used to unburden the lovers of any guilt. The invalidation of the role of the love philtre in *Tryščan*, where Ižota's father, King Lenviz (Anguin) even encourages her love for Tryščan, does not necessarily indicate a less Christian-moral approach to the poem. It rather reveals the absence of interest in the love story altogether, clearly represented by the lack of romance or intimate episodes between the two protagonists. In *Tryščan* they do not escape to the Forest of Morrois, since there is none in the Belarusian version, and therefore the time they spend in other versions secretly living their love in isolation is missing from our version. Likewise, their early departure from King Marko's court 'precludes all clandestine love-making between the lovers' (Kipel 1988, xvi), which is precisely one of the reasons for their medieval, and modern, success. The Belarusian *Tryščan* is, paradoxically, not a story about love, either doomed or of any other kind. It is an account of the deeds of a bold hero and his fights, adventures and death.

The lack of the romantic element is consistent with the translations and versions of other epic poems and romances in Slavic, such as the various adaptations of the Alexander Romance and of the Byzantine romance of Digenis Akritas. Whether this is due in the case of Bohemia, as Thomas has argued (2000, 254–5), to the mentality of the merchant elites, or in East Slavic to the stern control of the Church, the point is that it is, in actual fact, the unifying feature common to all translations made throughout the Slavic realm and one of the defining characteristics of heroic poetry in Slavonic (Torres Prieto 2009). Consequently, it is also absent from the Russian tradition of oral heroic poetry, the *byliny*. This lack of interest in the romantic element, in sheer contrast to the devotion to the heroic one, along with the social and production reasons mentioned above, made of the adapted Tristan the most suitable hero for a society in bad need of military prowess.

Notes

[1] The earliest Arthurian romance in a Slavic language is the Czech *Tandariáš a Floribella* from around 1380 and preserved in three fifteenth-century manuscripts. This is a translation of the relatively unknown thirteenth-century German romance *Tandareis und Flordibel* by Der Pleier, which focuses on the love of the eponymous couple and their conflict with King Arthur who opposes the union. A second Czech Arthurian romance, *Tristram a Izalda*, dates from around 1400.

[2] On both these aspects, see Torres Prieto 2009.

[3] The best collection of *byliny* in English (introduction and translation) is still that by Bailey and Ivanova, 1998. In Spanish, see Torres Prieto 2003. There are many excellent studies on *byliny* by the Russian school, particularly those by B. N. Putilov (1988, 1999). For a general introduction in English to *byliny*, particularly their relation to history, see Torres Prieto, 2010.

[4] P. N. Rybnikov published the first collection of *byliny* (224 songs) in four volumes (1861–7). In 1804, another collection of 25 texts was published under the name *Ancient Russian Poems collected by Kirsha Danilov*, comprising songs from western Siberia, from the province of Perm. The latter, however, did not imply the direct collection of the texts from the singers of northern Russia, from the province of Olonets, as done by Rybnikov, a task that was to be followed by A. F. Gil'ferding's collection of songs from the same region (318 songs), which was published posthumously in 1873, since Gil'ferding fatally contracted typhus during his last trip to that province.

[5] On the mutual influences of this process, see Zumthor 1983, 35–7. In the case of the Russian *byliny*, there is a masterly study of this process by Novikov (2000).

[6] The different degree of improvisation was already noted by Vesterholt 1973, and further confirmed by Novikov's research (2000).

[7] This is a stress pattern, rather than a rhyme or stanza pattern, based on the long epic line (the asymmetric decasyllable), that usually ended on two syllables (Jakobson 1953, 22ff.).

[8] On the differences between the mythological and Kiev cycles, see Mendoza Tuñón and Torres Prieto 2009.

[9] The quest of the hero is the structural element that brings the *byliny* closer to the *romantz*. It is essential to the structure of the poem, since it is, in Jakobsonian terms, the *dominant*, but it differs from the Arthurian quest in that it lacks a romantic element, which in the *byliny*, if it does exist, brings about, precisely, the failure of the hero's quest. See Torres Prieto 2005, esp. 184–94.

[10] On the reflection of Christianization in the *byliny*, see Torres Prieto 2004.

[11] The city of Novgorod, as a geographic point from which to depart and at which to arrive, fulfils the same function in the *byliny* of the Novgorod cycle, those dedicated to Sadko and Vasilii Buslaev. It is also in Novgorod, where they have to prove their worth, like the *bogatyrs* in Kiev.

[12] This understanding could reopen the question of the place of origin of the *byliny*, which is beyond the scope of the present chapter. For further discussion of the time and place of origin of the *byliny*, see Torres Prieto 2010.

[13] Precisely this detail is absent in the Belarusian *Tryščan*, as we shall see.

[14] A parallel situation was proposed for the popularization in South Slavic oral epics of the Byzantine epic of *Digenis Akritas*. See Torres Prieto 2009, 121, n. 26.

[15] The two Slavic versions of the Tristan legend also reveal two of the main routes of literary influence from West to East. The most relevant one, in quantitative terms, came from fellow Orthodox South Slavic

territories (Bulgaria, Macedonia and Serbia) in two waves, the first at the time of the Rus' conversion to Christianity (988) and the second during the fourteenth and fifteenth centuries, with the arrival of hesychasm. The second route was from Central Slavic territories (Bohemia, Poland), initially through Novgorod and Galizia and, later on, through the Grand Duchy of Lithuania, since, at the time when it achieved its greatest degree of expansion, which included Poland and Belarus, into which Bohemia had been absorbed, the Grand Duchy bordered directly on the Holy Roman Empire in the west and on Muscovy in the east.

[16] Heinrich von Freiberg's continuation was in fact composed in Bohemia for the nobleman Raimund von Lichtenburg in the late thirteenth century.

[17] For a discussion of the Czech Arthurian romances, *Tristram a Izalda* and *Tandariáš a Floribella*, adapted in Bohemia, see Thomas 2000.

[18] Since *Tristram a Izalda* has been discussed by Thomas (2000) in *The Arthur of the Germans*, I shall focus on the Belarusian *Tryščan*.

[19] This Belarusian translation of a Croatian recension of the romance made in Dalmatia, most likely in Dubrovnik, could have been the source for the Russian translation of the latter, *Повесть о Бове короле-биче*, which enjoyed enormous popularity until the nineteenth century, both in manuscript form (over one hundred manuscripts are preserved) and in *lubki* (nearly 200 editions). There are specialists who think the Russian version could have been made either from a Polish translation or from the Yiddish *Baba-boek*, which was ultimately also translated from the Italian version.

[20] Brückner (1886, 351) admits this date as valid for the entry of the codex into the family patrimony, while Veselovskii (1888, 130–1) considered that this annotation had been made retrospectively in 1598. The details of both positions can be found in Sgambati 1983, 4–5. See also Kipel's more succinct survey of the available data (1988, xi–xiii).

[21] Починается повесть о витезях с книг сэрбъских, а звлаща о славном рыцэры Трысчан[е], о Анцалоте и о Бове и о иншых многих витезех до[брых], translation by Kipel (1988, 3). Apart from Kipel's English translation, and Sgambati's into Italian, there exists another translation into English by S. Dekanić-Janoski (1977).

[22] Sgambati suggests that the codex could have been purchased by a member of the Unikhovski family in a visit to Vilnius, regardless of where it was made. In any case, the controversy will continue concerning a text whose embryonic stage of literary language does not allow a clear ascription to any of the East Slavic branches and which was, furthermore, made in a territory that was neither politically nor sociologically Belarusian at that time.

[23] Sgambati (1983), in her excellent and unsurpassed study of the Belarusian *Tryščan*, proposes the existence of two intermediary prototypes to explain the particular differences between the texts. All references to chapters and paragraphs are to Sgambati's edition.

[24] The break between the first and the second part of *Tryščan* is also a contentious issue. While Kipel places it quite 'arbitrarily' (*sic*) at the recounting by King Marko of his dream to Ižota, on page 100 of her translation (corresponding to Sgambati, chapter 31a), to judge from a change in the spelling of proper names and vocabulary (Kipel 1988, xv), Sgambati, after presenting a complete episodic collation of *Tryščan* with all other possible sources (Sgambati 1983, 405–86), concludes that the second part starts with the departure of both lovers to Domolot (Camelot) after the escape of Palamidež (Palamedes), who in *Tryščan* does not fight with Tristan but simply escapes when he hears him approaching (chapter 32a). It should be remembered that the whole codex was written by the same hand, and the differences in orthography cannot be attributed to the copyist of our manuscript.

[25] If Kipel's bipartite division is accepted, it will also include Marko's dream, Ižota's attempt at having Braginia put to death, her rescue by Palamidež, his introduction to King Marko's court and his winning of Ižota in exchange for Braginia, and the visit of Ižota and Palamidež to the church where Tryščan turns up (chapter 31a–n).

[26] This interpretation of Tristan and Yseut's love, in comparison to Lancelot and Guinevere's, was advanced by the French School in the 1830s and it is further discussed by A. S. Fedrick in his introduction

to Béroul's *Tristan* (1970, 22ff.). On definitions and developments of courtly love, see Brownlee 2000. On the social functionality of the myth and its modernity, see Le Goff's succinct remarks (2005, 236–42).

Reference List

Texts and Translations

The Belarusian Trysčan

The Byelorussian Tristan, trans. Z. Kipel (New York, 1988).

The Serbo-Russian Romance of Tristan and Isolt (Povest o Tristanu i Ižoti), trans. S. Dekanić-Janoski, in *The Tristan Legend: Texts from Northern and Eastern Europe in Modern English Translation*, ed. J. Hill (Leeds, 1977), pp. 47–143.

Il Tristano biancorusso, ed. and trans. E. Sgambati (Florence, 1983).

Other Texts and Translations

L'Akrite. L'épopée byzantine de Digénis Akritas, ed. P. Odorico and J.-P. Arrignon (Toulouse, 2002).

An Anthology of Russian Folk Epics, trans. J. Bailey and T. G. Ivanova (Armonk, NY, 1998).

Béroul. *The Romance of Tristan. The Tale of Tristan's Madness*, trans. A. S. Fedrick (Harmondsworth, 1970).

Cantos Épicos Rusos. Ciclo Mitológico, Ciclo de Kiev, Ciclo de Nóvgorod, trans. S. Torres Prieto (Madrid, 2003).

Danilov, K. Drevnie rossiiskie stikhtvoreniia, sobrannye Kirsheiu Danilovym (St Petersburg, 1804).

Gil'ferding, A. F., Onezhskie Byliny zapisannye A. F. Gil'ferdingom letom 1871 goda (St Petersburg, 1873).

Rybnikov, P. N., Pesni, sobrannyia P. N. Rybnikovym, I-IV (Moscow, 1861–7).

'The Tale of Devgenij', trans. H. F. Graham, Byzantinoslavica, 28 (1968), 51–91.

Studies

Alexander, A. E. (1973). Bylina and Fairy Tale: The Origins of Russian Heroic Poetry, The Hague.

Bodianskii, O. M. (1846). 'O poiskakh moikh v Poznanskoi publichnoi biblioteke', Chteniia v Imperatorskom obshchestvie istorii i drevnostei rossiiskikh pri Moskovskom universitete, 1, 27–32.

Brownlee, M. S. (2000). 'Medieval Spanish paradigms and Cervantine revisions', in R. L. Krueger (ed.), The Cambridge Companion to Medieval Romance, Cambridge, pp. 253–66.

Brückner, A. (1886). 'Ein Weissrussischer Codex miscellaneus der Gräflich-Raczynskischen Bibliothek in Posen', Archiv für Slavische Philologie, 9, 345–91.

Franklin, S. (1998). 'The invention of Rus(sia)(s): some remarks on medieval and modern perceptions of continuity and discontinuity', in A. P. Smyth (ed.), Medieval Europeans: Studies in Ethnic Identity and National Perspectives in Medieval Europe, New York, pp. 180–95.

Jakobson, R. (1953). 'The kernel of comparative Slavic literature', Harvard Slavic Studies, I, 1–71.

Jauss, H. R. (1982). Toward an Aesthetic of Reception, Minneapolis.

Kay, S. (2000). 'Courts, clerks and courtly love', in R. L. Krueger (ed.), The Cambridge Companion to Medieval Romance, Cambridge, pp. 81–96.

Le Goff, J. (2005). Héros et merveilles du Moyen Age, Paris.

Mel'nikova, E. A. (1996). The Eastern World of the Vikings: Eight Essays about Scandinavia and Eastern Europe in the Early Middle Ages [Gothenburg].

Mendoza Tuñón, J. and Torres Prieto, S. (2009). 'The atypical hero in the bylinic tradition: the mythological cycle', in J. A. Álvarez-Pedrosa Núñez and S. Torres Prieto (eds), Medieval Slavonic Studies: New Perspectives for Research, Paris, pp. 25–36.

Novikov, I. U. A. (2000). *Skazitel'i bylinnaia traditsiia*, St Petersburg.

Obolensky, D. (1971). *The Byzantine Commonwealth: Eastern Europe 500–1453*, London.

Picchio, R. (1972). 'Questione della lingua e Slavia Cirillometodiana', in R. Picchio (ed.) *Studi sulla questione della lingua presso gli slavi*, Rome.

Putilov, B. N. (1988). *Geroicheskii epos i deistvitel'nost'*, Leningrad.

Putilov, B. N. (1999). *Ekskursy v teoriiu i istoriiu slavianskogo eposa*, St Petersburg.

Shepard, J. (2003). 'Courts in East and West', in P. Linehan and J. L. Nelson (eds), *The Medieval World*, London, pp. 14–36.

Thomas, A. (2000). 'King Arthur and his Round Table in the culture of medieval Bohemia and in medieval Czech literature', in W. H. Jackson and S. A. Ranawake (eds), *The Arthur of the Germans: The Arthurian Legend in Medieval German and Dutch Literature*, Cardiff, pp. 249–56.

Torres Prieto, S. (2004). 'La Cristianización en las *bylinas*', *Ilu. Revista de Ciencias de las Religiones, Anejos*, XIII, 133–9.

Torres Prieto, S. (2005). 'Travelling in the Russian byliny: the hero and his trips', unpublished Ph.D. thesis, Universidad Complutense, Madrid.

Torres Prieto, S. (2009). 'Found in translation? Heroic models in Slavonic', in J. A. Álvarez-Pedrosa Núñez and S. Torres Prieto (eds), *Medieval Slavonic Studies: New Perspectives for Research*, Paris, pp. 115–27.

Torres Prieto, S. (2010). 'Slavic epic: past tales and present myths', in K. Raaflaub and D. Konstan (eds), *Epic and Ancient History*, Oxford.

Veselovskii, A. N. (1888). *Iz istorii romana i povesti: materialy i izsledovaniia. Vypusk' II: Slaviano-romanskii otdel'*, St Petersburg.

Vesterholt, O. (1973). *Tradition and Individuality. A Study in Slavonic Oral Epic Poetry*, Copenhagen.

Zumthor, P. (1983). *Introduction à la poésie orale*, Paris.

GENERAL BIBLIOGRAPHY

Icelandic names are alphabetized by given name and patronymic.

Álfrún Gunnlaugsdóttir (1978). *Tristán en el Norte*, Reykjavík.

Anderson, S. M. and Swenson, K. (eds) (2002). *Cold Counsel: Women in Old Norse Literature and Mythology*, New York.

Andersson, T. M. (2006). *The Growth of the Medieval Icelandic Sagas (1180–1280)*, Ithaca, NY.

Bandlien, B. (2005). *Strategies of Passion: Love and Marriage in Old Norse Society*, trans. Betsy van der Hoek, Turnhout.

Besamusca, B. and Brandsma, F. (eds) (2007). *Arthurian Literature*, XXIV: *The European Dimensions of Arthurian Literature*, Cambridge.

Bekker-Nielsen, H., Damsgaard Olsen, T. and Widding, O. (eds) (1965). *Norrøn fortællekunst. Kapitler af den norsk-islandske middelalderlitteraturs historie*, Copenhagen.

Bjarni Einarsson (1961). *Skáldasögur. Um uppruna og eðli ástaskáldasagnanna fornu*, Reykjavík.

Bjarni Einarsson (1976). *To skjaldesagaer. En analyse af Kormáks saga og Hallfreðar saga*, Bergen, Oslo and Tromsø.

Boberg, I. M. (1966). *Motif-Index of Early Icelandic Literature*, Bibliotheca Arnamagnæana, XXVII, Copenhagen.

Böðvarr Guðmundsson, Sverrir Tómasson, Torfi H. Tulinius and Vésteinn Ólason (eds) (1993). *Íslensk bókmenntasaga*, II, Reykjavik.

Bornholdt, C. (2005). *Engaging Moments: The Origins of Medieval Bridal-Quest Narrative*, Ergänzungsbände zum Reallexikon der Germanischen Altertumskunde, 46, Berlin and New York.

Boyer, R. (ed.) (1985). *Les Sagas de chevaliers (riddarasögur). Actes de la Vᵉ Conférence Internationale sur les Sagas (Toulon, juillet 1982)*, Paris.

Clover, C. J. and Lindow, J. (eds) (1985). *Old Norse-Icelandic Literature: A Critical Guide*, Ithaca, NY; (2005). Preface to the second printing, by T. M. Andersson.

Clunies Ross, M. (ed.) (2000). *Old Icelandic Literature and Society*, Cambridge.

Einar Ól. Sveinsson (1929). *Verzeichnis isländischer Märchenvarianten mit einer einleitenden Untersuchung*, FF Communications, LXXXIII, Helsinki.

Fry, D. K. (1980). *Norse Sagas Translated into English: A Bibliography*, New York.

Gibbs, M. E. and Johnson, S. M. (1997). *Medieval German Literature*, New York and London.

Glauser, J. (1983). *Isländische Märchensagas. Studien zur Prosaliteratur im spätmittelalterlichen Island*, Beiträge zur nordischen Philologie, 12, Basel and Frankfurt a. M.

Glauser, J. and Kreutzer, G. (eds) (1998). *Isländische Märchensagas*, I, Munich.

Green, D. H. (2002). *The Beginnings of Medieval Romance: Fact and Fiction. 1150–1220*, Cambridge.

Grimbert, J. T. (ed.) (1995). *Tristan and Isolde: A Casebook*, New York and London; paperback 2002.

Groos, A. and Lacy, N. J. (eds) (2002). *Perceval/Parzival: A Casebook*, New York and London.

Hallberg, P. (1971). 'Norröna riddarasogor. Några språkdrag', *Arkiv för nordisk filologi*, 86, 114–37.

Hallberg, P. (1973). 'Broder Robert, *Tristrams saga* och *Duggals leizla*. Anteckningar till norska översätt-ningar', *Arkiv för nordisk filologi*, 88, 55–71.

Halvorsen, E. F. (1959). *The Norse Version of the Chanson de Roland*, Bibliotheca Arnamagnæana, 19, Copenhagen.

Helle, K. (1968). 'Anglo-Norwegian relations in the reign of Håkon Håkonsson (1217–63)', *Mediaeval Scandinavia*, 1, 101–14.

Hermann Pálsson and Edwards, P. (1971). *Legendary Fiction in Medieval Iceland*, Studia Islandica, 30, Reykjavík.

Jackson, W. H. and Ranawake, S. (eds) (2000). *The Arthur of the Germans: The Arthurian Legend in Medieval German and Dutch Literature*, Cardiff.

Jochens, J. (1995). *Women in Old Norse Society*, Ithaca, NY.

Johanterwage, V. and Würth, S. (eds) (2007). *Übersetzen im skandinavischen Mittelalter*, Studia Medievalia Septentrionalia, 14, Vienna.

Jónas Kristjánsson (1988). *Eddas and Sagas: Iceland's Medieval Literature*, trans. Peter Foote, Reykjavík.

Jones, G. (1968). *A History of the Vikings*, London.

Kalinke, M. E. (1981). *King Arthur, North-by-Northwest: The matière de Bretagne in Old Norse-Icelandic Romances*, Bibliotheca Arnamagnæana, 37, Copenhagen.

Kalinke, M. E. (1985). 'Norse romance (*Riddarasögur*)', in C. J. Clover and J. Lindow (eds), *Old Norse-Icelandic Literature: A Critical Guide*, Islandica, 45, Ithaca, NY; rpt 2005, 316–63.

Kalinke, M. E. and Mitchell, P. M. (eds) (1985). *Bibliography of Old Norse-Icelandic Romances*, Islandica, 44, Ithaca, NY.

Kalinke, M. E. (1986). 'Scandinavian Arthurian literature', in N. J. Lacy (ed.), *The Arthurian Encyclopedia*, New York and London, pp. 473–78.

Kalinke, M. E. (1988). 'Riddarasögur', in *Dictionary of the Middle Ages*, X, New York, pp. 389–97.

Kalinke, M. E. (1990). 'Arthurian literature in Scandinavia', in V. M. Lagorio and M. Leake Day (eds), *King Arthur through the Ages,* New York and London, pp. 127–51.

Kalinke, M. E. (1996). 'Scandinavia', in N. J. Lacy (ed.), *Medieval Arthurian Literature: A Guide to Recent Research*, New York, pp. 83–119.

Kalinke, M. E. (2005). 'Scandinavian Arthurian literature', in N. J. Lacy (ed.), *History of Arthurian Scholarship*, Cambridge, 2006, pp. 169–78.

Kramarz-Bein, S. (2002). *Die Þiðreks saga im Kontext der altnorwegischen Literatur*, Beiträge zur nordischen Philologie, 33, Tübingen and Basel.

Kretschmer, B. (1982). *Höfische und altwestnordische Erzähltradition in den Riddarasögur. Studien zur Rezeption der altfranzösischen Artusepik am Beispiel der Erex saga, Ívens saga und Parcevals saga*, Hattingen.

Kulturhistorisk leksikon for nordisk middelalder fra vikingetid til reformationstid (1956–78), I–XXII, Copenhagen.

Lacy, N. J. (ed.) (1986). *The Arthurian Encyclopedia*, New York and London; 1987, 1988.

Lacy, N. J. (ed.) (1991). *The New Arthurian Encyclopedia*, New York and London; 1996.

Lacy, N. J. (ed.) (2008). *The Grail, the Quest, and the World of Arthur*, Arthurian Studies, 72, Cambridge.

Leach, H. G. (1921). *Angevin Britain and Scandinavia*, Harvard Studies in Comparative Literature, VI, Cambridge, MA and London.

Lindow, J., Lönnroth, L. and Weber, G. W. (eds) (1986). *Structure and Meaning in Old Norse Literature: New Approaches to Textual Analysis and Literary Criticism*, Viking Collection, 3, Odense.

McTurk, R. (ed.) (2005). *A Companion to Old Norse-Icelandic Literature and Culture*, Oxford.

Meissner, R. (1902). *Die Strengleikar. Ein Beitrag zur Geschichte der altnordischen Prosalitteratur*, Halle a. S.

Mitchell, P. M. (1959). 'Scandinavian literature', in R. S. Loomis (ed.), *Arthurian Literature in the Midddle Ages*, Oxford, pp. 462–71.

van Nahl, A. (1981). *Originale Riddarasögur als Teil altnordischer Sagaliteratur*, Frankfurt a. M.

Nedoma, R., Reichert, H. and Zimmermann, G. (eds) (2000). *Erzählen im mittelalterlichen Skandinavien*, Wiener Studien zur Skandinavistik, 1, Vienna.

O'Connor, R. (2005). 'History or fiction? Truth-claims and defensive narrators in Icelandic romance-sagas', *Mediaeval Scandinavia*, 15, 101–69.

Ordbog over det norrøne prosasprog. Registre: A Dictionary of Old Norse Prose (1989), Copenhagen.

Polomé, E. C. (ed.) (1969). *Old Norse Literature and Mythology: A Symposium*, Austin, TX.

Poole, R. (ed.) (2001). *Skaldsagas: Text, Vocation, and Desire in the Icelandic Sagas of Poets*, Ergänzungsbände zum Reallexikon der Germanischen Altertumskunde, 27, Berlin and New York.

Pulsiano, P. and Wolf, K. (eds) (1993). *Medieval Scandinavia: An Encyclopedia*, New York.

Quinn, J., Heslop, K. and Wills, T. (eds) (2007). *Learning and Understanding in the Old Norse World: Essays in Honour of Margaret Clunies Ross*, Turnhout.

Reichert, H. (1986). 'King Arthur's Round Table: sociological implications of its literary reception in Scandinavia', in J. Lindow, L. Lönnroth, G. W. Weber (eds), *Structure and Meaning in Old Norse Literature: New Approaches to Textual Analysis and Literary Criticism*, Odense.

Les Relations littéraires franco-scandinaves au Moyen Age. (1975). *Actes du Colloque de Liège (avril 1972)*, Paris.

Sävborg, D. (2007). *Sagan om kärleken. Erotik, känslor och berättarkonst i norrön litteratur*, Uppsala.

Schlauch, M. (1934). *Romance in Iceland*, Princeton.

Seelow, H. (1989). *Die isländischen Übersetzungen der deutschen Volksbücher. Handschriftenstudien zur Rezeption und Überlieferung ausländischer unterhaltender Literatur in Island in der Zeit zwischen Reformation und Aufklärung*, Reykjavík.

Shepard, J. (2007). 'Rus'', in N. Berend (ed.), *Christianization and the Rise of Christian Monarchy: Scandinavia, Central Europe and Rus'c. 900–1200*, Cambridge, pp. 369–416.

Skårup, P. (ed.) (1998). *Traductions norroises de textes français médiévaux*, in *Revue des langues romanes*, CII.

Smyser, H. M. and Magoun, F. P. (eds) (1941). *Survivals in Old Norwegian of Medieval English, French, and German Literature, together with the Latin Versions of the Heroic Legend of Walter of Aquitaine*, Baltimore.

Spiegel, G. (1993). *Romancing the Past: The Rise of Vernacular Prose Historiography in Thirteenth-century France*, Berkeley, CA.

Thomas, A. (2000). 'King Arthur and his Round Table in the culture of medieval Bohemia and in medieval Czech literature', in W. H. Jackson and S. A. Ranawake (eds), *The Arthur of the Germans: The Arthurian Legend in Medieval German and Dutch Literature*, Cardiff, pp. 249–56.

Togeby, K. (1972). 'L'influence de la littérature française sur les littératures scandinaves au Moyen Âge', in H. U. Gumbrecht (ed.), *Généralités*. Grundriß der romanischen Literaturen des Mittelalters, I, Heidelberg, pp. 333–95.

Tulinius, T. (2002). *The Matter of the North: The Rise of Literary Fiction in Thirteenth-century Iceland*, trans. R. Eldevik, Odense.

Turville-Petre, G. (1953). *Origins of Icelandic Literature*, Oxford.

Vésteinn Ólason (1982). *The Traditional Ballads of Iceland: Historical Studies*, Reykjavík.

Wahlgren, E. (1938). *The Maiden King in Iceland*, Chicago.

Würth, S. (1998). *Der 'Antikenroman' in der isländischen Literatur des Mittelalters. Eine Untersuchung zur Übersetzung und Rezeption lateinischer Literatur im Norden*, Basel and Frankfurt am Main.

INDEX OF MANUSCRIPTS

GENERAL INDEX